PIMLICO

197

RIDING THE RETREAT

Richard Holmes is professor of Military and Security Studies at Cranfield University and the Royal Military College of Science. He was educated at Cambridge, Northern Illinois, and Reading universities, and carried out his doctoral research on the French army of the Second Empire. For many years he taught military history at the Royal Military Academy, Sandhurst.

A celebrated military historian, Richard Holmes is the author of the best-selling and widely acclaimed *Tommy* and *Redcoat: The British Soldier in the Age of Horse and Musket*. His dozen other books include *Dusty Warriors*, *Sahib*, *The Western Front*, *The Little Field Marshal: Sir John French*, *The Road to Sedan*, *Firing Line*, *The Second World War in Photographs* and *Fatal Avenue: A Traveller's History of Northern France and Flanders* (also published by Pimlico).

He is general editor of *The Oxford Companion to Military History* and has presented eight BBC TV series, including 'War Walks', 'The Western Front' and 'Battlefields', and is famous for his hugely successful series 'Wellington: The Iron Duke' and 'Rebels and Redcoats'.

RIDING THE RETREAT

Mons to the Marne – 1914 Revisited

———

RICHARD HOLMES

PIMLICO

Published by Pimlico 2007

2 4 6 8 10 9 7 5 3

Copyright © Richard Holmes 1995
Preface to the Pimlico 2007 Edition copyright © Richard Holmes 2006

Richard Holmes has asserted his right under the Copyright, Designs
and Patents Act 1988 to be identified as the author of this work

This book is a work of non-fiction. The author has stated to the publishers
that the contents of this book are true.

First published in Great Britain in 1995 by
Jonathan Cape

First Pimlico edition published in 1996

Second Pimlico edition 2007

Pimlico
Random House, 20 Vauxhall Bridge Road,
London SW1V 2SA

www.randomhouse.co.uk

Addresses for companies within The Random House Group Limited can be
found at: www.randomhouse.co.uk

The Random House Group limited Reg. No. 954009

A CIP catalogue record for this book
is available from the British Library

ISBN 9781845951092

The Random House Group Limited supports The Forest Stewardship
Council (FSC), the leading international forest certification organisation.
All our titles that are printed on Greenpeace approved FSC certified paper
carry the FSC logo. Our paper procurement policy can be found at:
www.rbooks.co.uk/environment

Printed and bound in Great Britain by
CPI Cox & Wyman, Reading, RG1 8EX

This book is dedicated, with gratitude, to
Lady Patricia Kingsbury
who set me on the road to Mons
in the footsteps of her grandfather
Sir John French

CONTENTS

ILLUSTRATIONS AND MAPS

The publishers are grateful to the Imperial War Museum for permission to reproduce the following illustrations: Nos. 1, 4, 5, 10, 11, 12, 15; to Tony and Valmai Holt for No. 13; and to the author for nos. 2, 3, 6, 7, 8, 14, 16, 17.

PREFACE TO THE
2007 PIMLICO EDITION

It hardly seems possible that twelve years have elapsed since I rode the route of the Retreat from Mons with my trusty companions, human and equine. I actually feel no older than I did when I mounted that grey ruffian Thatch just south of the Mons-Condé canal on the first day of the ride, but every morning my shaving mirror tells me a different story. In the interim my life has hurtled on, the years flickering by ever faster, and a good deal has happened. I presented the first series of *War Walks* for BBC television not long after writing this book (fittingly, one of its six episodes dealt with Mons) and that led to six further series on various military-related topics.

In one sense *War Walks* showed the way I was developing as a historian. Going back to memoirs, letters and diaries to write *Riding the Retreat* reinforced my growing reservations with what we might term 'arrows on maps' military history, and drew me ever closer to the men who make up the warp and weft of armies. Indeed, the experience of the ride and the writing that followed it provided what was, at least to me, a new perspective on the subject. I became more interested in 'microterrain', that tiny detail of ground and vegetation that means so much to men in battle. You cannot fully grasp the significance of, say, the sugar factory near Elouges or the sunken lane at Le Cateau until you have actually seen them: and yet the moment you glimpse them, a piece of the mental jigsaw puzzle clicks into place. I grew more and more fascinated with what soldiers wore and what they carried: not from the costume print point of view (although there are enough of those on my study walls) but from considerations of sheer utility. A long journey, with limited opportunities to wash dirty clothes, procure forgotten necessities, accommodate the cuts and bruises which are the inevitable result of moving cross-country on horseback between the hammer of the sun and the anvil of the earth, teaches you something about the rough edge of campaigning, even without the knowledge that the *Garde Ulanen* are kicking on at a fast trot half an hour behind.

The seed of an idea, planted when I was writing this book, grew into *Redcoat*, *Tommy* and *Sahib*, my trilogy on the British soldier across two centuries. I could never have written them had I not already worked on *Riding the Retreat*, but there was more to it than that. I was a Territorial colonel when I wrote this book. I became a brigadier soon afterwards, serving one tour at headquarters Land Command at Wilton and another, for which I was able to nudge my professorial 'day job' towards the back burner, as Director of Reserve Forces and Cadets in the Ministry of Defence, becoming what was then the country's most senior serving reservist.

Towards the end of my time on the active list I was invited to become Colonel of the Princess of Wales's Royal Regiment (Queen's and Royal Hampshires). The post – effectively non-executive chairman of an infantry regiment with two regular battalions and a Territorial battalion – is a relic of the days when colonels were essentially the proprietors of their regiments. They were given 'beating warrants' which enabled them to raise recruits by beat of drum in market-places; purchased the clothing, arms and equipment for their men, using government funds provided for the purpose, and pocketing the difference between this grant and what they actually paid for shoddy cloth and skimpy leather; and they had an interest, often both personal and financial, in their regiment's officers.

Today the role of a regimental colonel is, quite properly, much reduced. He chairs the board of trustees who manage the regiment's assets, the result of legacies and bequests made over the years and, God willing, invested productively. He takes a close personal interest in regimental benevolence – the grants and loans given to former members of the regiment and its historical predecessors who need a hand up. He is involved in the selection of the regiment's officers, and is consulted on the choice of commanding officers for his battalions. He has a good deal to do with establishing and maintaining his regiment's cultural ethos, in reinforcing its relationship with its recruiting area, and in using his influence to help ensure its equitable treatment in the matter of postings, domestic and foreign, and tours of operational duty.

I had joined the Territorial Army as a private soldier in 1994, and by the time I wrote this book I had commanded at platoon, company and battalion level, felt easy with soldiers and hoped that they were as comfortable with me. But my military horizons were bounded by the unfought war on the north German plain. Like many of my generation, I knew the Sibesse gap, the Landwehr canal and the bridge at Hessische Ohlendorf all too well. My regimental colonelcy, however, broadened my view as the comfortable certainties of the old world were replaced by the conflicts which characterised the 'new world disorder'. I visited my regular battalions on operations in Northern Ireland, the Balkans and Iraq, and my first visit to the latter, at a time of heavy fighting in 2004, provoked me to write *Dusty Warriors*, the story of a battle group engaged in the 'three block war' where humanitarian relief, peace enforcement and all-out violence might be mingled simultaneously across three city blocks.

I had imagined, when I started to write *Dusty Warriors*, that it would sit uncomfortably alongside my previous books. In fact I was constantly struck by the similarities between the young men I saw in Maysan province in the late summer of 2004 and the soldiers I had followed across the battlefields of history. Although weapons and equipment have changed beyond all measure, the infantrymen crammed into their Warrior armoured vehicles would not have seemed out of place in a marching column slogging back from Mons. True, the old, hard, self-confident and deferential society which spawned the men of 1914 has gone, and today's soldiers are the product of a very different background. But in the claustrophobic world of the rifle platoon the bonds of comradeship are still rock-solid. The strict formal discipline of 1914, which saw an isolated private soldier, at the end of a chaotic battle, come to attention and shoulder his rifle smartly before asking a passing officer for instructions, has long disappeared, but the easier informality of modern discipline seems no less effective. Men, in 2004 as in 1914, sought to gain and retain the respect of those whose judgement they respected: the regimental system, then as now, was at its best when it made them feel both valued and valuable.

When I first thought of riding the retreat I had no real idea how it would work, and how I would manage to stitch together history and contemporary narrative in the book. I found the whole process so illuminating that I have done three long military rides since then. In 1996 I followed the old Spanish drove road, the Cañada Real, from near Badajoz in Extremadura to Avila in Old Castile, taking in several of Wellington's battles on the way. It was physically far tougher than the French trip, and I can see why many of the *conquistadores*, who crossed the Atlantic to hew out a Spanish empire in the new world, had come from Extremadura: it was a good place to escape from. The arid landscape south of the Tagus does not encourage one to linger, and there was an almost palpable sense of relief as we crossed the river and climbed the empty hills behind it to reach the high pastures of Castile.

Two years after that I rode across South Africa from the Northern Cape to KwaZulu Natal, visiting most battles of the Zulu war and the second Boer War in the process. The trip enabled me to gallop the route of the British charge at Klip Drift, just outside Kimberley, to climb Hlobane mountain, scene of a sharp British defeat at the hands of the Zulus and, perhaps most evocatively, to spend a night on the battlefield of Isandlwana. The inimitable David Rattray drove out from nearby Fugitives' Drift on the Buffalo River to give us his account of the battle, so much of it gleaned from Zulu oral history.

At Isandlwana the British dead lie beneath whitewashed cairns, and they felt uncomfortably present as I tried to sleep, with clouds scudding past a full moon and the sphinx-like mass of Isandlwana mountain crouched on the near horizon. I had just dropped off when the horses, tethered to a rope at one end of our little camp, fell into a panic, probably because one of them had kicked a water-bucket, and streamed off into the drizzly darkness. By the time we had eventually recaptured them, with much bad language, I had come to terms with the place. Nevertheless, the night's alarums and excursions did not leave us in the best frame of mind to follow the Fugitives' Trail from the battlefield to the Buffalo. Only the first few hundred yards of it were rideable, and leading a horse down a steep and bounder-strewn track was hard enough, even with no Zulus behind.

In the spring of 2001 I embarked upon my most ambitious excursion to date, following the route taken in 1895 by a little column of Indian army troops who set off from Gilgit, on the edge of the Karakoram, to Chitral, close to the Afghan border, whose tiny garrison was besieged by disaffected locals. The landscape was breathtaking and the hospitality generous. For all the traditional harshness of the North-West Frontier and our proximity to Afghanistan, then ruled by the Taliban, I never felt a moment's unease about the dangers posed by human beings. But I have no head for heights, and I crossed swaying bridges with my eyes firmly shut, trusting to what I hoped might prove the good sense of my thick-necked Afghan pony. Sometimes our track had been hewn out of the mountainside, with a wall of rock on one side and a sheer drop on the other, and I presented an unedifying spectacle as I kept the pony as close to the cliff-face as I could while he, with the perversity of his breed, attempted to skitter outwards and kick stones into the river a thousand feet below. Like our predecessors just over a century before we entered Chitral to a triumphant welcome, with the pipes and drums of the Chitral Scouts striding out ahead of us, resplendent in Royal Stuart tartan, playing tunes more familiar to another race of tough highlanders. There were earnest hopes that tourists would visit this enchanted spot in growing numbers, but the aftermath of 9/11 put paid to that, and I fear for the future of so many of our generous hosts.

A year ago I followed the route of Prince Rupert's 'York March', his trans-Pennine expedition to relieve the beleaguered city of York in the early summer of 1644, to raise money for the Army Benevolent Fund. One of the trip's most memorable moments was persuading Thatch to ford the Ribble with water up to his girth and my boots. The ride culminated on the field of Marston Moor, in a gallop up the gentle slope on the Royalist left, following the line of George Goring's charge. By then there were perhaps sixty of us, in various forms of seventeenth-century costume (the less said about my grey wig the better) and if I did not already understand why the Royalist horse so often got out of hand, believe me, I know now.

Were I writing *Riding the Retreat* today I would make a few changes. A day riding with the King's Troop Royal Horse Artillery has taught me just how difficult it is to drive a pair of horses in a gun-team, even if I was only entrusted with the relatively undemanding 'centre pair'. I would certainly have written with greater fluency about the role of artillery drivers had I known in 1994 what I know now. A steady patter of dignified letters has pointed out that I was wrong to say that it was the Canadians who took Le Quesnoy by escalade in 1918. It was, *mea maxima culpa*, the New Zealanders, as their splendid memorial in the town's well-preserved wall points out. A slower trickle of more forceful protest takes issue with some of my picture captioning. Although photograph 10 is often captioned as infantry on the retreat from Mons, it is probably from a sequence showing troops moving through Vermelles, on the road that bisects the battlefield, during the battle of Loos in September 1915. Some men are carrying early gas helmet bags, and at least one has a soft 'gor blimey' hat that was not in use in 1914. Similarly, photograph 11 must postdate August 1914 as the soldier is wearing 1914 pattern leather equipment, not the 1908 pattern Mills webbing equipment worn by the BEF in the summer of 1914, and also has a soft 'trench cap'. The absence of a steel helmet, however, suggests a date before the spring of 1916. Even so, the face is pure, timeless Tommy.

Evelyn Webb-Carter, now a retired general and a knight, has been the one constant factor in all my rides. Indeed, without his organisational ability, unshakeable good humour and old-world courtesy I doubt if any of them would have proved feasible. My other comrades (and my daughters too, now veterans of Spain, South Africa and the frontier) deserve my thanks for putting up with my grumpy mornings, woeful horsemastership, and a mind that keeps slipping out of the present into the past. And yes, before you ask, Thatch, far less wearied by age than his master, is alive and well, staring out across his Hampshire farmyard as I write.

Richard Holmes
Ropely
October 2006

I

A Sense of Time, an Eye for Place

Battles long ago

At 9.30 a.m. on the morning of 10 August 1993, I nudged my heels into Thatch's rough grey flanks and we ambled off to the war. Not to climb a Balkan ridgeline or splash across a Cambodian paddy-field, girt about with flak-jacket and cameras, but to follow the route of the British Expeditionary Force, which had passed that way seventy-nine years before. The First World War has always lurked just over the edge of my memory. It is as near as my grandfather's stories and the assorted sheaves of diaries, letters and reports which have cluttered so much of my professional life, but as far away as picture-book images of biplanes, battle-cruisers and French cavalry in helmet and breastplate. This is neither a book about strategy and tactics nor a travel book in any conventional sense of the word: it is a trip back through history, a journey over the horizon to glimpse the summer the old world ended.

It was not one war but many. Operations on the Western and Eastern fronts had their own hallmarks, while those in more distant theatres, like Gallipoli, Mesopotamia or East Africa, were as different again. Even the Western Front played host to a series of campaigns, not a single war. Its geography varied from the slime of Flanders, through the dry limestone of Champagne to the misty hills of Alsace. Intensity oscillated between the grimy squalor of trench life, where the real enemies were vermin, weather and mind-numbing tedium, and the white heat of battles like the Somme or Passchendaele. Even hostility was inconstant, with yesterday's avuncular Bavarian replaced by today's more martial Prussian, and the precarious arrangements of live and let live, typical of much of trench warfare, disrupted by official goading or private vengefulness.

It is close yet distant. When I first took an interest in military history, thousands of survivors were alive, many in their fifties or early sixties. I could, had I put my mind to it, have spoken to an army commander, for Sir Hubert Gough, relieved of command of the 5th Army in 1918, did not die till 1963. I have tramped many a battlefield in company with veterans who pointed out the difficulty of dealing with the *Springfield* pill-box on the Ypres–Langemark road, swore about the repetitive servitude of humping 'trench stores' up the line, and touched a comrade's headstone so tenderly that they might have been reaching down to close his eyes. Now, most of them have gone, and for many of the fast-dwindling band of survivors reminiscence has been polished so lovingly that its meaning is all but illegible.

The first weeks of the war were a watershed. The events of August and early September 1914 have as much in common with clashes a century before as with battle even three months later. 'Suddenly there was a loud yell and a rush of galloping horses round the corner,' wrote Lieutenant-General von Poseck.

> Red and blue uniforms and glittering sabres were visible through the dust. A squadron of the French 10th Hussars, the captain well in advance of his men, came on at full gallop. 'Charge,' shouted Captain von Ploetz, and the two squadrons came together with a mighty crash. It was an unequal contest, the big Cuirassiers on their heavy horses and the little southern Frenchmen on their cat-like Arab mounts. The collision of the heavy Irish charger of Captain von Ploetz rolled over the little thoroughbred of the French captain. Even as he fell he gave his adversary a sabre-cut in the face. There followed a hand-to-hand encounter in the roadway, the long German lances against the keen sabres of the Frenchmen.

We may be forgiven for thinking that this occurred at Waterloo, or at least during the Franco-Prussian war of 1870–71. Not at all: von Poseck is describing an action between German *Guard Cuirassiers* and French hussars at Zorées, south of Maubeuge, on 26 August 1914.

Back in the Saddle

I have never been a real cavalryman. The closest I came to it was to slip into the local Yeomanry regiment during my last term at school. It had been converted to artillery years before, but clung to its Yeomanry identity and was proud of the 'Royal Horse Artillery' in its title, which marked it off from the great mass of Territorial artillery. The officers, senior NCOs, and a few junior ranks whose pockets matched their zeal, shimmered about, when opportunity offered, in dark green tunics with shoulder chains and dark green overalls with double red stripes strapped over spurred Wellingtons. The regiment had a fine fighting record, as cavalry on the Western Front in the First World War and as artillery in the Second. Our motto was *Decus et Tutamen* — an ornament and a safeguard — but I could not help feeling that in the twilight of our regimental life, as we fired our elderly 25-pdrs over heather and downland, we were rather more of the former than the latter.

Typically, I never got beyond itchy battledress of an unflattering cut that made the Battery Sergeant-Major's comparison with a pregnant camel seem undeniably apt. My grandmother, whose grasp of pre–1908 army organisation was somehow a good deal more robust than her memory of what had happened the previous day, gained some comfort from my Yeomanry shoulder-titles. 'That's not so bad,' she said, patting my sleeve encouragingly. 'There's no harm in being a private soldier in the Yeomanry. But I wouldn't want to see you in the Militia or the Volunteers.' The 1967 reorganisation of the Territorial Army all but extinguished the Essex Yeomanry, though it lives on, much-diminished, as a Royal Signals squadron. I had already concluded that lack of numeracy was likely to prove a serious handicap to a career as a gunner, and stepped smartly sideways into the infantry. I have no complaints, for my career has taken me as far as brigadier, and has brought me some of my best friends and most rewarding moments. But when the port goes round after dinner and I see, somewhere through the cigar-smoke, the high collar and shoulder chains of cavalry No. 1 Dress I cannot quite stifle a tiny regret that my time as a 'donkey-walloper' was so brief and inglorious.

If I am ambivalent about the cavalryman, I am scarcely more consistent about what the French cavalry theorist F. de Brack called 'his legs, his safety, his honour and his reward': the horse. I have ridden on and off since I was a boy: indeed, on and off is not a bad description of my style and its consequences. When I joined the academic staff of the Royal Military Academy Sandhurst I took the short course known as the Cadet Ride, trotting round the outdoor school on many a freezing morning, careering down the jump lane, without reins or stirrups, and then going off to lectures with the gunslingers' crouch which bore silent testimony to the strain on little-used muscles. The fact that I was on the staff brought me no privileges as far as the riding school was concerned, and my frequent falls were greeted with an ironic demand as to why I had dismounted without permission or the hope that I might manage to find some potatoes down there. There was a test at the end of the course: one could fail, pass to hack or pass to hunt. I passed to hunt, and few exam results have given me greater satisfaction.

There could be no denying the fact that I am an untidy horseman. When I was young, with more courage than imagination, I rode with short stirrups and an aggressively forward seat, cramming my horse into crowded fences with the Staff College Drag. When I came to grief it was straight through the front door, and I still wonder why I did not finish up on one of those bone-cracking drag lines across Barrossa Common with a broken neck. I hunted occasionally — suburban Surrey rather than high Leicestershire — and found it a good deal safer.

Even now I am not wholly comfortable about the morality of hunting (the spade-and-terrier business has always worried me), but would profoundly regret its demise. It has helped shape the land-scape I love, and is part of my comfortable world of covert and downland. Though I would be ashamed to live in a country which did not permit peaceful protest, in a world where so much is so wrong I remain genuinely surprised that the sudden death of a predator can arouse such emotion. Certainly, if I was allowed to plan my own demise I would prefer a split second of snapping jaws to days of gutshot anguish. But of course there is more to it than that. Just as the hunt's quarry is the fox, so the protestor's is the hunt: this symbiotic relationship says at least as much about tribal markings and tensions between town and country as about killing foxes.

And there is the age-old friction between the man on horseback and the man on foot. Bruce Chatwin thought that 'equitation engen-ders a sort of Olympian grandeur'. The great horse empires were built by men who shared what Colonel Nikolai Przewalskii saw as the Kalmuk nomad's 'contempt for pedestrianism [which] is so great that he considers it beneath his dignity to walk even as far as the nearest *yurta*'. The Huns, Chatwin reminds us, bought, sold, slept, ate, drank, gave judgement, even defecated without dismounting. Wallenstein's trooper of the Thirty Years' War would have understood it well: 'Free will I live, free will I die; none will I rob, I am no man's heir; and I look proudly from my horse upon the rabble beneath me'. It requires a conscious effort not to seem literally *de haut en bas* when mounted and speaking to someone on foot, and it is not an effort which is made quite as often as it might be.

Eventually, re-enacting Civil War battles with the Sealed Knot came close to succeeding where the Drag had failed, and a spectacular fall in buff-coat and plumed hat put me into hospital with a cracked skull. When I had regained my wits, I resolved to take things more steadily in future, and the pressures of marriage, paternity and career all combined to help keep me out of the saddle.

But not for long. My daughters Jessie and Corinna rode, and their criticism, winged with the artless honesty of the young, grew more strident as we hacked out together. There were suggestions that a leading rein might help, and earnest enquiries as to whether everybody really rode that way in the old days. Swallowing my pride I crept back to riding school, and was patiently told that everything had changed. I should grip with my legs, not with my knees; ride with wide-open eyes to maintain peripheral awareness; breathe through my whole body; find my physical centre and breathe down through it, and balance my body from feet through head. Getting new ideas into my brain is a good deal easier than getting old ones out, and I find myself caught between two worlds. In good moments I am a passable advertisement for Sally Swift's *Centred Riding*. Yet in bad moments my old ways return and I look like what one instructress called 'a hunting farmer'. She meant it as a criticism, but I was secretly flattered.

An Eye for the Ground

For most of history the horse played a quintessential role in military affairs. As late as 1940 a German infantry division had 5,375 horses on its establishment and we shall see just how dependent the armies of 1914 were on the services of *equus caballus*. Across the centuries horses hauled guns, wagons and senior officers' coaches, and mounted not only the glittering shoals of cavalry but also infantry officers of company commander's rank and above. Officers were taught equitation at military academies, although usually this simply confirmed existing skills, for in most European armies they came from backgrounds where riding was, at one extreme, the only way of casting an eye over the family's broad acres or, at the other, a step on the ladder to social respectability. When George Barrow, who was to find himself on the staff of the Cavalry Division in 1914, was at Sandhurst he discovered that military instructors did not view riding in quite the same way as civilians. 'Lady novelists speak of the noble animal pawing the ground and champing his bit,' thundered the riding master, 'but I say what damned fools their riders were to let 'em paw and champ.'

In the British Army, hunting attracted a particular following. This had its dark side, for it was partly responsible for what Wellington (no mean man to hounds himself) called 'the trick our officers have acquired of galloping at everything and their galloping back as fast as they galloped at the enemy. They never consider their situation, never think of manoeuvring before an enemy . . . never keep nor provide for a reserve.' At Talavera, in July 1809, the 23rd Light Dragoons charged without discerning that a ravine lay between them and the French. Some jumped it and others scrambled across, but not a few remained stuck in the obstacle. The survivors hurooshed on and crashed through the leading French regiment only to be cut to ribbons by lancers close behind. The 23rd lost just over half its strength in the action. In contrast, the 1st Hussars of the King's German Legion (KGL), moving behind the 23rd at a slower pace, managed to cross the ravine, form up on the far side, and charge with complete success and trivial loss. Sergeant Edward Costello of the 95th Rifles wrote of the high respect his comrades entertained for the KGL, 'not only on account of their humanity and general good feeling towards us, but from their determined bravery and discipline in the field'. He observed that nobody paid much attention to British horsemen darting about the camp, but if a German came up at the gallop soldiers at once stood to their arms. Indeed, one of the most remarkable feats of arms of the entire horse and musket era, the breaking of three French squares, drawn up on good ground at Garcia Hernandez in July 1812, was the work of KGL horsemen.

Colonel Eley of the 23rd told his sister that his charge was witnessed by the entire army 'with a mixture of exultation, anxiety and astonishment'. When William Havelock was killed at Rahmaduggur in 1846 as the 14th Hussars charged down a dry river-bed in an effort to reach an invisible enemy, his brother Henry was far from astonished. 'Old Will was a foxhunter,' he reflected, 'before he became a cavalryman.' The connection was not lost on R. S. Surtees' inimitable sporting character Mr Jorrocks. 'Should there be a barracks in the neighbourhood,' he announced, 'some soger officers will most likely mix up and ride at the 'ardest rider amongst them. The dragon soger officer is the most dangerous and may be know by the viskers under his nose.'

In the years before the First World War, hunting was encouraged because it was believed to give officers a good eye for the country and keep them in good physical trim. Prince Kraft zu Hohenlohe-Ingelfingen, who commanded the Prussian Guard artillery in 1870–71 and wrote prolifically on military matters, warmly agreed, declaring: 'Hunting and campaign riding are on the same level; both require the same degree of training; in both the rider must retain constant control over his horse'. In practice, officers required little encouragement. When George Barrow attended Staff College in the 1890s he found that: 'Although a few officers rode with the hunt as a painful duty, the majority went out with the Drag for the simple purpose of pleasure. A few did not hunt at all and made no pretence of their dislike for riding across country.'

The reluctant minority had common sense on their side, for the 1914 *Army List* was, in its way, a catalogue of equestrian injuries. Sir John French, commander-in-chief of the BEF, had broken his hand steeplechasing as a young officer, and a badly-healed finger (known as the crochet hook to his family) is some excuse for his execrable handwriting. Sir Horace Smith-Dorrien, who commanded II Corps, smashed his knee hunting, and the future Field-Marshal Lord Birdwood recalled how: 'Going fast on the abominably hard Annandale ground, my pony crossed his legs and rolled over me. I was lucky to escape with three broken ribs . . .' In his diary entry for 8 August 1914, Captain James Jack of the Cameronians admitted that he 'loathed the outlook' of the coming war, blaming 'a hard if not dangerous fifteen months in the South African War together with many racing, hunting and polo accidents'. Even during the war hooves vied with shot and shell to cause death and injury. While on a visit to the front, King George V was injured when his horse threw him after a guard of honour startled it, and hunting was eventually banned in the BEF's sector after a brigadier-general fractured his pelvis. Major-General Drummond, commander of 19th Infantry Brigade, survived the battle of Le Cateau only to be kicked by his weary charger and hurt so badly that he had to give up his brigade (subordinates cursed the horse because Drummond's replacement was 'a dear old gentleman but no soldier').

In 1899 Lieutenant-Colonel Edwin Alderson (who came to grief as a corps commander in France in 1915) published *Pink and Scarlet, or Hunting as a School for Soldiering*. It went into a second edition, this time with illustrations by Lionel Edwards, in 1900. The originals, a pair of military and hunting paintings illustrating each of Alderson's points, hang in the upstairs ante-room of the Officers' Mess at Sandhurst. As we solved the problems of the world over coffee, we sometimes mocked the patronising comparisons between hounds scouring a covert and Indian infantry advancing through scrub, but the book did underline some of the eternal truths of soldiering. Officers must put their men before themselves (our hero sees that his hunter is warmly stabled before he thinks of his own dinner); lower your guard before an enterprising enemy and you risk disaster ('Shan't find — here, they shot it last week' says a red-coated thruster at a covert's edge as a fox steals to safety behind him); and there comes a time when, cost what it may, you must lead from the front ('Be with them *I will*,' grunts our paragon, kicking his grey on up a steep thorny slope).

The military twin of the pair depicting the importance of terrain was the painting that most appealed to me. It showed a regiment of hussars moving fast through a dusty landscape, its commander reflecting that by taking ground in the valley, down by the farm with the poplar trees, he would be able to get the squadrons into charging distance without being seen. It makes the point perfectly. In this sort of scenario, ground makes the difference between success and failure, between horses and men in kicking heaps and an enemy taken helplessly in the flank. There is precious little time to choose a line, and the officer who makes the decision will be at least as tired as any of the men he commands. Well might Prince Kraft write of a leader of cavalry:

He must first be a good rider across country, better indeed than any of those under him. He must, moreover, be hard, so that neither exertions by day and night nor the longest gallop affect him in the least. He must have the eye of an eagle, for he has not time to use his field-glass, which will probably be useless owing to the dust and rain. He must be a man of quick decision and strong will, for he has not time for consideration and counter-orders.

Just as hunting has lost the military cachet it once possessed, so too the impact of ground is often poorly appreciated by historians and soldiers alike. Part of the reason for the failure of historians stemmed from a tendency for 'respectable' scholars in the 1960s and

1970s to shun the hard old world of battle to apply themselves to engaging topics like military sociology. But the pendulum has now swung back. In *The Face of Battle*, nothing less than a landmark in historiography, John Keegan touched a profound truth by declaring: 'Military history, we may infer, must be in the last resort about battle'. He was echoing not only Clausewitz, who saw combat as 'the central military art', but also Engels, who told Marx in 1857 that: 'Fighting is to war what cash payment is to trade, for however rarely it may be necessary for it actually to occur, everything is to be directed towards it and eventually it must take place all the same and must be decisive'. This is not a view which pleases all historians. However, the statement of editorial intent launching the new (1993) journal *War in History* strikes a sensible balance by observing that though 'the study of war is the study of combat', it would be a sterile document which failed to consider the economic, social and political aspects of war.

Battle was relatively infrequent even in what seemed like high-intensity war. The Napoleonic Wars contained perhaps two hundred days of pitched battle in some twenty years, and a very experienced soldier would be unlucky if he hazarded his person in more than half a dozen major engagements. This book is concerned with the battles of Mons, on 23 August 1914, Le Cateau, fought three days later, and the retreat of the British Expeditionary Force which went on till 5 September and was accompanied by a number of smaller actions. Some units were all but wiped out: the Cheshires at Audregnies, the Suffolks and the Gordons at Le Cateau, and the Munsters at Etreux. But others were scarcely touched. The South Wales Borderers did not lose a single man to enemy action during this time, while the Royal Welch Fusiliers lost only three wounded.

Even in an age where an army's combatant 'teeth' were large by comparison with its administrative 'tail', many soldiers found themselves near a battlefield but not actually in combat. Napoleon's army began the Austerlitz campaign with a total effective strength of 210,500 men. About 73,000 were present at Austerlitz, and certainly not all of them fired a shot in anger. One of the BEF's two corps fought at Mons, and only one of its divisions was seriously engaged. Of the total British loss of some sixteen hundred men almost half was sustained by three battalions of 8th Infantry Brigade.

Even if battle is relatively uncommon, and may not directly involve the majority of soldiers in the combatant armies, the battlefield is the place where soldiers close their deals. Over the past twenty years historians have looked at the business of battle with sharper eyes than ever before. John Keegan blazed the trail with *The Face of Battle*, and he has been followed by several writers who have concentrated on what Field-Marshal Lord Wavell called 'the "actualities of war" — the effects of tiredness, hunger, fear, lack of sleep, weather . . .' John Ellis produced *Eye-Deep in Hell*, a slim but penetrating study of trench warfare, and the weightier *The Sharp End of War*, the best study to date of British and American combat experience in the Second World War. In *The Western Way of War*, Victor Davis Hansen applied what we might not unfairly term the Keegan method to infantry battle in classical Greece, producing an account of hoplite warfare that has me there in the sweating, stamping ranks of the phalanx as it rocks forward from walk to jog-trot and on into the last run-in before impact. Most recently, Charles Carlton has done the same for the English Civil War in *Going to the Wars*, to provide an unmatched view of the conflict from behind the bars of a lobstertail helmet or beneath the sweaty rim of the musketeer's felt hat.

All these authorities make much of Wavell's actualities of war, those Clausewitzian variables of chance, chaos, fear and courage. Their chief concern is with the men who do the fighting and the dying, and their achievement has been to get behind the rhetoric of Official History or the deceptive polish of oft-repeated half-truths to discern what battle was really like. Our concern for individuals, however, can sometimes bring its own form of selective blindness. We talk about the impact of terrain and climate on combatants but sometimes forget the central role that ground plays in the land battle. Military theory does not always help: in an age where professional soldiers are increasingly concerned with manoeuvre warfare, and strive to focus on the enemy rather than the ground, we are inclined to underrate terrain.

Usually its value is relative rather than absolute. Hougoumont in 1815, Passchendaele Ridge in 1917 and Tumbledown Mountain in 1982 were important because of what could be done with them and from them, rather than simply because of what they were. Yet it is easy enough, once a piece of ground has been bought or leased at an exorbitant cost in lives, to forget why it was sought in the first place or, like a headstrong bidder at an auction, to push the price up. The fighting at Hougoumont, the great farmhouse complex in front of Wellington's right centre at Waterloo, sucked in the greater part of a whole French corps after the leading French divisional commander, Prince Jerome, lost sight of the overall plan and sent attack after frontal attack roaring in to wither before the defenders' musketry.

It is easy to assume that ground matters most to tactical commanders, whose troops actually do the fighting on it. But as we ascend the levels of war, from the tactical to the operational and on to the strategic, getting further away from the field of battle as we do so, then ground becomes more likely to possess intrinsic qualities. A commander at the operational level of war, responsible for the conduct of campaigns in a given theatre — General Joffre in 1914 or General Schwarzkopf in the Gulf — has non-negotiable terrain requirements. He needs secure administrative bases or points of entry, huge tracts of suitable ground on which his logisticians can ply their essential trade, and all-weather routes to take supplies forward.

For war cabinets and their professional advisers the importance of ground can hardly be overstated. The lowest common denominator amongst coalition objectives in the Gulf War was the need to remove the Iraqis from Kuwait, while in 1982 no amount of slick propaganda could suggest that one side had won if the other remained in occupation of the Falklands. NATO officers who planned the Unfought Battle in West Germany were caught on the dilemma of terrain. Defending close to the Inner German Border threatened to put the majority of their troops in an easily-broken shop window. There was much tactical logic in fighting a mobile battle, trading space for time, but such a manoeuvre, which would have left much of the Federal Republic's territory devastated, would have met with muted applause from Bonn.

In 1914, Paris was immensely important. The French government left for Bordeaux, promoting a disgruntled populace to sing a ribald version of the Marseillaise:

> *Aux gares, citoyens*
> *Montez dans les wagons . . .*

But the city remained a cultural and psychological focal point. Its capture would have helped convince the Germans that they were winning the war and shown the French and British that they were losing it. If the Germans had taken Paris — and they were within measurable distance of doing so — it is hard to conceive of France surviving the blow.

For most of history obdurate practical problems made it hard for commanders to recognise the implications of terrain. Maps were either non-existent or so sketchy as to be all but useless. In 1260, those doughty warriors Bela IV of Hungary and Ottokar II of Bohemia were striving to get to grips with one another, only to discover that the River March lay inconveniently between their armies. The monarchs had a gentlemanly discussion and Bela was allowed to cross the river and draw up his army unhindered. Ottokar then proceeded to destroy it, and Bela was lucky to escape with his life. When Frederick the Great attacked the Austrians at Kolin in 1757 he began his orders with the less than encouraging preamble: 'Gentlemen, many of you must remember this neighbourhood from the time we stood here in 1742. I am certain I have the plan somewhere, but Major von Griese cannot find it.'

By the Napoleonic era, acceptably accurate maps were available, but their issue fell lamentably short of what any modern army would regard as essential. When the *Grande Armée* invaded Russia in 1812, only divisional commanders (and by no means all of them) had maps. One, no doubt with bitter memories of wrestling with a large rolled map on horseback, had his cut up into squares and stuck, in the interests of durability, onto two dozen red and white checked handkerchiefs. When it took the field in Belgium in 1815, the British Army had generations of experience of fighting there, but the best one senior officer could do for a map was to tear one out of a history book. It still hangs in the Army Staff College in Camberley, its owner's inky annotations easily visible. With maps in such short supply, for generations armies relied on guides, often a pressed man who spent anxious days with his hands tied to a trooper's stirrup, with much stern tapping of a holster to remind him of what would happen if he led his captors astray — by design or accident.

Some battles of the horse and musket era were decided largely by one side's ability to turn the ground to its advantage. Early on the morning of 23 May 1706, the Duke of Marlborough was riding westwards through Brabant, with his Quartermaster-General, William Cadogan, and a small escort well to his front. To his rear the Allied army, some 50,000 strong, stepped out in three great columns. Cadogan brushed with a party of French cavalry, glimpsed, through the mist beyond, the white coats of French regulars drawn up on rising ground behind the marshy Geete around the village of Ramillies, and spurred back to tell the Duke that the French were offering battle. It took Marlborough at least three hours to deploy, and as his men wheeled from column into line (with a good deal of flam and paradiddle from drummers and as much bad language from officers and sergeants) he rode across the front of the French position. The Duke noticed a small re-entrant running north-south just east of Ramillies: troops in it would be invisible to French observers. When battle was joined, he used the re-entrant to shift troops covertly from his right flank to his centre, concentrating combat power at the decisive point and routing the French.

Twentieth-century commanders have generally had reliable and detailed maps — often reinforced by air photographs — at their disposal. Indeed, some sort of 'map appreciation' — a study of the ground from the map — comes early on in their planning process. Yet mistakes are still made. The trench maps issued before the Battle of the Somme began on 1 July 1916 not only showed the German front line in admirable detail, but also sketched out the German second position, lying well behind it and out of range of the majority of British field batteries. General Rawlinson, commander of the 4th Army, which assaulted that day, had already expressed doubts as to how deep his attack might be expected to go, and favoured 'bite and hold' operations of a methodical kind. His initial plan did not meet with the approval of Sir Douglas Haig, who had replaced French as commander-in-chief the previous December, and 4th Army found itself committed to an attempt to achieve a full-blooded breakthrough. Quite what would be done about the German second position was never properly explained.

For another spectacular example of failure to grasp the real meaning of ground we must look to Marshal G. K. Zhukov's attack on Berlin in April 1945. His 1st Byelorussian Front held a narrow bridgehead over the River Oder. To reach Berlin (and to do so before Zhukov's rival, Koniev, took the city) the attacker had to cross the boggy Oderbruch and then storm the Seelow heights beyond it. Zhukov's plan was based on his abundant recent experience. He would hammer the heights with artillery — the intensity of whose fire was to remind some older Germans of the drumfire of Verdun — and then use his combined arms armies to clear the Oderbruch and take the heights before his tank armies broke clear to thrust on to the German capital. Zhukov had reckoned without the finesse of his opponent, Colonel-General Gotthard Heinrici, who withdrew his first line just before the bombardment hit it, and underestimated the sheer difficulty of moving tanks and men across what was by then a heavily-mined swamp. Not only was the area well mapped, but from a command post on the Reitwein spur

Zhukov enjoyed an excellent view of the ground. But he did not listen to what it could have told him. Like Rawlinson a generation before, he was spurred on by a demanding superior (in his case Stalin) and this time it was Russian, not British, lives which paid for information which the map provided free.

Historians have mixed fortunes when they try to assess the effect of ground on battle. Crammed diaries and empty bank accounts may make it impossible to visit the battlefield. But the uncomfortable fact remains that whenever I have written about a battle and subsequently visited the field I have always regretted an error or omission. However hard you look at the map, there are things it is easy to miss. Austerlitz is bigger than I expected and Malplaquet smaller. The Seelow heights, like Passchendaele Ridge, would be insignificant almost anywhere else in the world: to recognise their importance you must see them in context.

The big farms of Brabant and Hainault — like Gemioncourt on the field of Quatre Bras and Hougoumont at Waterloo — are not farmhouses as the English-speaking world might understand them. Nor is it much help to call them châteaux, which tends to bestow a stately dignity they do not quite deserve. They are huge farm complexes, with thick external walls on four sides of a massive square, and house, stables, byres and other buildings around a central courtyard which might be lawned today but was once the site of a reeking dunghill. They are often very old, much older than the façade of the house might suggest, and were built at a time when luminaries like Everard de la Marck — whose behaviour, as much as his coat of arms, earned him the nickname 'wild boar of the Ardennes' — might sweep down with rape and murder in mind. Stout walls designed to keep out the likes of Everard were effectively impenetrable by field artillery until the late nineteenth century, but it is only by looking at these complexes that one can really grasp what value they could have as bastions for a defensive position.

The visitor with time and money to spend still faces obstacles. It is hard to be absolutely sure of the location of some seventeenth-century battlefields. I live almost on the field of Cheriton, where Sir William Waller beat his old friend Sir Ralph Hopton on 29 March 1644, but still have some doubts as to what happened in which fold of ground. Captain Jones of the London Trained Bands did his best to help, but saying 'we fought in East Down between Cheriton and Alesford [sic]' is a trifle unspecific. Difficulties multiply as time passes. There is a ghastly possibility that the fine visitors' centre at

Bosworth Field (1485) is actually not on the field at all, while urbanisation has effectively blotted out the site of St Albans (1455 and 1461), leaving the bemused visitor confronting car parks and supermarkets. Even Ordnance Survey maps can prove delusive. The crossed swords marking the site of Preston, where Cromwell beat the Scots in 1648, are certainly in the wrong place. The worthy cartographers were induced to place them where cannon-balls were discovered in the last century, but what ought to have made this find less than conclusive is the fact that neither side had cannon at the battle.

Attempts to commemorate battles may mislead or conceal. The Marston Moor monument (1644) is well towards the field's eastern flank, while the memorial to the cavalry actions at Naseby stands squarely in the centre of the infantry line. There is a dignified monument to *Husaren-Regiment 'von Zeiten'* on the Roman road which marks the left flank of the 'death-ride', where von Bredow's brigade charged the gun-line of the French 6th Corps on 16 August 1870. But although the Zeiten hussars had a good day (losing their commanding officer in the process) they were not actually in the charge.

The more elaborate the commemoration the greater the risk that it will extinguish the spirit of the place or, worse still, actually change the ground. The Lion Monument at Waterloo is a notorious example. Collecting the earth needed to build it transformed the topography of this crucial part of the battlefield. Even if the field could support cafés and Naporamas, it is bent out of shape by the weight of the lion and his mound. First World War British cemeteries on the Western Front are a mixed blessing. On the one hand they convey their own sense of place and — like those strewn along the British front line of 1 July 1916 — help relate troops to ground in the most poignant way. But on the other they get between the visitor and the landscape. Unless the traveller is remarkably strong-willed a battlefield visit easily drops into a cemetery-crawl, with a double DSO here and an unusual cap-badge there.

Hacking into history

This book puts personal accounts of the events of August-September 1914 into the context of the ground on which they took place. In a few cases, war or urbanisation has altered it, sometimes beyond recognition. But one of the beauties of following the drums of 1914

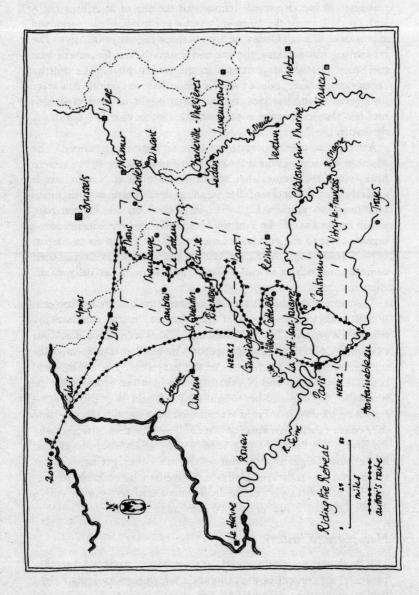

is that the ground has generally changed little, and in most cases its minutiae — which means so much to an infantryman scratching for cover or an artillery driver whipping his team into a sunken road — are as evident now as they were a lifetime ago.

I and my companions followed the line of the retreat and crossed the battlefields of Mons, Le Cateau, Cerizy, Guise, Néry and Villers-Cotterêts on horseback. We did so partly because it is far easier to cover ground on horseback than on foot, and a good deal of wheeling and countermarching was going to be required if I was to squeeze all the information from the terrain. If we had marched the retreat, we would still be hard at it, looking for some way of crossing that autoroute that curls inconveniently across the field of Cerizy. And there were other good reasons for going *à cheval* not *à pied*. Most of the commanders of 1914, down to humble infantry captains, were mounted, and their decisions were often made on a horse's back. There is no better way to glimpse the problem facing Major-General Allenby, commanding the Cavalry Division, on 24 August 1914 than to trot into Audregnies, to the road junction where a junior officer saw him glaring, face as red as his collar-tabs, at the oncoming torrent of German infantry.

When I first conceived the notion of riding the retreat, eighteen months before I actually did it, everything seemed wonderfully simple. I would turn up in Mons, get hold of a horse, and ride to the Marne, putting up for the night wherever I could. It would be relaxed and low-key with no rigid timetable. I would have plenty of time to think: indeed, one of the project's attractions was that it would be a retreat in both senses of the word, giving me the chance to look at my own life from the plateau of my middle years. But the more I thought about the scheme the more the difficulties multiplied. Horses are notoriously badly-designed. The old saying 'no foot, no horse' has it precisely, and lameness can strike without warning: a sharp flint here, an unexpected furrow there, and the horse is literally off the road. Accommodation might not be easy to find, and routes, too, would require serious consideration unless I expected to spend most of my time on metalled roads. By mid–1992 I had decided that I would need at least one human companion and that (as is often the case with matters military) logistics would dominate the entire operation.

I was saved by a chance remark. In June 1992 I was taking 19th Infantry Brigade to Sedan, where Guderian's panzers had crossed the Meuse in 1940. I had written about the episode in a book I had just finished, and found myself discussing my next book with the brigadier, Evelyn Webb-Carter. I already knew him quite well, having taught him on the Higher Command and Staff Course at Camberley. This had convinced me that his appearance — he has the sort of 1930s face that would be at home with Bertie Wooster and Gussie Fink-Nottle amongst the whizzing bread-rolls of the Drones Club — is somewhat deceptive. Behind exactly the façade that Central Casting might come up with if asked to produce a Grenadier officer there buzzes a sharp brain with a particularly good grasp of military history. What I did not know at the time is that he is a keen horseman, and when I told him that I planned to ride the route of the retreat from Mons I was taken aback when he riposted: 'Not without me, I hope!' The next ten minutes convinced me that I would indeed be rash to attempt the venture without him. Fewer first impressions have been more correct: his forethought was to avert many a potential disaster, and, having seen him in sunshine and in shadow, at jovial Gallic lunches and fraught two-in-the-morning horse lines, I like him more now than I ever did.

The remainder of our little band slipped together without great effort. We needed a horse expert. Corporal of Horse John O'Flaherty had been running the Guards Saddle Club stables at Melton Mowbray and was about to leave the army. Evelyn thought that he was the man for the job, and our first meeting confirmed it. John was stocky, with a shock of dark hair and a Liverpool accent that squeezed every bit of mileage out of his sergeant's mess repartee. He ran through a list of possible horses with the easy certainty of a colonel cataloguing wayward subalterns. One had 'been allowed to yahoo', another 'can be a maggot in a box' and a third was 'a drama horse'. He had spent twenty years in the Life Guards, most of them at mounted duty in London, and the majority of that time as a troop corporal of horse, the Household Cavalry's idiosyncratic term for sergeant.

In some respects John's job was to be the hardest. He was the only man qualified to drive our horse-box, and piloting this and its unstable occupants along an assortment of continental roads was in itself enough to try the patience of a saint. And although we all worked hard at grooming the horses, overall responsibility for them sat heavily on his shoulders. A girth-gall here or a cracked hoof there were matters of deep concern, for it was a point of honour to him that we should not loose a horse, however temporarily. It is a measure of John's triumph that when, at the very end of our trip, we took the horses over jumps at the French army's equitation centre at Fontainebleau, our hosts could hardly believe that they had just trekked down from Mons.

Captain Ollie Richardson became our administrator and logistician, either because he volunteered for it or, as I suspect was the case, because he had not been able to say 'no' quite as if he meant it. Ollie had been selling shoes in a shopping mall in Chicago in 1981 when he had decided to join the army, and he was commissioned just in time to join the Welsh Guards as they left for the Falklands. He was aboard the Royal Fleet Auxiliary *Sir Galahad* when it was bombed in Bluff Cove and, although he was anything but the caricature Falklands veteran, the experience had moved him deeply. It had also left physical scars, and even a blazing French summer could not cure the trench foot which returns to plague him every winter. Our planning was well advanced when Ollie heard that he had caught the selector's eye for redundancy, and would leave the Army in March 1994. These unwelcome tidings coincided with the news that his wife was expecting their first child, but he pushed ahead with planning for the ride, and nobody hearing his Basil Brush laugh or fractured French — both inevitably delivered at maximum volume — would have guessed that uncertainty veiled his future.

The fifth member of the team was Clive Webb-Carter, Evelyn's son. Clive was about to start the final year of his A-levels when we returned from France, and intended going to university or to Cirencester, with a short-service commission in the Grenadiers after that. Clive was sixteen, uncomplicated and quite wonderfully disorganised. Few mornings were not enlivened by questing cries of 'Dad, have you seen my breeches?' or 'Dad, do you know where my boots are?' The sole of one his jodhpur boots parted company from the uppers even before we left England, but he bore the inconvenience (no small matter when a fair amount of one's time was spent standing in manure) with characteristic humour. We called him 'HMO' (Her Majesty's Oaf) and this, too, he tolerated with good grace.

We planned to take four horses, which would ensure that our two principal riders, Evelyn and I, could change horses at lunchtime each day. Two of us would set out on horseback, leaving our companions to drive on and meet us with the horse-box and fresh horses at a pre-arranged rendezvous. Each day's march could, at a pinch, be completed by one horse so that we could continue to field two riders even if two of the horses became unsound. If we were unlucky enough to lose three horses, one rider could still complete the journey. This may seem a high degree of over-insurance, but many similar projects have been marred by sickness, or by a horse which is simply not up to its work. Riding the whole length of the retreat was always the essence of the book, and I had the uneasy feeling that my publishers would have felt contractually dissatisfied with something that ended in St Quentin or lingered on diseases of the hoof and the inadequacies of the public transport system in the Aisne valley.

One of the four horses was easily selected. Clive is as inseparable from Thomas as from his eternal jeans and t-shirt. Thomas is a nine-year-old thoroughbred cross gelding, chestnut with a white blaze, 16.3 hands high (or, to the non-horsy, 5ft 7ins/170cm from the bottom of his hoof to the top of his shoulders, the withers). Thomas was the only one of our equine quartet whose breeding and manners would unquestionably have made him a charger in 1914. 'Charger' has a specific military meaning: it is an officer's warhorse. A private soldier or NCO is mounted on a troop horse. Somehow the other horses knew it, and poor Tom-Tom found himself the low man on the totem pole, like the public school boy who finds himself, by some ghastly mischance, in the toughest of barrack-rooms. Just as Clive put up with our barbed humour so Thomas tolerated a certain amount of roughness in stable and paddock, and we all understood his motives when we were bivouacked in a field at Néry and he strolled over to join us for dinner, leaving his mates talking smut on the picket line.

Two of the horses were army remounts from Melton Mowbray, good examples of what troop horses would have been like in 1914. Jeopardy (Army No. 7129) is a ten-year-old 16.2 grey gelding, bought, like most army horses then and now, from a stud in Ireland. He was initially destined to be a trumpeter's horse in the Household Cavalry. Trumpeters traditionally have mounts whose colours contrast with those of chargers and troop horses. This is not just an aesthetic contrivance. A trumpeter was as essential in the horse and musket age as a radio operator is now, and dressing and mounting him distinctively enabled his officer to pick him out. Trumpeters' greys retained something of their old purpose as long as the House-hold Cavalry expected to take the field mounted: a film taken on training in the inter-war years shows greys being used as markers on a night march, standing out well against the blackness which swallowed up their sombre stablemates.

Jeopardy did not retain his status for long. Bought by the Army in 1987, he was re-classified as a riding horse the following year and spent the rest of his career at Melton Mowbray rather than the Household Cavalry's barracks at Knightsbridge. Although he is a handsome fellow, and a livelier ride than his military stablemate, his defects soon emerged. His wind was poor, and after a moderate canter he sounded like a kettle at boiling point. His front hooves were prone to cracks, and towards the end of our trip the state of his feet was a growing concern. He had long ago discovered that a horse's lead-rope is tied to a short length of bailer twine so that if the horse does decide to break loose he snaps the twine, not the headcollar. Jeopardy scorched through bailer twine as a chain-smoker gets through cigarettes, not with a sudden jerk but with a long, steady pull which, as we were to discover, could easily lead to architectural remodelling if the twine refused to break. Finally, he sometimes forgot himself in the matter of biting, and even as I write, in the gloaming of a Hampshire autumn, I cannot fully use my right forefinger, which Jeopardy attended to at an already tense lunch halt.

Mr Magoo (Army No. 7289) came, like his stablemate, from Waterford in the Irish Republic. He is eight years old, brown with a star, and stands 16.1 hands. Magoo was the least fit and idlest of our horses, but there was something about him which grew on us as the trip went on. He remained obstinately well-mannered to his riders: dogs, combined harvesters, Parisian boy racers thrumming past in their Porsches, all failed to shake him. Where the other horses were concerned, Magoo's word was law: he enforced discipline with much baring of teeth and the occasional nip. I noticed John's manner towards him change, and by the end of the first week there was something identifiable as mutual respect. John would mutter 'Magoo' — not 'maggot' or worse — as he entered his stall, and Magoo would snort, brace up for a moment, and then relapse into watchful lethargy. One old warhorse had the measure of another.

My horse never looked like being a problem. I intended to borrow Josepha, a great-hearted polo pony I rode often. She is shorter than the other horses on the trip but this was not in itself a disadvantage. Chargers and troop horses alike were often much smaller than we imagine — the Dragoons of Napoleon's Imperial Guard were mounted on horses averaging 15 hands, and Commanche, Captain

Miles Keogh's charger and the only survivor of the destruction of Custer's 7th Cavalry at the Little Big Horn, is 15.2. I use the present tense advisedly, for Commanche can still be seen, stuffed and slightly moth-eaten, in the University of Kansas. But, as is sometimes the case with ladies of a certain age, Josepha's spirit was willing but her flesh was weak. We were less than three months away from departure when I realised what I should have known all along: that she was a brave old girl but was simply not up to the journey. This left me with the task of finding a suitable horse with all too little time available.

For a frantic week I did nothing but search. A neighbour, Charlie Corbett, an unfailing source of sound advice in matters equine, supplied me with a list of telephone numbers and I ploughed on from there, increasingly aware that I was exactly the sort of person most likely to make an expensive mistake. Buying a horse makes buying a used car look effortlessly simple. Even if a vet can detect every physical defect, matters of character and temperament are far harder to ascertain, and may lie hidden until it is too late. I was to ride across the field of Mons with a Belgian gentleman mounted on what even I could see was a stunning horse, with the dished face and high-set tail of the Arab. 'That', I said with perfect frankness, 'is a wonderful looking horse.' 'You are precisely right,' he replied sadly. 'It is wonderful looking, but quite useless. I rode it out to meet you, but I shall certainly change it for a better horse as we pass my stables. This looks fine, but falls over whenever it canters, which, as you will agree, is something of a disadvantage.'

I narrowly missed half a dozen horses that would, as their ex-owners explained at length, have done admirably if only I'd phoned a day before. My eyes grew blurred skimming down columns of advertisements in the horsy press, and in the process I gained a working knowledge of adspeak, the sort of terminology that is anything but confined to estate agents. Every phrase had a hidden meaning, and a brief glossary ought to include the following:

Has been hunted — Terrified me on my one morning out
Would suit keen teenager — Would suit nineteen-year-old youth with nerves of steel and muscles to match
Not a novice ride — Definitely not a novice ride
Has been seen to weave — Known on the yard as The Whirling Dervish
Good to shoe and clip — But a real beast to get into a box

Eventually, a contact from the widening ripples of Charlie Corbett's friends told me of a horse in Sussex. His niece had considered buying it but looked 'like a pea on a drum' on its back. It was, predictably, at exactly the top of my price-range, and my informant's voice dropped conspiratorially as he told me of another problem. The horse was, he whispered, 'a bit common about the head'. By this stage in proceedings I did not much care whether he had zebra-stripes and luminous hooves, provided that he was unfailingly good-natured and tough enough to carry me up hill and down dale from Mons to the Marne. I made an appointment to see him the following day, though I was warned that somebody was already ahead of me in the queue.

I drove over to Pulborough on a warm Saturday afternoon, half sure that the horse would have been sold. His owner's farmhouse, tucked away at the end of a lane in a fold of the downs, was not easy to find, but I arrived, more by luck than good judgement, at exactly the right time, and saw the large Viyella-clad figure of John Parker standing beside the stables, talking to a groom in her late teens. I was climbing out of my car when a large grey head appeared over a stable door to my right: thus Thatch, the Horse That Ate Europe.

Thatch's distinctive features had already deterred that morning's prospective purchaser. 'Ah, yes . . .' he had exclaimed, as the great face materialised. 'Thank you, thank you, but that's not quite what I'm after,' and he had vanished down the lane just as quickly as he had come up it. It was hard to miss the Roman nose, not usually deemed a sign of fine breeding, knicker-pink against a grey face. And as Amy, his groom, led Thatch out the reason for his name became evident: there was a big splash of Appaloosa brown on his quarters. Damon Runyon would have described him as a hammered-down horse. His stocky body is carried on legs which are a good deal shorter than those found on a diagram of The Proportionate Horse. He may not have 'a head like a lady's maid' but, in the cob tradition, certainly has 'a bottom like a cook', though he is a good hand and a half taller than the cob's show-ring limit of 15.1.

His mighty hooves give a clue to his ancestry. Thatch is part Irish Draught, not the classic hunter pedigree of Irish Draught cross Thoroughbred, but Irish Draught mixed with something rather heavier. His colour and the low soles of his hooves point to Percheron amongst his forebears. Horses of Thatch's build had a military background every bit as distinguished as that of more finely-bred chargers. They once carried armoured warriors into battle, and in the First World War their strength and stamina provided the motive power for field artillery. He is perhaps, in the cutting words of a Wellingtonian confidential report, more fitted to carry the hod than the epaulette, but I wanted a workman not a dancing-master.

I watched Amy put Thatch over some simple jumps, and then rode him myself. We made a passable attempt at twenty-metre circles at walk, trot and canter, but it was clear that this sort of thing was not much to Thatch's taste, scarcely surprisingly, for he understood hunting, not this riding-school nonsense. He was much happier hacking out, and passed all his tests with flying colours. He squeezed past a tractor, stood stock-still while I opened a gate, and then hurtled obediently down a long grassy track — it was like being in a flying armchair — coming to a dignified halt at the end without the need for any white-knuckled tugging. Amy evidently loved him dearly, which was a good sign, and John Parker seemed exactly what Thatch's subsequent behaviour has confirmed him as: one of that disappearing breed of gentlemen whose word is their bond. By the time we drank tea in the farmhouse kitchen I had bought Thatch, subject to the vet's verdict, and there have been few decisions I have regretted less.

We all have failings, and Thatch is no exception. He is not always steadfast in his dealings with dogs, a matter of some concern in dog-infested France. There is not an ounce of malice in him, but he is what John terms 'a piss-taker'. Groom him inside and he stands still, but groom him outside and he skitters about, waiting only for you to apply a brush to his luxuriant tail before hopping sideways. When you try to do up his girth he turns his head to say: 'There must be some mistake, master: that little thing can't possibly fit *me*'. Once the girth is safely on, he resists every attempt to do it up more than a hole at a time. Then you come to mount: he breathes in, the saddle revolves with your weight in one stirrup, and the assembled stable-yard is treated to an outburst of unscholarly language. Lastly, he is an inveterate snacker. Trees, bushes and grass all fall prey to swift grabs by those pink and rubbery lips. Carry a whip and he behaves immaculately. Forget it and you arrive at your destination with the evidence of picnicking shining green about his muzzle; he then compounds the felony by nuzzling you enthusiastically in the back when you dismount and turn to run his stirrups up, thereby writing off a shirt that might, with luck, have staggered on for another day.

I bought Thatch with just enough time to get us both fit for the journey. In the meantime, Evelyn, Ollie and John made their own final arrangements. Evelyn and Ollie dealt with an assortment of French and Belgian agencies and individuals, the latter largely the product of a network of contacts which persuades me that the mafia has nothing on the Household Division, putting the finishing touches to details of route and accommodation. For the former we were heavily dependent on the *Association Nationale de Tourisme Equestre* (ANTE), whose regional branches supplied us with details of off-road routes which took us between battlefields. It is fair to say that not all branches were as efficient as some, and the southern end of our journey was destined to remain under what might best be termed as intelligence blackout. Our accommodation, much of it provided by friends of friends, varied dramatically: one of the attractions of the trip was that one might wake under a hedge and sleep in a château. John was deep in the world of jute rugs, nosebags and surcingles, and by late July had amassed, I know not how, enough equipment to deal with almost any eventuality.

As the date of our departure approached, my morale grew increasingly fragile. I became the horse boutique's best friend, hoovering up all sorts of patent devices designed to prevent Thatch or myself from falling victim to anything from a sore back to sunstroke. Most of them remain in virgin packaging. The week before we left I drove up to Catterick — Evelyn's brigade had moved there from the more convenient Colchester — to collect his horse trailer, our belt-and-braces way of transporting two of the horses in case anything happened to the box. It was a long time since I had towed a trailer (far less backed one) and by the time I found myself leading Thatch aboard it early on the morning of Saturday 7 August to join the others in London, I was convinced that this was all a piece of consummate folly. Armchair history did not seem so bad after all, and if I really had to ride across a battlefield I could do Cheriton and still be home for tea.

II

HORSE, FOOT AND GUNS

The fighting troops of an army are composed of cavalry, artillery, engineers, infantry, cyclists and the flying corps. These arms are in certain proportions which have been fixed as the result of experience. Each has its special characteristics and functions, and is dependent on the assistance of the others.

Field Service Regulations Part 1 1909

Something old, something new

The armies of August 1914 were a pastiche of ancient and modern. The killing-power that thumped from Lee-Enfield, Mauser and Lebel, clattered out of Maxim, Spandau and Hotchkiss, and spun away from 18-pdr, 75mm and 77mm, was a quantum leap from that used in the previous major European conflict, the Franco-Prussian War of 1870–71. But in so many other respects 1914 would not have been beyond the comprehension of Wellington or Marlborough. Although railways whisked men to concentration areas with a comfort their grandfathers would have envied, once they had detrained they were scarcely more mobile than the warriors of Agincourt or Crécy.

Communications, too, were as much Marlburian as modern. Guglielmo Marconi had sent a radio signal across the Atlantic in 1901, and in 1910 the murderer Hawley Harvey Crippen was arrested in mid-Atlantic after a suspicious captain contacted Scotland Yard by radio. There were radios in the armies of 1914 — the BEF had a single wireless section — but they were almost useless for communication below army level, and sometimes did more harm than good: the cataclysmic Russian defeat at Tannenberg was made possible because the Germans listened to radio conversations and learnt that the Russian 1st and 2nd Armies would be unable to offer mutual support.

The civilian telephone system was invaluable, armies were good at laying cable of their own, and signallers wagged away with semaphore flags or winked, when weather permitted, with heliographs. Yet the worse the crisis, the harder it was to communicate. Shellfire cut land-line and tore down telephone poles, and semaphore and heliograph had acute limitations on a fire-swept battlefield. When a senior officer sought to command in mobile battle he was back in the eighteenth century. He could go forward himself and risk becoming a casualty. Some seventy British generals were killed or died of wounds on the Western Front during the war; four were killed and one mortally wounded in its first six months. It was a natural impulse for a man used to riding with a forward seat to push on and take command in person, but he might perish in the attempt, depriving his men of leadership just when they needed it most. Gallopers, motor-cycle dispatch riders, cyclists and runners helped, but there were times when a desperate rearguard fought on to extinction, unaware that orders for withdrawal lay in a dead man's pocket somewhere behind it.

The British Expeditionary Force, in whose steps I rode, was a creature as distinctive as the spotted hyena or the two-toed sloth, and if we are to make much sense of its behaviour we must indulge in a little basic zoology. The beast was conceived in that burst of military reform which followed a lacklustre performance in the South African War of 1899–1902, when Britain had flexed all her imperial muscle to defeat the tiny armies of the Boer republics and irregulars who drew the war out into an enervating guerrilla struggle.

Almost no part of the military organism emerged from the war undamaged. The Army's central direction, unevenly balanced between the Secretary of State at the War Office and the Commander in Chief at Horse Guards, failed to exercise effective strategic control. Commanders were brave but unschooled: the replacement of Sir Revers Buller by Lord Roberts, with the dour and monkish Kitchener as his Chief of Staff, brought some improvement, but even this formidable pair made avoidable errors.

Each arm of the service had a mixed record. The artillery used tactics not unworthy of Waterloo and was outclassed by the few Krupp guns in the hands of regular Boer gunners. The cavalry tried valiantly to take sword and lance to the Queen's enemies, but its record in horsemastership was appalling: 326,000 horses perished, one officer calculating that his regiment used up a horse every three and a half miles, expending 3,750 animals in all. The infantry often showed its traditional steadiness under fire, but there was a woeful catalogue of frontal attacks and dawn surprises, and it was uncomfortably true that Boer civilians generally shot better than British regulars. Volunteers flocked to the colours — 'Cook's son, Duke's son, son of a belted Earl' — but poor training took its toll, and the song 'The Boers have got my Daddy' became lamentably popular in the music-halls.

The postwar reforms, chiefly associated with R. B. Haldane, who became Secretary of State for War when the new Liberal government took office in late 1905, had both political and military motives. It was becoming increasingly clear that Britain's main military and economic rival was Germany, not France, and that German aggression in Europe would be a more likely *casus belli* than friction with Russia on the North-West Frontier of India. In 1904 Britain and France concluded a friendly understanding, the 'entente cordiale', and in 1906 Haldane authorised the Director of Military Operations, head of one of the three branches of the newly-formed General Staff, to open unofficial 'conversations' with the French. The Army had its own reasons for welcoming these discussions, for commitment to a continental strategy would help ensure its own funding and status, whereas a more traditional view of defence priorities gave pride of place to the Navy. In 1910 Major-General Henry Wilson, an ardent francophile, became Director of Military Operations, and under his tutelage plans for sending an expeditionary force to France were finalised.

The Expeditionary Force, Britain's first-line army, was to consist of six infantry divisions and one cavalry division: we shall see, very shortly, just what these comprised. There was no operational reason for making the force this size: it was simply the largest that could fit within the confines of a tight military budget. General Headquarters (GHQ) did not exist in peacetime, but the senior officers who were to join it knew of their dormant appointments and carried out war games (in the rather dusty surrounding of the gymnasium at Sandhurst) as well as manoeuvres in open country. There were no permanent corps headquarters linking GHQ and the divisions, although Aldershot command provided the nucleus of one corps staff. It was only on mobilisation that the decision was taken to form corps to conform with French practice and there was, in consequence, a good degree of improvisation.

The departure of the Expeditionary Force would denude Britain of regular soldiers, and the Boer War had shown that the hotch-potch of non-regular troops — Yeomanry, Volunteers and Militia — needed radical reform before it would be fit to undertake major tasks unassisted. Following Haldane's remorseless logic, the defence of the national territory was entrusted to a remodelled second-line army, the Territorial Force (TF). This came into being on 1 April 1908, and comprised fourteen brigades of Yeomanry cavalry and fourteen divisions of infantry. Its officers and men served part-time, with a fortnight's annual camp and assorted training weekends and drill nights. There was a small full-time cadre, and the divisions were commanded by regular major-generals with regular staffs.

There was much muttering about the TF's efficiency or lack of it. The conscription lobby, with Lord Roberts as its most influential advocate, argued that the Territorials were a pale substitute for the compulsory service which the worsening international situation urgently demanded. Many professional soldiers argued that some tasks were inherently too complex for non-regulars, and there was a heated debate over the wisdom of giving Territorials their own artillery. Falling numbers and lack of experience — in 1913 the TF was 66,000 below its establishment strength of 300,000, and eighty per cent of its members had served for less than four years — caused further concern. It was assumed that six months' training would be required before the TF could take the field, and during that time an element of the Expeditionary Force would have to be retained within the United Kingdom. We shall not encounter the Territorials on our march, because none arrived in France in time to fight in August or September. Yet though they were not liable for overseas service and were expected to require six months' train-ing, the first of them were in action by October and acquitted themselves far better than their detractors could ever have expected. Sir John French, commander-in-chief of the BEF, freely admitted that 'we could not have held the line without them'.

The TF swept together the Yeomanry and Volunteers. The Mil-itia, always closer to the Regular Army than the Volunteers were, emerged as the Special Reserve. Each infantry regiment had its Special Reserve battalion, usually the 3rd, whose officers and men served for an initial period of six months and then returned for a fortnight each year. They joined their regiments on mobilisation, and provided drafts, as required, for the regular battalions. Similar arrangements applied in other arms and services and there were, quite exceptionally, two Special Reserve cavalry regiments, the North Irish Horse and the South Irish Horse, who provided GHQ with its mounted squadrons in 1914.

The reform of army training began with the publication of Colonel G. F. R. Henderson's *Combined Training* in 1902. The Directorate of Army Training was one of the three branches of the new General Staff, and in 1909 *Field Service Regulations* appeared in two parts, the first covering operations and the second organisation and administration. It is impossible to read *Field Service Regulations* without being struck by their good sense. They pay particular attention to co-operation between arms, and stress the contribution which relatively new devices like machine-guns and aircraft could make to the battle. In 1914 there was a rewritten version of every arm's training pamphlet and by and large these publications embodied the best of recent experience and sound judgement. Where they erred it was generally in attempting to superimpose offensive theory on the realities of firepower, and there was, as we shall see, some excuse for this.

New weapons and equipment arrived. The artillery obtained the excellent 13-pdr and 18-pdr quick-firers, the infantry the Short Magazine Lee Enfield, and the cavalry, in the shape of the 1908 pattern, the most effective sword it ever carried. New khaki uniform appeared in 1902, initially worn with the peakless Brodrick cap which perished unlamented to be replaced by the familiar peaked field service cap with its brown leather chin-strap.

It is one thing to lay a shiny veneer of reform on an army, but another to ensure that change seeps into every drill-shed and barrack-room. For all the efforts of Haldane and his supporters, in some respects the Army changed little. Its regimental system remained that bequeathed it by Cardwell's reforms of the early 1880s. These had combined pairs of numbered regiments into the 1st and 2nd battalions of a regiment with a county connection. As we look back with shining eyes at all those bright cap-badges, most now gone for ever, we should not lose sight of the fact that they were initially accepted with misgivings. There were anguished demands for the return of 'our numbers wreathed in glory', and an officer of the 67th Regiment declared that 'damned names mean nothing', and furiously refused 'to come to anything called a *Hampshire* Regimental Dinner. My compliments, Sir, and be damned'.

The essence of Cardwell's system was that one battalion would serve at home and train recruits which were sent out to the other battalion abroad. In practice, home battalions were almost constantly understrength. In May 1914 the Regular Army was 10,932 men, or 6%, short of its establishment, and it was predicted that changes in terms of service and recruitment trends would soon take this to at least 19,000. Most men who enlisted in the Army were unemployed, and only half even laid claim to a trade. This was scarcely surprising, for the Army was very poorly paid. An infantry private received weekly pay of 11s 4½d on joining, a full 2s a week less than an agricultural labourer. A cavalryman got 2d a day more. Proficiency pay and the bonus that came with good conduct badges (more easily lost than won) would increase this. Conversely, deductions ate into it: 6d a week went to the towel club (so that the soldier could dry himself after a bath), 6d a week to the barber's club, and so on. After an initial free issue of uniform, replacement items had to be bought from a quarterly allowance: a soldier received any unspent balance but could easily find himself in arrears, especially if an unscrupulous quartermaster sergeant 'put him down' for unused items in order to balance his books.

Most recruits came from a life of hardship and grinding poverty, which often showed in rickety limbs, hollow chests and tubercular coughs: just over half would-be recruits failed their medical examination in 1910. There were more 'town casuals' than unskilled agricultural workers, and the ranks of many an infantry regiment with a broad-acre set to its shoulders and perhaps 'The Farmer's Boy' as its march were actually filled with urban unemployed. The same was true of the cavalry: the 16th Lancers recruited in the west Midlands, but was known as 'The Brummagem Spearmen'. One sample of fifty men who enlisted into the cavalry between 1908 and 1912 shows that forty-one came from towns and cities and only nine from the countryside. David Ascoli is probably right to suggest that most country boys understood the work-creating nature of the horse far too well to risk becoming trapped in the world of wheelbarrows and muck-heaps.

London not only filled its local regiments like the Royal Fusiliers and the Middlesex — both of them reflected their fertile recruiting areas by having four regular battalions. It also sent Cockneys far afield, where they turned up as kilted highlanders, trewsed lowlanders and quick-stepping riflemen. Birmingham, with more young men than jobs, produced not just rank upon rank of Royal Warwicks but also more than its fair share of Royal Welsh Fusiliers. Captain Robert Graves recalled his company sergeant-major, a Birmingham man, giving a stern ticking-off to a German who had been captured with a collection of lurid photographs. There were Irishmen everywhere, not only in Irish regiments, horse and foot, but also in overtly English ones: not for nothing was the York and Lancaster Regiment styled (safely out of earshot of its members who were likely to respond to slights with a playful tap) the Cork and Doncaster. The King's Liverpool Regiment and the Manchester Regiment snapped up many an Irish lad not long after he stepped off the Liverpool ferry.

Reasons for taking the King's shilling varied. Often it was 'unemployment and the need for food' as one 1913 recruit put it. But sometimes, perhaps rather more often than historians are inclined to admit, a young man's taste for adventure, and a need to feel valued and valuable, persuaded him to go for a soldier. William Nicholson had been well educated at a Board School and had a job as a telegraph messenger. His grandfather had charged with the 13th Light Dragoons at Balaklava and three of his uncles were regular NCOs. Family opinions, which so often militated against enlistment — the future Field-Marshal Sir William Robertson's mother said that she would rather bury him than see him in a red coat — encouraged him to join. 'I was also attracted,' he admitted, 'by the full-dress uniform of mounted regiments.' Herbert Wootton felt much the same. He was:

> Very keen on becoming a soldier. I had two uncles, both regulars who served through the South African War of 1899–1902. As a youngster I was thrilled with their stories. I became a keen reader of G. A. Henty's books on war, and later read Rudyard Kipling's books. I loved to be in the company of old soldiers.

Sometimes family tradition or personal preference made a man's choice of regiment quite specific. R. A. Lloyd joined the Life Guards in 1911. It was not a difficult decision, for: 'I had always wanted to be a soldier, and a cavalryman at that.' R. G. Garrod would have agreed. He was a junior clerk when he saw 'a gorgeous figure in blue with yellow braid and clinking spurs and said to myself "that's for me . . ." ' Fred Milton, in contrast, simply fell into the Army. He was a farm worker at South Brent, and went off with a friend one Saturday to see the bright lights of Newton Abbot. 'About four o'clock we were spied by a recruiting sergeant', he remembered, 'and within a couple of hours we found ourselves in the Devons. And I stayed there for twenty-two years.'

John Lucy and his brother Denis had 'gone a bit wild' after their mother died.

> We were tired of fathers, of advice from relations, of bottled coffee essence, of school, of newspaper offices. The soft accents and slow movements of the small farmers who swarmed in the streets of our dull southern Irish town, the cattle, fowl, eggs, butter, bacon, and the talk of politics filled us with loathing.

They enlisted in the Royal Irish Rifles, and found its ranks filled largely with 'scallywags and minor adventurers', as well as a few strange characters:

> There was a taciturn sergeant from Waterford who was conversant with the intricacies of higher mathematics ... There was an ex-divinity student with literary tastes, who drank much beer and affected an obvious pretence to gentle birth; a national school teacher; a man who had absconded from a colonial bank; a few decent sons of farmers.

What Private Frank Richards of the Royal Welch Fusiliers termed 'booze and fillies' were a constant preoccupation. George Barrow was commissioned in 1884 and joined the Connaught Rangers in India. 'Drink', he wrote sadly, 'was the besetting sin of the Connaught men.' But then, few regiments had a fiercer reputation for drinking and fighting. In 1916 a benevolent lady visited a Ranger in hospital. 'This is a terrible war, my poor man,' she lamented. 'Yes ma'am,' he replied, ''tis a terrible war, but 'tis better than no war at all.' The Army Temperance Society — its adherents unkindly termed 'tea busters' or 'bun wallahs' by the beery majority — made some impact on the drunkenness which ravaged the Victorian army. The Garrison Institute Coffee Shop offered heat, light and newspapers at trivial cost, but the wet canteen continued to do a roaring trade. In 1912–13, 9,230 men were fined for drunkenness, and this figure is the tip of the iceberg, for many offenders were dealt with less formally by NCOs, or received other punishments from company commanders. Drink was a constant lure. The 11th Hussars' history ruefully acknowledges that as soon as the regiment disembarked in France it discovered that the *Hangar des Cotons* — a huge warehouse which contained their brigade — 'also accommodated the BEF's rum casks, and two men fell to the temptation'. A Field

General Court Martial awarded the miscreants three months' imprisonment apiece.

Fillies were at least as much of a problem. Although soldiers might marry, they could only 'marry on strength' if vacancies for wives existed. Marrying 'off the strength' meant that the happy couple were not entitled to accommodation and when the regiment moved the family had to follow at its expense. In practice, this meant that only senior NCOs were married, and most soldiers had to take their pleasures as they found them. There was a good deal of dalliance with housemaids and the like, which often ended with an identification parade, the regiment drawn up for the unlucky girl to peregrinate tearfully along its nervous ranks to identify the author of her woes.

Some brief pleasure could be had from ladies of the town. The fortress-like red-brick barracks built to house regimental depots in the Cardwell era — Brock Barracks in Reading, Roussillon Barracks in Chichester or Le Marchant Barracks at Devizes — were partly surrounded by iron railings which were far enough apart for commerce to be carried on between them. The lady pocketed the proffered 6d — there was much heavy humour about the fact that this was a marksman's daily proficiency pay — and backed gingerly onto the railings while her client made the appropriate arrangements from his side.

The appetite for fillies grew rather than diminished with war. Frank Richards recalled that most of his comrades left cap and collar badges with the French girls they had been walking out with at Vicq, in their concentration area. 'I expect in some cases [they] had also left other souvenirs which would be a blessing or a curse to the ladies concerned,' he added. The imminence of death could infuse a wild urgency into such relationships. Sergei Kournakoff, an officer in the Caucasian Native Cavalry Division, argued that 'slaughter and procreation are blood-kin'. In early 1915, an officer going up into the line at Ypres saw a young Highlander making passionate love to a shop assistant, impelled, perhaps, to create a new life as his own seemed so terribly fragile.

We should be neither surprised nor shocked by this, for Kipling was right to warn his readers that 'single men in barracks don't grow into plaster saints'. But, equally, we should guard against the easy assumption that every regular soldier was a beer-swilling, filly-faking thug. I never cease to be struck by the very high quality of so many of the letters and diaries left by pre-war regulars. William

Nicolson's elegant copperplate pays eloquent tribute to the achievements of his Board School. Ernest Shephard, a regular NCO in the Dorsets, left school at fourteen, yet his diaries are not only beautifully written but testify to a lively intellect. After hearing Professor Atkins of Cambridge University speak on the position of Turkey in Europe and the Slav question in the canteen at Blendecques he wrote: 'I should very much like to get the chief points of these lectures in their sequence for study at leisure.' R. A. Lloyd read for his degree at London University while a serving Life Guard NCO, and eventually left the army to become a schoolmaster.

If the BEF's soldiers came from backgrounds which had changed little since Wellington's day, the origins of its officers, too, would not have surprised the Duke. Most came from traditional officer-producing backgrounds — the peerage, gentry, military families, the clergy and the professions, with a smaller admixture from commerce and industry. 'The county communities continued to provide the bulk of officers in the early twentieth century,' suggests Edward Spiers. 'Within their confines an uncomplicated patriotism and sense of duty flourished alongside an unbridled enthusiasm for field sports.' The officer corps was two-thirds rural, in part because of the tendency of families who had made their money in industry to set the seal on social ascent by buying estates and becoming landed gentry. While service in the ranks was the kiss of death to a middle-class boy, a commission was entirely the reverse. Service as an officer conferred status and respect and, in brusquely practical terms, was one of the few alternatives open to a youth who failed the competitive examinations to the Indian Civil Service but wished to pursue a 'gentleman's' career.

Well over half of regular officers came from public schools. Many had 'army classes' which specifically prepared boys for entrance to The Royal Military College Sandhurst (for infantry and cavalry) and the Royal Military Academy Woolwich (for gunners and sappers). Most had Officers' Training Corps which granted certificates of military training to diligent cadets and thereby eased entry into the Regular Army, Special Reserve and Territorial Force. The OTCs did not produce as many officers as Haldane hoped, but his assumption that many ex-cadets would come forward to take commission in the event of war was amply justified, as rolls of honour in chapel and cloister proudly proclaim. When the Bishop of Malvern dedicated the war memorial of Malvern College he described the loss of public school boys in the war as 'the wiping out of a generation'. It was an understandable exaggeration, though the truth was scarcely less sombre: when J. M. Winter examined what he termed 'the slaughter of social elites', he concluded that public schools lost on average one boy killed for every five who served.

Neither the public schools nor the military crammers who often took over where they failed in an effort to get a boy into Sandhurst or Woolwich were hugely successful in purely educational terms. The 1902 Akers-Douglas Committee on military education reported that most young men seeking commissions were 'deficient in general education'. But the Army valued public schools precisely because of those qualities which impelled so many public school boys to volunteer in 1914. As we approach the end of a century littered with blighted hopes and broken promises it is easy to poke fun at public schools with their emphasis on self-denial, team spirit and manly sports. The fact remains that public schools did produce young men inculcated with loyalty and prepared to accept responsibility; in short, first-rate officer material.

But a more tangible commodity was required. In order to pass into the Indian Army from Sandhurst or the Royal Engineers from Woolwich a cadet had to come towards the top of the order of merit. This did not simply reflect a desire to serve in India or to master the intricacies of field engineering; it was because it was impossible to accept a commission in a British infantry or cavalry regiment or the Royal Artillery without private means. A subaltern had to meet initial costs (of say £200 in the infantry and £600 in the cavalry) to provide his uniform and other requisites, and then maintain his uniform, pay a soldier-servant, meet a monthly mess-bill, the costs of field sports and the incidental expenses of moving from one garrison to another.

Expenses varied from regiment to regiment. In 1913 E. G. W. Harrison survived as a gunner subaltern on an allowance of £18 per annum, which brought his annual income to £92. Survived is exactly the word because, as he admitted, 'Mess bill without a drink or a cigarette [was] £6 monthly, soldier servant and washing £1 monthly, so a penny bus fare was a matter of deep consideration'. Alan Hanbury-Sparrow joined the Royal Berkshires with an allowance of £175 per annum, a little above the £160 per annum that a 1903 War Office committee estimated to be the minimum necessary allowance for a line infantry officer: the Footguards demanded at the very least £400 a year.

The cavalry was even more expensive because an officer had to provide at least one charger and could scarcely avoid hunting and playing polo. He might just scrape by with a private income of £300 a year, but the average was some £600–£700, nearly eight times a second-lieutenant's annual pay and twice a lieutenant-colonel's. When he wrote *Our Cavalry* in 1912, Major-General M. F. Rimington acknowledged that it was becoming increasingly difficult to find the right sort of cavalry officer. The new seriousness which had infected the mounted arm meant that work was getting harder. Once an officer could hunt every day but now, Rimington observed with alarm, officers were expected to work till 1.00 or even 3.00 p.m. 'We particularly want the hunting breed of man,' he declared, 'because he goes into danger for the love of it . . . we draw on a class who have not been used to much brain work . . . the young officer should for choice be country bred, fond of sport, a 'trier' and there must be some private income.'

In the years before the First World War, a series of committees reviewed allowances because it was becoming harder to find an adequate number of cavalry officers, and resignations from the cavalry reached epidemic proportions. The 1905 Hutchinson Committee concluded that: 'The average English boy would prefer cavalry to other branches of the Service if he could afford it, and this is confirmed by the fact that there is no difficulty finding recruits for the Indian cavalry'. It recommended that an officer should receive his field service kit, chargers and saddlery at public expense, and although the cost of serving in the cavalry was reduced it remained so high as to deter many young men. There was a serious shortage of cavalry officers in 1914. A total of 792 were required, but only 632, including reservists, were available at home — a shortfall of 20.2 per cent.

The young officer spent the first few months of his commissioned service back amongst the new boys, learning his trade with the recruits until he was deemed competent to take charge of his platoon. At first he might find life in the mess rather frosty. Second-lieutenants were known collectively as warts — for a wart is a useless fleshy excrescence — and some officers saw 'toning up the warts' as part of their duty, just as prefects had kept the fags on their toes. The overwhelming majority of a regiment's officers lived in the mess. It was said that 'subalterns must not marry; captains might marry, majors ought to marry and lieutenant-colonels must marry'. Officers were older than we might expect: there were subalterns in their thirties and captains in their forties. As a young officer became more confident, and ran with the wolf-pack below the salt, he would grow to appreciate the informal style that prevailed in most messes. There was no sirring in the mess in most of the infantry and cavalry: officers called one another by their surnames (first names or nicknames were for close friends) and the commanding officer was 'colonel'.

There was inevitably a gulf between the officer and the men he commanded. In many regiments a private soldier could not address an officer without an NCO acting as go-between. John Lucy thought that 'the pre-war officer, despite his pleasant fancy to the contrary, was not very much in touch with his men, whose temper and habits were better known to the non-commissioned officers'. R. A. Lloyd made precisely the same point. His commanding officer, Lieutenant-Colonel E. B. Cook, 'was a thorough gentleman, sympathetic and approachable'. However, 'If he had a fault, it was that, in common with all the senior officers, he did not get about enough among the men. Hence much that he would never have tolerated went on in the regiment without his knowledge.'

This remoteness should be kept in proportion, and in any event war quickly broke it down. Ernest Shephard was genuinely delighted when his company commander was decorated. 'He is a real sample of the Regular "Officer and Gentleman",' he wrote in his diary. 'One of the old 1st Bn officers. Absolutely fearless and first and last thought for his men.' Later, when Captain Algeo was reported missing, Shephard lamented: 'The loss of my gallant Captain to the Battalion, my Company and myself cannot be estimated. He was the bravest officer I have met . . .'

In good units mutual affection and respect bridged the barriers of rank. Indeed, in some respects the British army, for all the rigidity of its hierarchy, was actually less class-conscious than the German army. Five hundred warrant officers and NCOs were commissioned in the first month of the war, and as the war went on the officers' mess was enriched by a steady flow of sergeants. Alan Hanbury-Sparrow thought that Colour-Sergeant Foster, who became sniping officer and then adjutant when he himself was commanding officer, was: 'most valuable . . . He must have killed over twenty German snipers and had his warnings been taken seriously about the location of enemy MGs, the 8th Division would never have lost so heavily on the first day of the Somme.'

Ernest Shephard was commissioned in November 1916, and wrote proudly that: 'The man who passes through the ranks to a commissioned rank is the better for his experience.' He commanded a company as a second-lieutenant, but had precious little opportunity to savour his new star. His company was counter-attacked after taking an objective: professional to the last, he told the commander of a flanking company to fall back because the position was untenable, and died as German infantry swarmed in with stick-bomb and bayonet. John Lucy, too, was commissioned, and as he mounted the steps to the officers' mess he looked back at his chum, Big Jim, motionless against the lighted windows of the sergeants' mess. 'I was proud now to be an officer,' he mused, 'but prouder far to have been a Regular sergeant with those chaps.'

An officer's first months with his battalion were anything but easy, but most private soldiers found the first months of their service decidedly hard. The Lucy brothers 'became insensitive, bored and revolted and talked seriously of deserting after three months of the life.' R. G. Garrod spent weeks at foot drill before he even saw a horse, and was not allowed to walk out in the frogged tunic which had so attracted him until he had perfected picking up a dropped whip or glove: the braces of his leg-hugging overalls were so tight that he had to cushion them with cotton wool to prevent them from chafing his shoulders. Then he was allocated a horse, and with it came the repetitious drudgery associated with that noble beast: 'First sponge out eyes, nose and dock, then pick out feet, then start to brush, using only the brush on the horse, while the curry comb, held in the left hand, was used only for cleaning the brush'.

Horse maintenance dominated the day in the cavalry and artillery. Routine varied from regiment to regiment and with the time of year, but a young soldier in a mounted regiment would find his dawn-to-dusk existence crammed full of saddle-soap and stable-forks. Reveille was at 5.30 a.m., and beds were made up and rooms swept before warning for stables sounded at 5.45. First stables was at 6.00: horses were mucked out and groomed before breakfast and the squadron leader's inspection. Men spent the first half of the morning in the riding school, before another round of stables at 11.00 a.m., followed by saddlery cleaning till lunch at 12.45 p.m. Afternoon work began at 2.00 p.m., and might consist of foot drill and gymnastics. The day's third stables began at 4.45, and the 'tea meal' and more kit cleaning followed it. By 9.00 p.m. our hero was free to walk out if he had permission to do so and could pass the guard commander's inspection, but with only an hour to lights out he might be forgiven for collapsing on his bed.

After about six months of this unrelenting pressure, most of it applied by NCOs, men changed. Physically, because a combination of regular food and exercise filled them out. 'I felt really fit,' remembered George Ashurst, 'with the cross-country running and the gym exercises we had daily . . .' Mounted men toughened up after those hours in the riding school. Private Garrod (private soldiers in line cavalry were not officially called troopers till 1922, though the term 'troopers' was used for cavalrymen generically) graduated from the recruit ride to exercises in the Abbey Field in Colchester: 'To practise figure of eight, jumping, balloon bursting, and taking the rings, which was a really interesting exercise as there was a great competition to see who could get the most rings on his sword blade'. He was promoted to first class ride, with spurs, sword, rifle and double reins, and took fencing lessons — although this meant that he missed tea — gaining the mounted skill-at-arms proficiency badge of crossed swords and the extra 6d a day that went with it. By the end of the process, as he recalled: 'we were very well trained in horsemanship, doing attack riding, vaulting, which entails jumping off your horse at full gallop and leaping up again into the saddle. We took jumps with no reins and no stirrups, just with folded arms.'

Mentally, men changed as self-confidence and pride hardened, and the pervasive discipline seemed less obtrusive. John Lucy linked these physical and mental transitions: 'Our bodies developed and our backs straightened according to plan. We marched instead of walking, and we forced on ourselves that rigidity of limb and poker face that marks the professional soldier. Pride of arms possessed us, and we discovered that our regiment was a regiment, and then some.'

The regimental system defied logic. It was intended to bring men from the same area together, but, as we have seen, often failed to do so. It also strove to promote cohesion on active service by ensuring that robust bonds of mateship held men together. While this may have worked well enough for colonial soldiering, it was not uniformly successful in 1914. About half the BEF's soldiers were reservists, and in some battalions the proportion was much higher. 4th Battalion The Royal Fusiliers, which was to be one of the three hardest-hit units at Mons, needed 734 reservists to bring it up to war establishment.

Yet the system conferred tangible benefits, in great measure because it gratified that heartfelt British need: to belong to a tribe with its own distinctive war-paint. It was, in part, a club for the officers, and the prevalence of royal colonels-in-chief — The Kaiser had 1st Royal Dragoons — gave membership a cachet no money could buy. It helped put a rural patina on new money, and conferred a county connection which underlined a family's ascent from 'trade'.

For soldiers, the regiment was a team which trained hard for a rough game. It was much more than simply what the psychologist Wilfred Trotter called 'a body solidly united for a single purpose'. The body had existed for centuries, and would abide when those who composed it at any one time did not. Suffering and even death could be minimised by being placed in a regimental context. The system encouraged men to emulate not only the bravery of their comrades to left and right but the achievements of their ancestors. Sir Henry Lawrence, who defended the Residency at Lucknow during the Indian Mutiny, argued that: 'Courage goes much by opinion, and many a man behaves as a hero or a coward according as how he considers he is expected to behave'. The regimental system bestowed this expectation of courage on men who, in the harshest terms of social analysis, were often grubby urchins or feckless bumpkins. It gave them, perhaps for the only time in their lives, something to look up to, something to admire, even something to worship.

Instead of showing team loyalty by a coloured scarf, the point was made by cap-badge and shoulder title. Past successes were borne as battle honours on the colours and recalled on Regimental Days. Sometimes past disasters were tricked out in such dazzling heroism that they became victories of a kind. The Footguards remembered that they had beaten the French Guards at Fontenoy (1745), but forgot that the French had won the battle. The Royal Berkshires were rightly proud of Maiwand (1880). Whimsical portrayals of their last stand graced everything from the officers' mess to corporals' bunks: the group even included a dog, Maiwand Bobby, a terrier-like chap of uncertain parentage who survived the battle only to perish beneath a cab outside the regimental depot in the Oxford Road, Reading. It was an uncomfortable fact, however, that the Afghans had actually won Maiwand.

Most regimental tradition was carried, sometimes with a good deal of sleight of hand, back beyond the Cardwell reforms. Much was simply invented. The Royal Sussex wore the Roussillon Plume as part of its cap-badge, having allegedly won it from the Roussillon Regiment at Quebec in 1759. The Roussillon Regiment, alas, did not wear a plume. We probably have to thank a quick-thinking Commanding Officer — 'Won it from the French, Sir' — for the survival of what began as an unofficial bit of campaign costume jewellery, feathers stuck in hats to show that I was there and you were not.

Charles Wilson — subsequently ennobled as Lord Moran — who was commissioned into the RAMC in October 1914 and spent much of the war as a Regimental Medical Officer with the Royal Fusiliers argued that: 'Loyalty to a fine battalion may take hold of a man and stiffen his purpose'. His experiences helped him write *The Anatomy of Courage*, in which he argued that regimental loyalty helped deepen a man's well of courage. The regiment was 'the source of their strength, their abiding faith, it was the last of all the creeds that in historical times have steeled men against death'. Bill Slim, junior officer in the First World War and army commander in the Second, declared that: 'The moral strength of the British army is in the sum of all these family or clan loyalties. They are the foundations of the British soldier's stubborn valour.' The regimental system was not the only reason why the BEF fought hard in August 1914 and there were times when all its strengths could not prevent men from running or surrendering. But it was one of the BEF's unmistakable characteristics, and made its own unique contribution to enabling men to cope with the trials of that lime-kiln summer.

Eight 'undred fightin' Englishmen, the Colonel, and the Band

So much for the creature's physiology. Now let us look at its behaviour, and stand beside one of those endless poplar-lined roads of northern France to watch the infantry come by, trudging to a hundred destinations but a common fate: most of the soldiers we see will be dead or wounded before the year is over. At the head of the battalion column rides the commanding officer, a lieutenant-colonel in khaki barathea tunic, Bedford cord breeches and high, brown field-boots, the splash of medal ribbons marking him out as a man who smelt powder in South Africa over a decade before. He is already well into his middle years, and that thoughtful look may tell us that he already knows what others suspect: he is not quite the man he was, more worrier, now, than warrior, with late nights and early starts far more of a strain than when he was chasing de Wet or mounting bridge-guard in the Karroo.

The colonel has a little headquarters. His adjutant, a captain, rides with him; his second-in-command, a major, is enjoined by regulations to follow at the rear of the battalion as whipper-in, but do not be surprised if he escapes from the dust to trot forward for a pipe and a chat. The pioneers under their sergeant — the only man in the battalion allowed to wear a beard — stump along behind, on hand in case a gate needs taking off its hinges or a broken-down wagon has to be heaved onto the verge. Next comes the Corps of Drums, fighting soldiers as well as musicians, ready to strike up 'The Young May Moon' or 'It's a Long Way to Tipperary' if they are from an English regiment, or to set fingers to chanters for 'Black Bear' or 'Hielan' Laddie' if they are Scots.

The buglers are both notice-board and public address system. Their calls regulate the day in barracks and camp, and even now we may hear them on the battlefield. Soldiers have memorised the calls by putting words to them. There is an official version, inevitably corrupted. 'Come and do your guard, my boys! Come and do your guard! You've had fourteen nights in bed, so it won't be hard' suggests *Trumpet and Bugle Sounds for the Army*. 'Come and do a picket, boys, come and do a guard! You think it's fucking easy but you'll find it's fucking hard' chant the irreverent soldiery. Such rudery was international. Russian cavalrymen remembered the call for 'Mount' by giving it the words 'The devil got hold of me, and I mounted a nun'.

The unmistakable figure of the Regimental Sergeant-Major, a warrant officer and the battalion's senior non-commissioned member, strides along ahead of the leading rifle company. Each of the four companies has a nominal strength of six officers and 221 men. A major or captain, mounted like the officers at the head of the column, commands each company, with a captain as his second-in-command. The subalterns — lieutenants and second-lieutenants — command the four platoons, each consisting of a sergeant and forty-six men, and subdivided into a small headquarters and four ten-man sections under a corporal.

This organisation is unfamiliar to many of the soldiers in its four-deep ranks. For although the British Army, unique amongst the combatant powers, has no conscripts, not all its soldiers are regulars. Many are reservists, snatched back from civil life. Frank Richards had served eight years with the colours and had become a timberman's assistant in a mine. He was enjoying a beer with his mates in the Castle Hotel at Blaina when somebody came in with the news that the police sergeant was hanging up a notice recalling reservists. Richards duly reported to his Regimental Depot at Wrexham the following day, having stayed at a nearby pub till 'stop tap' and arriving at the barracks 'in a jovial state.' He was posted to 2nd Royal Welch Fusiliers, and recalled that his fellow reservists were 'a little muddled' by the four-company organisation, having been used to the pre-1913 eight-company system.

Not only has the new organisation robbed half the battalion's captains of their former status as company commanders — James Jack, junior captain in his Cameronian battalion, finds himself leading a platoon — but the company commander's erstwhile right-hand man, the colour-sergeant, has also declined in importance. With the change to four companies, the four senior colour-sergeants in each battalion became company sergeant-majors, although it will not be until 1915 that they receive their own badge of rank — a crown on the cuff — and the status of Warrant Officer Class 2. The four juniors retain the rank of colour-sergeant and have become company quartermaster-sergeants, responsible for administration within their companies.

Toiling along at the rear come the odds and sods. Here is the medical officer, a lieutenant or captain attached from the Royal Army Medical Corps, with his sergeant and stretcher-bearers, the latter the regiment's bandsmen (serious musicians, these, not the fife and drum boys at the head of the column) who have returned their instruments to store on mobilisation. There are the signallers, encumbered with semaphore flags, heliographs, field telephones and cable. The machine-gun officer, his sergeant and twelve men accompany the battalion's two .303 belt-fed Maxim machine-guns. These are old models with brass cooling jackets round their barrels; the new Vickers gun has been introduced but few are to be seen. Each gun is carried on a two-wheeled wagon which tows a two-wheeled limber; there are 3,500 rounds with each and a reserve of 8,000 on a third wagon. Ammunition carts, five in all, carry some 100,000 rounds more, forming a regimental reserve of 100 rounds per man.

Last, but by his own practised reckoning anything but least, comes the quartermaster. He has been commissioned from the ranks; not too long ago he was the regimental sergeant-major. He is the colonel's logistic staff officer, though call him that and you will have your fortune told in a way no soothsayer would risk. The quartermaster is responsible for the receipt, safe-keeping and issue of food, clothing, ammunition and much else besides. His myrmidons, headed by the regimental quartermaster-sergeant, have a cushioned and knowing look, for if you spend your life counting blankets you do not want for an extra one when the nights grow chilly. The quartermaster's impedimenta travels on the horse-drawn GS (general service) wagons that rumble along with the cookers and water-cart at the very end of this long and martial snake.

The battalion is marching at ease. The men have undone the collars of their khaki tunics, rifles are carried anyhow, and stubby little pipes jut beneath many a moustache. A few push their luck by smoking cigarettes; pipes are permitted on the line of march but cigarettes are not, though as Private Harry Beaumont, shouldering his pack with 1st Queen's Own Royal West Kent, remembered, 'this rule was unfair, and died a natural death on the first day'. Marching at ease; but not an easy march. The road is high-cambered *pavé*, made of four inch square granite blocks set half an inch apart. Some of the younger regulars find the going hard, and not a few of the reservists are in real difficulties. On 21 August Count Gleichen, commanding 15th Infantry Brigade, reported that there were many stragglers after a fifteen-mile march: 'all of them reservists . . . They had every intention of keeping up, of course, but simply could not.'

Packs are another problem. The men wear 1908 pattern webbing equipment, much better, as any old soldier will tell you, than the leather it replaced. Shoulder straps suspend ammunition pouches: five left, five right, with ten rounds in each. Another twenty rounds are carried in the haversack which is on the left hip, balancing the water-bottle, blue enamelled tin covered in khaki felt, on the right. The entrenching tool hangs at the base of the spine, its handle strapped to the bayonet scabbard beneath the haversack. The pack hangs squarely in the middle of the back. Crammed with spare clothing — a 'worsted cardigan jacket', spare grey flannel shirt, socks, underwear, and here and there a board for the forbidden gambling game of Crown and Anchor — it brings the total weight carried, by Harry Beaumont's reckoning, to almost eighty pounds. Small wonder that as his battalion moved up on a scorching day: 'within an hour [we] began to feel the effects of the intense heat. Some were more or less in a state of collapse, and had to be supported by their comrades, while others carried their rifles.'

His rifle was the infantry soldier's *raison d'être*. The .303 Short Magazine Lee-Enfield weighed 8lb 10½oz and was 3ft 8½ins long.

Its magazine held ten rounds, loaded by thumbing in two five-round clips. The British infantryman of 1914 could dispose of these to good effect. He fired 250 rounds on his annual musketry course, which consisted of slow, rapid and snap practices at ranges up to 600 yards. In the 'mad minute' he was expected to fire fifteen rounds at a target 300 yards away, and Major Frederick Myatt suggests that: 'there were very few infantryman who could not put all their shots into a two-foot (61-centimetre) circle in that time; many indeed could almost double that rate of fire with no appreciable loss of accuracy'. *Field Service Regulations* 1909 described ranges of 600 yards and under as being 'close' as far as infantry was concerned; 600 to 1,400 was 'effective', 1,400 to 2,000 (the limit of the standard back-sight) was 'long', and only 2,000 to 2,800 was 'distant'.

The soldiers who tramp past us take their musketry seriously. Proficiency brings extra pay: 'How do I stand for Marksman?' was the urgent question as butt-markers passed the scores down the range telephone. Officers fired the same course as their men, and were expected to do well. 'There is nothing so disgusting', said Major-General Thompson Capper, 'as an officer who is a second class shot'. When young George Ashurst, who joined the Lancashire Fusiliers in 1913, scored nineteen points out of a possible twenty at 600 yards, his colonel gave him five shillings on the spot. Officers carry sword and pistol. Swords have been sharpened by the armourer on mobilisation, but few will kill Germans: Lieutenant George Roupell of the East Surreys will find that his comes in handy for beating prone soldiers on the backside and telling them to fire low.

The fact that the sword and magazine rifle — ancient and modern yet again — were carried in such close proximity emphasises the dilemma facing the armies of 1914. There was widespread recognition that the firepower revolution brought with it the risk of very heavy casualties. In 1912 General Friedrich von Bernhardi warned: 'Anyone who thinks that great tactical successes can be achieved in modern war without staking a great deal of human life is, I believe, very much mistaken'. For his part, on mobilisation young Hanbury-Sparrow expected 'a short war with heavy officer casualties. I warned my parents to prepare themselves not to see me again.'

Theorists and practitioners were unsure whether firepower favoured attack or defence. The Polish banker, Jan Bloch, author of the perceptive *Future War*, declared that it simply ruled out frontal attack, and British experience in South Africa seemed to prove that

Bloch was right: both British and French infantry regulations were modified to reflect the reality of the fire-swept battlefield. But it was not that simple. The weight of military opinion believed that wars were won by offensive action, and it followed that an army which allowed itself to be paralysed by firepower — 'acute transvaalitis' — could not expect to win. Moreover, as Colonel Charles Ardant du Picq had acutely observed even before the Franco-Prussian War, on the new battlefield 'cohesion is no longer ensured by mutual observation'. What would happen if these loose, flexible formations met the enemy's fire? Officers would be unable to lead effectively, and soldiers' courage would not be buttressed by the close physical proximity of comrades. Men — short-term conscripts, most of them — would go to ground and not get up again; impulsion would be gone and stalemate would result.

The reaction was predictable. If war was not to be mere sterile butchery, soldiers must be imbued with the desire to press to close quarters and win. This would prove costly in the short term, but it was preferable to have a short, bloody and victorious war than a long and inconclusive conflict. In Germany, von Bernhardi proclaimed that 'those troops will prove superior who can bear greater losses than the others', and in France, General Joffre (chief of the general staff and commander-in-chief designate from 1911) demanded 'the spirit of the offensive'. All this, as its proponents recognised, called for more than merely the transformation of military training: it demanded the forging of a new national will.

This task was already well under way in Germany, where society was infused by a pervasive militarism that made 'a young officer into a god, a reserve officer into a demi-god'. In France, the popular novelist Ernest Psichari demanded 'a proud and violent army'. The philosopher Henri Bergson expounded to huge audiences his conviction that the creative urge, not natural selection, lay at the heart of evolution: what better way to show *l'élan vital* than to impose your will on an enemy in battle.

In Britain, the 'unconquerable and determined offensive spirit' was championed by Thompson Capper, an infantry officer who had entered Staff College in 1896, and became inspector-general of infantry in February 1914. Capper believed that German tactical doctrine, which emphasised attacking the enemy's flanks and rear, was superior to French teaching. However, he argued that victory was essentially a matter of morale, of 'determination to conquer or die'. Like continental theorists, he argued that 'organised abnegation of self' was the basis of the offensive spirit, and felt that this must be reflected in the community at large, attributing Germany's success in 1870–71 to her schoolmasters who had imbued youth with national ethics.

Though Capper's position was more extreme than that of many of his colleagues, he was not exceptional in demanding a national revival. The National Service League argued vigorously in favour of national service rather than more restrictive professional soldiering. Popular culture radiated the new mood. Guy du Maurier's play, *An Englishman's Castle*, warned of invasion by a thinly-veiled Germanic enemy, and Erskine Childers' bestselling book, *The Riddle of the Sands*, was a spy story with the Germans as its villains.

In the decade before 1914 military doctrine was recast on both sides of the Channel. Although the most extreme expression of offensive spirit was contained in the French Regulations of 1913 which declared that: 'The French Army . . . recognises no law save that of the offensive', the British were scarcely more measured. The 1909 edition of *Field Service Regulations* abandoned the cautious note which pervaded the 1905 edition, written while the Boer War was fresh in the collective memory. The new regulations proclaimed that: 'Success in war depends more on moral than on physical qualities', and added that 'decisive success in battle can only be gained by a vigorous offensive'. This view was echoed in the regulations for the individual arms. *Infantry Training 1914* was unequivocal, and made a rare excursion into bold type to lend emphasis to crucial points:

> The main essential to success in battle is to close with the enemy cost what it may . . . **The object of infantry in attack is therefore to get to close quarters as quickly as possible**, and the leading lines must not delay the advance by halting to fire until compelled by the enemy to do so . . . **The object of fire in the attack, whether of artillery, machine guns, or infantry, is to bring such a superiority of fire to bear on the enemy as to make the advance to close quarters possible**.

A battalion might push a company or two forward to form a firing line and its immediate supports while the remaining companies waited in reserve. The forward companies, assisted by artillery and machine-guns, would set about winning the fire fight. The slackening of the enemy's fire and the sight of demoralised individuals sloping off to the rear would prompt the local commander to order his bugler to sound the charge. And now we slip back a century: 'the call will be taken up by all buglers, and all neighbouring units will join in the charge as quickly as possible. During the delivery of the assault the men will cheer, bugles be sounded, and pipes played.' Successful assault would be followed by relentless pursuit: the enemy's army would be broken and the war won.

Defence, in contrast, could not in itself produce a decisive result and was acceptable only as an adjunct to offensive action: firepower would enable a commander to reduce the forces committed to a specific sector and thus free them for an attack elsewhere. **'The choice of a position and its preparation must therefore be made with a view to economising the power expended on defence in order that the power of offence may be increased,'** declared *Infantry Training*.

Our thoughtful colonel, then, has much on his mind. Experience has taught him just what damage his battalion's firepower can do, but his training emphasises the need to 'demand the impossible and not think of sparing his men'. As the campaign develops he will find his resolve sorely tried, all the more because he is so close — physically and psychologically — to the battalion he commands. The first casualty will be his sense of perspective, his ability to balance his loyalty between the sweating column behind him and the chain of command stretching above him.

He answers to a brigadier-general, who commands four such battalions with the aid of a small staff headed by his brigade-major. Count Gleichen (soon to avoid his title's foreign ring by styling himself Lord Edward Gleichen) noted that his brigade numbered 127 officers, 3,958 men, 258 horses and 74 vehicles when it was ready to leave for France. It is not until we ascend to the next level of command, the division, that we see the beginnings of a combined arms force. The major-general commanding it has a colonel as his chief of staff — officially General Staff Officer Grade 1, abbreviated to GSO1. Full colonels are rare birds in the British army of 1914. In the French and German armies they command three-battalion infantry regiments, and have lieutenant-colonels as their second-in-commands and majors commanding their battalions. In the British army the word 'regiment' has no tactical significance in the infantry: different battalions of the same regiment are seldom in the same brigade in 1914.

Down in the lead with the wheel at the flog

The division is a well-balanced instrument. Of its war establishment of 18,000 all ranks, 12,000 are infantrymen, marching in the twelve battalions of its three brigades. The 4,000 gunners serve seventy-six guns: fifty-four 18-pdrs, eighteen 4.5 inch howitzers and four 60-pdrs. For all the lethality of the infantry's musketry, these guns will do much of the killing in the weeks that follow, and as the war goes on will drench the ever-deepening battlefield with their iron torrent.

Between 1899 and 1924, the Royal Regiment of Artillery had three branches, the Royal Horse Artillery (RHA), manning guns intended to support the cavalry; the Royal Field Artillery (RFA) serving field guns and howitzers, and the Royal Garrison Artillery (RGA) with heavy guns. There was a sharp cultural divide between horse and field, both mounted branches, and garrison gunners. The latter were unkindly nicknamed 'Gambardiers', but were taking a lively interest in indirect fire and the effect of meteorology on ballistics long before the war. In contrast, in the judgement of one modern artillery officer, the RFA was 'renowned for its unscientific approach to gunnery, admiring intuition and subjective judgement, not calculation, when opening fire'. We should not be too hard on it. In 1899, British field guns achieved a mere 2,000 yards, and the middle-piece gunner officers of 1914 had been brought up in a world where getting into action briskly, smacking shells down-range and standing the enemy's pounding were really what mattered.

The battery was the gunner's spiritual home. In 1914, batteries were combined into brigades, a source of potential confusion, for an artillery brigade — RFA brigades had three batteries and an ammunition column, RHA brigades two batteries and an ammunition column — was a lieutenant-colonel's command. Introduction of the term regiment, long after the war, ended the ambiguity. Field artillery batteries were numbered, and RHA batteries had distinguishing letters. A division's artillery comprised three brigades of 18-pdrs, one brigade of 5.4 inch howitzers and a battery of 60-pdr heavies, the whole under the command of the Brigadier-General Royal Artillery, assisted by his Brigade Major Royal Artillery. These posts had been instituted in 1912 and 1913 respectively, and their occupants confronted a sharp learning curve as centralised control of artillery became increasingly important. They were not helped by the fact that they had no communications whatever, and we should not be surprised to discover that Brigadier-General N. G.

Findlay, BGRA 1st Division, was the first British general to fall in the war, killed as he went up to his batteries.

The 18-pdrs of the RFA and the 13-pdrs of the RHA were quick-firers, very much the state of the art in 1914. For centuries, guns had bounded backwards on firing as recoil was transmitting through carriage wheels, imperilling the toes of unwary gunners and compelling the detachment to heave the weapon back into position. The development of hydraulic buffers enabled recoil to be absorbed by the top carriage, which meant that the layer, crouched over his sight, might need to make only a tiny adjustment before the next round was fired. The ammunition was 'fixed', the shell fitting into a brass shell-case, which greatly simplified the business of loading. The famous French 75mm, introduced in 1897, was first in the field, but in 1914 there was little to choose between it and either the 18-pdr or the German 77mm. At the beginning of the war British field guns had a range of some 6,500 yards, which could be increased to 7,500 by digging in the trail to give extra elevation. The 4.5 howitzer's 35lb shell had a similar range, while the 60-pdr threw its shell to 10,300 yards.

British horse and field artillery fired only shrapnel until October 1914. The shrapnel shell was a hollow iron canister with a brass fuse at its tip. Its upper half was filled with lead balls about the size of a marble. A thin tube, passing through them, connected the fuse to the burster charge at the base of the shell. The forward observation officer's target information was converted, on the gun position, into an elevation and bearing on which the gun should be laid, and a fuse setting. The object was to burst the shell above and in front of its target; the shell-case acted like the barrel of a stubby shotgun, and the balls whistled down to kill and maim.

British affection for shrapnel dated back to the Boer War, when air-bust rounds had been ideal for use against scattered riflemen. It had limitations in 1914, for shrapnel was all but useless against buildings and trenches with overhead cover. Field howitzers and heavy guns fired high explosive (HE) rounds, filled with Lyddite and fitted with a fuse which burst them when they hit the ground. As the war became static high explosive was the real killer, and even in the summer of 1914 the most profoundly shocking results of artillery fire were produced by HE. Captain Arthur Osburn, medical officer of the 4th Dragoon Guards, heard a single heavy shell smash squarely into a nearby farmyard full of troops.

Fragments of stone, manure, pieces of clothing and hair came falling about me as I ran through an archway into the yard and beheld one of the most heartrending sights I have ever seen, even in war. The detachment of 9th Lancers had almost completely disappeared. In the centre of the yard where I had seen them but a moment before, there was now a mound four or five feet high of dead men and horses . . . Around this central heap of dead men the wounded lay on all sides. Some had been blown to the other end of the yard, their backs broken. One sat up dazed and whimpering, his back against a wall, holding part of his intestines in his hand.

Catastrophes like this provided combatants with the sternest test of courage. Capricious death and butcher-shop mutilation rustled overhead, pulverised trenches, headquarters and horse-lines, snatched a latrine queue here and a gambling school there, levelled woods and villages, and stove in caves and crypts. The British cursed the German heavies, whose black-bursting shells were nicknamed 'coal-boxes' or (after the negro boxer) 'Jack Johnsons'. The Germans were certainly better provided with heavy guns than their opponents. They had formidable 150mm and 210mm howitzers at corps and army level. Their super-heavy weapons, like the 305mm and 420mm siege mortars, were intended for use against fortresses but might be deployed, with earthquake-producing effects, against strongpoints in the field.

Even in 1914, before many heavy guns were available to the British, the long arm of the RGA reached out to search German back areas. Captain Rudolf Binding, commanding a German divisional cavalry squadron, met a much-decorated infantry officer who could not even bring himself to describe heavy shelling. 'The history of this War will never be written,' reflected Binding. 'Those who could write it will remain silent. Those who write it have not experienced it.'

Modern in its effect, but ancient in its appearance. Let us watch a battery of British horse artillery clipping across beet-field and stubble at a belly-to-ground gallop, its six guns — which, with their limbers, weigh a ton and a half apiece — bounding from furrow and tussock. The battery commander, a major, is going like a good 'un, one eye on the ground well ahead and the other on his map-case; his horse-holder is a stride or two behind. A few yards further back hurtle the battery sergeant-major and a handful of signallers: they will eventually set up the battery command post and establish communications with the observation officers. The three subalterns gallop ahead of their two-gun sections, watching for ruts or bumps which, taken at this speed, may flip a gun onto its back.

The gunners pound along behind. As this is an RHA battery, expected to keep up with galloping cavalry, all are mounted: RFA gunners sat on limbers and in wagons. A team of six useful-looking horses pulls each 13-pdr. The Board of Agriculture's remount manual describes a model artillery horse as: 'A bay gelding 15.3, thirteen years old. Can gallop and looks as if he should have spent his life as a hunter, short legs, deep through the heart and a good shoulder.' A driver bestrides the nearside horse of each pair. His is an undramatic title for a white-knuckled job, for he has to control his own mount and lean across with his whip to keep the offside horse in order. His right boot has a steel reinforce to give some protection from the jabbing and jostling which goes on in the best of teams, especially at corners. If he comes off he can expect scant mercy from the iron-shod wheels behind him:

> But down in the lead with the wheel at the flog
> Turns the bold Bombardier to a little whipped dog.

Although horses are expected to be interchangeable, the gun's No. 1, a sergeant, will have his own favourites for the very different jobs that need to be done. The front pair — the leaders — must above all be plucky, and their driver needs nerves of iron. The centre pair matter less, but must be good honest workmen. The rear pair — the wheelers — ought to have more wit than most, for they are in effect the brakes. All the horses transmit motive power through breast-harness connected to the traces which pull limber and gun. But the wheelers also have breeching, a wide belt fastened about a foot below the root of the tail and connected to the end of the limber-pole. The gun is braked when the wheelers slow down and bring their weight to bear on the breeching. When it goes down hill they will be 'sitting on the breeching' and much depends on their good sense and their driver's skill.

To bring his battery into action, our galloping major spurs ahead and selects a suitable gun position. *Artillery Training 1914* tells him that it will be 'covered, semi-covered or open'. In the former, the gun and its flashes are concealed from enemy. A semi-covered position shields the gun but not its flashes, and an open position is in full view of the enemy. Ideally, he will seek a reverse slope, where the ground ahead rises sharply enough to offer protection but not so steeply as to limit the battery's fire. This is a counsel of perfection, for his room for manoeuvre will be limited by his brigade commander's orders and the presence of other troops.

The observation officers have gone forward in an effort to get the best available view. 'The use of haystacks, buildings etc was recommended,' wrote one gunner officer, 'but . . . these rarely obliged by situating themselves in the right places . . . ' Observation officers have to be close enough to the guns for their signaller to run cable back to the command post or, failing that, to attract its attention with semaphore. In practice, they are often very close to the gun-line — sometimes up a ladder attached to an ammunition wagon. In some actions we will see them almost redundant as the guns engage over open sights, firing from open positions at an enemy who is all too visible.

The guns are brought into action twenty yards apart, with a limber and its twenty-four rounds or an ammunition wagon alongside each gun. Using dial sights, a military theodolite called a Director, and basic trigonometry the guns are laid so that their lines of fire are parallel. A target hit by any single gun can now be taken on by the whole battery without the need for every gun to register its fire.

The teams and most of the officers' and gunners' horses go back to the wagon lines, a safe distance behind the guns, where they wait under the direction of the battery captain. He has the task of keeping the guns supplied with ammunition, and will do this by sending wagons — they hold another 152 rounds for each gun — forward as the situation demands. When the time comes to bring the battery out of action, he takes the teams forward and the guns are hooked in and brought away.

Easy to describe: hard to accomplish. *Infantry Training 1914* emphasised that: 'Artillery coming into action, limbering up or in movement is a vulnerable target against which rapid fire or even fire at long infantry ranges is justifiable'. Getting a battery out of action during the retreat often meant galloping teams onto a position that was being shelled and was threatened by German infantry into the bargain. The sight contrasts all too poignantly with our earlier vision of a battery changing ground. Some guns have been hit and there are dead and wounded beside those still in action. As the teams gallop up, the drivers have no time to spare more than a glance for their chums, though there is a heart-stopping moment as the drivers of A Subsection, on the right of the line, realise that theirs is a fruitless journey. Their gun is on its side — an incoming 77mm has caught it square on the axle-tree — with old Sergeant Brown and his lads in a dreadful jumble around it.

As he gallops in, the lead driver has to swing his team so that the hook on the limber is as close as possible to the towing-eye on the gun's trail. German infantrymen, now very close, rise to their feet, lean into their rifle-butts and try to bring down the wheelers. Horses fall here and there. The harness has quick-release fittings, but cutting out a wounded horse still takes time, with bullets kicking earth out of the stubble all around. You are expected to shoot it — the manual generously explains that you put the bullet through the centre of an imaginary cross connecting ears and eyes — but there is simply no time. Yet it is an old friend, and leaving it trying to hobble on behind as the team lurches off to safety is perhaps the worst moment in a ghastly day.

With the rank and pay of a Sapper

The officers and men of the division's two Royal Engineer field companies cut less of a dash than their gunner comrades, but without their help the division would be hard-pressed to operate effectively. Each company had a war strength of six officers, 200 NCOs and men and sixty horses, and consisted of a headquarters and four sections, each commanded by a subaltern. The sappers were trained to carry out all sorts of field engineering. They could construct a strongpoint, reinforce a farm track so that a 60-pdr could use it or blow a bridge so that the enemy could not. They could throw a pontoon bridge across a river, or, if pontoons were lacking, improvise something scarcely less serviceable with whatever timber they might lay hands on.

Sapper officers had a reputation for being serious or eccentric — 'mad, married or Methodist'. During the retreat they were called upon to perform tasks which often seemed hard for their modest rank, like blowing bridges on whose destruction the safety of the Army depended. Their NCOs took their lead from this easy shouldering of wide responsibility. Lieutenant James Pennycuick, who served with 5th Division's 59th Field Company, recalled that the senior NCO in his section 'J. Buckle by name, was a man of exceptional character and merit'. The remainder of his section was no less impressive.

In the Engineers we then recruited tradesmen, carpenters, bricklayers, masons and the like and taught them to be soldiers — firing exactly the same musketry course as the Infantry. Even in that good company our tradesmen soldiers were of outstanding quality. Many and varied were the jobs the Engineer companies were called upon to do and our sappers could do anything. It was the greatest of privileges to serve with them.

Sappers enjoyed higher rates of pay than infantrymen: a sapper drew 3s to the infantry private's 1s. The fact that the latter increasingly found themselves providing working parties under the direction of engineer officers of NCOs inevitably caused friction. Ernest Shephard jotted the chalked doggerel of some unnamed trench poet in his diary:

> God made the bee
> The bee makes honey
> The Dorsets do the work
> And the REs get the money

The division's Signal Company was part of the Royal Engineers Signal Service. Its members still wore sapper badges but their brassards of dark and light blue set them apart from their comrades in the field companies, though it was not until 1920 that the Royal Corps of Signals came into being. *Field Service Regulations 1909* opened its chapter on inter-communication and orders by stressing that: 'The constant maintenance of communication between the various parts of an army is of urgent importance.' It went on to warn that the 'elaborate means of communication provided under modern conditions should not be used in such a manner as to cripple the initiative of subordinates by unnecessary interference'.

The more static the operations the more elaborate the communications. Wireless, as we have seen, was of very limited value, and most of the energies of the divisional signal companies and the signal units controlled directly by GHQ went into the laying and maintenance of line. The French civilian telephone network was valuable, and it soon became apparent that railway telephones, which connected the numerous stations of the very extensive railway network, had particular advantages. Wise commanders would establish their headquarters in stations or *mairies* so that their numbers could be found easily. However, it was unwise to rely on civilian communications, and in any event no telephones were to be found in the haystacks, cowsheds and hedges where some commanders inevitably found themselves.

Divisional signal companies were concerned with establishing and manning the signal office at divisional headquarters, for communications by telephone and telegraph, and with running line out to brigade headquarters. Line parties worked from a wagon containing cable which unrolled as the wagon moved on. An accomplished team could lay line at the gallop, its senior NCO picking the route as he went, a horseman behind adjusting the lay of the cable with a tool rather like a shepherd's crook, and a follow-up party dealing with road-crossings, where the cable would have to be hoisted out of harm's way or protected against hooves and wheels.

The limitations of a system which relied on line had been foreseen, and on mobilisation the army not only accepted the services of gentlemen who offered to serve with their private cars — the Royal Automobile Club produced twenty-five such volunteers — but used newspaper appeals to call for motor-cycle dispatch riders. W. H. L. Watson, an Oxford undergraduate, duly contacted the War Office and was instantly transformed into a corporal, Royal Engineers; he joined 5th Division's signal company in Ireland, and found himself in a ringside seat for the whole 1914 campaign. The cars whisked officers between headquarters, and dispatch riders roared dangerously along the *pavé* with messages.

The divisional commander had two other useful communication assets. His cyclist company provided scouts and messengers. Cyclists were useless off roads, but on them could make better average speed than cavalry. Military cyclists later found themselves in the Army Cycling Corps, whose bicycle wheel cap badge makes an occasional incongruous appearance on headstones in military cemeteries, but in 1914 cyclist companies were formed on mobilisation from soldiers drawn from other units. Sergeant T. H. Cubbon went to war with 3rd Division's cyclist company. His Field Message Book records that on mobilisation he drew from his Company Quartermaster-Sergeant, amongst other things, nine compasses, two eight-gallon paraffin bottles, four six-foot flag poles, twelve 3ft 6in flag poles, 112 maps and a grease tub. The flag poles, for use with semaphore flags, would be attached to the cross-bar of the bike, the six-foot version dividing in half for ease of carriage.

Sergeant Cubbon was an old soldier in the full sense of the word. On 16 August he recorded: 'Cadged dinner with an old French couple. Cleaned rifle and bicycle.' On the following day, hospitality lavished during a visit to Wassigny proved too much for him: 'Got mouldy. Returned about 6pm. Went to bed.' Eventually his taste for creature comforts led to his downfall. On 3 September, he wrote: 'Had row with [Lieutenant] Sharpe and [Captain] Lloyd on account of being absent last night. Had to hand everything over to Sgt Giles as QMS.' Later he added: 'Have just heard that Mundy, O'Gorman and myself are being returned to our units on crimes . . . My bicycle taken from me.' He reported to the King's Regiment on 8 September, was severely reprimanded by his commanding officer, and found himself back in the war with a vengeance. 10 September was: 'The most awful day I have had. Shells bursting on all sides, bullets within a foot. Before entering firing line prayed and had a look at [a photograph of] Flo . . . I was in charge of the burial party. Terrible sights. Jakes had to be picked up in pieces and buried in a ground sheet. Took Kenny's razor, [shoulder] titles and cap badge.'

Blow the trumpet, draw the sword

Let us leave Sergeant Cubbon on his journey to Golgotha and consider the last of the divisional commander's mobile resources, his divisional cavalry squadron. The troop, under a captain, had traditionally been the cavalry's sub-unit. Troops could be combined into squadrons commanded by one of the regiment's field officers, but it was not until 1892 that squadrons were permanently established, a reform which foreshadowed the infantry's adoption of four large companies rather than eight small ones. In 1914, cavalry regiments, commanded by lieutenant-colonels, had three squadrons each of four troops: two squadrons were commanded by majors and one by a captain. Troops were led by subalterns, and consisted of four seven-man sections.

There was a two-gun machine-gun section, again a subaltern's command, with regimental headquarters. It has been unkindly suggested that cavalry commanding officers were not *aficionados* of the machine-gun. In his *History of the 4th/7th Royal Dragoon Guards* Major-General J. M. Brereton describes an incident in the 1910 autumn manoeuvres when a machine-gun officer approached his commanding officer: 'What shall I do with the Maxims, Sir?' asked the subaltern. 'Can't you see I'm busy,' spluttered the colonel. 'Take the damn things to a flank and hide them.' This advice was not as lunatic as it may sound: concealed machine-guns on a flank were precisely what a cavalry regiment needed, whether it was attacking on horseback or defending on foot. Lieutenant-Colonel W. T.

Willcox of the 3rd Hussars certainly took the view that there were too few machine-guns, venting his feelings with a sporting metaphor. They were, he affirmed, 'as scarce as woodcock in a day's covert shooting'.

In August 1914, cavalry regiments put twenty-five to thirty officers and around 530 men into the field. The 3rd Hussars went to war with twenty-six officers, 523 men, 528 chargers and troop horses, seventy-four draught horses — for the machine-guns and the eighteen wagons of the regimental transport — and six pack horses. Not only was a cavalry regiment just over half the size of an infantry battalion, but if it fought dismounted its strength was reduced by the need for one man in four to act as horse-holder.

In *Cavalry Studies*, published in 1907, Major-General Douglas Haig outlined three roles for cavalry. Independent cavalry carried out deep strategic exploitation, working directly under the orders of the commander-in-chief. Protective cavalry provided security for the army and its lines of communication, while divisional cavalry helped protect the division and provide it with communications. In August 1914, the 15th Hussars found the squadrons for 1st, 2nd and 3rd Divisions, and the 19th Hussars for the 4th and 5th Divisions.

Commanding divisional cavalry was an instructive experience for the squadron leader, who worked closely with divisional headquarters and had his finger on the pulse of events. But it was not a job which appealed to most cavalry officers. They aspired, not to be tied to the apron-strings of the infantry, but to be operating as part of a cavalry division at the army's cutting edge. In August 1914 the BEF included a cavalry division of four brigades, each brigade containing three regiments and the division as a whole fielding 9,269 officers and men and 9,815 horses. There were two two-battery brigades of horse artillery, permitting a battery to support each brigade, four cavalry field ambulances, an engineer field squadron, a signal squadron and divisional transport. In addition, there was the independent 5th Cavalry Brigade with its own little slice of support, including J Battery RHA.

We have already seen how pre-war doctrine had attempted to grapple with the linked issues of firepower and offensive action. The debate on the relationship between fire and shock was particularly heated where the mounted arm was concerned. Even in the horse and musket age, cavalry had been hard put to break infantry who formed square, stood their ground and fired. When they succeeded it was usually because of leadership which was brave to the point of suicide. Lieutenant Moore, adjutant of 3rd Bombay Light Cavalry, set his horse at a Persian square in 1857, letting his sword swing from his wrist by its sword knot to leave both hands free for the reins. He jumped right over the infantry, losing his horse in the process, but the *sowars* followed his resolute lead to break the square.

The development of effective breech-loading weapons in the second half of the nineteenth century led many commentators to proclaim that cavalry could not achieve useful results by shock action. In 1863 a French cavalry officer ruefully admitted that 'cavalry is in disfavour; it is a fact'. The cavalry lobby riposted by claiming that well-handled horsemen could make clever use of ground and smoke to burst in on unsuspecting opponents, breech-loaders or no.

In the Franco-Prussian War, French cavalry showed itself deficient in almost everything but courage. On 6 August 1870, General de Bonnemains' cuirassier division thundered to destruction at Froeschwiller. Ten days later, the Cuirassiers of the Guard charged Prussian infantry at Rezonville and lost twenty-two officers and 244 men in the process. The 5th Cuirassiers launched a similarly heroic but catastrophic charge at Mouzon, trying to buy time for shaken French infantry to cross the Meuse, while at Sedan, on 1 September, General Margueritte's fine division of Chasseurs d'Afrique attacked with such magnificently wasted gallantry that the Prussian King, watching from a nearby hilltop, could not resist exclaiming: 'Ah! The brave fellows.'

Much the same evidence had emerged from the American Civil War, where even in mounted engagements fire seemed to have the edge over shock. The Confederate General John H. Morgan armed all his troopers with firearms: some had Enfield rifles and some shotguns, and nearly every man had a pair of revolvers. When charged by Union cavalry, Morgan shouted: 'Here, boys, are those fools coming again with their sabres; give it to them'. In November 1864, a pistoleering Confederate squadron took on a sabre-wielding Union squadron: the former lost one man killed and several wounded, while the latter lost twenty-four killed, twelve wounded and sixty-two prisoners.

The Boer War made much the same point. Although there were successful cavalry charges — on 21 October 1899 a squadron of the 5th Dragoon Guards and one of the 5th Lancers cut up a retreating Boer force at Elandslaagte — by the end of the war most horsemen had given up carrying sword or lance. Major A. W. Andrew observed that the accuracy of Boer fire made it 'unsafe to sit still on horseback at 1,500 or 1,600 yards', and thought that 'five determined mounted riflemen will scare a whole division of cavalry'.

Lord Roberts already had reservations about the *arme blanche* — sword and lance — when he arrived in South Africa. When campaigning in Afghanistan in 1879, he had watched men of the 9th Lancers trying to cope with lance and carbine while fighting dismounted, and his experience in South Africa confirmed his worst suspicions. He bent all his influence as Commander-in-Chief of the Army — he was the last holder of that office — to reforming the cavalry, and contributed a preface to the 1904 edition of *Cavalry Training* which left no doubt as to his view 'that instead of the firearm being the adjunct to the sword, the sword must henceforth be an adjunct to the rifle; and that cavalry soldiers must become expert rifle shots and be constantly trained to act dismounted'. The cavalry lobby protested vigorously, and the following year the Army Council struck a typically unsatisfactory compromise: *Cavalry Training* would be issued without its preface, but the lance would be abolished as a weapon of war.

The Roberts preface was the high-water mark of the reformers' success. The field-marshal's departure from Horse Guards and the presence of cavalry officers — notably French and Haig — in a number of key posts helped sway the debate the other way. The 1907 edition of *Cavalry Training* decreed that 'thorough efficiency in the use of the rifle and in dismounted tactics is an absolute necessity', but went on to affirm that: 'It must be accepted as a principle that the rifle, effective as it is, cannot replace the effect produced by the speed of the horse, the magnetism of the charge, and the terror of cold steel'. Symptomatically, the lance was reinstated in June 1909.

This was not quite the folly it seemed. We have already seen how tactics generally were becoming more offensive in order to avoid the perceived danger of bloody stalemates. Moreover, the cavalry lobby argued that the evidence of history could not be construed in quite the way the reformers claimed. There had been successful examples of cavalry dash in all the wars under discussion, and Lieutenant-Colonel F. N. Maude, an intelligent sapper and anything but a caricature horse soldier, argued that the lack of properly trained cavalry made the American Civil War an unfair example in any case. He went on to maintain that the Boer War was 'entirely abnormal'; a future European war would be very different. The charge of von

Bredow's brigade at Rezonville on 16 August 1870 was arguably
the single most battle-winning element of German tactics that day,
and the British 'charge' at Klip Drift on 15 February 1900 — in
fact a divisional rush in open order rather than a classic knee-to-
knee charge — opened the way to the relief of Kimberley.

The cavalry lobby also claimed that the Russo-Japanese War
pointed to the continuing value of shock action. French complained
that the Russians 'thought of nothing but getting off their horses
and shooting' and claimed that this had contributed to their defeat.
Here he was guilty of generalising from inadequate evidence, for
the report of one of the official British observers pointed out that
Russian cavalry were poor at dismounted work.

It was also possible to argue that as armies grew bigger and placed
increasing reliance on short-term conscripts and reservists, there
would be plenty of opportunities for cavalry to sweep in and complete the destruction of an already-demoralised force. Finally, most
commentators agreed that the first act of any major European war
would be a huge clash between the opposing cavalries. Sending
horsemen into this gigantic mêlée without the self-confidence that
came from being trained to charge home would result in a failure
of willpower when it mattered most.

The controversy generated as much heat as light. Reputation and
careers were bound up in it, able publicists supported both sides,
and organisational politics complicated matters. During the Boer
War many infantry units had been mounted, and Mounted Infantry
survived the war. However, even the commandant of the Mounted
Infantry school at Aldershot felt that MI was essentially a hybrid,
with limited opportunities in war, while Colonel H. B. de Lisle —
Durham Light Infantry officer turned Royal Dragoon — argued
that MI should take over protective duties, freeing cavalry proper
for strategic action.

Yet there was a good deal of middle ground. From the Mounted
Infantry flank, Major F. M. Crum, using the pseudonym 'A Rifleman', wrote: 'we claim, not that "the days of cavalry are past", not
that "shock action is impossible", but that the rifle and the rifleman
come more to the front each war, and that the difficulties in the
way of shock action increase "generation after generation".' Douglas
Haig, ostensibly on the other wing of the debate, freely conceded
that fire action was nine-tenths more likely than shock action. Even
Sir John French, in his preface to the English edition of Lieutenant-
General von Bernhardi's *Cavalry in Future Wars*, was 'absolutely

convinced that the Cavalry Spirit is and may be encouraged to the utmost without in the least degree prejudicing either training in dismounted duties or the acquirement of such tactical knowledge on the part of leaders as will enable them to discern when and where to resort to dismounted methods'.

The 1912 edition of *Cavalry Training* modified previous emphasis on shock action, and French's successor as Inspector-General of the Forces suggested that the cavalry should spend more of its time shooting. Sir Horace Smith-Dorrien, commanding at Aldershot, summoned all the cavalry officers under his command to a meeting in the 16th Lancers' mess on 21 August 1909 and ordered them to take musketry more seriously. In fact, the cavalry's shooting was anything but derisory. Private Bertie Seed of the 3rd Hussars won the Indian musketry prize at 600 yards in 1903, and in 1908 the 14th Hussars had 354 marksmen, 212 1st class shots, thirty-five 2nd class shots and a mere four 3rd class shots. It was a record which many infantry battalions would not have been ashamed of. In 1910, Lieutenant-Colonel Edwards summed up what many cavalry officers saw as a decent compromise. 'The *desire* to use the sabre or lance should be predominant,' he wrote, 'but it must be held in restraint by a thorough knowledge of the power of the firearm.'

There was a world of difference between British cavalry and their allies and opponents, all of whom took a decidedly more *arme blanche* view of things. Vladimir Litauer of the Russian 1st Sumskii Hussars recalled that:

> The goal set before us had been the mounted charge, whose most important element was speed, for on the latter largely depended the impact with which we could enter the enemy's formation. And since we had also been brought up to believe that no one was a match for us when it came to hand-to-hand fighting, our one desire was to reach the enemy's ranks as soon as possible. Once, when we were unhappily fighting dismounted and were pinned to the ground by German fire, I remember our regimental commander rising up and shaking his fists in the direction of the enemy, exclaiming: 'If we could only get *to* you!'

Lieutenant-General von Poseck, Inspector-General of the German cavalry, thought that German and French cavalry tactics were outdated:

> The greatest emphasis was placed by us on the skilful grouping of forces in the mounted combat since, at the beginning of the campaign, we calculated more particularly on this kind of fighting . . . Despite the

improvements made in fighting dismounted, there was nevertheless a lack of schooling in firing practice in the larger units . . . As late as 1913, in France . . . special importance was placed on tactical instruction for mounted combat . . .

1914 found British cavalry, in contrast, entirely capable of using fire or steel as the situation demanded. In a leather bucket on the offside of his saddle, the British cavalryman carried the same rifle as the infantry, not the stubby short-range carbine favoured by continental horsemen. On the other side of his saddle hung the 1908 pattern sword, with a pistol-grip hilt moulded to the shape of the hand, a large dish guard, and a straight blade offset so as to be in line with the straight arm.

For most of the previous century British cavalry had been armed with a series of less than effective swords, many of them 'cut and thrust' weapons which neither cut nor thrust efficiently. It was the natural inclination of most soldiers in a hand-to-hand fight to lay about them, and a sabre with the muscle of desperation behind it could do horrific damage. 'At Essling,' wrote Brack, 'I saw Cuirassiers' helmets quite cut through with sabre cuts . . .' The hirsute Orcadian, George Broadfoot, one of the paladins of British India, emerged from a skirmish in which he had killed three Afghans musing on 'how *soft* a man's head is'. While it requires a blow of not less than 90 foot-pounds to fracture the front of the skull, half that will shatter the temporal area and a mere 18 foot-pounds — well within the capability of a ten-year-old with a heavy stick — will break the side of the skull above the jawbone.

But a man's head is a hard target, easily protected by helmet and sabre. Moreover, a soldier who tries to hack at an opponent's head will be inside the man's reach, and the most probable result of his efforts will be nasty bludgeon-work, more likely to produce a broken collar-bone than a cloven skull. Indeed, Brack concluded that 'the strokes which kill are the thrusts: the others merely wound'. A horseman leaning forward could deliver a thrust long before his enemy's cut went home, and there was a good chance that a penetrating wound anywhere in the torso would prove fatal. The research which preceded the adoption of the 1908 sword concluded that a weapon specifically designed for thrusting would encourage the soldier to use it as he had been taught and not simply swing it about wildly.

George Barrow echoed the view of many cavalry officers when

he proclaimed the lance 'a weapon . . . much superior to the sword, when it is a question of using the *arme blanche*, not only for putting one's opponent out of action, but even more on account of its moral effect'. In 1914, a proportion of French, German and Russian cavalrymen — whether or not they were lancers by name — carried the lance. In these cases it was an all-metal weapon, unlike the British steel-tipped and steel-shod bamboo lance, and was issued on a wide scale to enable the front rank of a charging unit to gain the maximum reach. If training was all-important when thrusting with the sword, it was every bit as crucial with the lance, for controlling an excited horse with a ten-foot spear in one hand was a difficult business.

The new sword influenced the way men rode. In the nineteenth century, British military equitation had been heavily influenced by the 'Old German Seat'. Men were trained to ride with long stirrups and straight legs, and sat at the trot so as to present a more uniform appearance and, it was argued, use their weapons more effectively. Many experienced officers disagreed, arguing that if bumping down the Mall was an aesthetic necessity, a more practical seat, with shorter stirrups and a bent knee, should be used in the field. At Laswaree, in 1803, Colonel Thomas Pakenham, commanding a brigade about to charge infantry, ordered his men to take their stirrups up two holes, and in the action that followed the troopers cut with good effect. In the 1880s, British cavalry at last abandoned the sitting trot on all occasions except on parade, but they retained long stirrups.

Major Noel 'Curly' Birch, an RHA officer who was to rise from lieutenant-colonel to lieutenant-general during the First World War, complained that 'the outbreak of the South African War in 1899 found our mounted troops sitting on their forks'. The war showed, once and for all, that this seat was 'most wearing for man and horse on the march, and quite unsuitable for crossing obstacles'. By 1909, when Birch wrote *Modern Riding*, the army had adopted what was in effect a hunting seat. Birch hoped that in view of this 'the remark of a famous master of hounds . . . that his son rode very well until he entered the Army and passed through a cavalry riding school, should not hold good nowadays'. In 1914, then, British horsemen rode with short stirrups and a bent knee, taking rough country in their stride, and able to lean forward, sword thrust out in the 'straight arm engage', to gain a slightly longer reach than a continental lancer.

Some of the crucial discoveries of the Mons campaign were made, not by enterprising horsemen on deep reconnaissance, but by what would soon establish itself as 'the cavalry of the clouds'. The Royal Flying Corps sent four squadrons to France in 1914, and by 20 August had assembled 105 officers, 755 other ranks and sixty-three aeroplanes at the aerodrome at Maubeuge and also formed an aircraft park at Amiens. Sir John French admired the RFC, and on 15 August 1914, the day after he landed in France, he visited it at Amiens and wrote: 'I was much impressed with the general efficiency of the aircraft force. I saw the squadron commanders and told them so.'

French soon developed a high regard for the RFC's reconnaissance. However, at this stage in the war its limitations were striking. Aircraft were tiny and temperamental — sadly, the RFC's first fatalities came from crashes rather than enemy action. Pilots felt their way across country with the aid of roads and railway lines, and the early-morning mist, so typical of northern France in August, made flying almost impossible. Low cloud blinded even the most zealous pilot, and one intrepid aviator managed to fly across Brussels, by no means an elusive target, and failed to spot it.

As rations came to hand

It is sometimes said that most British officers are 'G snobs', fascinated by operations but scorning logistics. Until the army slipped painfully into line with NATO terminology in the 1980s the staff was divided into three branches. Its A Staff, working under the adjutant-general, were responsible for administration and discipline. The G Staff, under the chief of staff, dealt with operational matters and were traditionally the most prestigious branch. The Q Staff, responsible to the quartermaster-general, did for the force as a whole what the quartermaster did for his battalion: they fed and watered it, and issued it with everything from ammunition to zinc ointment. Logisticians are the Cinderellas of warfare. Nobody pays much attention to them when they succeed; ask someone with a nodding acquaintance with military history to name three famous logisticians and watch him turn pale. When they fail, colonels fulminate, privates curse and horses die.

In 1914, logisticians had the task of patching together ancient and modern. Men and supplies could be moved by rail with unparalleled efficiency, but the gap between railhead and fighting troops had to be bridged by road transport. Each British infantry division had a

Divisional Train, horsed wagons of the Army Service Corps —
nicknamed Ally Sloper's Cavalry, after a popular music-hall character. An Army Troops Train was controlled directly by GHQ, and
in the rearward world of the Inspector-General of Communications
an assortment of Divisional Supply Columns, Field Butcheries and
Field Bakeries plied their trade. The Divisional Supply Columns
were motorised, and were responsible for taking stores up to a
nominated rendezvous where they met the divisional trains who
hauled their loads forward to refilling points where units collected
their requirements.

As the war went on, ammunition came to dominate logistics. In
1914, however, ammunition requirements were relatively modest.
A British 18-pounder had 24 rounds in limbers, 152 in battery
wagons, 76 in brigade ammunition columns and 126 in divisional
ammunition columns, a total of 378 rounds. Holdings in ammunition parks and depots took the total to 1,000 rounds per gun in
the theatre of operations. In 1916, the 4th Army's 18-pounders
had 1,000 rounds per gun actually on the gun position before the
bombardment started for the Battle of the Somme, and British
gunners fired four and a quarter million shells during the preliminary
bombardment for the Third Battle of Ypres. Despite the grotesque
appetite of the guns, fodder for horses was the heaviest item sent to
France during the war: 5,438,602 tons of it, as opposed to 5,253,538
tons of ammunition. In August 1914, von Kluck's First Army, with
which the BEF had most of its dealings, had 84,000 horses consum-
ing almost two million pounds of fodder every day. The BEF needed
rather less than half this but the provision of fodder was a constant
drag on the line of supply. Reduce horses' rations and the whole
army's efficiency dwindled, for without fit, full horses neither men
nor guns could be properly fed.

And without horses little could be done for soldiers whose luck
ran out. Pre-war assessments envisaged heavy casualties. For
example, if fighting went on for a year (the longest period deemed
credible), the 327 cavalry officers serving with the BEF would have
incurred such 'wastage' that another 227 would be required. About
one-third of casualties would be killed, one-third badly wounded
and one-third slightly wounded. When a man was hit immediate
aid came from within his own unit. *Infantry Training* dourly
informed the casualty that he was to place his unexpended ammunition in a conspicuous place for his comrades to use, and went on
to warn that 'no man is permitted to leave his platoon in action to

take wounded to the rear . . .' Walking wounded would make their own way back, and the battalion's stretcher-bearers would collect immobile wounded and take them to the Regimental Aid Post. There the doctor would do what he could for them, and make a quick estimate of their chances. Some could be saved only by speedy evacuation. Others could be patched up to wait their turn. An unlucky few were already beyond hope, and were given morphia or chloroform.

We must spare a thought for medical officers, who required every inch of their professional armour-plate to cope with the decisions which faced them in a busy aid post, with old friends arriving *in extremis*. Arthur Osburn was a seasoned regular and had served in South Africa, but found his resolve tested to destruction by:

> one big man whose ear-splitting screams were racking the nerves of those less seriously wounded, whose lives we were trying to save . . . In spite of the drenching dose of chloroform it was a long time before that six-foot-three of agonised humanity stopped screaming. Perhaps it would have been more merciful to have shot the worst and obviously fatal cases at once, as some of the wounded and some of the spectators urged me to do.

Other medical officers were more matter-of-fact, even when faced with horrors like this. Henry Owens was a hunting doctor from Norfolk who volunteered on the outbreak of war, telling the War Office that: 'I wanted to see something of the war, if possible as soon as possible, and wanted some job with a horse to ride in it'. He was commissioned a temporary lieutenant in the RAMC and posted to 3rd Cavalry Field Ambulance. His diary suggests that he coped by walling up the awful aspects of his job in the very back of his mind. Horses, food, and the French countryside in late summer all feature more prominently than the business of the day, though stark juxtapositions hint at the burden on his shoulders. 'Had to see a staff officer, a major,' he wrote on 27 August, 'who had just shot himself in the head with a revolver in a motor car. He was still living. Had a very nice tea here.'

Field ambulances, like that in which Owens served, were allocated on a scale of three per infantry division and four for the cavalry division, so that one could be deployed with each brigade. A field ambulance had three sections, each comprising a bearer subdivision and a tent subdivision. The bearer subdivisions would go forward to recover wounded who might already have been treated by their regimental medical officer, and would take them back to the tent subdivision which constituted an Advanced Dressing Station. The wounded were moved back, in horsed ambulances, to Clearing Hospitals (soon renamed Casualty Clearing Stations) which sent them to general hospitals or ambulance trains.

As all a division's brigades would normally not be in action at the same time, it was often possible for a brigade to be supported by more than one field ambulance. However, a major battle like Le Cateau simply swamped the available medical facilities. For most wounded the ancient aspects of the war — painful journeys on stretchers or across a comrade's back, confusing waits in crowded aid posts or dressing stations, and the unspoken competition for the attentions of an exhausted doctor — were more apparent than the modern.

Men who were beyond help were buried in the field, sometimes in a civilian cemetery if one was close by. In the early stages of the war, procedures for identifying the dead and marking graves were poorly developed: indeed, as Fabian Ware, founding father of the Imperial (now Commonwealth) War Graves Commission was to discover, there was no proper army policy for noting and maintaining grave sites. Things were not helped by the fact that British killed in the retreat were hastily buried by their chums or interred by Germans who were trying to cope with mountains of their own dead. The mechanics of casualty identification had not been brought up to date: the soldier's Pay Book gave all his relevant details but was easily damaged or rendered illegible by damp. Officers had no pay books and, unless they had chosen to wear privately-purchased identity discs or bracelets, identifying their bodies was often a matter of grisly speculation beside an open grave, under the fetid breath of war at its most ancient.

III

CONCENTRATING THE MIND

The process by which an army is brought into the theatre of operations is called the strategical concentration. This is effected by sea, by rail, by water or by road, or by a combination of these means. In the case of an operation conducted outside Great Britain the concentration must be begun by sea, whilst it may be necessary to complete it either by rail, water, or road.

Field Service Regulations

Plans of War

I lectured at Sandhurst for fifteen years, and am the first to admit that the job had delightful aspects. The setting was beautiful: few views at Oxford or Cambridge could beat the Georgian crispness of Old Building early on a summer morning. The students, by and large, were congenial young men (and, latterly, no less pleasant young women), who posed few of the problems glumly described by my friends who had followed more conventional academic paths. My departmental colleagues, with the odd spectacular exception, were a pleasure to work alongside, and I still miss the delights of unravelling the morning with them over coffee in Topper's Bar, tucked away behind the pillars of the Grand Entrance. True, the job had its disadvantages, notably the suspicion that we were regarded by the Civil Service, which employed us, much as a receiver might view the staff of a bankrupt firm.

For many years the disadvantages of this snug world of corduroy and tweed were manifestly outweighed by their advantages. Not least of these was the fact that although the syllabus changed, facts did not. A lecture polished up in 1970 might stand scrutiny a decade later. In a sense I had much in common with the hard-working ladies who operated on the corner of the street where I lived when reading for my doctorate in Paris: we were selling the same product many times over.

How things have changed. With the end of the bipolar world, all my lectures on NATO and the Warsaw Pact, nuclear deterrence and Soviet operational doctrine have joined the Albigensian heresy and Byzantine cavalry tactics in the dusty loft of history. Yet even the dramatic changes of the past few years are not without precedent, and the senior officers who commanded the BEF in 1914 would have performed feats of mental gymnastics which, in their way, were no less taxing than those carried out by military men striving to make sense of the puzzling new world arising from the ashes of Communism.

In the 1860s Britain feared the expansionist France of Napoleon III: the redbrick forts that line Portsdown Hill above Portsmouth testify to the perceived danger of a French landing — perhaps near guiltless Chichester or sleepy Bosham — to threaten the naval base from inland. The Franco-Prussian war left France a much-reduced threat, and in the 1890s Russia shambled into the role of bogey-man. Learned reports worryingly observed that a British force of a quarter of a million could face a Russian army three and a half million strong, and naval power, traditionally Britain's strong suit, was of limited value in a war with Russia.

After the Boer War the picture changed again; by 1904 the General Staff was considering the possibility of a German offensive through Belgium into France meeting Anglo-French opposition. Momentous strategic decisions often reflect tensions within the defence community as the different services struggle for status and their share of an endangered budget, and the run-up to the First World War is no exception. Over the next decade the Army ensured that its strategic view triumphed over that of the Navy, which had long preferred to see the Army as a small bullet fired by a large Navy. It did so partly by outmanoeuvring the Admiralty in the knock-down drag-out world of defence politics. At a crucial meeting of the Committee of Imperial Defence on 23 August 1911, three years to the day before the Battle of Mons, Henry Wilson expounded the Army's plans with what the CID's secretary described as 'remarkable brilliancy' when compared with the Navy's visibly outdated scheme.

It was no accident that British planners were considering a German turning movement through Belgium as early as 1904. After the Franco-Prussian war, the French had fortified their common border

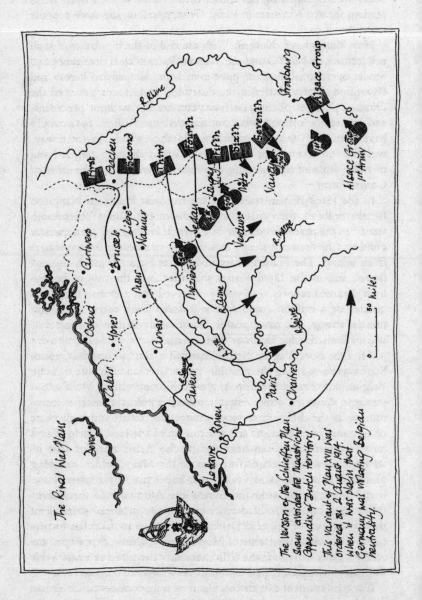

The Rival War Plans

The Version of the Schlieffen Plan shown avoided the Maastricht Appendix of Dutch territory.

This Variant of Plan XVII was ordered on 2 August 1914 when it was plain that Germany was invading Belgian neutrality.

First · Aachen

Second · Liège

Third

Fourth · Sedan

Fifth · Longwy · Metz

Sixth · Verdun

Seventh · Verdun

Alsace Group · Strasbourg

Alsace Group 1st Army

Antwerp
Ostend
Brussels
Bruges
Ypres
Namur
Dover
Calais
Arras
Mézières
Amiens
R.Somme
R.Oise
R.Aisne
R.Marne
R.Aisne
Paris
Chartres
Le Havre · R.Seine
R.Rhine
R.Rhine

0   50 miles

with Germany, making direct German attack a risky venture. More-over, the rapprochement between France and Russia boded ill for Germany, which would be unlikely to enjoy the luxury of being able to fight on a single front. Her chief advantage was her central position and excellent strategic railways which could enable her to concentrate against each opponent in turn. But where should she strike first? Count Alfred von Schlieffen, who became chief of the German General Staff in 1891, was convinced that invading Russia was fruitless — history loudly applauds his wisdom. The Germans could win only 'ordinary victories', and the Russians would simply withdraw into the deepest recesses of their enormous empire. The French were different. They could be beaten in a truly decisive engagement — Schlieffen was a keen military historian, and regarded Hannibal's victory over the Romans at Cannae in 216 BC as the supreme example of a successful battle. On 31 December 1905, Schlieffen wrote a memorandum which acknowledged that the French fortifications were essentially impenetrable, and envisaged swinging the mass of the German army through Belgium — and part of Holland to boot — so as to attack the French on the line Verdun–Dunkirk.

Schlieffen was too accomplished a staff officer not to recognise that the scheme faced staggering obstacles. Paris itself was a fortress, and if left outside the German wheel its garrison would undoubtedly jab in against the open flank. This being the case, the attackers would have to turn outside Paris, to encircle it, together with the bulk of the French armies, from west and south. There was also the very real danger that the French, obsessed — as Schlieffen knew them to be — with the burning desire to recover the provinces of Alsace and Lorraine, lost after 1871, would launch a determined thrust straight into Germany, into precisely that area denuded of troops by the demands of the great outflanking march. Schlieffen concluded that such an attack could in fact 'only be welcome to the Germans'. It would make the French less able to defend themselves against the turning movement, and the terrain over which they would have to advance, strengthened as it was by German fortifi-cations, was decidedly unpromising for an offensive. Schlieffen was confident that he would be able to hold the crucially-important Metz area while his right wing bit deep into the French left rear.

The wisdom of the Schlieffen Plan — a piece of historical short-hand for a series of projects evolved by Schlieffen and his successor — remains a matter of dispute. Gerhard Ritter's old but sprightly study is sharply critical of its lack of flexibility and the enormous risks, political and military, that it ran. In his preface to Ritter's book, Basil Liddell Hart acknowledges the plan's 'Napoleonic boldness', but casts doubt on the feasibility of moving troops on foot in a huge arc from the German-Belgian border, where they would detrain, right round Paris. Other commentators have suggested that it was not the plan's inherent defects, but specific errors in execution, which led to its failure in August 1914. Gordon Craig argues that: 'The daring of this conception must arouse a reluctant admiration, and it is possible that, if this plan had been carried out in 1914 in its original form and under the direction of an energetic and stubborn commander-in-chief, it would have achieved an overwhelming initial success'. Walter Goerlitz draws much the same conclusion, but goes on to maintain that even if France had been 'hurled into the dust' by the plan's triumph, Britain and Russia would have fought on.

In 1906 Helmuth Johann Ludwig von Moltke succeeded Schlieffen as Chief of the General Staff. He was the nephew of Helmuth Karl Bernhard von Moltke, architect of German victory in 1866 and 1870–71, and self-deprecatingly — and perfectly rightly — referred to himself as 'the lesser thinker'. He made important changes to Schlieffen's work. First, he abandoned the idea of violating Dutch neutrality, so as to retain Holland as 'the windpipe that enables us to breathe'. This made good sense politically, but imposed a heavy logistic burden on the armies of the German right wing, which would have to pass through the bottle-neck of Liège, between the 'Maastricht appendix' of Dutch territory to the north and the militarily difficult ground of the Ardennes to the south, before they could begin their march through Belgium proper. Second, he altered the balance of the right and left wings by allocating more troops to the defence of Lorraine.

There is no unanimity amongst historians as to the wisdom of Moltke's amendments to Schlieffen's project, and the details of their squabbles do not concern us here. But two key aspects of the final plan will loom large in the pages that follow. The first concerns Liège. Its rapid capture was regarded as the prerequisite of German success, and what Ritter terms the 'unbelievable haste' of German steps towards war in late July 1914 was conditioned by the need to take Liège. Violating Belgian neutrality would place the Germans at a moral disadvantage from which they would never fully recover, and would be likely to bring Britain, a guarantor of that neutrality, into the war. As early as 1906 Schlieffen assumed that a British force of some 100,000 men would be sent to the continent. He thought that it would probably land at Antwerp, where it would be shut up with the remnants of the Belgian army. He had little respect for the fighting power of the British, and his military attaché in London wrote hungrily of 'giving them a reception they will remember for centuries'. Quite what the Royal Navy was expected to make of all this did not concern Schlieffen. However, the population of Germany, enduring the privations produced by the Allied blockade, would have to have good reason to lament his lack of vision.

The Schlieffen plan rapped out the giddy tempo of the dance of death which whirled Europe to war in the summer of 1914, and in subordinating political caution to military imperatives it helped coax Britain onto the floor. It also stretched military feasibility to snapping point. Schlieffen was insistent that concentration on the right flank was essential — 'only make the right wing strong'. Moltke has been heavily criticised for weakening the right wing to strengthen Lorraine, but even after his modifications there were still over 760,000 men in the three armies — Kluck's *First*, Bülow's *Second* and Hausen's *Third* — that were to march through Belgium. Most of them would have to elbow their way through the choke-point of Liège, and then march at least as far as the River Seine. Even then their journey would not be at an end, for Kluck's men were expected to cross the river west of Paris before swinging eastwards. At the very least they would have to march 400 kilometres — carrying, like their British and French adversaries, some 80 lbs of rifle and pack — even if the plan worked flawlessly.

The French and Belgians could be expected to destroy railway bridges and viaducts as they fell back, and for all the energies of German railway troops there would inevitably be a widening gap between railheads and advancing troops. Schlieffen had hoped that the troops could live off the country, and expected that motor transport, bridging the gap between railhead and guns, would meet the army's ammunition needs. Moltke took supply more seriously, and ran logistic staff exercises, termed 'Flour Rides' — in contrast to the more usual Staff Rides — by officers who, one suspects, were no less G-snobs than their British counterparts.

The practical problems confronting the German armies on the right wing were enormous, even if the possibility of enemy action is discounted. Finding road-space for tens of thousands of men, horses, guns and wagons would tax the brains of even the hard-headed *Kriegsakademie* graduates for whom march-tables were meat and drink. On 17 August, *First Army* crammed 18,000 men into each mile of front, and *Second* and *Third Armies*, at 13,000 and 12,000 respectively, were only slightly less densely concentrated. Moltke and Schlieffen both expected that the decisive battle would be fought somewhere in Champagne, and hauling forward enough artillery ammunition to win it was a prodigious task, which would only be made harder if the Germans were forced to fight, burning off ammunition, in Belgium or northern France. There must be very serious doubt as to whether German logistics could have supported a stronger right wing than Moltke deployed, and there can be none whatever that the physical challenge facing the human ingredients of Schlieffen's plan was, quite literally, awesome. I thought this in the bookish chaos of my study, scratching dividers across maps: I knew it after a fortnight in the saddle had etched those miles deep into me.

A German advance through Belgium should have come as no surprise to the French. Intelligence reports based on details of the rail network around Aachen, and more sketchy information gleaned from pilfered documents, suggested that some Germans would indeed march through Belgium. But it was hard to assess how many would carry out the manoeuvre, and how deep they would go. The French army's mistrust of its own reservists — 'These reserve divisions exist on paper, but who can guarantee their solidity?' observed a senior general in 1911 — encouraged it to doubt that the Germans would employ reserve divisions in the front line, and without large-scale use of such formations the Germans would have insufficient troops to mass in both Alsace-Lorraine and the north. It seemed fair to assume, therefore, that the troops concentrating around Aachen would mount a secondary thrust to distract French attention from Alsace-Lorraine, and would probably not cross the Meuse into central Belgium. There were certainly strong indications to the contrary — in 1904 a German officer obligingly sold the French a plan which strongly resembled that drawn up by Schlieffen — but as Douglas Porch observes in *The March to the Marne*, 'French commanders were prisoners of their own preconceived ideas'.

When Joffre took over as Chief of the French General Staff in 1911 he inherited a war plan which neither guarded against an attack through Belgium nor provided for the rapid offensive which French military doctrine and his own inclinations demanded. He set about recasting it, and at the same time pressed the Foreign Office for information on Russian and British attitudes. Those worthies at *Quai d'Orsay* assured him that the Russians would undoubtedly support France, and subsequent discussions with the Russian General Staff produced a firm guarantee of a prompt offensive. British intervention, however, hinged on German violation of Belgian neutrality. Henry Wilson, francophile though he was, warned Joffre's deputy that a French pre-emptive advance into Belgium would drive the Belgians into the arms of Germany and place Britain 'in a very embarrassing situation'.

British insistence on the maintenance of Belgian neutrality helped dissuade Joffre from mounting an attack through the Belgian Ardennes. He accepted that the Germans might launch a subsidiary drive down towards Mézières, but this would be merely an adjunct to their major concentration in Lorraine. His own project, Plan XVII, was well-developed by the spring of 1913. It gave Joffre considerable flexibility as to the precise location and timetable of his offensive, but left no doubt that French fortunes were irrevocably wedded to a general assault. 'Whatever the circumstances,' it trumpeted, 'it is the Commander-in-Chief's intention to advance with all forces united to attack the German armies.' The five French armies, comprising a little over a million men in all, were concentrated along the Franco–German border, with the 5th, on the left, extending only as far as Mézières. The 110 miles between Mézières and the sea were entrusted to the BEF, whose arrival, as Joffre saw it, 'remained doubtful'.

The aura of doubt was no less evident to the British. Plans for mobilisation and concentration were well-developed. Six infantry divisions — or four if all six could not be spared — and a cavalry division would be shipped to France, most of them landing at Le Havre. They would be moved by rail to a concentration area between Avesnes and Le Cateau, and would be ready to advance on the sixteenth day after the order for mobilisation had been issued. However, Britain was not bound by the military discussions that had led to the finalisation of a plan so detailed that it included, in Henry Wilson's words, *'dix minutes pour une tasse de café'* at Amiens station. There was 'no definite agreement nor understanding that she should send assistance to France, and the British Government was free to decide, untrammelled, for peace or war', confesses the Official History. In view of the fact that the British were expected to deploy in exactly that area not threatened by the Germans, their uncertain arrival caused Joffre no great concern. Indeed, at around

100,000 strong the BEF was only a visiting card by the standards of continental war. But as the American historian, S. R. Williamson, has pointed out: 'The French regarded British intervention as a form of insurance, useful at a war's outbreak, imperative if the war was prolonged'. In 1909, Henry Wilson had asked Ferdinand Foch, then commandant of the Ecole de Guerre and destined to become general-issimo of the Allied armies in 1918: 'What would you say was the smallest British military force that would be of any practical assist-ance to you in the event of such a contest as we have been consider-ing?' 'One single private soldier,' replied Foch, 'and we would take good care that he was killed.' Few undertakings have been honoured with grimmer effect.

Some damned foolish thing

Old Bismarck had predicted that 'some damned foolish thing in the Balkans' would start the war which had seemed so close for so long. There had been several grave international crises in the first few years of the century, and there was initially no apparent reason why the Balkan crisis of 1914 should not be another in a line of near misses. On 28 June the Archduke Franz Ferdinand, heir to the Austrian throne, was assassinated in Sarajevo, capital of the recently-annexed Austrian province of Bosnia, by a Bosnian Serb. The Austro-Hungarian government, confident of German support, pre-sented a harsh ultimatum to Serbia and when she failed to give way on all points duly declared war on her.

The Serbs hoped for support from their fellow Slavs, and Russia duly began partial mobilisation in an effort to deter the Austro-Hungarians. The Germans had assured Austria-Hungary that they would prevent Russia from intervening, and on 29 July warned that they would answer a Russian general mobilisation with one of their own. The Russians, undaunted but still hoping for a diplomatic solution, raised the stakes by ordering full mobilisation the following day.

With all that we know about German preparations for war, we should not be surprised that Russian mobilisation shunted the crisis down the track which led inevitably to war. Speed was the essence of Germany's plan, and giving Russia time to mobilise could fatally weaken her chances. Russia was ordered to cease military prep-arations forthwith, and when she failed to do so Germany declared war on her on 1 August. France, asked for a guarantee of neutrality in a Russo-German war, replied that she would act in her own interests: fictitious tales of French violation of German territory (something the French were in fact anxious to avoid) were used to justify German declaration of war on France on 3 August.

This bald account does little justice to the many undercurrents of personal preference and public policy which carried Europe over the lip of the crater and into hell. There were many on both sides who strove, in good faith, for a peaceful solution. On 1 August the Imperial Chancellor, Theobald von Bethmann-Hollweg, genuinely believed that he had averted the worst by obtaining a guarantee from Sir Edward Grey, the British Foreign Secretary, that France would not attack Germany provided she herself was not attacked. Moltke responded that 'the deployment of an army a million strong was not a thing to be improvised', and it was simply impossible to jettison the plan in favour of a war with Russia alone. The Kaiser, characteristically swinging between belligerence and conciliation, firmness and pliability, snapped: 'Your uncle would have given me a different answer'.

The German military had some reason for wanting to press on. Not only would it have been difficult (though, on the evidence of the head of Moltke's railway department, by no means impossible) to change arrangements for deployment, but if war was indeed inevitable there was much to be said for fighting it sooner rather than later. The Russian army was improving following its poor showing in the Russo-Japanese war, and the French army seemed certain to become a more formidable opponent once the three-year service law of 1913 had taken full effect. In the event, it became clear that there could be no question of British assurance of French neutrality, and Moltke was eventually told to get on with the planned mobilisation. The day's meetings had sapped much of his moral strength and had destroyed his confidence in the Kaiser. Moltke had once told Prince Bülow that: 'I lack the capacity for risking all on a single throw, that capacity which made the greatness of such born commanders as Napoleon, our own Frederick II, or my uncle'. As he sat in his office on the Königsplatz, late on the night of 1 August, Moltke must have realised that he had hurled the dice in a gambler's throw, and he knew well that he was no gambler.

Shortly before the Morocco crisis of 1911, the British government ordered the Committee of Imperial Defence to prepare a War Book which would incorporate all Britain's approved defensive measures. Its most recent pre-war edition had, quite fortuitously, been

approved by the Committee on 14 July 1914, and in the words of
Maurice Hankey, its secretary, it was:

> so arranged that one could see at a glance the exact state of preparation
> on every subject, e.g. whether messages had been drafted; by what
> method they were to be sent, etc. Documents requiring the King's
> signature always accompanied His Majesty on his travels. In addition
> they were kept set up in type in the printer's office, ready to be struck
> off at a moment's notice.

On the afternoon of 28 July the Home Fleet was ordered to proceed
to its war station, and on the following day the Army's Precaution-
ary Period began. Regular officers and men were recalled from leave
and the coast defences were manned. However, the Government
shrank from ordering general mobilisation in case it worsened an
already grave situation. It was not until the afternoon of 4 August,
by which time German troops had entered Belgium, that the cabinet
agreed to mobilisation, which was to commence the following day.
A formal British declaration of war on Germany took effect from
11.00 p.m. that night.

The Empire was at War

The news came as no real surprise to Field-Marshal Sir John French,
who had long expected war with Germany. He had resigned as
Chief of the Imperial General Staff over the Curragh affair in March,
but a new commander-in-chief designate had not been appointed,
and he had been assured on 30 July that he would indeed command
the BEF if war broke out. On the afternoon of 5 August he attended
a Council of War at 10 Downing Street, accompanied by Lieutenant-
General Sir Archibald Murray, his chief of the general staff, Major-
General Henry Wilson, sub-chief of staff, and his two corps commanders, Lieutenant-General Sir Douglas Haig of I Corps and
Lieutenant-General Sir James Grierson of II Corps. Also present was
Field-Marshal Lord Kitchener, snatched from the boat-train at
Dover — he had been on his way back to resume his proconsular
duties in Egypt — to take over as Secretary of State for War.

  H. H. Asquith, the Prime Minister, was right to call it 'rather a
motley gathering'. Kitchener was a man of formidable energy and
determination, but he knew nothing of the tidy departmental world
of Whitehall, worked uncomfortably with colleagues, and got on
badly with French. French, for his part, was a mercurial cavalryman
who had risen to eminence following well-publicised successes in

the Boer War. John Terraine has rightly termed him the most distinguished English cavalry leader since Cromwell. He was certainly not the unthinking buffoon of popular mythology, and Alan Clark's assessment of him as 'a weak-willed man of medium height' is cruelly superficial. On the credit side were his unquestioned physical courage, personal charm and magnetism, and what Winston Churchill called his 'sacred fire of leadership'. On the debit side were his inconstant temperament, lack of deep intellectual capacity and tendency to pick advice from unreliable sources. Sir Philip Chetwode, commanding 5th Cavalry Brigade in 1914, later wrote that French 'loved life, laughter and women', and his private life was colourful, even by the gaudy standards of the age. When Captain the Honourable Arthur 'Jack' Annesley of the 10th Hussars was killed that autumn, French wrote a letter of condolence to his mistress, Winifred Bennett, and was soon involved in an affair which belied his sixty-four years.

French always considered himself 'far more a regimental than a Staff Officer', and his back-slapping style of command demanded first-rate staff support. Archie Murray's tragedy — and, in a broader sense, the BEF's too — was that he could not provide it. He had made a bad recovery from a stomach wound received in South Africa, and lacked the physical or mental robustness to sustain a rigorous campaign against a numerically superior foe. Brigadier-General Sir James Edmonds, a sapper officer who was to become the official historian, harshly described him as 'a complete nonentity'. The quartermaster-general, Major-General Sir William Robertson, was altogether more reliable and eventually succeeded Murray. But in the crucial months of 1914 Sir John, deprived of effective guidance from Murray, relied heavily on Henry Wilson, whose devotion to the French strapped blinkers onto GHQ at the very moment when it needed all-round vision.

French knew both corps commanders well. Grierson was a bluff Scots infantry officer who had served as Director of Military Operations at the War Office, worked closely with French when war seemed imminent in 1912 and accompanied him on his visit to French manoeuvres in Champagne in 1913. He had been chief of staff designate of the BEF, but after the 1913 manoeuvres French decided that he would be better placed as a corps commander. Grierson was jovial and outgoing, spoke good French and German, and joked that the collection of medal ribbons on his well-filled chest commemorated many a hard-fought battle with knife and fork. In the summer of 1914 he looked so dangerously apoplectic that his staff had been issued with scalpels with which to bleed the great man in case he became *too* florid.

Haig was altogether different. A quiet, Lowland Scot, aged fifty-three, Haig had served as French's brigade major at Aldershot before the Boer War, and had come to his assistance when a rash investment (French was no more level-headed with money than with ladies) brought him to the edge of bankruptcy. He performed well in staff and minor command appointments in South Africa, serving as one of Haldane's military advisers and as Director of Military Operations. He had not covered himself with glory in the 1912 and 1913 manoeuvres. A staff officer thought that in 1913 he was 'so completely outmanoeuvred that the operations were brought to a premature end', and in the following year his dispositions left a three-mile gap in the British centre. For his part, Haig thought that French's performance had been poor, and he privately doubted 'whether his temper was sufficiently even or his military knowledge sufficiently thorough to enable him to discharge properly the very difficult duties which will devolve upon him. In my own heart I know that French is quite unfit for this great command in a time of crisis.'

Unfit or not, French lost little time in outlining the War Office plan to the Council of War. He acknowledged that as Britain was now behind both France and Germany in the business of mobilisation, Amiens might be a safer concentration area than Maubeuge, but stressed that the entire BEF should be sent to France as quickly as possible. Having toed the party line thus far, French then veered off on a tangent and suggested that it might, after all, be possible for the BEF to operate from Antwerp against the German right flank. There was a majority view in favour of adhering to the original plan, although no definite decision was taken as to the number of divisions to be sent or their precise concentration area. The following morning the cabinet approved the dispatch of four infantry divisions and the cavalry division, but at another Council of War that afternoon there was a sharp dispute between French, who pressed for five divisions, and Kitchener, who foresaw a long conflict and urged caution. It was not until detailed discussions with French staff officers that it was at last decided, on 12 August, that the BEF should indeed concentrate around Maubeuge.

While Sir John and his staff were poring over maps in the Edwardian splendour of the Hotel Metropole in Northumberland Avenue, the army's machinery of mobilisation clattered smoothly on. Reservists were recalled to bring regular regiments up to war strength, the Territorial Force was called up, and units comprising the selected divisions of the BEF — 1st and 2nd Divisions in I Corps and 3rd and 5th Divisions in II Corps — were moved by rail to their ports of embarkation. Most troops stationed in England sailed from Southampton, while those stationed in Ireland departed from Dublin, Cork and Belfast.

The mobilisation of August 1914 saw the old world blaze up in a splendour that was to make the night which followed seem even blacker. There were scenes of wild enthusiasm in European capitals. 'Whoever failed to see Paris this morning and yesterday', wrote the poet Charles Péguy on 3 August, 'has seen nothing.' The Kaiser, gratified by the disappearance of factionalism, was able to say: 'I do not see parties any more: I see only Germans.' Sergei Kournakoff watched a woman rip her dress open and throw herself on the feet of a young officer in field service uniform: 'Take me! Right here, before these people! Poor boy . . . You will give your life . . . for God . . . for the Tsar . . . for Russia!' Even staid old London was not immune from hysteria. There was noisy enthusiasm outside Buckingham Palace when war was declared — although George V confided to his diary his fears for the safety of his eldest son — and a few of the capital's inhabitants managed to combine patriotism with self-interest by looting German-owned shops.

The men in whose footsteps we will march received news of mobilisation with mixed feelings. For the young, with no experience of war and no dependents, the spirit of adventure raged unchecked. Alan Hanbury-Sparrow entrained at Aldershot, thinking how those waving goodbye must envy him. 'Now we are to find out if our training has been right,' he exulted: 'now we are to find out what war is really like, and now we are to find out if we are really — men.' Major 'Sally' Home felt that he was particularly lucky: 'a weary year as a teacher at the Staff College has brought its reward and I find myself a GSO (General Staff Officer) 2nd Grade with the Cavalry Division.' A German student was equally enthusiastic. 'Hurrah! at last I have got my orders: to report at a place here at eleven o'clock tomorrow,' he rejoiced. 'I have been hanging about here, waiting, from hour to hour. This morning I met a young lady I know, and I was almost ashamed to let her see me in civilian clothes.'

Some joined for the sheer excitement, or to escape from a

humdrum life of inky clerking or repetitive drudgery. Others were affected by a profound sense of manly obligation. North Whitehead, waiting to go up to university that autumn, told his mother that 'I see in all the papers that all able bodied men are implored to join'. He assured her that 'in all probability I shall never go beyond the drill ground and that if I do I shall never be more than a reserve', and duly obtained a Special Reserve commission in the ASC. Just how wrong his prediction was may be gauged from the fact that his next letter, written from a railway carriage in France, reported that: 'Travelling on a troop ship is the most killing experience that I have ever had'.

Even a few of the young guessed that something terrible lay over the horizon. Herbert Sulzbach joined the German artillery as a war volunteer, feeling that 'a stone has begun to roll downhill and that dreadful things may be in store for Europe'. Lieutenant Billy Congreve, a regular officer in the Rifle Brigade, sensed the poignancy of the moment as far as his own family was concerned: his father was a serving general and his mother had so much to lose. 'It must be hard to be a woman now,' he wrote. 'I am mighty sorry for them all, but should be a deal more sorry if we were not to go, or, if we went, to find ourselves too late.' Young Billy was too late for Mons. He went out with 6th Division in September 1914, and was killed on the Somme less than two years later, winning a posthumous Victoria Cross.

Unlike the majority of their French allies and German opponents, most senior and middle-ranking British officers had already been under fire. This did not stop Lieutenant-Colonel G. T. G. Edwards of the 20th Hussars from assuring his sister that:

> It will be a big show and I am lucky to be able to go out as CO of the Regiment I have done all my service in. I would not change my position with anyone and praise God I hope we shall be able to give a good account of ourselves . . . This war had to come and it has come at the right time for us and I suspect the Germans will have to take a back seat when it is all over.

James Jack, however, was shocked to receive the telegram announcing that Britain was at war with Germany. It was 'quite mad, as well as being quite dreadful'. His comrades were in 'high fettle at the prospect of active service. But hating bloodshed as I do, and having had a hard if not dangerous fifteen months in the South African War . . . I personally loathe the outlook. A queer soldier!'

On 15 August, Arthur Osburn, who had just taken up his mobilisation appointment of Medical Officer to the 4th Dragoon Guards,
found himself trying to snatch a little rest and wondering:

> if I should come back to England or fall into a perpetual sleep in France.
> And then, alas! I was a doctor. I began to wonder whether other and
> worse things than death might not befall me. Would I lose my nerve
> and be shot for cowardice? Would a fragment of shell or bullet ricochet-
> ting from the ground and lodging in my spine paralyse my legs, my
> bladder and my bowels, leaving me foul, incontinent and helpless, an
> offence to myself and others — to die from bedsores and gangrene after
> twelve years of wasting agony in Netley Hospital. After all I had seen
> many others have to endure this, after the Boer War.

For fathers of families, the wrench of parting was especially cruel.
Walter Bloem, a forty-six-year-old novelist and drama critic mobilised as a captain with *12th Brandenburg Grenadiers*, had the professional writer's feel for a phrase, and observed that: 'The tear
season had begun . . .' With his kit packed and saddlery loaded, he
enjoyed a last bottle with his family: 'And when I thought of the
morrow, when my life would be taken up in the clutches of that
remorseless monster, War, I realised as never before, looking round
at my family, how intensely happy and fortunate I'd been in my
life and how truly grateful I should be.' Captain Wilfrid Dugmore
of the Cheshires, writing to his wife long after his capture, recalled
'previous to going to bed on the night of the 13th, going to my
children's beds and gazing at their darling little faces and heads!
Kissing them for the last time in their beds, perhaps for ever!' He
had his last glimpse of his wife and children, 'a lovely and sorrowful
little group', as the train taking him to Belfast pulled away. Dugmore was torn by that feeling, so common to men going to face
death, that he had simply run out of time to say the things that
matter. 'How . . . I reproached myself with not having made the
most of you,' he wrote, 'with having found fault with you constantly and without reason, with having treated you so unkindly on
frequent occasions!'

Rites of passage tug the heartstrings. Marc Bloch, a French historian mobilised as a reserve NCO in the infantry, reached the Gare
de la Chapelle in Paris in a market gardener's wagon (thereafter he
associated the smell of cabbage and carrots with that early-morning
departure) and saw how 'an aged, white-haired father made heroic
but unavailing efforts to hold back his tears as he embraced an

artillery officer'. Lieutenant John Campbell of L Battery RHA told his mother that they would not be able to meet before he left for France. 'Goodbyes are very harrowing,' he wrote, 'so do not try and come and see me. You will understand what I mean.'

Sometimes the friction of leave-taking was lubricated by alcohol. Lieutenant-Colonel G. A. Carden, leaving Glasgow for Ireland to take command of an ammunition column, was irritated to share the passage with 'a mob of reservists — many drunk'. When George Ashurst reported at Bury barracks he found that 'public houses were doing a roaring trade . . . There was a lot of hand-shaking, kissing and good wishes; women were crying and laughing and quite a number of the men were drunk.' Many reservists, denizens of a hard world where expectations were low and pitfalls numerous, took mobilisation in their stride. Private A. Wells of the 9th Lancers remembered things in a very matter-of-fact way. He was working in the gardens of the Hon. Mrs Portman with three other reservists, and on 6 August was told to report to Woolwich. He was sent thence to Tidworth, and arrived there only to find the regiment had already left for France. He rejoined it in the concentration area, and had barely enough time to get back into the swing of things before he found himself charging the German guns at Elouges.

Once a reservist, enthusiastic or not, reached his unit the machinery took over. He was issued with uniform and personal weapon, and was caught up in the business of preparation for war. Sergeant William Edgington, a rather serious thirty-five-year-old, was with D Battery RHA at the Curragh. The reservists rejoined on 7 August and turned his orderly world upside-down. 'Harness in barrack rooms, men sleeping on floor,' he observed. 'Very hard getting reservists back to discipline.' He was happier a day later, writing: 'Mobilisation completed. All ranks anxious to fight.'

Lieutenant Pennycuick thought that 'the arrival of the horses more than even the arrival of the reservists . . . made the greatest impression'. From his own very different perspective Walter Bloem might have agreed:

> Then there were the horses — snorting, rearing, stamping everywhere. Sturdy cart-horses, powerful runners, light hacks from gentlemen's stables, prancing thoroughbreds, steeple-chasers, browns, blacks, chestnuts, bays, all sorts and colours, excited by the change from their daily routine, the railway journey, this great gathering of their kind, by the cracking of many whips and the shouting — all sweat and commotion.

The British army's appetite for horses was scarcely less voracious than its hunger for men. During the Boer War it lost 326,000 horses. This was in part due to the harsh climate, and to an outbreak of glanders at Cape Town which resulted in many remounts being destroyed. It also reflected a shortage of veterinary officers, and low standard of horsemanship, even in units which should have known better. Major William Birdwood, staff officer with a mobile column, gently suggested to Colonel Steele of the Canadian cavalry regiment Lord Strathcona's Horse that his men might dismount to ease their horses since there was a pause in operations. 'Ye sons of — ,' bellowed the good colonel. 'Why the — — — — are ye sitting on your — horses?' 'Whereupon,' noted Birdwood, 'the regiment dismounted.'

The First World War did not witness the escalating demand for mounted men which had contributed to the difficulties in South Africa. And some of the lessons of the Boer War had been well learnt, in matters equine as in so many others. A Committee on the Supply of Remounts met in 1902, and made eminently sensible recommendations. The Army Veterinary Corps was established in 1903, and was steadily enhanced over the next few years, receiving a major-general as its director in 1906. It numbered 122 officers and 797 NCOs and men on mobilisation, and took the field with a Director and Assistant Director of Veterinary Services with HQ Lines of Communication, an Assistant Director of Veterinary Services with each division, and veterinary officers with mounted units. There were six veterinary hospitals, each of which could hold 250 patients, eleven mobile veterinary sections, and two base depots.

In the event this provision, although a real improvement over Boer War arrangements, proved inadequate. It was impossible for the Director of Veterinary Services, back down the lines of communication, to control the mobile sections working in forward areas. Five sections were soon placed directly under divisional control, and the remainder were grouped to form hospitals at Amiens, Rouen and Le Havre. Even so, as the official history of veterinary services admits, 'the enormous aggregate wastage from animal casualties of modern war was under-estimated, and in consequence it is conceivable that the service dealing with the sick and wounded animals was not . . . given the attention it merited'.

Just as the Army needed men to bring it up to war establishment, so too it needed horses. There were 25,000 on the strength on 4 August 1914, and at least another 120,000 were required to meet the requirements of the mobilised army. The 1909 Board of Trade publication *Types of Horses Suitable for Army Remounts* defined the sorts of horse that were required, and a horse census had established just where suitable animals might be found. The Army had traditionally relied upon buying its horses from the trade, and there were neither government studs nor any of the schemes, widely used on the continent, of state stallions being used to cover privately-owned mares.

The existing arrangements suited the Army, which was able to meet its peacetime needs with little difficulty. The cavalry of the line, for instance, required an annual intake of a thousand troop horses, a typical example of which was defined as being 'of hunter stamp. Height 15.2 hands, cost £40 in Ireland, a black gelding.' The Household Cavalry needed something rather bigger, likely to cost £65 as a four-year-old: 'A real nice-looking heavyweight horse with plenty of bone'. Providing the Army with horses like this suited breeders, who were able to sell remount officers perfectly satisfactory horses which had just failed to make the grade as top-quality hunters.

The Boer War had shown that the Army could not rely on normal commercial channels when it wanted a large number of horses quickly. Many of the horses which perished in South Africa should never have been sent there in the first place. Although remount officers in North America were looking for 'medium-sized, clean limbed, sound, active horses, between the age of five and ten, preferably broken to saddle', their arrival in town unleashed a flood of questionable dealers with strange-looking animals in tow. There were greys stained brown, whistlers dosed with a variety of patent cures, and elderly horses who had been 'bishoped' by having their teeth rasped to make them seem younger. In May 1901, the remount officer in Quebec announced that he would take no more, and there was a serious riot amongst the throng of disappointed would-be sellers. There were suggestions that some remount officers, while jolly good horsemen, were less sound judges of horse-flesh and were out of their depth in the cut and thrust world of dealing. There were also accusations of impropriety, which were to be repeated during the First World War: it was not difficult for a remount officer to get a dealer to agree to sell a horse for £40, show the price in his purchasing ledger as £50 and split the difference with the dealer.

It had been decided, therefore, that on mobilisation for a major war purchasing officers would be given justice's warrants which would permit them to requisition horses, and in August 1914 most of the 165,000 horses procured for the Army were obtained by compulsory purchase. Results were mixed. Some conscientious purchasing officers scoured their localities for good horses and paid sensible sums, coming as close as they could to their guideline prices (£70, for instance, for an officer's charger), neither overspending nor robbing the sellers. B. E. Todhunter mounted C Squadron of the Essex Yeomanry, travelling over 900 miles in the process. On 14 August, he told the remount officer in Brentwood that 'Essex has been pretty well skinned of her horses by this time and I had to go poaching in Suffolk before I could get the six that I sent you yesterday'. Acquaintances of government bureaucracy will not be astonished to discover that the authorities were remarkably dilatory in reimbursing Todhunter. Some Army Forms N 1547, horrifying to relate, had 'been rendered in an incomplete state', and the dispute dragged on till 9 September 1915. By this time not only had some of the horses died, but many of the 'jolly Yeo-boys' who had ridden them off to war had fallen when the Essex Yeomanry counter-attacked on foot at the Second Battle of Ypres.

Other purchasing officers were less astute than Todhunter. Irish dealers had a field day: twelve per cent of the horses they sold to the Army had to be disposed of almost immediately, and gullible buyers often soared above the guideline price. In England, many of the horses purchased came from private stables, and it needed all a household's resolve to steel itself to the loss of trusted friends and workmates. When remount sergeants visited Tysoe in Buckinghamshire: 'Every farmhouse . . . had some . . . shock and grief that day'. Kathleen Ashby's family lost the old carthorse, Captain, who was still useful 'if you humoured him and knocked off promptly after his stint of work, but under new men and at hard tasks he must break down'. Even big ponies were not safe, and there were tearful stable-yards as children heard that Sammy and Rob Roy had gone to be soldiers: empty stalls today, empty beds tomorrow. The remount authorities were no respecters of persons: James Jack was packing up to leave for France when a note informed him that his two remaining hunters, 'Ardskull Boy and Home Park, have been taken for the army — the first war wrench . . .'

There was a good deal of disinterested patriotism. Captain Lumley of the 11th Hussars recorded that 'Colonel Pitman's brother sent eight hunters all of which came through the war successfully. The master of the Meynell Hunt sent a number of hunt horses, and others came from Mr Fernie's and from the Pytchley.' Weymouth corporation was generous with its omnibus-horses; so generous that none were left to pull the buses. One way or another, by June 1915 the Army had taken some eight per cent of the heavy horses used on the land in June 1914, and no less than twenty-five per cent of the saddle horses had gone from farms. At one point in 1917 the Army had over a million animals — horses, mules, camels, donkeys and oxen — on its strength, 436,000 of them in France.

No less than 484,113 of the British Army's horses perished during the war. A few were lost at sea, but most died of disease or enemy action, or were destroyed when they were too worn out to be worth saving. A routine note from a RFA sergeant to his troop commander must serve as their epitaph.

> D/242 AFA
> Wagon Line, 3-4-17
>
> The following horses have been destroyed in my subsection
>
> | | |
> |---|---|
> | I Riding lead of gun | Baby |
> | II Riding lead 1st L[ine] Wagon | Black Bess |
> | III Riding centre 1st L[ine] Wagon | Broncho |
> | IV Rider Gnr Thorpe (Grey) | Dick |
>
> W C Stafford Sgt
> No 1 i/c A Sub Section

Fate could be as capricious with horses as with men. David served with 107th Battery RFA throughout the Boer War and First World War; Jones and Joubert, leaders of one of J Battery RHA's subsections, left Aldershot in August 1914 and when they returned in 1919 walked without hesitation into their old stalls; and four of F Battery's horses saw out the war on the Western Front and when safely back in England entertained visitors by tossing sugar lumps from their front hooves into their mouths. A moment's bad luck could change the story. Frank Pusey, a clerk with 31st (Howitzer) Battery RFA, recalled 14 September 1914 as his first bad day, when 'the Battery was shaken at the loss of so many old friends. One gun team of black horses — the pride of No. 1 Section — which were used for funerals at Woolwich, were all killed while standing with the gun limber on the flank of the battery.'

As the war went on attempts were made to spare British stock by securing horses from overseas, but it was not until 1918 that the amount of horses used for agriculture in Britain appreciably exceeded the July 1914 total. Some breeds were particularly hard hit. The big Clydesdales which pulled many of the heavy guns died like flies in the severe winter of 1917, largely because regulations dictated that horses would be clipped throughout the winter. Thereafter it was decreed that horses would not be clipped after 15 November.

In August 1914 horses went to remount depots and thence to units. Horsy officers had the time of their lives making selections from depots: it was not unlike letting a crop of modern subalterns loose in a showroom full of fast cars and telling them to take their pick. James Pennycuick remembered how: 'An enormous horse depot was formed at the Curragh race course to hold wonderful animals requisitioned from all over . . . Ireland, a sight never to be forgotten in that green land of horses. We young officers had great fun picking our requirements, and it was a great time for anyone with an eye for a horse.'

Henry Owens, doubtless thinking more about horseflesh than the need to find synonyms for nice, visited the Curragh on 11 August and found 'a lot of nice horses out. Have got a nice horse, a long tailed bay, well bred, nice mouth and manners and nice paces — 4 years old.' She did him well when he got to France, and on 21 August he wrote: 'My nag is a topping ride. Soft misty morning — nice cubbing morning.'

Young officers in all armies traditionally favoured good-looking, nippy mounts. Those who had bothered to read Hohenlohe-Ingelfingen would have recalled his strictures on the subject. In the Schleswig war of 1864 a Prussian staff officer went to war on a showy race-horse. He galloped up to the advanced guard with a message, failed to stop his steed, and was carried right through the rearguard of stocky Danish dragoons: mercifully the horse tore up the right-hand side of the road so they had to cut at him backhanded as he streaked past. In 1914 four subalterns in a Russian dragoon regiment obtained horses from the Moscow race-track. Their regiment charged, then halted abruptly, and they were carted right into enemy lines. The thoughtful Germans dropped a message from an aircraft the following day, announcing that: 'Lieutenant Count Rebinder won by two lengths, in case you had bets on the gentlemen'. More experienced officers made wiser judgements. Major Tom Bridges of the 4th Dragoon Guards secured 'one Umslopagaas, a powerful weight-carrying hunter with a wall eye, who could jump railway gates'.

Private soldiers had to put up with what they were given. Private

Garrod's first horse was a beauty. 'She was under fifteen hands,' he remembered, 'had the heart of a lion, would try to jump anything possible, and if a sword was cut down at the side of her eyes would never flinch or run.' She had to be put down after breaking a leg, and he was issued with the worst horse in the troop 'who was such a bastard that he was known as Syphilis' — presumably because nobody wanted to catch him. When the BEF embarked, its horses were either led up gangplanks or swung aboard by cranes. The latter process was not much to their taste. Pennycuick watched 59th Field Company's horses going aboard the Blue Funnel Line's *Bellerophon* at Dublin on 16 August: 'Most of our horses were slung aboard by means of a canvas belt fastened round the creature's stomach. The lift operator was skilful, but quick. As soon as the belt was adjusted the well-fed astonished "hairy" shot high into the air, exploding wind from both ends and kicking out feverishly to high heaven.' When the 20th Hussars were embarking at Southampton, Garrod saw how: 'Syph lashed out, broke the arm of the Farrier Sergeant-Major who was supervising the shipping of the horses, and when he stepped back old Syph plunged over the dock into the water and was never seen again'. Garrod got the Farrier Sergeant-Major's horse instead, and was well pleased with the exchange.

Movement to ports of embarkation and thence to France was carried out with a remarkable degree of secrecy. Sergeant Percy Snelling of the 12th Lancers admitted that 'we haven't the slightest idea where we are going', and Major Lord Bernard Gordon-Lennox of 2nd Grenadier Guards was no better informed, remarking on 12 August that 'we left Chelsea Barracks for an unknown destination to help the brave Frenchmen and Belgians'. The weather was generally good throughout the period. Lord Bernard recalled 'a lovely night, with not a ripple on the water'. But Corporal Watson, an Oxford undergraduate only a fortnight before, found the night 'horribly cold, and a slow dawn was never more welcomed. But day brought us a new horror. The sun poured down on us, and the smell from the horses packed closely below was almost unbearable.' Lieutenant A. A. Martin, hastily commissioned into the RAMC, found the horses a trial. There were 600 aboard *Cestrian*, and he 'managed to commandeer an old sofa cushion, and lay in the corner of the smoking-room and went to sleep, and dreamt of thousands of horses looking at me reproachfully out of boxes'. Bombardier Thomas Langston was also not at his best. His battery had left Deepcut after an address from the colonel, but 'I was at the back and did not hear one word'. Safely embarked on *Victorian*, he wrote: 'The troops are now singing "Hey ho, can't you hear the steamer." Everybody seems to be bent on war. Remain on deck till 10.00. Retire to *bed*.' The 3rd Hussars had a difficult time getting their horses onto *City of Lucknow*, almost losing the CO's charger in the process. Once aboard they discovered, as the regimental history drily observes, that 'sanitary arrangements . . . were totally inadequate'.

The majority of troops disembarked at Le Havre. Getting men off the ships was one thing, but unloading the horses was quite another. 'Very bad place to land,' noted Lieutenant-Colonel Edwards, 'and very difficult to get horses off.' It took much of the day to get XIV Brigade RFA off *Minneapolis*. No sooner had the 4th Hussars left *Atlantan* than C Squadron's horses stampeded and several were killed. The 5th Dragoon Guards arrived at Le Havre at 3 p.m. on 15 August, but Captain John Norwood told his wife that he did not manage to disembark till 11.00. He spent his first few hours in France in the *Hangar des Cotons*, which was 'so big that a cavalry brigade and a half with horses, 1 infantry battalion and 2000 huge barrels of beer and endless stacks of supplies only half filled it'.

Norwood managed to nip into Harfleur to have his hair cut by 'a most amusing barber' and then dined off bully beef in the warehouse before his regiment entrained. Most units, however, marched out of Le Havre to one of a number of rest camps on the hills above it. Count Gleichen disembarked on 16 August and discovered that it had been raining heavily:

> so the ground where we were to encamp was mostly sopping. It was not easy to find in the dark, especially as the sketch-maps with which we were provided most distinctly lived up to their names . . . There was of course no baggage, nor anything to sleep on except the bare ground under the tents, with our saddles for pillows; and as a pleasant excitement nearly all our horses stampeded about 2.00 a.m., tore up their picketing-pegs from the soft ground, and disappeared into the darkness in different directions.

Kitchener had written a short exhortation, issued to every soldier in the BEF on 10 August, telling him that he was 'ordered abroad as a soldier of the King to help our French comrades against the invasion of a common Enemy', and concluding, with what was indeed the triumph of hope over experience, that 'while treating all women with perfect courtesy, you should avoid any intimacy'. The latter suggestion amused French officers, one of whom quipped that the British had obviously shipped over a girl's school rather than an army. This being the British Army, there was a shortage of French-speakers. Aubrey Herbert MP materialised as an unofficial interpreter by the simple expedient of getting his tailor to run up an officer's uniform without badges of rank and joining the Irish Guards (full of fellow old Etonians who turned a blind eye to his irregular status) as it marched out of barracks. The guardsmen were at first inclined to be hostile to the French, until a Coldstream officer told them:

> 'The French are our Allies; they are going to fight with us against the Germans.' Whereupon one man said: 'Poor chaps, they deserve to be encouraged,' and took off his cap and waved it and shouted 'Vive l'Empereur!' He was a bit behind the times. I believe that if the Germans beat us and invaded England they would still be laughed at in the villages as ridiculous foreigners.

The warmth of the French welcome surprised many. Sergeant Edgington reported an 'enthusiastic reception by French population who shower us with flowers (and kisses) . . .', while Tom Langston received a kiss for his cap badge and another for each of his shoulder titles. Frank Richards' chum Billy, a seasoned colonial campaigner, had a robust approach to his generous hosts. 'Look here, Dick,' he told Richards, 'there is only one way to treat foreigners from Hong Kong to France, and that is to knock hell out of them.' Lieutenant Edward Spears, on temporary attachment to the French general staff when war broke out and then posted as British liaison officer with the 5th Army, believed that in one specific case 'the difference of language, far from being an impediment, tended, on the contrary, to closer, more rapid, and generally to more satisfactory relations'. A soldier wishing to enjoy the favours of a young lady would hold up a tin of jam, 'and the formula "*Mademoiselle, confiture?*" became well established.'

The French military authorities provided units with interpreters. Their numbers varied: the 3rd Hussars received a dozen, while the Household Cavalry Composite Regiment had two, promptly christened Weary Willy and Tired Tim. The former soon lost his horse, not entirely accidentally, and briefly rattled around on a bike before he vanished; the latter's dimensions put riding out of the question, but he 'stumped stolidly along, got a lift whenever he could, and remained faithful to the Composite Regiment until his well-earned promotion took him elsewhere'. Paul Maze, a young civilian, saw the Scots Greys landing at Le Havre on 18 August and at once decided to go to war with them. He offered his services to Lieutenant-Colonel Bulkeley-Johnson, who agreed to take him, and he spent his first night with the regiment:

> under the sky amongst the horse lines in a clover-field. The horses kept scraping the ground with their hooves, and the mechanical action of their teeth munching hay constantly woke me up. The warmth of their breath was pleasant. It was cold . . . Wet with dew, I was up at dawn . . . Fires were crackling — an odour of frying bacon drifted in the air. We washed ourselves. Only a night spent in the open can make an early morning meal taste as delicious as that one did.

Maze spent the whole of August with the BEF, and it was not until early September that he returned to Le Havre to enlist formally into the French army and be posted to the BEF as an interpreter — this time officially.

Units were summoned at intervals from the rest camps above Le Havre to entrain for the concentration area. Count Gleichen's brigade moved from three different stations between midnight on the 17th and 5.45 the following morning. The French had allowed four hours for the entraining of a battalion, but although the trucks were unfamiliar the brigade entrained in forty minutes, though not without the usual equine dramas. 'Silver (my first charger) was very bobbery as usual,' wrote Gleichen, 'and it took a good half hour to persuade him to enter his truck. Once in, he slept like a lamb.' The trucks held forty men or eight horses — four at either end, with their saddlery and two men on bales in the centre. As trains shuttled back and forth the condition of the trucks worsened, and Lieutenant C. L. Brereton RFA saw how by the time 4th Division moved up on 24 August: 'The floors of the horse boxes were very slippery and the horses were falling about all night. One horse shot at Rouen. Spent most of the night pulling horses up.' The Composite Regiment moved up earlier but had similar problems. Horses fell but there was no way of contacting the engine-driver, so Surgeon-Major Cowe crawled along the carriage-tops in the best Wild West style to tell him to stop the train.

Horses were not the only casualties of the rail move. Jimmy Grierson died of a heart attack on the train at Amiens on 16 August; Frank Richards was one of the party which brought his body from train to town hall, and then returned it to the station, whence a detachment of Cameron Highlanders escorted it back to Le Havre. French at once wired Kitchener, asking for Sir Herbert Plumer, GOC of Northern Command, as a replacement. Kitchener did not reply, but on 19 August sent out Sir Horace Smith-Dorrien. It was a deeply controversial choice. The bad relations between French and Smith-Dorrien were, as Major-General Sir Charles Callwell recognised, 'almost a matter of common knowledge within the service', and Kitchener knew that French cherished 'great jealousy of and personal animosity towards' Smith-Dorrien. When Sir Horace took over Aldershot Command from French he made changes which French resented, and to make matters worse he was believed to have a 'down' on the cavalry. He was a deeply moral man, happily married to a young and pretty wife, and made no secret of his disapproval of the Field-Marshal's light cavalry lifestyle. And when Smith-Dorrien reported for duty on 20 August he told French that the King had asked him to report directly on the doings of II Corps, by-passing the chain of command; it was not a good beginning.

Sir George Arthur, Kitchener's private secretary, believed that Smith-Dorrien was appointed because Kitchener feared that Plumer would be too compliant. Kitchener 'was sure it was important that the corps commander should be imbued with sufficient self-will to resist an order which, if implicitly obeyed, might spell disaster'. Of Smith-Dorrien's military competence or popularity with the rank and file — who knew him as 'Smith Doreen' — there can be no doubt. But even if appointing a corps commander who was known to get on badly with the commander-in-chief was not in itself unwise, there were other reasons why Kitchener should have paused. Smith-Dorrien had an appalling temper. It was legendary even in an army of short-fused generals, and there were suggestions that there it had some deeper cause than the neuralgia to which it was usually attributed. Lord Crewe, an old school friend of the general's, turned him down for the post of commander-in-chief of the Indian Army on the grounds that his health and temper were not equal to the task. 'When unwell,' warned Crewe, 'the unlucky result is loss of temper and self-command, to an extent which might be serious in such a position.'

By the time that Smith-Dorrien reported to him, French himself was not in the best of tempers. He had landed in Boulogne from the cruiser *Sentinel* on 14 August and travelled to Paris via Amiens, reaching the Gare du Nord on the afternoon of the 15th. His meeting with President Poincaré was not auspicious. The President thought that he looked more like a plodding engineer than a dashing cavalry-man (French would have been cut to the quick had he known it), and added reproachfully that 'he speaks our tongue with great difficulty'. Poincaré was perfectly right. Although Sir John had spent some time in France in the autumn of 1906 with the specific intention of learning the language, his French would not have disgraced the script of *'Allo 'Allo*: on one occasion he translated footman as *pied-homme*, and even when he lived in Paris after the war he found it hard to persuade a taxi driver to take him back to his hotel. An encouraging meeting at the War Ministry was followed by dinner at the Ritz, where Sir John was surprised to hear 'silly reports of French "reverses" ', though he was sure that they were 'all quite untrue'. The next day he travelled out to Vitry-le-François, south-east of Rheims, to meet Joffre.

French and Joffre formed a generally favourable impression of one another, which was as well, for much would turn on their relationship in the days that followed. Joffre said that while infor-mation on German movements was still too imprecise for him to issue firm instructions, he hoped to attack as planned and expected the BEF to advance, in the general direction of Nivelles, on the left of the French 5th Army. Sir John replied that although his army would not be ready to move till the 24th, he would do his best to start sooner.

French then drove to Rheims, where GHQ was temporarily estab-lished amidst the moquette and veneer of the Hôtel Lion d'Or. All was not well. The code book had been lost, and several War Office telegrams had arrived, to remain as unintelligible to friend as to foe. Edward Spears drove over from 5th Army's headquarters at Rethel with his code books, but they were no use. Spears met Murray, who greeted him with his customary kindness, but who was worried 'not so much by the situation, which he was trying to unravel on all fours on the floor, where enormous maps were laid out, as by the fact that chambermaids kept coming in and he had only his pants on'. Murray's *déshabille* was a consequence of the temperature. It was a glorious summer, and Spears acknowledged that discussing strategy was not an easy matter when it was ninety in the shade.

On the 17th, French drove across to Rethel to visit General Charles Lanrezac, commander of the 5th Army. The meeting could scarcely have gone worse. Colonel Huguet, a French liaison officer with GHQ, was greeted by the trim little General Hély d'Oisel, Lanrezac's chief of staff, with the less than cheery cry of: 'Well, here you are — it is just about time. If we are beaten it will be thanks to you.' The commanders spent a little time in Lanrezac's office, failing to communicate, and then emerged for a brief and stilted general discussion. Sir John, wrestling with his execrable French, choked out an enquiry as to whether the Germans were going to cross the Meuse at Huy. Lanrezac replied that, in his opinion, the Germans had simply gone there to fish. The meeting ended with Lanrezac, already inclined to lump British and Belgians together with his own reserve divisions as equally useless, convinced that Sir John did not propose to use his cavalry for reconnaissance but planned to keep them in reserve; in view of French's tribal markings nothing could have been farther from the truth.

Spears, by no means a biased witness, blamed the misunderstanding on Lanrezac rather than French. Its consequences were far-reaching; Spears thought that French was 'as bad an enemy as he was a good friend, and that is saying a great deal'. Once he lost confidence in a man he was finished, and the 17 August meeting began the demolition of Lanrezac, a process the sledgehammer of war would soon complete. Yet if little can justify Lanrezac's deliberate rudeness, we must pause to consider the man's state of mind. He was one of the lions of peacetime, regarded, Spears tell us, as 'the star turn' by Joffre's headquarters. Podgy, opinionated and abrupt, Lanrezac was given to pontificating to his staff with his glasses hooked over his right ear. But his reputation for sagacity was not misplaced. As early as 31 July he had drawn Joffre's attention to the possibility of a German sweep through Belgium, and as the days went on, alone amongst the French Army commanders, he scented that 'the real danger lay in the north where the great upper jaw was beginning to close down'.

This was not the sort of news Joffre wanted to hear. A series of *Instructions Particulières* had modified the general provisions of Plan XVII, but all discussed variants of the offensive scheme. Lanrezac met Joffre on 14 August and tried to persuade him that pushing 5th Army forward into the Ardennes would be suicidal if the Germans were advancing west of the Meuse in strength. Joffre eventually allowed Lanrezac to shift his weight towards the north-west, and sent three Territorial divisions off to screen the area between Maubeuge and Dunkirk against possible incursions by German cavalry. By nightfall on 18 August 5th Army was holding the line Philippeville–Maubeuge. In the process, it had taken under command formations it had not worked with before, and the equilibrium of its headquarters was further disturbed by news that the Germans had forced Liège and were pouring across the Meuse between Maastricht and Visé. Lanrezac could see his worst nightmare coming true, but this increasingly accurate vision of the real operational situation was not shared by GQG, which came to regard him no longer as a star turn but as a high flier who was about to crash.

No thought of all this friction in high places clouded the minds of the British soldiers who arrived in their concentration area in the third week of August. Much of I Corps detrained at Hautmont, on the southern edge of Maubeuge. Sergeant Edgington thought it a 'very dirty place, coal mines, consequently when we had finished we all looked like sweeps'. Tom Langston's unit detrained at Etreux, further south, and then marched up to Maubeuge. 'This is strongly-fortified and looks impregnable,' he wrote approvingly, 'wire entanglements and trenches surrounding the place and it is evident that they are expecting the Germans.'

What impressed a bombardier might not have seemed as imposing to an engineer officer. Maubeuge was a fortress of long standing. In 1914 its ramparts and bastions, installed by the great Vauban, were intact: it was not until 1962 that the demolition of fortifications on the southern bank of the Sambre broke Vauban's neat geometrical belt, and even now the defences around the Porte de Mons, beautifully restored by the local *Renaissance Vauban* society, provide a wonderful snapshot of the golden age of artillery fortification. After the Franco-Prussian War a ring of outlying forts had been built round Maubeuge with the intention of keeping a besieger out of bombardment range of the body of the town, but these had not been as well developed as many of the forts on the Franco-German border — like those around Verdun — and in 1914 the place was vulnerable to heavy guns. Indeed, the Liège forts, far bigger and more modern than those at Maubeuge, had just been battered into submission by German artillery: the last blew up on 15 August.

Many units of II Corps arrived further west. James Pennycuick's 59th Field Company RE detrained in the dark at Landrecies, and then marched northwards, sustained by gifts of fruit, eggs and milk. 'I got quite good at cracking an egg on my saddle and swallowing it raw,' he wrote, 'or drinking milk while a child ran beside my horse to collect the borrowed cup.' Second-Lieutenant Kenneth Godsell of 17th Field Company, also in 5th Division, had less idyllic memories of the same route. The fruit was 'washed down with the red and white wine of the country to the disaster of the gastronomics of the less strong. Falling out among the troops became very frequent and men were seen rolling in agony by the roadside.'

By 20 August the British concentration was all but complete. The BEF was deployed ready for an advance north-westwards, with the cavalry east of Mauberge, patrolling out towards Binche and Thulin. I Corps headquarters was at Wassigny, just west of the Oise to the south of Le Cateau, and II Corps headquarters was further north at Landrecies, on the southern edge of the great Forest of Mormal. The infantry divisions were billeted in villages a few kilometres to the east of their respective corps headquarters, making the most of local hospitality, carrying out some limited training largely with the aim of welding the reservists back into the regimental team, and preparing to advance. 'We are to support three French Cavalry Brigades who are in pursuit of a German Army Corps,' wrote Percy Snelling with eager anticipation. Little did he know how different the truth was.

Thatch goes east

Our own journey to France went just as smoothly as our grand-fathers'. Although our plans were marginally less elaborate than those which took the BEF to war in 1914, they were none the less comprehensive, and there were moments when I thought that we could have shipped a whole cavalry brigade to France, let alone the four horses, five men and two vehicles making up our little expedition. We began planning a year before setting out. The BEF retreated from Mons on a wide front — it might stretch across fifty miles on an average day — using a mixture of metalled roads and occasional tracks. For this book to make much sense, our own route had to follow that of the BEF and to take in the battles of Mons and Le Cateau and the smaller actions at Cerizy, Néry and Villers-Cotterêts. This would involve following II Corps for part of the way, for Smith-Dorrien's men bore the brunt of the early fighting, and then swinging across to get onto I Corps' route: Villers-Cotterêts was fought by 2nd Division's 4th (Guards) Brigade, and with a Grenadier in our party it was inconceivable that we should not spend a day on the battlefield.

Our first meetings were in 19th Brigade's headquarters, then conveniently located in Colchester, and we drank endless cups of coffee sitting in a half circle beneath a wall-map consisting of 1:50,000 maps of northern France stuck together in a vast mosaic. 'Riding the Retreat from Mons' had looked so good on the synopsis. But which route would we take? How long would we need to do it? Where would we stay? It was easy enough to find Mons, and scarcely more difficult to discover the limit of the BEF's retreat south of the Marne. We began by marking corps' withdrawal routes onto the maps, and then added transverse lines which we hoped would represent a reasonable day's march. Our guiding principle was to choose marches of around twenty-five miles a day, which could be safely carried out by one fit horse. We hoped to box two of the horses on to a lunchtime halt while the remaining two were ridden, and then ride the fresh horses during the afternoon, but we needed to be able to complete the journey even if we lost up to three of our horses.

There were other good reasons for being modest in our expectations. This was not an endurance ride. We wanted to enjoy ourselves, take in the country, and it would be churlish not to do justice to a bottle or two at lunchtime. We hoped to cover ground at about the same pace as the BEF, and to be able to spend a day on each of the battlefields we crossed. Finally, there was the question of routes. We would try to use metalled roads as little as possible, but by using tracks we would be likely to cover much more ground than if we stuck to the most direct route.

Evelyn and Ollie took on the task of finding a detailed route and suitable accommodation. This was simpler in France than it would have been in Britain. The *Association Nationale de Tourisme Equestre* (ANTE) was founded in 1963 and became part of the *Fédération Française d'Equitation* (roughly equivalent to the British Horse Society) in 1987. ANTE has some 30,000 individual members and 1,300 Riding Centres. Its headquarters is in central Paris, and it has twenty-three regional offices (ARTEs) as well as local *Associations* in most *départements*. It is funded by a mixture of membership fees, government grants and income from sponsorship and competitions: the National Stud (*Administration des Haras*) and local authorities contribute towards the cost of running the regional ARTEs. Government — local and central — contributes to ANTE because it recognises that horse tourism generates income for rural areas where agriculture is in steady decline and the population is drifting to the towns.

The entire set-up is very French. Although it is run from Paris and gets a good deal of its money from central government, ANTE draws its real strength from the regions, whose relationship with Paris, and with one another, is rather looser than the wiring diagram described above might suggest. Some local ARTEs answer letters and telephones with commendable speed; others might as well have adopted the motto of the defenders of Verdun, *on ne passe pas*, for it is difficult to get a word out of them. It has to be said that most of those that we dealt with were very helpful, and in the case of Nord–Pas de Calais so hospitable that bladder and liver were more stressed than backside and thighs when we rode through their patch.

As the ARTEs responded to our request we were able to plan our route in more detail. Sometimes this was simplicity itself. I phoned Jean Petitprez of Nord–Pas de Calais, and we got down to brass tacks at once. No, he had no jurisdiction over Belgium but he knew a man who did, and was sure that he would guide us along the rather tricky route from Mons to Malplaquet, where we wanted to cross the border. There was the obligatory banter over who had actually won the battle of Malplaquet. I claim a victory on points, but it was as inconclusive as the bloody contest in 1709. And I undoubtedly lost the next round. Which side of the mighty Forest of Mormal did we wish to travel? To the west, I replied. There was a long pause. This was not so easy, said M. Petitprez. The routes were not good and he anticipated difficulties. To the east, then. This too presented problems. Had I considered going through the forest? I had not, because I was under the (mistaken) belief that no British soldiers had crossed it. Hm, said M. Petitprez, audibly pressing his advantage. He would see what he could do about the flanks, but he thought we might have to go through the forest after all. There were worse things, he added: 'Mormal will be lovely at that time of year and you'll regret not seeing it'. And, of course, he was absolutely right. By the time we left England most of the ARTEs whose ground we were covering had come up trumps, providing us with details of off-road routes and abundant advice on places where men and horses might stay.

I was keen to find billets right on our line of march to avoid lengthy wheeled moves at the end of one day or the beginning of the next. At those early meetings I banged on relentlessly about the need to have as much texture as possible in our accommodation. Although living out of a saddle-bag would be a little too spartan, sliding from smart hotel to smart hotel was definitely not what I had in mind. Eventually I used 'texture' so often that it was banned, and later, as we approached the occasional rather medieval-looking establishment where we were to spend the night my companions would look darkly in my direction and mutter something barely audible about the T word.

At the same time that we sought advice on accommodation from the ARTEs we also cudgelled any of our friends who might possibly be able to help. We struck gold quite quickly. I knew Brigadier Johnny Rickett, military attaché at the British Embassy in Paris, from his time as Chief of Staff at Headquarters South-East District in Aldershot. He is a keen horseman with good contacts, and immediately made some useful suggestions. The Grenadier mafia also turned up trumps. Charlie Bennett, who had served with Evelyn but had since exchanged scarlet for pinstripe, put us into contact with Maurice Velge, a Belgian businessman who spends most of his time in Antwerp but owns a stunning château rather more than half-way along our route. Not only did Monsieur Velge offer to put us all up for a night, but he also spread the word among his hunting friends, and we were to owe some of our most delightful evenings — and one unforgettable harum-scarum morning — to his kindness. By the spring of 1993 the travel and accommodation plots had hardened nicely. Evelyn had arranged a mixture of accommodation which would take us from châteaux at one extreme to sleeping-bags in a cornfield at Néry at the other. The horses would be stabled for all but two nights, when we could use John's cavalry expertise to picket them in the field, as our grandfathers would have done seventy-nine years before.

Getting men and horses to France was no problem. The regulations on the export of livestock had changed on 1 January 1993, greatly reducing the bureaucratic burden. We would need to have the horses inspected by a vet within twenty-four hours of their departure, but there appeared to be no other hurdles. Pessimistic as ever, I expected some last-minute administrative requirement to curl in from a flank, but none materialised. Three days before our departure I drove up to Catterick — 19th Brigade had inconveniently moved north since the project began — to collect Evelyn's horse trailer.

We had agreed to meet at Hyde Park Barracks at 10.00 on the morning of Saturday 7 August. The others — men and horses — would have travelled down from Catterick to Melton Mowbray two days before and driven the last leg of the journey on the Friday. Hyde Park Barracks, rebuilt in the 1960s, now houses the two

Household Cavalry mounted squadrons; in 1914 it was the home of 1st Life Guards. There were then three regiments of Household Cavalry: 1st Life Guards, 2nd Life Guards and the Royal Horse Guards. They sent a Composite Regiment to war in 1914, with a squadron from each regiment, the whole commanded by Lieutenant-Colonel Cook of the 1st Life Guards. The guards were issued with live ammunition at the outbreak of war and Sir George Arthur described it as 'a most exhilarating exercise, and increasingly interesting when it was explained that anyone failing to answer a challenge would be fired on. The net result of this caution was a succession of "friends" vociferated at all entrances to the park without any chance being given to a sentry to challenge, let alone fire.'

I was up early that Saturday. Karen, who ran the stables, and Ginny, her second-in-command, were there to help me get Thatch dressed for the journey — tail-bandage, tail-guard and travelling boots — and safely onto the trailer. He went aboard with no fuss, and was steadfastly addressing his haynet when we left Newton Valence for London. My wife Lizie and Jessie, my eldest daughter, came with me to provide moral support, and there were moments when I needed it as Thatch shifted his not inconsiderable weight while we percolated our way through London traffic to Knightsbridge.

Evelyn, Ollie, Clive and John were already there, and the other horses were comfortable ensconced up a long ramp to the left in the stables that normally harbour mounts for footguards officers. We led Thatch up to meet his chums. I then said goodbye to Lizie and Jessie, who were to return home on the train, and waited while Major Douggie MacDonald gave the horses their veterinary inspection. It was a rather lengthy process because body whorls and striated hooves had to be laboriously recorded on the horses' travel papers. At last we loaded Magoo, Thomas and Jeopardy on the horse-box, put Thatch back onto his trailer, and set off for Dover, going out under the old portico, retained when the barracks were rebuilt, in the footsteps of the service squadron of the 1st Life Guards who had passed beneath it on 15 August 1914. 'There was no crowd to see them off,' remembered R. A. Lloyd.

> That was just as well. The men and horses looked fit. Joe Ratcliffe and I stood together just outside the gate as they passed, exchanging a word here and there, and now and then a handshake, with one or another of our special chums. The Band turned out to play them off. It struck up

the most inappropriate tune that could be found, 'Where are the boys of the old brigade?' I felt like going across and throttling the bandmaster.

The only crowds we encountered were south of the river, where the Saturday afternoon traffic was shimmering away in a haze of diesel through Kennington and Blackheath. We paused at a motor-way service area to eat what was unquestionably the worst sandwich of the trip — you have to try to eat badly in France, but I am afraid that in England you can manage it with almost no effort — and reached our destination, Elms Farm, at Hougham, just outside Dover, at 4.00. Its stables had a rather forlorn look. Until the rules changed at the beginning of the year, outgoing animals had to spend a night at their port of embarkation, and business had been brisk. Now there was almost no demand for stabling, and the owner, tucked away in his valley, was concerned about the future. We left the horses for the night and drove the short distance to Shorncliffe, where we were to stay in the mess at 2nd Infantry Brigade.

I had dressed in my best country gent outfit so as not to let my friends down on their home turf at Hyde Park, and by the time I collapsed into my room at Shorncliffe I was in a sorry state. Thatch had responded to the vagaries of London traffic by filling his trailer with dung. I had mucked it out once in London and again at Hougham: and the process had not done much for my favourite cords, whose turnups, normally a harmless sartorial affectation, were now rather crusty. Although the mess staff made us very welcome, there was the occasional raised eyebrow and, dare I say, wrinkled nostril amongst the mess's occupants, so we decided to bathe and change before finding dinner elsewhere.

The crossing, next day, was an anti-climax. The expected bureau-cratic glitch failed to materialise. We were through the freight office in minutes, and there was no official interest in the horses. I explained to a passing customs man that there was a horse on the trailer we were towing. He genially rejoined that he was not in the least surprised, because people rarely travelled with empty trailers, and went on his way.

The Army has a fondness for briefing sessions known as orders groups — O Groups for short — at which a commander explains his intentions to his subordinates. Evelyn had planned to have an O Group on the boat, but by the time we had pillaged the Duty Free and had a cup of coffee Calais was in sight: the O Group would have to wait. Getting through Calais was simplicity itself, and soon we were driving north-east along the new coastal autoroute. The Isuzu with its trailer made rather better speed than the horse-box, and it was easy to forget that John and Clive were thundering along behind us: when we slowed down to rejoin the box after outdistancing it on long upward slopes I could almost see the air above the cab turn blue as John outlined his views on my driving.

We swung inland at Dunkirk, and stopped for lunch at Steenvoorde, not far from Meteren, where Lieutenant B. L. Montgomery of the Royal Warwicks won his DSO in 1914. The A25 took us on past Lille — whose fine citadel, 'Vauban's masterpiece', caused Marlborough so much trouble in 1708 — and then squarely across the battlefield of Fontenoy, over the ridge-line so painfully crossed by the Duke of Cumberland's infantry on 11 May 1745. Just west of Mons the A25 joins the A2, and the result of this union, the A7, follows the line of the Mons–Condé canal, with the onion-domed bell-tower of Mons in sight long before the town itself can be glimpsed, past the grassed-over slag-heaps which show that this is *Le Borinage*, Belgium's Black Country. The mines have long since closed, but in 1914 the whole area was a hive of industrial activity with a web of light railways connecting busy pitheads to the main line.

North-east of Mons we left the autoroute and headed for the village of Thieusies, where the horses were to stay for the next two nights. We found the stables, redbrick and prosperous on three sides of a large courtyard, easily enough. Awaiting our arrival — and taking the edge off another scorching day with a cool beer — were James Scott-Clarke and Alec Finlayson. Both are lieutenant-colonels, James a Grenadier and Alec a Queen's Royal Lancer, on the staff of Supreme Headquarters Allied Powers Europe (SHAPE) which moved to Casteau, near Mons, after the French evicted it from the more stately surrounding of Fontainebleau when they withdrew from NATO's integrated military structure in 1966.

We planned to spend Monday in Mons, letting the horses recover from the journey and re-loading box and trailer. Until the very last leg of our journey, from Fontainebleau to Calais, we would not use the trailer for horse transport unless there was a problem with the box. Instead, it would hold the table and chairs (with a good supply of clean table cloths, for standards must be preserved from the assaults of Camembert and Corbières) for alfresco lunches, food for the horses (we had brought almost as much cavalry mix as they would require, to avoid sudden changes to diet) and a good deal of other horsy impedimenta. The remainder of our kit went into the groom's section at the front of the box. This was a warren of saddles, bridles, headcollars, sweat rugs, nosebags, grooming kit, shovels, forks, brooms and muck sacks, with our own luggage, which ranked junior to rollers and tail-bandages, chucked in for good measure.

Evelyn and Clive stayed with James and Jenny Scott-Clarke at Obourg, just north of the canal, and the remainder of us squeezed into Alec and Kate Finlayson's cottage, not far from the stables and, as it happens, literally within earshot of the first and last shots of the First World War. On Monday, Evelyn and I exercised the horses, leaving John and Clive to get on with loading. I rode Thatch, who had been a little fractious after his journey but was now his usual good-natured self, and led Magoo. Although we were only a few miles from Mons it was hard to recognise that we were even in the same country. Instead of slag-heaps and miners' cottages there were wide fields, many shouldering luxuriant crops of maize, and big farms, standing proud in self-contained isolation, their massive barns decorated with dated iron wall-ties, 1765 here and 1794 there.

This part of Belgium has a complex history which bears closely on our story. In the fourteenth century the provinces making up what are now Belgium and Holland fell into the unyielding grip of the Dukes of Burgundy. When the duke known in English as Charles the Bold, but in French, more appropriately, as *Charles le Téméraire* (Charles the Rash), died in 1477 — his head laid open by a Swiss halbert at Nancy — his territories were inherited by his daughter Mary, wife of the Holy Roman Emperor Maximilian. They were passed on to Maximilian's son Charles, and thence to Philip II of Spain in 1555. Although the treaty of Westphalia, which ended the Thirty Years War in 1648, formally stripped Spain of the northern Netherlands, which had become the Dutch Republic, she remained in possession of the provinces of Hainault (whose capital Mons is), Brabant and Flanders, as well as a broad band of what is now northern France.

The Spanish Netherlands formed an uncomfortable glacis between Catholic France and Protestant Holland. As French power increased in the seventeenth century so Spanish possessions were whittled away. First the Spaniards were dislodged from France itself: Condé's great victory in 1643 near the little town of Rocroi, away to the south-east of Mons, struck them a blow from which they were never to recover. Then the armies of Louis XIV ground their way

up into the Low Countries. Mons was besieged by the French on
17 March 1691 and fell less than a month later. In 1709 an Allied
army under the Duke of Marlborough and Prince Eugene invested
the place, and when the French approached in an effort to raise the
siege Marlborough attacked them at Malplaquet, winning a costly
victory, and went on to take Mons.

The Treaty of Utrecht, which ended the War of Spanish Succession in 1713, brought about the cession of the Spanish Netherlands to Austria. For much of the eighteenth century, white-coated
Austrian infantry mounted guard on the gates of Mons and, no
doubt, sought good luck by patting the head of the Main Guard
Monkey, a cast-iron figure on the front wall of the Town Hall,
much as passers-by do today. In 1792, with the stiff armies of old
Europe in arms against the threadbare volunteers of revolutionary
France, Mons was the centre of a concentration of Austrian troops
under the Archduke Albrecht. The Austrians had been threatening
Lille, and in early November the French — commanded by an
officer who had replaced his politically incorrect surname du Perier
du Mourier with the more democratic Dumouriez — attacked
them. The French won a scrambling and disorganised battle at
Jemappes, now effectively a suburb of Mons, and the town surrendered the next day.

Mons spent the Napoleonic period in French hands, and in 1815
it became part of a short-lived Kingdom of the Netherlands. The
second Treaty of Paris, signed in November that year, gave France
the pre-Jemappes border of 1790, rather than the 1792 boundary
further to the north. Diplomats who redraw national borders in the
heady atmosphere of military victory usually do their descendents a
disservice. We have already seen how the French loss of Alsace-
Lorraine in 1871 was not least amongst the causes of the First World
War, and the Balkan tragedy of our own times owes much to the
efforts of peacemakers to forge a state out of incompatible national
fragments. The marriage of Holland and Belgium was not a happy
one, and in 1839 Belgium became independent after a civil war, her
neutrality guaranteed by a great-power agreement to which Britain
was signatory. This was the 'scrap of paper' which a perplexed
Kaiser thought hardly merited British intervention but which, spinning on with a trajectory of grim inevitability, brought British
soldiers to Mons in 1914.

Seventy-nine years later we lunched in one of the many little
restaurants on the Grande Place — having that much-delayed

Oe Group with our *frites* — paused on the square where A Company, 4th Royal Fusiliers had been photographed on 22 August 1914, and walked across to the military museum in the Jardin du Mayeur behind the Town Hall. This being a Monday it was shut — continental museums often stay closed on Mondays to compensate for being open on Sundays. I had visited it many times, but it was a pity not to be able to take my friends round its crammed showcases.

They might have been perplexed by the fact that it deals as much with 1918 as 1914, but for the British armies Mons was the alpha and omega of the First World War. On 23 August 1914 a corporal in the 4th Dragoon Guards fired the first British shot on mainland Europe since Waterloo almost a century before, and on 11 November 1918 a Canadian soldier, Private Price, had the melancholy distinction of being killed just outside Mons two minutes before the armistice came into effect. He is buried in the touching little military cemetery at Saint-Symphorien, just east of Mons, with the first British soldier killed in the war, Private J. Parr of the Middlesex Regiment, attached to 3rd Division's cyclist company, who died on 21 August 1914, and the last, Private G. E. Ellison of the 5th Lancers who fell on 11 November 1918 — albeit slightly earlier than Private Price.

The Finlaysons threw a party for us that night. I went to bed in the small hours and slept fitfully, dreaming of grey horses and trying to remember the French for colic. It was a concern eminently symbolic of all those other silly worries. Few of the hurdles ahead were to prove as bad in practice as they did in my wretched half-sleep that Monday night. The French for colic is, of course, *colic*, not that I need have worried, because nobody — equine or human — was to suffer from it for the next fortnight. Had I concentrated on finding diplomatic ways of declining another glass of champagne, then my night would have been wasted to much better effect.

IV

FIRST BLOOD

An army advances covered by its tactical advanced guards . . .
At this stage collisions may be expected to occur between the
opposing protective troops covering the movements of the main
forces behind them.

Field Service Regulations

On 19 August 1914 the Royal Flying Corps flew its first
reconnaissance on active service, sending a Bleriot and a BE
from Maubeuge to Brussels, Tournai and Courtrai. It is one of the
war's many little ironies that the Bleriot was piloted by Captain
Philip Joubert de la Ferté, an officer of Huguenot ancestry whose
forebears had left France after the revocation of the Edict of Nantes
in 1685. The German *4th Cavalry Division*, trotting out on its big
Hanoverians and Trakheners somewhere beneath him, was led by
another Huguenot, Lieutenant-General von Garnier, and away on
the Eastern Front General von François was about to play a distinguished part in winning the battle of Tannenberg. At a more humble
level, Major P. A. Charrier, commanding 2nd Battalion The Royal
Munster Fusiliers — who made no sartorial concessions to the fact
that his was the only line battalion in 1st (Guards) Brigade and
insisted on wearing pith helmet and shorts — was inordinately
proud of his Gallic ancestry and regarded the war as an admirable
opportunity to get to grips with France's ancient foe. I am Huguenot
on my mother's side, and Ollie's distinctive middle name de Rouge-
mont marks his own French descent: how different things would
be had our industrious forbears not fallen victim to Louis XIV's
intolerance.

No large bodies of troops were seen by the RFC's recces on 19

August, but on the following day another flight reported 'a column of enemy troops stretching through Louvain as far as the eye could reach'. This was part of the German *First Army*. Kluck had sent a corps, shortly followed by another, to shepherd the Belgian field army back into Antwerp, while the remainder of his divisions marched due west. Elements of General von der Marwitz's *II Cavalry Corps*, moving ahead of Kluck's infantry, entered Brussels that day. Marwitz's men had not had things all their own way. On 12 August the Belgians fought a skilful rearguard action at Haelen, midway between Liège and Antwerp, mauling *4th Cavalry Division* and killing the Commanding Officer of the *18th Dragoons*, Baron Digeon von Monteton, yet another Huguenot, in the process.

Already the strains of the advance had provoked frightened and tired Germans into over-reaction. Lieutenant-General von Poseck complained that 'many a good cavalryman had become the victim of the bullet of a cowardly assassin in ambush', and his comrades were not always nice in their distinctions when seeking the guilty. The little town of Andenne was burned and 200 of its inhabitants were shot, and nearly 400 of the citizens of Tamines perished. On 25–26 August part of the ancient city of Louvain was burned, including the library with its priceless collection of medieval manuscripts. Not all German 'atrocities' were the result of deliberate policy, though Moltke admitted that 'our advance through Belgium is certainly brutal', but Allied propagandists lost no time rearing an edifice of exaggeration on foundations of fact.

Word of German entry into Brussels was scarcely encouraging, but rang few alarm bells at GHQ. After all, if the Germans turned south, as there was reason to expect they might, their flank would not extend beyond Mons, and the BEF, poised on the left of the French 5th Army, would threaten their right. And though there was little information on the progress of the main French offensive, launched by Joffre on the 20th, GHQ was cheered by news that 4th Division was to be sent out to join the BEF; four of the five battalions employed on lines of communication duties were to be combined into 19th Infantry Brigade; and the French I Cavalry Corps under General Sordet, which had been scouting up in the Ardennes, had been ordered to swing round to the British left.

As far as Sir John French and his staff were concerned, then, things were not going badly. The French were pushing ahead with their offensive, the BEF was to be reinforced, and although the Germans had moved deeper into Belgium than had been expected there were as yet no hard facts to invalidate Allied assumptions. Indeed, Sir John, sustained by copious draughts of Wilsonian optimism, thought that Lanrezac was just about to plunge forward and 'rather chaffs at the delay'. However, the fact that the German spearhead was buried deep in the belly of Belgium compelled GHQ to tinker with its plans. When French had briefed his senior officers on the 18th he concluded: 'Should the German attack develop in the manner expected we shall advance on the line Mons–Dinant to meet it'. Dinant is on the Meuse south of Namur, and such a line of advance — east-south-east from Mons — presupposed that the Germans had not crossed the Meuse in strength. By the 20th such an advance was patently suicidal because it would expose the BEF's left flank to Kluck, and that evening GHQ, now established in the school in the centre of Le Cateau, issued orders for a march northwards over the next three days. It would leave the BEF facing northeast from Binche in the east to Lens, north of Mons, in the west. The Cavalry Division was to cover the advance, finishing up on the left of the line, while 5th Cavalry Brigade (nominally independent, but operating under the Cavalry Division's orders) was to protect the right flank during the move and end up screening the right front.

The advance began on the morning of 21 August in a thick mist which kept the RFC on the ground. Cavalry patrols heard that there were Germans to the north, and 2nd Cavalry Brigade, which crossed the Condé canal east of Mons, saw German horsemen near the bridges at Nimy and Obourg. II Corps moved up behind the cavalry to the Maubeuge–Valenciennes road, with I Corps, which halted for the night on the line Avesnes–Landrecies, half a day's march to its right rear. The RFC flew once the sun had burnt off the mist — suffering its first loss from enemy action when Lieutenants Bayley and Waterfall were brought down by ground fire — and reported a strong body of cavalry, with infantry and guns, south-east of Nivelles. This was later identified as the *9th Cavalry Division*, and traces were found of Marwitz's other two divisions, one of them so far to the west that it was 'evidently intended to explore the area as far as the sea'.

On the British right, Lanrezac's men were in contact with the infantry of *Second Army* along the Sambre astride Charleroi, and that afternoon the Cavalry Division was ordered to fill the gap between Mons and the French left. Shortly before midnight GHQ modified the orders for the next day's march: instead of moving across the canal with Mons on its right, II Corps was to take up a line like a collapsed L. The long leg would stretch along the canal from Nimy towards Pommeroeul, with the short leg kicking down towards Givry, south-west of Mons. Once this line was secured the Cavalry Division would turn in behind it to halt in the triangle Thulin–Quiévrain–Baisieux. These changes were evidence of a whiff of caution at GHQ. With German horsemen so far west it made good sense to shuffle the cavalry round to cover the exposed flank, and by ordering II Corps to pause on the canal with its right wing drawn back Sir John went part of the way towards recognising that the two corps, initially laid out for an advance eastwards, were less well deployed for a northward move.

Major Tom Bridges, commanding C Squadron 4th (Royal Irish) Dragoon Guards was no stranger to Belgium. He had been there as a temporary lieutenant-colonel in 1912, and had failed utterly in an attempt to persuade the Belgians to agree to what was in effect a secret alliance, leading the exasperated chief of the Belgian general staff to declare that his countrymen would fire on any would-be British rescuers. Bridges admitted that his comrades were not men of delicate political sensibilities. They would, he said, have cheerfully fought the French: 'Our motto was, "We'll do it. What is it?" ' The morning of 22 August 1914 saw him on outpost duty between the villages of Maisières and Casteau, on the main road which runs from Mons through Soignies to Brussels. Bridges put two troops in ambush positions alongside the road, and kept the other two, under Captain Charles Hornby, on their horses just over the crest-line behind. At about 7.00 a.m. ('a responsible officer who was there' told a newspaper that it was in fact 5.00 a.m., demonstrating just how difficult it is to keep track of time during even a tiny battle) a small German patrol appeared, led by an officer smoking a cigar. The 4th Dragoon Guards' account describes them as uhlans because they carried lances, but they were in fact from the *4th Cuirassiers* of *9th Cavalry Division*, lance-armed like all German cavalry.

A little way short of Bridges' position the Germans smelt a rat and turned back. Bridges shouted: 'Now's your chance, Charles — after them with the sword' and Hornby galloped off with 1st Troop, with 4th Troop close behind. There was a brief skirmish in Casteau itself: one German was wounded with a sword-thrust and others were captured. The survivors, driven back onto the troop of which they formed part, dismounted east of the village, and as 4th Troop galloped up Hornby sent it into action on foot. Corporal Edward

Thomas, a bandsman until the outbreak of war, ducked into cover behind a wall. 'I could see a German cavalry officer some four hundred yards away standing mounted in full view of me,' he remembered, 'gesticulating to the right and left as he disposed of his dismounted men and ordered them to take up their firing positions to engage us. Immediately I saw him I took aim, pressed the trigger and automatically, almost instantaneously, he fell to the ground.'

After a brief fire-fight the Germans remounted and galloped towards Brussels with Hornby in hot pursuit. Private Ted Worrell thought that:

> the chase went on for a mile but we were better mounted and caught up with them on the outskirts of Soignies and there was a proper old melee. Captain Hornby ran his sword through one Jerry and Sgt. Major Sharpe got another. I got a poke at a man but I don't know what happened to him. There was a fair old noise what with the clatter of hooves and a lot of shouting. The Jerries couldn't manage their long lances at close quarters and several threw them away and tried to surrender but we weren't in no mood to take prisoners and we downed a lot of them before they managed to break it off and gallop away. Our horses were pretty blown so Capt. Hornby decided not to give chase. I suppose it was all over in five minutes but we certainly showed them that the 4th were hot stuff.

The pursuit actually ended at a hamlet called after its tavern (itself named in honour of the Empress Maria Theresa) as *A La Reine de Hongrie*, where the Thieusies road crosses the main Brussels highway. The cuirassiers had rejoined their squadron, and there were some lorried *jäger* in evidence, doing much the same for German cavalry in 1914 that panzergrenadiers were to do for tanks a generation later. Several Germans were killed and five captured. Charles Hornby was the son of a quartermaster captain in the Durham Light Infantry, and perhaps some of his father's concern for equipment had rubbed off on him. In any event, he had left his embossed 1912 officer's pattern sword at home and taken a trooper's plain 1907 pattern to war. He rode back up the Brussels road with this weapon drawn, and Captain Arthur Osburn — who thought that the enemy troopers were rather sad figures, 'Bavarian ploughboys in German uniforms' — noticed that 'about four inches of the blade near the tip was smeared with blood'. Second-Lieutenant Roger Chance saw the prisoners: 'Halted under guard, but mounted, all grimed with dust they stared back, like animals in a cage . . . Alive but taken, were they glad or shamed at an early release from war?'

Brigadier-General de Lisle of 2nd Cavalry Brigade had promised to recommend for a decoration the first officer to kill a German with the sword and he was as good as his word, although Hornby's DSO was not gazetted until February 1915. Hornby survived the war but was badly wounded. Corporal Thomas later transferred to the Machine Gun Corps and was awarded the Military Medal. He was discharged in 1923, and became a cinema commissionnaire in his home town, Brighton, where he died in 1939.

While 2nd Cavalry Brigade screened the BEF's right front to such good effect, 5th Cavalry Brigade covered the right towards La Louvière, between Mons and Charleroi. It heard that the Germans were advancing from the north and the French were falling back across the Sambre, and in mid-morning elements of *13th Infantry Division* (from *Second Army*'s right flank corps) approached the bridges over the little Samme at Binche and Péronnes. They were held by the Royal Scots Greys, which had last distinguished itself on European soil by charging at Waterloo, a morning's ride to the north. Napoleon had spoken of 'those terrible grey horses', but would not have recognised the Greys by the colour of their steeds today. The regiment was particularly well-mounted: local hunts had been generous, and many officers had sold their own hunters to the Army at the recommended remount price, well below their real value. However, the authorities deemed that the presence of so many greys would reveal the regiment's identity to German observers. The horses had therefore been dyed with permanganate of potash which had turned them all a reddish khaki. The dye was meant to last a month in fine weather but would disappear more quickly in frequent rain.

Paul Maze, the regiment's unofficial interpreter, saw the Germans, through Lieutenant-Colonel Bulkeley-Johnson's telescope, as 'a number of little grey figures'. They made no attempt to force the bridges but shelled the Greys heavily, though only one officer was hit. 'We saw the first blood-stained field dressing,' wrote Maze: 'it marked a moment.' 3rd Cavalry Brigade was in support around Bray, on the Mons–Charleroi road, and from the fields north of the road D and E Batteries RHA fired the first British shells of the war. The Greys drew off at about 2.00 p.m., having inflicted thirty to forty casualties. As they retired a troop of the 16th Lancers, sent up to support them, came under fire from some Germans behind corn-stooks and charged at once, losing three horses killed and a man wounded. Official and regimental histories alike paint the incident in rosy colours, but Lieutenant Trevor Horn, the regiment's machine-gun officer, was less sure. 'Tempest-Hicks got rather ambushed by some Germans hiding in corn stooks and had his horse shot,' he confided to his diary.

News from the cavalry and RFC suggested that German cavalry, with a corps close behind, was moving south-west, with its main body between Soignies and Ath. There were also signs that 5th Army was fighting hard for Charleroi: the town and many surrounding villages were in flames. French had already decided to switch the Cavalry Division to his left flank, but in view of the news from Charleroi this might leave his right, screened only by 5th Cavalry Brigade, dangerously exposed. In consequence, I Corps, which reached its designated halting-places in mid-afternoon, was ordered to push further forward, halting for the night south-west of Binche. The last of Haig's men did not reach their new position till 3.00 on the morning of the 23rd: the march had, as the Official History baldly admits, 'tried the troops severely'.

Edward Spears had visited GHQ that morning. On his way to Le Cateau he met French, who was in search of Lanrezac, and reiterated his warning, made the day before to Sir John's staff, that Lanrezac was unlikely to advance. He added that 5th Army's intelligence staff had concluded that 'the far-flung German movement to the west could mean one thing and one thing only, an enveloping movement on a huge scale'. Hearing that Lanrezac was up with his troops rather than at his headquarters, Sir John decided that he could not afford the time to go so far, and gave Spears a lift back to Le Cateau. Here Spears found that Colonel Macdonough, GSO1 (Intelligence), shared his view of the situation. But the robust optimism of the operations sections remained unshaken. George Barrow of the Cavalry Division staff had already had the bright idea of phoning post offices in Belgium to trace the progress of the German advance, only to receive a pained rebuff from GHQ: 'The information which you have acquired and conveyed to the Commander-in-Chief appears to be exaggerated. It is probable that only mounted troops supported by *jägers* are in your immediate neighbourhood.' GHQ was, in fact, contemplating an advance on Soignies at exactly the moment that its own intelligence section knew that the Germans were likely to get there first.

As Spears made his way to Lanrezac's forward command post at

Mettet, between Dinant and Charleroi, he could see that 5th Army was in real trouble. He first met a stream of wounded, and then exhausted, unofficered battalions in retreat. In Mettet itself the news worsened hour by hour, and eventually a badly wounded divisional commander was driven through the square. He gasped to Hély d'Oisel: 'Tell the General that we held on as long as we could,' and was driven off, leaving the watchers transfixed by the image of a division which had suffered so badly that its commander had been hit by rifle-fire. Spears could glean no official information, but by talking to officers coming from the front and taking short trips forward in his car he established that 5th Army had been forced back well behind the Sambre. The BEF was now ahead of the main French line.

Spears drove back to Le Cateau at once, arriving so wearied that only half a bottle of champagne, husbanded by Macdonough for just such an emergency, could revive him. Macdonough walked him across to the commander-in-chief's quarters, where he told French and Murray of the condition of 5th Army, stressing that: 'General Lanrezac had no intention of attacking, even were he in a position to do so, which he was not'. Spears was then ushered into the dining room, where he found the corps chiefs of staff, Johnny Gough — whose brother Hubert was commanding 3rd Cavalry Brigade — of I Corps and Forestier Walker of II Corps. With them was Colonel Vaughan, Allenby's chief of staff — who, like Murray, was already feeling the strain — and a few of French's personal staff. They were bent over the table in a welter of maps, field-service notebooks and coffee cups, tying up details of the next day's advance. The door opened and Murray stood there framed against a dark hall. 'You are to come in now and see the Chief,' he said. 'He is going to tell you that there will be no advance. But remember that there are to be no questions. Don't ask why. There is no time and it would be useless. You are to take your orders, that's all. Come on in now.' Shortly before midnight a French staff officer arrived with formal confirmation of Spears' news, and a request that the BEF should fall on the right flank of the German formations attacking Lanrezac. French refused — given the position of Kluck's right wing to have complied would have been nothing short of folly — but agreed to hold his position on the canal for another twenty-four hours.

It was a short night for the BEF. I Corps was on the road till the small hours, and II Corps was scarcely more fortunate. Kenneth

Godsell, moving up to St Ghislain on the canal, saw 'infantry falling out like flies', and Count Gleichen, riding ahead of 15th Brigade, on the corps' left flank, watched his men making heavy weather of the march. 'The beastly paved road with cobbles,' he wrote, was 'just broad enough for one vehicle and extremely painful to the feet, whilst the remainder of the road on both sides was deep in dust or caked mud, was a most offensive feature.' Some units of 5th Division, on the corps' left, were up on the canal by midday, but others of 3rd Division, on the right, did not arrive till after nightfall.

Smith-Dorrien sensed that something menacing was groping towards him north of the canal and ordered his divisional commanders to prepare hasty defences when they reached it. Godsell's sappers helped 2nd Royal West Kent of 13th Brigade, 5th Division's left-hand formation, to dig in at St Ghislain, trying to convince the infantry that a bullet-stopping parapet a foot wide really was worth the extra effort. They might have gained satisfaction from the fact that the Official History speaks approvingly of 'some excellent trenches by the railway bridge'. The divisional commander, Major-General Sir Charles Fergusson, rode up, with an aide de camp and a lancer escort, and chatted to Lieutenant Smythe, one of Godsell's colleagues,

> who he knew from the hunting field at the Curragh . . . In the evening sun they were a charming group. Beautifully mounted and sitting their chargers easily, they conversed freely, the lancers standing motionless with the evening breeze fluttering their pennons. As the general moved off, he said to Smythe 'Don't work your fellows too hard, I should knock off now as we may be here for ten days'.

Godsell and Smythe did not have the heart to spoil the general's evening hack by telling him that they had spotted Germans north of the canal. Pennycuick saw Fergusson on the same ride, and asked him how long they might expect to be there. 'I cannot tell you,' laughed the general. 'We may be here a week, or perhaps going on tomorrow.'

While Smith-Dorrien's infantry were digging in on the canal, the Cavalry Division rode from east to west behind them. Gleichen watched the 4th Dragoon Guards pass through his brigade, near Dour. 'They crossed at a trot,' he wrote, 'men and horses looking very fit and workmanlike, and disappeared westwards through the haze of the factories; any more impossible country for cavalry — except perhaps the London Docks — I have never seen.' The cavalry felt rather less fit. 'Fifteen miles over paved roads,' recorded Sally Home of the divisional staff in his diary, 'the worst march I have ever done, on a tired horse and in the dark.' Arthur Osburn thought the ride 'a nightmare; a thin drizzle had turned the coaldust that lay everywhere into a greasy slime; our horses, half asleep like ourselves, had staggered on, stumbling over the uneven cobbles and cinder heaps, slipping and falling on the endless network of tram and trolley lines'. Henry Owens reckoned that he rode 25 miles to Quiévrain that night, astride his 'topping nag' with 1st Cavalry Field Ambulance: 'Very dark and "pavé" slippery roads.' He arrived at 1.00 on the morning of the 23rd, 'Sleepy and with a rare old twit on'.

The British high command was about early on the misty, drizzly morning of 23 August, long before the inhabitants of Mons and the surrounding villages had set off for Mass in their Sunday best. French briefed his commanders in Smith-Dorrien's headquarters in the château at Sars-la-Bruyère, midway between Bavay — where a small forward element of GHQ was now set up — and Mons itself. It is more than usually difficult to be sure of what was said at this meeting, as both French and Smith-Dorrien have left substantially different accounts of the discussion. It opened inauspiciously. Sir John announced that the Army would give battle on the line of the Mons–Condé canal, and when Smith-Dorrien asked if he was to attack or to stand on the defensive, Murray told him not to ask questions but to do as he was told. French later claimed that he informed his commanders of the doubts that were now in his mind, and warned them that they might have to advance or retreat. Smith-Dorrien, however, initially found the field-marshal 'in excellent form', and believed that he intended merely to use the canal line as a springboard for a continuation of the advance. Sir Horace recalled that it was he himself who expressed doubts about his far-flung front, and put forward plans for a local retirement in case German pressure became too great.

It is safe to conclude that Smith-Dorrien's position was discussed in detail, and neither French nor Smith-Dorrien can have been unaware of the vulnerability of the Nimy–Obourg salient to the north of Mons, held by elements of 8th and 9th Brigades of Major-General Hubert Hamilton's 3rd Division. The evidence also suggests that French was frankly uncertain whether he would be advancing or retiring. He scrawled in his diary that the Germans were 'merely trying to "feel" our position all round', and considered things safe enough to drive off to Valenciennes to see how the newly-formed 19th Brigade was shaping up. Smith-Dorrien thought matters more serious, and his staff set about laying out a fall-back position, running roughly Dour–Frameries–Paturages, which could be occupied if the canal line became indefensible.

When we approached Mons on 8 August 1993 the A7 autoroute wafted us straight across the front of Smith-Dorrien's position. It follows the line of the Condé canal all the way from Ville Pommeroeul to Maisières, just north of Mons, and from it the driver — even one encumbered by a trailer housing an increasingly fractious horse — can gain an excellent impression of the battlefield. Where it marches alongside the autoroute the canal is smaller than it was in 1914, for construction of the *canal du centre* in the inter-war years shifted barge-traffic to this new watercourse which runs parallel with the old canal and a couple of miles to its north. It is not until you approach Nimy and look southwards that the canal appears in a form that the combatants of 1914 would have recognised.

Exits from the autoroute lead to the villages that were to be fought over on 23 August 1914 and still feature in paintings on the wall of many an officer's mess: St Ghislain, Jemappes — there is a stunning Gilbert Holiday of the Royal Scots Fusiliers holding the bridge — Nimy and Obourg. In 1914 these housed the miners who toiled in the pits of the *Borinage*, and glum rows of terraced houses stared blankly out across narrow cobbled streets. With the mining boom of the 1890s many of the villages had grown into one another: Count Gleichen observed with irritation that even the inhabitants could not tell him where Dour ended and Boussu Bois began. Navigation was difficult, and many promising looking roads led nowhere, while good through-routes were not shown on maps. W. H. L. Watson had a dismal time piloting his motor-bike through it all: 'The roads wandered round great slag-heaps, lost themselves in little valleys, ran into pits and groups of buildings. Each one tried to be exactly like all its fellows. Without a map to get from Elouges to Frameries was like asking an American to make his way from Richmond Park to Denmark Hill.' Even now, equipped with the *Institut Géographique National*'s detailed 1/50,000 map, I have no difficulty at all in getting lost in the post-industrial sprawl south of the canal, where Paturages, Colfontaine, Wasmes and a dozen villages like them wallow in a morass of blind junctions and empty squares.

Railways still lace the landscape, main lines sliding through the folds of ground used by the autoroutes and Brussels trains thundering across the box girder bridge at Nimy as they did in 1914. The narrow-gauge tracks — contemporary accounts call them 'mineral railways' — have now disappeared, but in 1914 they trundled from pit-head to main line past the slag-heaps which sprouted from the landscape like pustules on a grimy face. West of St Ghislain the ground opens out, and on both sides of the canal it is slashed by dozens of drainage ditches which make movement off roads, even today, a matter of wet feet and nettled hands.

Mons is Latin for mountain, a rather grand description of the low hill upon which the town stands. There is a loftier eminence to its south-east, where the wooded hill of Bois la Haut rises northwards from the valleys of the By and Trouille streams near Hyon and dips briefly before emerging as Mont Panisel, where the old roads from Charleroi and Beaumont meet on the edge of Mons. To an army which had done so much of its training on Salisbury Plain or the Berkshire Downs it was a queer place for a battlefield, made even odder by the fact that the inhabitants were going about their business even as soldiers began to loophole their garden walls and pile bedstead and wardrobe in the street to dam the grey flood. A shunting engine puffed its complacent way across the railway bridge at St Ghislain while the sappers were laying their charges, and the driver politely doffed his hat to the men who were about to blow the source of his livelihood sky-high.

Whether French had told him to do so or not, Smith-Dorrien immediately set about preparing the bridges in his sector for demolition and strengthening his outpost line. The former was more easily said than done. II Corps held twenty-one miles of canal. It was an average of sixty-four feet wide and seven feet deep, and was crossed by eighteen road and rail bridges; it would have taken the sappers many hours to prepare all of them for demolition. Moreover, the destruction of lock gates — which could be crossed by infantry — presented a delicate diplomatic problem. The cavalry's flank march had already been complicated by the fact that troops were enjoined to stay off private property and stick to roads, and the GHQ's permission had been sought before buildings were loopholed for defence. Young Godsell had just measured the railway bridge in St Ghislain and returned to his command post to work out what charges would be required to blow it when the opening German salvo arrived, making 'a very funny sound which we

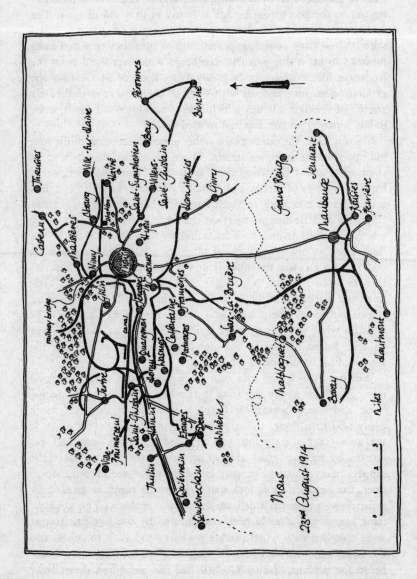

Mons

23rd August 1914

couldn't make out until I saw the shells burst. Rather a short fort-night.'

The morning's first clashes came as German cavalry patrols col-lided with British outposts in the salient north of Mons. Most battalions had pushed small parties across the canal: 4th Royal Fusil-iers had a detachment in Maisières station, and at St Ghislain A Company 2nd Royal West Kent, the divisional cavalry squadron and cyclist company were north of the canal. At Obourg, 4th Middlesex engaged a group of horsemen at about 6.00, and shortly afterwards 4th Royal Fusiliers, on their left, wiped out a patrol and captured its wounded commander, Lieutenant von Arnim of the *3rd Hussars*, corps cavalry in *III Corps*. Further to the west, the Royal Scots Fusiliers killed a trooper of *IX Corps* cavalry, and still further west, at Ville Pommeroeul, two horsemen were killed, this time from *9th Cavalry Division*.

This pattern of contacts, with the Germans rolling onto II Corps' position obliquely from the north-east, was to continue throughout the day. It is worth noting that by mid-morning British intelligence, working from known orders of battle which enabled them to ident-ify a corps once a unit within it had been found, knew that the BEF was in contact with at least two German corps and a cavalry corps.

The Germans were fighting blind. In *The March on Paris* Alexander von Kluck admits that he did not expect to meet the British in strength at this juncture. The Germans believed that the BEF would land at Calais, Boulogne and Dunkirk and knew, from the action at Casteau and the destruction of an aircraft, that at least part of it had arrived. It seemed 'not unlikely' that the British would move up through Lille, and although a captured letter spoke of strong British forces south of Mons the bad weather on the morning of the 23rd prevented German pilots from verifying this information. Kluck thought that there might only be cavalry to his front, and could expect to brush it aside with little effort. However, once he had encountered substantial bodies of British infantry there was much to be said for attacking resolutely to pin forward units to their positions on the canal, while his flanking formations, which would soon overlap II Corps to both east and west, closed in for a battle of encirclement.

If British infantry had time for a Woodbine and a moment of self-congratulation after emptying German saddles, their mood soon changed. The Germans had long recognised the importance of keeping artillery well to the fore on the line of march, and by 9.00

that morning the positions of both the Middlesex and Royal Fusiliers were swept by a blizzard of shellfire. One German battery commander rashly unlimbered so close to the Middlesex that its machine-guns drove him off, but elsewhere the British could make little effective response to the shelling. A few guns had been worked forward amongst the infantry — there were four guns of 120th Battery on the tow-path with the West Kents — but the bulk of II Corps' artillery had been held back to deal with an attack from the left, and it was difficult to make effective use of guns amongst the slag-heaps and terraces south of the canal.

The shellfire endured by the British that morning may have been unimpressive when compared with the bombardments fired later in the war, but to generally inexperienced troops, many of them in flimsy field defences, it was certainly unpleasant. One shell burst squarely in a house whence a party of Northumberland Fusiliers was covering the bridge at La Mariette, between Jemappes and St Ghislain, and killed the entire garrison, while the Middlesex company at Obourg lost its commander and second-in-command before the German infantry appeared.

Massed infantry came in on the heels of the shellfire. Although the ground made for local variations, what happened then was much the same across the whole front under attack. John Lucy's battalion, 2nd Royal Irish Rifles, was not engaged until mid-afternoon, but his description of the impact of British musketry on German flesh is especially evocative.

> For us the battle took the form of well-ordered, rapid rifle-fire at close range, as the field-grey human targets appeared, or were struck down. The enemy infantry advanced . . . in 'column of masses', which withered away under the galling fire of the well-trained and coolly led Irishmen. The leading Germans fired standing, 'from the hip', as they came on, but their scattered fire was ineffective, and ignored. They crumpled up — mown down as quickly as I tell it — their reinforcing waves and sections coming on bravely and steadily to fall over as they reached the front line of slain and wounded . . . Such tactics amazed us, and after the first shock of seeing men slowly and helplessly falling down as they were hit, gave us a great sense of power and pleasure. It was all so easy.

Kenneth Godsell, listening just behind the firing line, could trace the progress of the attack as whistle and shout unleashed rapid fire, husbanded until the moment of assault: 'all other sounds appeared to fade, to be drowned in the magic roar of the mad minute. It started on our immediate right and rolled across the front, then became settled. Every man on the ground must have been firing like mad . . . it was the most exhilarating sound I have ever heard.'

It may have been easy for the Irish Rifles but it was less so for the troops in the salient. The Germans soon abandoned their massed attacks on the Middlesex at Obourg in favour of infiltrating troops across the canal to the east, where the bridges were intact and undefended, and although 2nd Royal Irish Regiment moved up to support the Middlesex they were speedily in difficulties themselves, with the machine-gun section wiped out by shellfire and infantry hammering its way in by sheer weight of numbers. Early in the afternoon both battalions began to fall back southwards, eventually converging on the northern slopes of Mont Panisel. A single soldier of the Middlesex, posted on the roof of Obourg station, covered the retirement of his comrades until he was killed.

The greatest threat to II Corps came from these attacks into the north-eastern face of the salient. The right-hand units of 3rd Division, 1st Gordon Highlanders and 2nd Royal Scots of 8th Infantry Brigade, held a thin line from the eastern edge of the Bois la Haut towards Harmignies. I Corps' left-hand division, 2nd, was on its way towards Harmignies to hold the ground between the right flank of II Corps and the 1st Division on Haig's right, and until it arrived the gap was filled only by 5th Cavalry Brigade. Worse still, there was a smaller but potentially more serious gap to the rear of the Middlesex and the Royal Irish, where the Charleroi road slips past the northern edge of Mont Panisel to drop down into Mons.

Shortly after midday, Regimental Quartermaster-Sergeant Fitzpatrick of the Royal Irish was engaged in the thoroughly quartermasterly task of issuing beer to nearby troops from the Segard Brewery, to the rear of his battalion's position. As he looked up to the right, towards the junction where the Beaumont and Charleroi roads meet, he saw some men of his battalion falling back across the road. He collected about forty cooks, grooms and storemen and took them up to the cross-roads, arriving just in time to engage the advanced guards of the *35th* and *85th Infantry Regiments*, moving in from the east.

During the afternoon he was visited by an officer of the Gordons, the battalion on his immediate right, with a handful of reinforcements, but the officer was wounded almost at once and the Germans continued to attack, now skirmishing forward through the cover east of the cross-roads. During a lull in the fighting Sergeant Redmond and some volunteers brought up ammunition and a damaged machine-gun, probably from the destroyed Royal Irish machine-gun section. Redmond repaired the weapon and brought it into action against the Germans, who renewed their attack after a bombardment which killed several civilians and set fire to the Château Gendebien, south-west of the cross-roads, which was being used as an advanced dressing station. Fitzpatrick held his ground until midnight, when he withdrew, having buried his fifteen dead and smashed the machine-gun, rejoining his battalion on the afternoon of the 24th.

At much the same time as the Middlesex and the Royal Irish began their retirement, the Royal Fusiliers, holding the canal at Nimy, also started to fall back, in their case on the orders of Brigadier-General Shaw of 9th Brigade following Smith-Dorrien's decision to withdraw on the Dour–Frameries–Paturages position. The battalion retired with 'peacetime precision', covered by its surviving machine-gun. The machine-gun section under Lieutenant Maurice Dease had started the day with a gun up on each side of the abutment of the railway bridge at Nimy. Although the guns had a superb field of fire — the bridge is clearly visible from the autoroute, which runs right across the assault line of the *84th Infantry Regiment* — they were cruelly exposed, and had not been in action long before one was knocked out by a direct hit. Lieutenant Dease, wounded several times, was eventually evacuated to a dressing station, where he died. The surviving gun was manned by Private Sid Godley, who fired on, covering his comrades' retreat, until he ran out of ammunition. He then smashed the gun against a girder, threw it into the canal, and stumbled off towards Nimy, where he collapsed, badly wounded, and was soon captured.

Not all the heroism at Nimy that day was British. The main road now crosses the canal east of the railway bridge over a modern concrete bridge. In 1914 there was a swing bridge on the site, with its mechanism on the south bank, and the Fusiliers had opened the bridge so that the *84th* could not cross. One brave German, Private Niemayer, swam the canal, clambered up to the mechanism and closed the bridge. He was shot dead as he did so, but his comrades were able to cross when the Fusiliers withdrew. As the Fusiliers fell back they ducked into shop-fronts and behind lamp-posts to keep the Germans at bay, and a platoon had been dug in to block the main road to Mons. However, it was unable to fire because several inhabitants of Nimy had been caught between retreating Fusiliers and advancing Germans. Local historians argue that they were being used as a human shield by the Germans, while the Germans maintain that the plight of these unlucky civilians was a genuine accident. It is certainly true that the Germans took the burgomaster of Mons hostage for the good behaviour of his citizens when they reached the town, but we can only find the case against them unproven as far as the Nimy allegation is concerned.

On the Royal Fusiliers' left, the Royal Scots Fusiliers had fought a successful action on the canal at Jemappes, but when they were ordered back in mid-afternoon the Germans crossed the canal over an unblown bridge and there was ugly fighting amongst the slag-heaps north of Frameries until the two reserve companies of Northumberland Fusiliers, whose forward companies were up on the canal at La Mariette, clipped down into the German flank and allowed the Scots Fusiliers to complete their retirement undisturbed. Two sappers won Victoria Crosses in this area. Lance-Corporal Charles Jarvis worked single-handed under a hot fire for an hour and a half to blow the lock bridge at Jemappes, and Captain Theodore Wright made repeated though unsuccessful attempts to blow the road bridge at La Mariette, swinging hand over hand beneath it to connect the charges.

Still further to the British left, 13th Infantry Brigade sat tight on the canal around St Ghislain under continuous shellfire. It was not until 6.00 p.m. that the King's Own Scottish Borderers, on the brigade's right, fell back across the canal, 17th Field Company blowing the bridge behind them. The Royal West Kent, the next battalion along, had a company in Tertre on the far bank, supporting the divisional cavalry squadron and cyclist company. The *Brandenburg Grenadiers* attacked them. Walter Bloem, the German novelist turned company commander, found some horses from A Squadron 19th Hussars in Tertre and had a pistol duel with 'a man in a grey-brown uniform, no, in a grey-brown golfing suit with a flat-topped cap'. The cavalryman was killed by Bloem's company headquarters, but as the Brandenburgers moved into the open between Tertre and St Ghislain they came under searching fire from invisible positions. 'Where was the enemy?' thought Bloem.

Not the faintest sign of him anywhere, nothing except the cows that had become restless and were gadding about. One, as I watched, rose on its hind legs and then collapsed in a heap on the ground. And still the bullets kept coming over, over our heads and all about us . . . To the right and left, a cry here, a cry there: 'I'm hit, sir! Oh God! Oh mother! I'm done for!'

'I'm dying, sir!' said another one near me. 'I can't help you, my young man, we must go on — come, give me your hand.' . . .

Behind us the whole meadow was dotted with little grey heaps. The hundred and sixty men that had left the wood with me had shrunk to less than a hundred.

Bloem would have been pained to know that his regiment's valour was derided by his enemies as clumsy tactics. Godsell and his NCOs were only half a mile south of him, preparing the road and rail bridges at St Ghislain for demolition, with wounded drifting back from the fighting north of the canal, and eventually unwounded soldiers crossing as the survivors of A Company — which had lost its commander and half its men — fell back. 'The men were in high spirits,' remembered Godsell. 'The assault was delivered by a mass of goose-stepping Germans who approached our lines arm in arm, singing and shouting. The effect of the mad minute on such a target was electrical.' Harry Beaumont of the Royal West Kents thought the Germans made 'easy targets', and saw that the ground in front of his position was strewn with bodies in field grey.

There were no jokes about German gunners. They drove the four guns of 120th Battery RFA back at about noon, and then concentrated on the bridges, putting 150 rounds into a 150 yard circle round one: Godsell's senior corporal, Marsden, 'a remarkably intelligent NCO' and inventor of the Marsden bridging trestle, was killed. Charges were blown off by shellfire but replaced at once, and when Godsell was ordered to blow the bridges, at 1.30 in the morning after the infantry had fallen back, 'all went up well'. As the sappers marched southwards they passed through a roadblock manned by Royal West Kents. 'All the men to my surprise were waiting in the road to see us through,' wrote Godsell. 'I shook hands with the Officer. I cannot imagine why, we have all been a bit strung up. "What a grand job you fellows did," said the subaltern, "What a wonderful show your fellows put up," I replied. It was all very awkward, there under the shining stars, men who had just realised it. I went goosey down the back and just itched to get away.'

German bugles had sounded cease fire at nightfall: 'Well I'll be damned,' said a sapper officer, 'they'll be asking us to breakfast next.' There was in fact urgent need to impose order amongst the exhausted attackers. Bloem met his battalion commander, to discover that all the other company commanders were dead. 'What a day, Bloem, perfectly ghastly.' muttered Major von Kleist.

'And the men?'

"The battalion is all to pieces — my splendid battalion,' and the voice of this kindly, big-hearted man trembled as he spoke . . . 'Watch the front carefully, and send patrols at once up the line of the canal. If the English have the slightest suspicion of the condition we are in they will counter-attack tonight, and that would be the last straw. They would send us all to glory.'

There was little activity on the western flank. The East Surreys of 14th Brigade covered the bridge at La Hamaide until it was blown at the same time as those at St Ghislain. Lieutenant Flint of 17th Field Company blew a bridge over the tiny Haine, just behind the canal. The Germans had worked a field gun forward and fired on his party over open sights, but Flint watched the gun through binoculars from the bridge parapet and as soon as he saw its muzzle flash yelled to his men to drop to cover. The Duke of Cornwall's Light Infantry, to the left of the East Surreys, drove off German cavalry, advancing from Villers Pommeroeul, late in the afternoon, and on the extreme left of the British line, 19th Brigade, which took over from the Cavalry Division in mid-afternoon, was left virtually undisturbed.

By midnight most of II Corps was back on the Dour–Frameries– Paturages line, though some units, imbued with what Sir James Edmonds, the official historian, called 'the characteristic obstinacy of the British infantry' were still up on the canal. As his two divisions fell back Smith-Dorrien had foreseen that there would be a gap between them in the area between Frameries and Paturages, and asked GHQ for a brigade from I Corps to fill it. Eventually he drove over to Haig's headquarters and borrowed 5th Brigade, which was in reserve near Genly, south of Frameries.

GHQ's reluctance to approve of the dispatch of 5th Brigade testifies to its failure to grasp what was afoot. French returned to his forward headquarters at Bavay in mid-afternoon and at once dictated a message for transmission to Spears. 'I am prepared to fulfil the role assigned to me when the Fifth Army advances to the attack,' he announced. 'In the meantime I hold advanced defensive positions . . . I am now much in advance of the line held by the Fifth Army, and feel my position to be as far forward as circumstances will allow, particularly in view of the fact that I am not properly prepared

to take offensive action until tomorrow morning, as I have previously informed you.'

We must blame Wilson for this blithe refusal to let military reality
interfere with Allied solidarity. He had spent the afternoon making
what he termed a 'careful calculation' which assured him that the
BEF was faced by a corps and a cavalry division, or two corps at
the most. In view of the information available as prisoners dribbled
back from the canal during the day this says little for Wilson's
calculating ability. He then 'persuaded Murray and Sir John that this
was so, with the result that I was allowed to draft orders for an
attack tomorrow'. Colonel Macdonough gave French his own rather
more accurate estimate at 6.00 p.m., but it was not until a message
from Joffre arrived an hour later, warning Sir John that he was
threatened by three German corps, that it became 'necessary for me
to radically change my dispositions for tomorrow'.

Even then French hoped to avoid retreat, wrote crossly of 'more
or less pessimistic messages' sent by Smith-Dorrien, and at 8.40 told
him that: 'I will stand the attack on the ground now occupied by
the troops. You will therefore strengthen your position by every
possible means during the night.' Eventually, at about 11.00, when
Spears arrived with news that Lanrezac was falling back, and hinted
that Lanrezac might have received bad news from the armies on his
right, French at last realised that the game was up. Corps chiefs of
staff were summoned at GHQ and told, at about 1.00 on the morning of the 24th, that the army was to make a general retreat of about
eight miles, to the line of the Maubeuge–Valenciennes road, from
La Longueville in the east, through Bavay, to La Boisrette in the
west. The retreat was on.

French issued his orders not a moment too soon. His own losses
had been light: some 1,600 killed, wounded and missing, all but
forty from II Corps and half of them from the Middlesex and Royal
Irish in the salient. German losses had been infinitely greater, perhaps
6,000 and possibly even as many as 10,000: some burial parties
resorted to mass cremation in an effort to cope with the piles of
dead north of the canal. Kluck expected that the British would offer
battle south of Mons on the 24th, and intended to envelop their left
flank, cutting off their retreat to the west and jamming them into
Maubeuge. Thus a successful defensive battle on the 24th, with both
corps in line south of Mons, would only have been the prelude to a
disaster, for Kluck's right-hand corps, assisted by Marwitz's cavalry,

would have swung round the British left flank to press in on its rear.

As it was, the fighting on the 24th of August was more dangerous and costly than that on the 23rd. GHQ, in a remarkable abrogation of responsibility, told corps headquarters to arrange details of the retirement between themselves, and II Corps faced the difficult task of withdrawing through the dreary urban sprawl south of Mons with the Germans close behind. Smith-Dorrien decided to interchange his two divisions, so as to place the 3rd Division on the outer flank. He did this because the army was falling back slightly south-westwards, and as 3rd Division would be able to start well before 5th Division, time and shoe-leather could be saved by permitting 5th Division to drop straight back southwards onto the right flank of the corps after 3rd Division had got clear.

The day began well enough. I Corps got away with little interference — but with much muttering in the ranks about the wisdom of marching all the way to Mons for the pleasure of marching back after scarcely firing a shot. There was some fighting in Frameries and Paturages, whence the British managed to extract themselves with little loss. On the western flank the Cavalry Division and 19th Brigade withdrew with 2nd Cavalry Brigade as rearguard; it slipped back, covered by L Battery RHA, up the gentle slope south of the Mons–Valenciennes road and through the village of Audregnies.

It was now about 11.00 a.m. and Sir Charles Fergusson of 5th Division received permission to retire as soon as 3rd Division, on his right, was clear. Not only had Hamilton's men already departed, but the Germans had begun to turn 5th Divison's right, and as 13th Brigade fell back, 2nd Duke of Wellington's was fiercely attacked north-west of Dour, losing 400 men. The Royal West Kent went forward to help, only to find the Germans already holding the trenches they hoped to occupy, and in a matter of minutes two companies were badly cut up. Harry Beaumont, already wounded in the groin, was almost buried by a shell and lay unconscious until the following day. He was sheltered by Belgians, and eventually made his way back to England through Holland.

No sooner were 13th and 14th Brigades safely on their way than Fergusson realised that the real danger came not from the right, but from the left. The Cavalry Division and 19th Brigade had already pulled back, and the whole of the German *IV Corps* was making good progress towards Quiévrain. Fergusson sent Allenby an urgent appeal for help, and at the same time ordered 1st Norfolk and 1st

Cheshire of 15th Brigade, taken from Gleichen the day before and kept under his hand as a divisional reserve, to advance northwards and counter-attack, supported by 119th Battery RFA. Lieutenant-Colonel Ballard of the Norfolks took command of the force, and led it forward until he was stopped by a staff officer and told to take up a position just north of the little road which connects Elouges and Audregnies.

It was a scorching day on 24 August 1914, but far duller on 10 August 1993 when I mounted Thatch just east of Quiévrain and looked up across the fields to the low crest-line held by Ballard's two battalions. My own mood matched the weather, a fact that was nobody's fault but my own. It had been my turn to drive down to check the horses the evening before and I had nothing much to drink at the Finlaysons' party until I returned, but then I made up for lost time, and remember helping with the washing-up, plying both tea-towel and what seemed to me extraordinary conviviality at two in the morning. Adrenalin and a head like an 18-pdr jerked me from sleep long before my alarm-clock, but John and Ollie were slower off the mark and we arrived later than planned at the stables, to be greeted by Evelyn in a slightly brigadierish vein. Alec Finlayson drove over as we made our final preparations for departure, bringing a flask of much-needed coffee and a slabby concoction of chocolate and nuts which I had admired the night before. Thus fortified, we loaded the horses. Evelyn, who could never stay very cross for very long, soon forgave us for being late at the rendezvous, and we set off. We drove westwards along the A7 as far as Ville Pommeroeul, swung down to Thulin, and then turned onto the Mons–Valenciennes road, and unboxed the horses — I was to start the day on Thatch, accompanied by Clive on Thomas — where the *Chaussée Brunehaut* crosses it a mile outside Quiévrain.

I had long been misled by the Official History's reference to 'the old Roman Road, famous under the name of the *Chaussée Brunehaut*' that featured so prominently in the fighting of 24 August. As our ride went on I kept finding the *Chaussée Brunehaut* on map-sheet after map-sheet, until I was eventually forced to recognise that they could not all be the same road. But it was not until we reached Bonnemaison Farm, on the limestone uplands north of the Aisne, at the end of the first week's ride, that our hosts the de Fays solved my problem. *Chaussée Brunehaut* on a French map has exactly the same connotation as Roman Road on an Ordnance Survey. The roads are named after Queen Brunehaut (Brunhilda in English) of the Frankish kingdom of Austrasia (567–613). She was a cultivated lady who tried to keep Roman civilisation alive and Roman roads in good repair. Alas, she was swimming against the dark torrent of her times, and her kingdom was invaded by Clotaire II of Neustria. When she declined his offer of marriage he had her dragged to death behind a horse. But she is better remembered than her victor, and as our journey went on we were grateful to those Roman and Gallo-Roman road-builders whose handiwork took us, straight as a die, across valley and ridge.

Our first day's ride was to take us across the battlefield of 24 August 1914, on past the site of Marlborough's bloodiest victory at Malplaquet, and then down to Jolimetz on the western edge of the Forest of Mormal. We had no ANTE routes for Belgium, and had been advised that off-road riding was more difficult there than in France, so were to be guided to Malplaquet by Monsieur Pauwels, proprietor of stables in Angre, on the Petite Honelle south of Quiévrain. We were tacking up when Monsieur Pauwels, a wiry gentleman in his thirties, arrived with two friends, one of them on a skewbald pony which was already pulling hard. We introduced ourselves and mounted. I had a last bite from the chocolate and nut slab. I knew lunch was a long way away; had I known just how far I might have taken the whole slab with me. And then we were off. Thatch fell into step beside Monsieur Pauwels' good-looking Arab and carried me across the sand-covered cobbles onto the scene of the first large-scale charge by British cavalry in the First World War.

That particular piece of Brunhilda's handiwork crosses the Mons–Valenciennes road (yet another Roman route) at right angles and then runs south-east towards the Roman settlement of Bavay which forms, like so many of the towns in the area, a hub of communications, with roads leaving it like the spokes of a wheel. To its west flow the Grande and Petite Honelle, easily fordable even by Thatch, who is not wholly convinced of the merits of immersing all four hooves in water, which join to form a unified — but still unimpressive — Honelle just north of Quiévrain. In the quadrant between the *chaussée* and the Mons road the ground rises to a gentle crest with the ill-defined villages of Elouges, Dour and Wiheries to its south-east. In 1914 there was a mineral railway connecting Elouges to the main line in Quiévrain, and although the track has gone, part of its route can still be traced, running across the slope like a languid Z. The old road from Baisieux to Elouges, sunken for part of its length, crosses the *chaussée* north of Audregnies. Also sunken

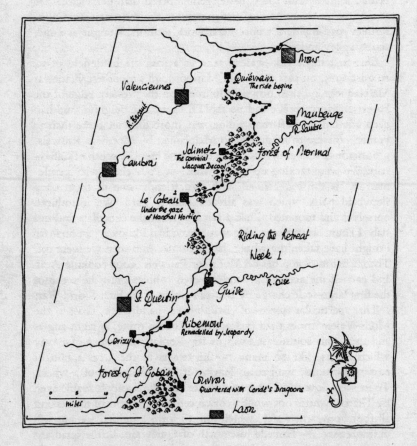

Mons

Quiévrain
The ride begins

Valenciennes

Maubeuge
R. Sambre

R. Escaut

Jolimetz
The convivial
Jacques Decool

Forest of Mormal

Cambrai

Le Côteau
Under the gaze
of Marshal Mortier

Riding the Retreat
Week 1

Guise
R. Oise

St. Quentin

Ribemont
Remodelled by Jeopardy

Cerizy

Forest of St. Gobain

0   5   10
miles

Couvron
Quartered with Condé's Dragoons

Laon

for the southern part of its route is the road which runs north-east from Audregnies to Elouges.

When we were a few hundred yards down the track my markers bobbed up comfortably: it would not do to be geographically embarrassed on the first morning. There, on the eastern edge of the track and just ahead of us, were the low redbrick buildings marked 'Sugar Factory' on the 1914 map: a sugar-beet processing plant then, farm cottages now. An old wall of brick redder than arterial blood, much knocked about, marked the original extent of the complex. The spire of Quiévrain church was behind my right shoulder, and to our front, across a potato field, I could make out the Audregnies–Elouges road. A prominent belt of trees, well over to my left, showed where the light railway had crossed it to run down the slope towards us before turning north to meet the main line, which parallels the Mons road just as it did in 1914.

Lieutenant-Colonel Ballard's battalions lined the slope, Cheshires to the west and Norfolks to the east. It was a breathless hugger-mugger business, and there was already a serious misunderstanding between Ballard and Lieutenant-Colonel Boger of the Cheshires. Fergusson had initially told Ballard to hold at all costs, but had later modified this instruction in a written order which stated that Ballard was to act as a flank guard and gave him discretion over withdrawal. Ballard assumed that Boger had the same orders. Unfortunately he did not. When posting his battalion, he thought that the original orders still applied, and told company commanders that they were to hang on to the end.

Three Norfolk companies lined out between the Elouges–Baisieux road and the mineral railway, with the fourth company by the railway bridge on the Elouges–Audregnies road and a platoon forward in colliery buildings in the centre of the slope. On the Cheshires' right, D Company linked up with the Norfolks and shoved two platoons forward towards the colliery. Captain Dugmore's C Company was in the middle of the line, with Captain Dyer's A Company on its left at the junction of the Elouges–Audregnies and Audregnies–Wiheries roads. Battalion headquarters was a nearby roadside cottage with the machine-guns beside it. When Captain Shore's B Company came in after watching the flank, it dropped off two platoons with A Company, while Shore himself took the other two to the north-west edge of Audregnies.

Wilfrid Dugmore remembered the deployment as the latest exasperating example of order and counter-order which had kept

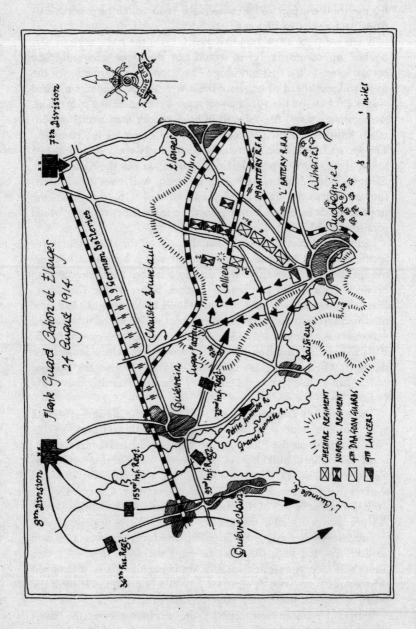
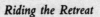

Flank Guard Action at Élouges
24 August 1914

CHESHIRE REGIMENT
NORFOLK REGIMENT
4TH DRAGOON GUARDS
9TH LANCERS

his battalion on the move, pausing here, digging in there, with little opportunity to eat or rest. It 'was lying down in a field with no cover of any description, except some stooks of corn, and occupying a front of about 2,000 yards, owing to the huge frontage the men were separated by big intervals'. Tom Lawrence, with the left-hand Norfolk company, was more matter-of-fact. 'We were on a little ridge,' he remembered, 'Cheshires on our left, 119th on our right, and a clear field of fire across cornfield to our north-west. Might have been back home in Norfolk.' 119th Battery came into action near the Elouges–Audregnies road, by the trees where the railway crosses it, and later on L Battery RHA, which had already been busy from a position further forward, unlimbered on the high ground on the eastern edge of Audregnies.

The Germans were now very close, coming on confidently in overwhelming strength. *IV Corps* was advancing with two of its divisions up: *8th Division*, to the west, poured through Quiévrain and Quiévrechain, with nine of its batteries wheeling into line on the Mons road: there were 77mms thumping away on the very spot where we had unboxed our horses. To the east, *7th Division* crossed the road and railway south of Thulin, dropped off some guns on the railway, and advanced on Elouges. Ballard's battalions found themselves, as was so often the case for infantry in a gunner's war, passive targets. 'The situation seemed pretty miserable,' wrote Dugmore, 'as the fire was so heavy as to defy description . . . I was dead beat not having touched a mouthful of food for over 24 hours, nor had I had a drink, less than 2 hours sleep; we had been marching in a sort of trance, receiving orders which were promptly countermanded . . . I think I would have welcomed a bullet through a vital spot.'

Things were even worse for the German infantry. Initially 119th Battery concentrated on the German gun-line on the main road, and L Battery, which came into action at about 1.00 p.m., took on the *72nd* and *93rd Infantry Regiments* as they debouched from the southern exits of Quiévrain. Tom Bridges saw its six guns tucked into a semi-covered position by the light railway embankment, the gunners at their work 'as steadily as if they had been on the range at Oke-hampton'. Sally Home watched the German infantry take the pun-ishment they administered: 'every shell burst low over them: they stood it for five minutes and then bolted.' Four German field batteries took on L. Their shrapnel burst too high and though most of the HE fell wide, one unlucky shell hit ten men.

Before this artillery duel was fully under way, Allenby, recalled
by Fergusson's appeal for help, appeared on the scene. He was a
burly man, marked with the stolid stamp of the East Anglian squire-
archy which had bred him. His nickname Bull reflected an obstinacy
that subordinates did not always find inspiring, and his obsession
with details of dress — at this stage in the war incorrectly-worn
chinstraps were his *bête noire* — ensured that there was much fid-
dling with kit as he pounded into view. Second-Lieutenant Roger
Chance of the 4th Dragoon Guards was letting his horse graze in
the dead ground south of Audregnies when the great man arrived,
his presence heralded by troop-sergeants desperately signalling men
to do up their chinstraps.

> The regiment waits, dismounted, in a field behind the village. I have
> slipped the reins over my charger's head, and he crops the lucerne. A
> remount, drafted from a hunting stable, he has not worked off a sum-
> mer's ease and sweat darkens his bay coat. Cley flies, out for blood,
> pester him. A lark sings out to me at a pause in the boom of the guns
> . . . 'We're for it, all right,' [Captain] Oldrey says, walking up to me.
> 'See who's coming.' And even as I turn a voice rasps, 'What Brigade is
> this?' — and my God it is 'Bull' Allenby himself, who lifts a hand to
> our salutes, nods at Oldrey's 'Second, Sir,' and rides off with one of his
> red-tabbed staff. 'Get girthed-up,' says Oldrey . . . 'Stand to your
> horses — prepare to mount — mount.'

Allenby sought out Brigadier-General de Lisle and, although we
cannot be sure of just what passed between them, for the muddled
events of the next half-hour helped ensure that there were several
versions of most of the conversations of that lunchless lunchtime,
the brief exchange galvanised de Lisle, no sluggard at the best of
times, into sudden action. He galloped up to Lieutenant-Colonel
David Campbell of the 9th Lancers, who was with A and C Squadrons of his regiment, dismounted and firing on the Germans, and
yelled: 'I'm going to charge the enemy. The 4th Dragoon Guards
will attack on your left. As soon as you see them deploy, attack on
the right with at least two squadrons.'

The Lancers had been making good practice with their rifle-fire,
as Corporal Harry Easton tells us:

> Directly in front of us was a field sloping downwards. The field had
> been cut and the sheaves of corn stooked and the first enemy line made
> a B-line for the stooks. We received the order 'Rapid Fire Commence.'
> They were such an easy target that I did not hear the order 'Cease Fire

retire' but found myself alone with a trooper, 'Farmer' Frond. We rejoined our troop just in time to hear Captain 'Revy' Grenfell say 'Get mounted, lads, we're going to charge the guns.'

Campbell was a lively and charismatic commanding officer, who had won the 1896 Grand National on Soarer, which had inevitably become his own nickname. He ordered his squadrons to mount, and sent scouts forward to check the ground, as one of them, Private Wells, recounted in a jerky scrawl in his diary: 'sent back to find Regiment. Ordered to halt. Draw swords from scabbards, the strain is beginning to tell now among us all. Call for wire nippers: find we had 4 pairs. Move off at trot and ride knee to knee. "Carry Lances." See figures running about in the distance. "Lance Engage." Gallop . . .'

The Official History, with its fondness for polishing jagged events into a glossy narrative that participants did not always recognise, declares that the lancers charged in column of squadrons — one squadron behind the other — and its map shows them advancing just east of the *chaussée*, with the 4th Dragoon Guards to its west. Harry Easton, however, thought that Campbell had ordered line of squadrons, with the 9th Lancer squadrons side by side. They were 'a very disordered mess — horses anyhow' as they came up into line, and he saw Campbell giving the signal for canter — a circular under-arm movement — as the regiment jolted off. For a moment everything was clear and sharp. 'I remember very distinctly seeing the whole line at a hand canter,' wrote Easton, 'and the trumpeter of the 4th DGs was Trumpeter Jackie Patterson a big friend of mine from early days in Canterbury where his parents kept a pub.'

Parade-ground formations did not last long amongst lancers or dragoon guards. Horses got away from their riders, hooves and shellfire kicked up dust, and obstacles caused bunching. 'Full of the spirit of the *arme blanche* and imagining that it was a matter of chasing away cavalry patrols,' remembered Tom Bridges, 'I debouched at the head of my squadron from the northern end of the village at a gallop, drawing swords as we went . . . ' Roger Chance hurtled down the *chaussée* behind him. 'All I can do now is follow my leader,' he admitted,

who forms troop in squadron column and is off at the gallop, swords pointed. We span the unmetalled road which runs straight, unfenced, through a stubble field dotted with corn stooks. A cloud of dust has risen ahead, pierced with the flash of shell bursts. If there is a hail of

bullets I am not aware of it, as with [Sergeant] Talbot glimpsed alongside, the men thundering after us, I endeavour one-handed to control
my almost runaway steed . . . He has gone — Talbot has gone down
in a crashing somersault, to be ridden over dead or alive, and no sooner
is he lost to us than I am among the ranks of those who, halted by wire,
veer right in disorder like a flock of sheep.

Harry Easton remembered the shrapnel bursting high and behind
him as German gunners failed to change fuse-settings fast enough
to keep pace with the charge. They did better with HE: the elegant
Vicomte de Vauvineur, an interpreter with the 4th Dragoon Guards,
was blown to tatters, and Roger Chance saw how 'a trooper
crouched in his saddle is blasted to glory by a direct hit whose
fragments go patter to earth'.

Sally Home, who watched the charge, thought that both regiments lost heavily but 'not so heavily as one would have thought'.
Shrapnel was little use against such a fast-moving target, and the
musketry of the German infantry, whose leading elements were
now just short of the sugar-factory, was poor. Popular imagination
carried the horsemen right onto the gun-line. A spirited painting,
The Taking of the Guns, showing lance and sword busy amongst the
guns was to hang in the Officers' Mess of the 9th/12th Lancers,
with a martial couplet by William Watson below it:

> At the cannon in ambush our horsemen spurred,
> Knights of liberty, glory's sons,
> and slew the gunners beside their guns

Richard Caton Woodville, who was to fill many a groaning canvas
before the war was over, painted *The First VC of the European War*
which now hangs in the National Army Museum. It catches the
lancers at the moment of impact. Grenfell, his sword at the drill-
book 'Engage', is about to run through a German officer, and a
trooper on his right has just recovered his lance from a supine
German. All combatants have evidently shaved and polished their
buttons that morning, and the lancers look remarkably impassive
for men who have just galloped a mile into the jaws of death.

It is, of course, pure moonshine. A few German scouts were
speared, but Francis Grenfell told Frederic Coleman, one of the
Royal Automobile Club members who had come out with his car,
that they 'never reached a point closer than 800 yards' from the
guns. Such was the dust, smoke and general confusion that a private

soldier confidently assured Coleman that he 'could not see what we were charging either going or coming'. Private Wells had a better view. 'Shouting and cheering we rolled on till near the guns,' he scrawled, 'and there we stopped. Few of [us] came in contact with Fritz as he moved off quick . . .'

The problem was wire, not fire. As we rode up the *chaussée* in 1993, the fields on both sides were open, though there was a low barbed wire fence on either side of the track. In 1914, the fields were smaller and there was far more wire, especially around the sugar-factory. Corporal Easton got that far unscathed, only to see 'a huge brick yard, surrounded by a twelve-foot high barbed wire fence'. This fence, and others like it, stopped the charge. 'We simply galloped about like rabbits in front of a line of guns,' wrote Grenfell. 'Men and horses falling in all directions. Most of one's time was spent dodging the horses.' Arthur Osburn, who 'pieced together the conflicting accounts and experiences of survivors' thought that the ground was impassable to cavalry: 'hundreds crashed amongst the railway lines, horses tripped on the low signal-wires or pitched headlong — breaking their riders' necks — into ballast pits near the railway, fairly terrifying the Germans — as a German told me afterwards in Cologne — by their reckless and meaningless onrush . . .' By now the cavalrymen were so close to the German infantry that rifle fire was bringing them down. Tom Bridges' horse was hit, and he fell heavily, to be ridden over by his squadron and, adding insult to injury, the machine-gun section. A horse smashed him in the face, depriving him of the power of speech, and he was carried, comatose, into the sugar-factory where there were a few dismounted men from both regiments.

Harry Easton was less lucky. His horse came down by the wire: he was never sure whether she had been hit or had stumbled. He stayed where he was on the ground, because his comrades had swung away — he heard Colonel Campbell shout 'Troops Right Wheel' but there was a good deal of confusion — and now that they no longer masked the Cheshire's fire, bullets were sizzling overhead. His sword and rifle were with his horse, and his lance was gone. 'I was very angry at being so near the German infantry . . . ' he told an interviewer late in life, 'I was reminded of the biblical saying "Though I walk through the valley of the shadow of death" . . . but I had no staff to comfort me.' The German infantry pressed forward, shoulder to shoulder, firing from the hip. 'I felt a hand on my shoulder and a German officer said: "You are a British Tommy." I said "Yes, Sir, I am." He took me back through the German infantry and handed me over to a German military policeman. Both spoke excellent English, one said: "You are fortunate. The war is over for you." '

The war came close to being over for Tom Bridges. Dazed and in pain, he looked out of the sugar-factory to see lines of German infantry with fixed bayonets only 200 yards away. At that moment a farrier led up a wounded chestnut horse, and, more dead than alive, he managed to mount it. It carried him back up the *chaussée* to Audregnies — 'sole target it seemed for a whole German army corps' — where it collapsed. Bridges shot it and sat down by the roadside to await developments. He saw Francis Grenfell 'with a bleeding hand tied up in a bandana handkerchief and bullet-holes through his clothes but very exhilarated', and was just thinking what he would give for a Rolls Royce when the brigade signal officer spun up in a blue and silver sports model and wafted him off to safety.

Most other survivors swung away to their right. 'I am among the ranks of those who, halted by wire, veer right in disorder like a flock of sheep,' wrote Roger Chance. They rallied near the trees where the light railway crossed the Audregnies–Elouges road, with a squadron of the 18th Hussars on their right. One party, under Captain Grenfell, helped the men of 119th Battery take their guns out of action, for the fire was too fierce to bring the teams right up. 'We pushed out one [gun] over dead gunners,' said Grenfell, 'but I do not think that we lost more than three or four men though it required more than one journey to get everything out.' Both Grenfell and the battery commander, Major Alexander, received the Victoria Cross for their gallantry that day.

Captain Dugmore, lying out on the ridge with shrapnel balls smacking into the earth around him, was not impressed by the charge. He thought, in common with other observers, that the cavalry had suffered more heavily than was in fact the case: 'my impression is that nearly all of them were knocked over, and the remnant with some riderless horses stampeded down a road on my right. It seemed to have been a useless waste of life, all to no purpose.' The Cheshires' official view was kinder. 'This gallant manoeuvre by the cavalry,' opined the regimental history, 'although procuring no material result, had some moral effect on the enemy and delayed his progress.'

The plight of the two battalions grew more serious by the minute.

Having propped up the flank long enough for the remainder of 5th Division to get clear, and seeing that the Germans would soon envelop his right, Lieutenant-Colonel Ballard prepared to withdraw. He sent his adjutant to tell 119th Battery and the Cheshires to retire, wisely dispatched a cycle orderly by a different route, and later confirmed the message by yet another runner before he set off. The adjutant was killed and neither orderly reached his destination, but when Ballard arrived in Wiheries stragglers told him that 2nd Cavalry Brigade was retiring southwards and they believed that the Cheshires were with them.

Nothing could have been further from the truth. Lieutenant-Colonel Boger held his ground, though he sent four orderlies to warn Ballard that German infantry — *36th Fusilier* and *153rd Infantry Regiments* with three battalions apiece — had turned his left flank, but all four ran into German infantry on the Norfolks' old position and were shot or captured. At about 4.00 p.m. he set off in an effort to find Ballard. On the way, he spoke to Wilfrid Dugmore, telling him to hang on as long as possible but not to get cut off. When he reached his battalion's right flank he was greeted by a brisk fire and knew the truth for the first time. As he retraced his steps Boger began to order men to fall back but was badly wounded before he had gone far, and his adjutant, who might have spread the word, was captured.

Major Sclater-Booth of L Battery was in a similar quandary. 119th Battery had already gone, and his own battery had fired 450 rounds and had little ammunition left. He was considering withdrawal when the brigade-major of 2nd Cavalry Brigade galloped up, shouting 'Good old L,' and ordered him to retire. The guns were manhandled back under the cover of the hedge which skirted the railway, and the teams thundered up, one by one, from Audregnies to take them all away safely.

The Cheshires' tragedy entered its last act. The two right-hand companies and a detached platoon of Norfolks held on until the Germans were almost on top of them and then tried to fall back by bounds. A few got back to Wiheries, but most, Dugmore amongst them, were killed or captured. Major Chetwynd-Stapylton, the second-in-command, tried to get the survivors away into Audregnies, where he thought Captain Shore was still holding out. The 'singularly quiet and unassuming' Captain Dyer was seen to draw his sword and lead the remnants of A Company and the two forward platoons of B in a bayonet charge in an attempt to relieve the pressure on what was left of the battalion's centre and let Chetwynd-Stapylton break clear, but the little band was shot to pieces: Dyer perished on the slope between battalion headquarters and the *chaussée*.

Shore had remained on the north-west edge of Audregnies with his two platoons, doing great damage to the *153rd Regiment*, as an unhorsed cavalry officer who limped back from Baisieux confirmed. He declined the suggestions of several cavalry officers that he should retire, and it was not until 3.00 p.m., when a staff officer formally ordered him back, that he consented to withdraw. Even then he tried to return to his old position when he could not find his battalion, and only a positive but erroneous report that the Cheshires had moved off safely to the south-east persuaded him not to go back.

Audregnies emptied soon after Shore left. A small party of 4th Dragoon Guards, who had been holding a cottage on the Baisieux road, dashed to safety. George Barrow rode into Audregnies at this very moment, trying to establish contact between the Cavalry Division and 5th Division. 'I had percolated only a short distance into the village,' he wrote, 'passing by a dead horse and overturned gun, when an officer came galloping round the corner of the street. He held up his hand and shouted "Don't go on; the Germans are just round the corner; they nearly got me." I needed no second warning and, turning round, galloped away with him.' The officer was Lieutenant-Colonel Noel 'Curly' Birch, author of *Modern Riding*, now commanding VII Brigade RHA. By the end of the war he was Major-General Royal Artillery at GHQ, and thus the commander in chief's principal artillery adviser. Barrow thought that he 'probably knew more about a horse at the beginning of the war than he did about any gun larger than a fifteen-pounder'. Barrow eventually made his way through Audregnies wood, south-east of the village, and reached Fergusson's headquarters safely.

The Cheshires fought on until, at about 6.30, Major Chetwynd-Stapylton ordered the survivors to cease fire. Surrendering during a firefight is never an easy business. Whatever military law or international conventions may say about the matter, a rough natural justice often induces victor to finish off vanquished with a shot or a bayonet thrust, muttering 'Too late, chum'. The defeated soldier has a much better chance of living long enough to become a prisoner if there is an element of formality to the surrender and his own leader comes to terms with an enemy officer. If this fails, he should divest himself of head-dress in order to look as human as possible, and he will appeal to both the humanity and the cupidity of his captor if he produces a photograph of his family — proclaiming that he too has dependents who will be blighted by his death — and ensures that lootable commodities like watch and ring can be grabbed with the minimum of fuss.

During the First World War, units rarely fought it out literally to the end; there usually came a moment when surviving officers realised that resistance was futile and duly surrendered. The Cheshires hung on longer than logic or honour demanded. There were only forty unwounded men still on their feet, and some officers and men had preferred to die rather than give in. Lieutenant Frost, a Special Reserve officer who had been understudying an experienced sergeant platoon commander, was seen by a wounded cavalry officer 'fighting like a demon, having refused to surrender' and was wounded several times before he was killed. Captain Jones, who led the rearmost platoons of D Company back to Wiheries, was surrounded but declined quarter, and aimed his revolver at the Germans, who shot him dead. The *66th Regiment* buried him with his arms with full military honours. Sergeant Raynor, commanding a platoon of C Company, was overpowered and, thinking that he was the only man left in his platoon, stopped struggling. His senior subordinate Corporal Crookes then appeared, and Raynor, in the grip of three Germans, growled: 'If I had known you were living I fucking well wouldn't have given in'.

In the minutes before the Germans overwhelmed them, the survivors carried out their last soldierly duties. In 1911, the wives of the officers serving with the 1st Battalion had embroidered a miniature regimental colour, a quarter the size of the original, which was presented on Meanee Day (17 February) to the best shooting company, which became Colour Company for the year. Captain Shore's B was Colour Company in 1914, and Shore decided to take the colour to France. Drummer Baker carried it with B Company's forward platoons at Audregnies, and as the position collapsed he managed to hide it under some straw in a loft. He was captured shortly afterwards. Private Riley, of the same company, was wounded and taken to a nearby convent for treatment. He knew where Baker had hidden the colour, and feared that the Germans would find it. Through the good offices of Sister St Leon, his nurse, he managed to persuade the *curé*, Père Soudan, to take responsibility for the colour. Aided by M. Alphonse Vallée, the village schoolmaster, the *curé* hid the colour in a succession of safe places. In 1918, the Armistice found 1st Cheshires twelves miles east of Audregnies, and on 17 November a colour-party was sent there to recover the colour, which eventually finished up in honourable retirement in the Regimental Depot at Chester. A machine-gun, hidden by the inhabitants of Audregnies at their peril, also survived; it still squats on its tripod in the entrance hall to the museum at Mons.

The battle earns a brief mention in the Official History as 'The Flank-Guard Action at Elouges'. It was actually more costly than Mons. The Cheshires had started the day nearly a thousand strong, and only two officers and two hundred men answered their names at St Waast that evening. The Norfolks had lost over 250 men, and even 119th Battery had lost thirty. Casualties in the Cavalry Division amounted to 250: the 4th Dragoon Guards had suffered eighty-one and the 9th Lancers, eighty-eight.

These casualties were not crippling: more serious was the fact that the battle had begun to fragment the Cavalry Division. Scattered groups of survivors made their way southwards. Private Wells wrote that 'we went through fields, villages, woods and roads not knowing or caring where we went'. On its long search southwards his group met some infantry which mistook them for Germans: 'I shouted "Don't fire we are troopers of the 9th Lancers," and being the oldest soldier I took charge of my . . . chums. I explained to the officer in charge that we had been roused from rest and ridden through the night and lost our regiment. He said he was placed the same way and did not know where he was.' Eventually he reached a railway, boxed up his horses and entrained his men. The train took them to Le Mans, where they met stragglers 'of every regiment and corps in France'. By the time they got back to the regiment the retreat was over.

Arthur Osburn had lost the 4th Dragoon Guards even before they charged. He reached Wargnies-le-Petit that evening with a party of 9th Lancer stragglers, and found his own regimental headquarters. 'Our CO was calm, but that night he was indignant, sorely grieved, wondering *who* had ordered *his* squadrons into this disastrous affair? No one could say! . . . Only about seven or eight officers could be found that night, yet, including various attached interpreters and French officers, we had had thirty-two that morning.'

My own retreat was scarcely less confusing. We soon reached the junction of the *chaussée* and the Baisieux road just north of Audregnies and rode through the village, past shuttered houses that had not changed since the Cheshires fired their last rounds and Curly Birch hammered along with the Germans close behind. As we turned into the Angre road, making for Monsieur Pauwels' stables, we passed the position of Captain Shore's two platoons — a well chosen slot with cover from fire from the north but a wickedly good flanking shoot across the Honnelle — and a few hundred yards down the road the village cemetery appeared on our right. There was a green Commonwealth War Graves Commission plaque by the gate, and from Thatch's broad back I could just see over the wall. Amidst florid memorials to successive generations of the inhabitants of Audregnies, polished marble here and crumbling granite there, were rows of plainer Portland headstones bearing a regimental badge.

The Cheshires' oak sprig cap-badge is one of the few to have survived unscathed by amalgamation or disbandment. I had seen it often enough at Sandhurst or Warminster, and here it was again, marking the last resting-place of young men from Runcorn or Chester who had died under the shrapnel or amongst the drab little houses when German infantry closed in with bayonet and butt. Looking northwards, I shared their last glimpse of the world: empty stubble, with Quiévrain spire stabbing up above the woods astride the Honnelle. There are more Cheshires in the communal cemeteries at Wiheries and Elouges. Captain Jones is at Wiheries, and lying amongst the British soldiers at Elouges is Louis Ouilico, *Maréchal des logis* (sergeant) in the 6th *Chasseurs à Cheval*, who fell charging with the 4th Dragoon Guards to whom he was attached as interpreter.

We cut off a long bend in the road by riding across a stubblefield; I was not sorry, because there was more traffic than I had expected and it had evidently not heard of slowing down for horses. By now we were beyond the Cheshires' position and on ground held by 3rd Cavalry Brigade, which had moved back northwards on Allenby's order, and, supported by D and E Batteries RHA, prevented the Germans from flowing down the Honnelle valley to roll up Ballard's line. Sergeant Edgington of D Battery had found the action frustrating: 'after what seemed to us wandering aimlessly about the country came into action (great confusion) lost my cap, teams came up without orders, both my waggons overturned'.

There must be a jinx on the place. The little piebald, which had been pulling like a train for the past hour, now excelled itself by edging crabwise into the deep ditch beside the road. For a moment I saw all four hooves thrashing in the air while its rider sprawled in the road. I was more than a little concerned, but there were whoops of delight from my companions. 'That's drinks all round,' they explained. 'It's just as well for him that there aren't more of us.' The rider, very evidently not sharing the prevailing triumphalist mood, remounted and followed us as we rejoined the road, by now on the outskirts of Angre.

The next piece of equine excitement came almost immediately. I was riding on the outside, chatting to Monsieur Pauwels on my right, when his horse suddenly skittered out into the road, upsetting Thatch, who pranced about, eyes wide and ears back. Monsieur Pauwels apologised most extravagantly, and I was congratulating myself on having made a suitably courtly response — 'My dear fellow, think nothing of it' does not trip easily off my tongue in French — when Thatch, whose horsy brain had now concluded that monsters must inhabit Angre if even the locals were scared of the place, plunged across the road into the path of the local dust-cart. It was the closest I came to a serious accident throughout the trip. Fortunately the dust-cart, going noisily about its malodorous business, was scarcely moving, and the road was temporarily free of other traffic.

I had expected to pause at the stables only long enough for Monsieur Pauwels to change his good-looking but impractical horse for something more useful. But as soon as we arrived it became clear that we were the centre of much local interest. A newspaper article — *Un général anglais sur nos chemins cavaliers* — had, unbeknown to us, drawn attention to our project, inviting all those attracted by 'horses, adventure, pleasure and good humour' to assemble for a jolly ride to the Forest of Mormal. Horses, adventure, pleasure and good humour were evidently much in vogue, for a substantial posse was drawn up waiting for us. It is kindest to describe the cavalcade as mixed in terms of age and ability. There were some very businesslike horsemen, smartly turned out and well-mounted: there were also some whose talents were fully stretched in getting their ponies into line in the stable-yard.

Eventually the procession was formed up and we clattered off, taking a track southwards out of the village and heading into the Bois d'Angre. Our path clung to the eastern bank of the Grande Honnelle and took us past the occasional disused factory or mine-working, yet more evidence of the industry that was at its height in 1914. Private Nobby Clarke of the Bays had come this way on 24 August. 'There must have been some kind of action ahead,' he wrote, 'because I can remember some riderless horses galloping back through our Squadron — they were some other Regiment's horses. By this time we and the horses were terribly tired, hungry and thirsty, but there was nothing for us to eat. So all we could do was to lie down with our horses in the open.'

All was well at the head of our column. Monsieur Pauwels was as informative as ever, and I did my best to chat up the pretty journalist who had written the article and was preparing a follow-up piece. I suspected that her striking blonde hair owed more to art than to nature, but she could certainly have made an old colonel very happy. 'Do you ride often?' I asked. 'This is the first time since I broke my arm in a fall,' she replied briskly, and conversation rather fell off. Meanwhile the clamour from the rearguard increased. There was contradictory advice. 'Can't we trot on a bit?' 'Can you slow down? Marie-Claire has lost a stirrup.' When we did trot on, the shouts grew more urgent, and soon there was a despairing cry of 'Marie-Claire has come off!' We peregrinated our way across the frontier between Autreppe and Gussignies — although I did not know it until I looked hard at the map, for there is no evidence of a border on the web of little roads and tracks — and rode westwards, heading for Malplaquet where we were to stop for lunch.

It was a late lunch. Marie-Claire was not alone in her misfortunes. The occasional thump and yell from behind announced that another of our posse had dismounted involuntarily, and one rider came by at speed, explaining as she passed that her horse would lead but not follow. We entered Malplaquet along the Mons road, the axis of Marlborough's central attack on the French position on 11 September 1709. It is easy to see why it was such a bloody battle, decided not by a Malburian masterstroke but by grim close-range volleying that left a quarter of the combatants dead or wounded. There are woods on both sides of the position, which made it difficult for the attackers to outflank it, and the central approach, down which we rode, was dominated by a row of redoubts on a low crest where the frontier now runs. An obelisk stands beside the road, erected by the French to commemorate the two hundredth anniversary of the battle, for Malplaquet was the closest they came to a victory against that formidable pair, Marlborough and Prince Eugene.

We lunched at a farm towards the northern end of the rather straggly village, in the area where the French and Allied cavalry had fought after Orkney's infantry had at last gained possession of the redoubts. Our army issue six-foot table was set up beside a high-eaved redbrick barn which post-dated the battle by seventy years, and we gave the horses their feed in nosebags — Thatch had not encountered one before, but is a quick learner where food is concerned. Our own lunch — *baguettes*, ham, cheese, pâté, tomatoes and apples, with wine and mineral water — was a rushed affair, because we were due to meet our next guide, Monsieur Jacques Decool, at the appropriately-named Carrefour du Blanc Cheval in the Forest of Mormal. In view of the morning's festivities we would not have time to get there on horseback, so we boxed up the horses and drove the ten miles through Bavay and into the forest.

Our drive took us through the BEF's position on the night of 24/ 25 August 1914. It finished up on a line east-west through Bavay, with 5th Cavalry Brigade, on the right flank, at Feignies, I Corps between Feignies and Bavay, and II Corps stretching from Bavay to Bermeries. The Cavalry Division — with 2nd Cavalry Brigade, as we have seen, much broken up — was at St Waast and Wargnies, and 19th Infantry Brigade covered the BEF's left flank at Jenlain and Saultain.

Sir John French was in a quandary. In the small hours of the 24th, he told Spears testily that if his left flank was seriously threatened he would withdraw on his lines of communication and Lanrezac would have to shift for himself. Daylight brought wisdom. He spent much of the day visiting the troops, a process which usually cheered him up. Haig's men 'looked very active and pushing', and he spared a nod of approval for the German gunners, whose shells 'seemed to burst very well'. He went on to Avesnes where he met General Sordet, whose cavalry corps had been sent across to the Allied left. Sordet, a regular-featured man who reminded the field-marshal of a piece of Dresden china, told French that he was perfectly willing to cover the BEF's left flank but he had not yet received orders to do so. In fact the relevant orders had been issued, but as Spears observed: 'It was strange how often cavalry corps got mislaid during the war of movement'.

When he returned to GHQ, French heard that the 5th Army was continuing to fall back. Two more reserve divisions had been added to the three already tasked with securing line between the British left and the sea, but it was evident that, even with the assistance of the 25,000 strong garrison of Lille, this force would not be able to cope with Marwitz's *Cavalry Corps*, its advanced guard already at Tournai, and *II* and *IV Corps* of Kluck's right wing, both now identified by the RFC to the BEF's left front. French flirted with the notion of hiding behind the fortifications of Maubeuge. Some of his wounded had already been sent there: Major Bailey of the 12th Lancers, who had accidentally shot himself in the leg with his revolver while running upstairs in his billet on 23 August, was the senior British officer in the garrison. However, the field-marshal remembered a line from Sir Edward Hamley's textbook *Operations of War* which warned that a commander who fell back into a fortress was like a sailor who, in a storm, clutched hold of the anchor. He was also certain that Kluck was trying to hustle him back into Maubeuge, and, indeed, on 24 August Kluck had ordered: 'The attack is to be carried out so that the enemy will be thrown back onto Maubeuge and his retreat to the west cut off'.

By mid-afternoon Sir John saw his way clearly: there was no more talk of acting independently or retiring under the guns of Maubeuge. He wired Joffre that he was falling back to the line Maubeuge–Valenciennes, which he hoped to hold with Sordet's help, and if driven back he would do his best to act in accordance with Joffre's wishes. At 8.25 that evening GHQ issued orders for withdrawal on the 25th. The Forest of Mormal, a compact block of oak and beech, nine miles long and three to four miles broad, lay due south of Bavay and threatened to split the BEF just as the cutwater of a bridge divides the torrent. There were some routes through it, but most were forest tracks, and, with the uncorrected maps at his disposal, French hesitated to commit a corps to what Sir James Edmonds called 'so large and blind a mass of trees'. French decided to send I Corps east of the forest and II Corps to the west: they would halt for the night of the 25/26th on the line Le Cateau–Landrecies, beyond its southern edge.

Bavay — Bagacum to the Romans — is girdled by a ring-road, but we wound our way through its centre, past the ruins of the forum and the archaeological museum, all looking slightly forlorn, because Bavay sees few tourists and there are precious few money-spinners locally. In the main square, in front of the contrasting brick clock-tower and granite town hall, is a female figure on a pillar. I would have looked at her harder had I then known what I discovered later about the *Chaussée Brunehaut*, for it is Queen Brunhilda herself, keeping a stony eye on a junction of those long, straight roads in which she took such an interest.

No sooner had we left Bavay on the Aulnois road than Mormal filled the horizon. We turned south-west down a road of Brunhilda-like exactitude, to arrive at the Carrefour du Blanc Cheval where we were to meet Jacques Decool. There was no mistaking him. A trim gentleman in late middle age, wearing grey blouson, breeches and long boots, he strode over and took us under his wing at once. We would of course take coffee and cognac before setting out; it was an invitation that brooked no denial. After a few minutes in the bar of the *auberge* the world was set firmly to rights, and we were all chatting away in a lingua franca that owed more to gesticulation than to phrase books.

As we walked over towards his horse, a good-looking chestnut with expensive and well-kept tack, Monsieur Decool asked me if I was a soldier too. I replied that I was actually the trip's historian, but also happened to be a colonel of Territorial infantry. 'Ah, then,' he said, 'you'll know all about colonel's trivia.' Colonel's trivia? Was this a military form of trivial pursuit? Or small-talk reserved for garrison drinks parties? I found out soon enough. 'In the old days,' said Monsieur Decool, 'colonels were men of a certain age, but had to be able to mount in front of their regiments. The colonel's trivia was designed to help them.' So saying, he undid a clip which fastened his stirrup-leather to the bar on his saddle, revealing an extra strip of leather which lowered the stirrup by a good six inches. He slipped a foot into the stirrup, mounted with ease and then clipped the leather back up again. There were times over the next two weeks when this colonel, one foot in the stirrup and the other on the ground, would have dearly loved some trivia.

Evelyn and Ollie rode Magoo and Jeopardy into the forest with Monsieur Decool while I set off with the Trooper and horse-box for Jolimetz, just off the *Chaussée Brunehaut* which runs along Mormal's western edge. I missed the first turning and ground slowly through the village looking for a road which would take us back on ourselves without having to turn round. There was a broken-down truck almost blocking the crucial turn, and John piloted the box past it with inches to spare: if the two Frenchmen looking disconsolately under the bonnet had been able to lip-read they would have profited from a free lesson in scouse vernacular.

Even when we were on the right road, finding Monsieur Gérard Chevalier's stable was not easy. I stopped to ask two ladies who assured me that they had lived in the village all their lives but had never heard of him: ought I to be in Le Quesnoy, or perhaps in Herbignies? Eventually, we met a postman who did know, and who directed us down a long drive with house and stables visible at the far end. Whatever else went down the drive regularly, large horse-boxes did not: there were overhanging trees which made it impossible for John to swing in front of the house to reach the yard. But finally he managed to tuck the box in at the end of the house, and we led Thatch and Thomas under the trees and into the stables.

John's face was a good barometer of collective morale where stables were concerned. It went very square when we encountered week-old deep litter, or if our requests for extra straw were met with blank looks: there were times when it was as well that John's command of French was less than extensive as I am not sure some of our hosts would have appreciated the O'Flaherty animadversions on the shortcomings of their stable management. But there were no problems at Jolimetz. The stables were old but clean, and if Monsieur Chevalier was a man of a few words he was on hand, unostentatiously, to help. Jean Petitprez, with whom I had discussed routes on the telephone all those months before, was also there to welcome us, in tweeds that put our travel-soiled kit to shame.

I added one new word to my vocabulary that day. I have spent so long researching in the *Service Historique de l'Armée* at Vincennes that nineteenth-century military French presents no problem. I can translate querulous demands for water-bottles and knapsacks, earnest discussions on the relationship between skirmish-lines and company columns, and learned reflections on the relative merits of latrines 'in the Turkish style' as opposed to the more comfortable variety 'in the English style'. But I did not know the French for wheelbarrow, and a glance into the horse-box where Thatch had been unusually productive made it all too clear that we would need one. I tried circumlocution: 'It's a sort of box with a wheel at the front.' No good. Then I tried charades, creaking forwards with my arms by my sides. Monsieur Chevalier had it in one. '*Ah, une brouette*,' he announced, and suggested that I could remember the word easily enough if I thought of *roue*, which gave me the wheel, and the rumbling sound conjured up by '*brrr*'.

We had got the horses squared away and the box cleaned out by the time that Evelyn, Ollie and Jacques rode in. They had had a marvellous afternoon in Mormal: Jacques Petitprez was absolutely right, it would have been a pity to have missed it. We believed that our hosts had organised accommodation for us, and were not a little surprised when they asked us where we were spending the night. Evelyn blithely replied that we hoped they would tell us. In fact a vital letter had gone astray, but Jacques Decool rose to the occasion. Discreet phone calls were made, and I was driven off into the forest to see whether the *auberge* at the Carrefour de la Touraille would suit us. It would suit us very well, and I felt no shame in demolishing the best beer of the day while arrangements were made. By the time I got back to Jolimetz most of the tack had been cleaned and the horses were bedded down. We piled into the Trooper, drove to the *auberge*, and staggered upstairs to skate through the quick change routine for which military training is a decided advantage: arrive hot and sweaty in one order of dress, and appear, bathed, shaved and scented in another only twenty minutes later.

The rush was dictated by the fact that we were bidden to dinner at La Forestière, deep in the forest, just outside the village of Loc-quignol on the Quesnoy road. As we drove past it to reach the hotel, we could see our hosts' cars there, and we were already late; by the time we returned in a more fragrant guise, we were very late indeed. It could not have mattered less. The proprietress ushered us into a long room, decorated with hunting trophies where our hosts, their wives and an assortment of family and friends were sipping kir. After several glasses on an empty stomach I was glad to sit down, though I thought it strange that the long table was laid for so many. Dinner arrived, course after course, simple, tasty food in the best bourgeois tradition. The menu had been chosen to show off the fruits of the forest: there was trout, venison and grilled Maroilles cheese with a salad. Bottles of Château Beauregard came on with all the determination of German infantry breasting the slope at Audregnies and were dealt with as steadily.

We were half-way through the meal when I heard familiar shouts outside: someone was suggesting that Marie-Claire might care to get a move on. The Belgians had arrived. Monsieur Pauwels led his squadron into the dining-room, almost two hours late but as indomitable as ever. I kept half an eye on Madame, expecting more than a hint of disapproval: but no, the kitchen yielded up more trout and more venison, and the march of bottles continued unchecked. We had devoured the Maroilles — I could see that John, a meat and two veg man, might have preferred something less pungent — when the speeches began. Jacques Decool graciously bade us welcome; Evelyn elegantly replied, and I translated with a verve that had more to do with claret than grammar. The flow of compli-ment and pleasantry became general. It had been such a marvellous evening at the end of a memorable day that I wanted to say some-thing that went beyond mere conventional politeness. There are not many times when it is worth having the sort of brain that can remember the details of Romanus Diogenes' defeat at Manzikert in

1071 but not my own phone number, but this was one of them. I recalled the lines engraved on the blade of a Hungarian light cavalry officer's sword in Konopiště Castle in Bohemia. They matched our mood precisely, and slipped easily across the table to our new friends:

> *Je te souhais dans ta vie*
> *Un bon cheval, une belle amie,*
> *Cent ducats quand tu voudras*
> *Et le paradis quand tu mourras.*

> (While you live I wish for you
> A good horse and a fair friend too.
> A hundred ducats when you desire
> And paradise when you expire)

As we left, I complimented Madame on the dinner, and said how much we had appreciated the wine, there being a special affinity between the British and claret. She smiled, produced a bottle of the 1985 Beauregard, and hoped that we would enjoy it. It stayed in the Trooper, lodged snugly between dog-guard and wheel-arch, until a night when we really needed it. I am not sure who drove the short distance back to the *auberge*: I only hope that it was not me.

V

A Bang at the Bastards

The guiding principle in all delaying action must be that when
an enemy has liberty to manoeuvre, the passive occupation of
a position, however strong, can rarely be justified, and always
involves the risk of crushing defeat; under these conditions a
delaying force must manoeuvre, so as to force an enemy to
deploy as often as possible, but should rarely accept battle.

Field Service Regulations

Another dawn, another hangover. Wednesday, 11 August was
to take us from Jolimetz to Le Cateau by way of Landrecies.
A 9.00 a.m. start meant that we needed to be at the stables by 8.00,
and this had us trooping down the winding stairs in the *auberge* at
7.00. It was as silent as the tomb. There was some gallows humour
(not least from the abstemious John) as we dragged suitcases through
the hall, and while I crouched in the back of the Trooper stowing
luggage in what I hoped would be the right order when we needed
it next I swore to give up alcohol for the duration of the trip. Coffee
would have helped, but it was slow in coming: one of the things
we had forgotten to do in the previous night's rush was to arrange
an early breakfast. A young and nervous waitress, looking, in her
black bombazine, for all the world like a novice in a nunnery, crept
out of the recesses behind the kitchen. Nobody else was about, and
she had only just started to work there so was not quite sure where
everything was, but she did her best and, sure enough, out came
orange juice, coffee and croissants.

One of the problems of owning a grey is that what are euphemistically called stable marks — the result of lying on hay which, in
the nature of things, is not entirely ordure-free — are both obvious

and obdurate. Thatch has the knack of acquiring stable marks in direct proportion to the importance of the coming day's events: because we were riding out with Jacques Decool we were anxious to be in good order, but Thatch was heavily mottled. We went through what was becoming a familiar routine. First, trot the horses up in hand under John's eagle eye to be sure that they were sound — a horse shows lameness by nodding when the sound foot of the pair comes to the ground — then feed and groom. The horses had three feeds of cavalry mix (a mixed feed with an appetising branny smell and the look of a rather chunky muesli) a day, and haynets in addition. We tried to leave a good hour between feeding the horses and riding them, and it was important that there was no radical change of diet, for if lameness was one potential show-stopper, colic (acute equine indigestion) was another.

I was still busy with a sponge removing the last of Thatch's nocturnal camouflage when Jacques and his friends arrived and mounted. They were very different from Monsieur Pauwels' rumbustious cavalcade. There were half a dozen experienced riders on their own horses: they knew Mormal well, and intended to give us a good morning. We crossed the *Chaussée Brunehaut* — for all its importance as a route, infinitely quieter than the A31 which roars past my garden wall as I write — and were in the forest. Over the next fortnight we were to ride through four of the great forests of Northern France: Mormal, St Gobain, Compiègne and Retz. Each has its characteristics: Mormal's tracks are clay, St Gobain's are strewn with flints, Compiègne's are sandy, and Retz has broad avenues between its oaks. And each has its devotees, who spend their spare time on horseback in the woods: there is a marvellous body called the *Association des Cavaliers Indépendants de la Forêt de Saint-Gobain*, which conjures up images of swashbucklers in plumed hats and bucket-topped boots.

But for Jacques Decool, Mormal had no rivals. He led us on Ague, his big chestnut gelding, down mile after mile of identical-looking forest rides without even thinking of a map, occasionally rising in his long stirrups to snap off a low branch that was beginning to obstruct the way, casting a proprietorial glance at damage done by the wild boars who root up the grass beside the wider tracks, and pointing out a handful of deer flitting through the shadows at the foot of the big oaks. We crossed a stream, a tiny tributary of the Sambre which flows through Landrecies, over a bridge built with money he had helped raise. Not much went on in Mormal that Jacques did not know about; he talked easily about its history (it had once been owned by the monks of the Abbey at Maroilles and had passed to the state after the Revolution) and politics (local government spends money on the forest, for it is recognised as a valuable amenity for the inhabitants of the teeming post-industrial towns of the north).

This was the sort of comfortable familiarity that one might have expected from a Hampshire farmer walking a visitor across Old Down, past Farringdon Firs and into Home Wood. It also highlighted a point which was to be underscored ever more heavily as our ride went on. Whatever Frenchmen and Belgians thought of politicians at the national level — and I was struck by the generally low esteem in which such creatures were held — local politics were a different matter altogether. They were a mainstream affair, part of daily life, and had much more to do with a view (often shared between those who might find themselves on different sides of the ideological fence) of what was best for the community. We found mayors — who exercise a wide range of administrative responsibilities, such as conducting marriage ceremonies — to be figures of pivotal importance in their towns and villages. From our point of view they were invaluable points of contact: they could organise access to a field, arrange accommodation in the village hall, or tell us who might have hay for sale. If we met a man who did not know the answer to our enquiry, the *mairie* would know somebody who did.

Jacques Decool was deputy mayor of Valenciennes — no sinecure, this, in a town with a population of more than 40,000 — and he was the first of many elected officials that we met. They turned out to meet us at lunchtimes, ambled over in the evening to make certain that we were happy, or ensured that the *garde champêtre* was on hand with the hose-pipe to fill our water-buckets. It is easy to scoff at portly, self-important figures in *tricouleur* sashes (the French equivalent of the mayoral chain), or to draw dark inferences about the intimate connection between political power and commercial success. I can only speak as we found, and in the deep France that opened up ahead of us mayors were the standard-bearers of their little communities, reflecting a local pride expressed in a genuine concern for our welfare which, I fear, we might not have found amongst our own countrymen.

A morning in the forest persuaded me that it was certainly not impenetrable to the armies of 1914, and when I got home and ransacked the sources it was clear that some soldiers, British and German, had indeed traversed it on 25 August 1914. L Battery RHA moved back through it, white markers on the rear of its guns and wagons enabling them to show up in the gloom, and Lieutenant Moore's troop of the 12th Lancers (part of 5th Cavalry Brigade, withdrawing on the eastern flank with I Corps) was wiped out in an ambush in Mormal. Paul Maze rode through it with the Scots Greys.

> The wood seemed completely deserted; there was no sound apart from the dangling chains and the steady strain of our horses. This sudden isolation relaxed my tension and for a while I gave myself up to its peace. Eventually we branched in to a broader alley nearly parallel, and the change from a rough to a smooth surface suddenly induced our horses to trot, as if they sensed the danger threatening.

We were ambushed at about 11.00 a.m. Our track crossed a metalled road somewhere south of Loquignol (I had long since given up trying to follow our route on my map) and a convivial posse of Jacques's friends were there, bottles at the ready. It was a warm morning — though not as warm as it was to become later in the week — and two or three glasses of Muscadet slipped down with no difficulty. We set off southwards at a good pace. Jacques led at a brisk mix of walk and trot, with plenty of opportunities for a canter where the tracks were not too slippery. Thatch has firm views on cantering. If he is going to put himself to the trouble of stretching out those rippling shoulders, then he likes to do it to some purpose. Why canter slowly when you can trot quickly? Jacques' horse was a delight: it had a soft, slurrupy action, and took him off at the most elegant of collected canters. Thatch did not know what to make of this running-on-the spot business. He could easily manage the same speed at a trot, and if he was going to canter, well, there was no virtue in hanging about. Jacques (who had no doubt got tired of a great grey head repeatedly appearing beside him) saw my problem. 'Why don't you lead for a bit?' he said. And off we shot at a decent canter, beeches whistling by on either side.

Then came the second ambush. This time it was the president of the Regional ANTE and his wife, well-armed with champagne. The canter had given me a thirst, and three or four glasses presented absolutely no problem. Or did they? Thatch's back began to seem rather less broad than usual, and there was sometimes less room between my knee and those passing trees than I had expected. Nor

was this all. John and I, English to the core, had stayed steadfastly
in the saddle at both brief halts, although there had been a certain
amount of dismounting and unzipping elsewhere in the troop. As
we neared Landrecies, I became increasingly aware that both brain
and bladder were not at their best, and I was delighted when we
dismounted to slacken off the girths and walk in the last half mile
or so to Le Rosembois, the hamlet between Landrecies and the forest
edge where we were to lunch.

The restaurant had just been refurbished with riders in mind, and
there was a large car park cum stable-yard on its forest side, surrounded by an imposing post and rail fence. We fastened haynets
to the fence, tied the horses to the haynets, and went inside. Another
ambush. Yet more well-wishers were there, including both the
morning's ambush parties and (this will come as no surprise) the
mayor. A brief speech of welcome and another glass of champagne;
and then at long last I was able to escape to unburden myself of the
morning's vinous mixture.

I tucked into lunch with a will. It was another example of masses
of good food coming out of a tiny kitchen as if by some gastronomic
conjuring-trick, and, chatting to a retired Belgian infantry officer
on my right and a keen local historian on my left, I definitively
abandoned my early-morning resolution (already badly dented by
the morning's ambushes) to shun wine. Although we were interested
in the First World War, it was the Second that stirred most local
emotions. The Maginot Line, built to defend France from German
attack, stopped near Longuyon, away to the east. In 1935, work
had begun on two prepared positions in the Avesnois, a *Ligne
Principal de Résistance* east of Maubeuge and a *Ligne d'Arrêt* behind
it, and there were more blockhouses scattered along the Belgian
border — we had ridden past one on the field of Malplaquet.

In May 1940, Rommel's 7th Panzer Division had churned its
way through both these lines and gone on to cross the Sambre at
Landrecies. For military historians the campaign is a stunningly
effective demonstration of the merits of boldy-handled armour and
air power, and the defenders feature only as confused victims of a
style of warfare they could not begin to grasp. Here, on the ground
they held, they are recalled with pride. The 84th Fortress Infantry
Division and the 1st North African Infantry Division have their
memorials: the North Africans strike a particular chord, and I have
seen the eyes of more than one middle-aged Frenchman fill with
tears when he describes those old regiments of the *Armée d'Afrique*,

turcos and zouaves, spahis and Chasseurs d'Afrique, taking on German tanks in 1940 with the same unreasoning valour that had nerved their fathers to face the Kaiser's legions in 1914 or to stand steady when Moltke the elder dismembered the imperial armies in the summer of 1870. There are local heroes, quietly remembered. Colonel Tachet de Combes of the 129th Infantry Regiment died — with 154 of his officers and men — at Yvoir, near Dinant up on the Meuse, and, closer to home, the blockhouses at Riame and Garennes, near Solre le Château, were defended to the death by their tiny garrisons under Lieutenants Pamart and Pinchon.

I was on my second helping of beef brochettes with Béarnaise sauce when somebody appeared and asked if one of the Englishmen could come out because there was a small problem with the horses. By the time I got there all was well: Jeopardy had broken loose but had been caught. John and Clive had now joined me, and arrived to see a small problem turn into a bigger one. A sudden gust of wind caught the trees beside the car park, and the noise startled Jeopardy who backed sharply away from the fence. Whoever had recaptured him had hitched him not to the haynet — which would have broken — but directly to the fence, which was more solid. It was evidently not solid enough. The whole upper bar, almost the size of a half-round telegraph pole, came away, and spun merrily through the car park with Jeopardy at one end and Thatch (needless to say) at the other. Onlookers skipped for cover. I saw one elderly French gentleman leap the oncoming bar with an agility which belied his years.

The whole arrangement came through the car-park entrance like a Leonardo da Vinci war-engine (Boudicca would, I think, have admired it), crossed the road and entered the forest. I had visions of the horses becoming terrified by the bar's clatter and really hurting themselves, but Thatch (who was actually tied to his haynet) broke loose when he passed an especially succulent bush and allowed me to catch him. Jeopardy soon lost interest in pulling the bar on his own and was apprehended by Clive. We led them back into the car park, to find that Monsieur Chevalier and one of his friends had stood to Thomas and Magoo, who were puzzled but secure. The restaurant owner was philosophical about his fence, and as we walked back to finish lunch the unlucky fence-builder, who was not there to defend himself, speedily assumed much of the blame for the incident. The bar was too heavy and the nails too short: it was as well that the fence's inherent unreliability had been discovered at this early stage, or somebody might have been hurt. As it was there was no real damage, apart from a hole punched in my saddle by one of the guilty nails (looking at it, I was secretly glad that the fence-builder had not used bigger ones), and the incident was a cheap reminder of a basic principle: never tether a horse without using a breakable link (bailer twine is the usual material) between lead-rope and hitching point.

That afternoon Evelyn and Clive were to ride through Landrecies to Le Cateau with Jacques while the rest of us took Thatch and Jeopardy on in the box. It was a short journey in 1993, but in 1914 this gap between Landrecies and Le Cateau was huge, for it marked the boundary between I and II Corps, split by the Forest of Mormal. On 25 August both corps had fallen back with the Germans snapping at their heels. For the officers and men of I Corps, most of whom had still not fired a shot in anger, the day was chiefly remembered as one of heat and confusion. Major Ma Jeffreys of the Grenadiers caught the mood of the day in his diary.

> Marched off 5 a.m. and marched by Pont sur Sambre to Landrecies, about 14½ miles. A very hot day again and a very trying march, owing to constant blocks and delays. Many refugees now on the roads, causing blocks and confusion. They were a pitiable sight — all ages and sexes, some in carts, many on foot. Some of the latter pushing barrows and hand-carts, piled up with bedding and belongings. Another cause of blocks and delay is double-banking, i.e. troops coming up alongside those in front of them so that the two columns are abreast. This generally means that no one can move either way.

The march was complicated by the fact that the French 53rd and 69th Reserve Divisions, on Lanrezac's left flank, were using the same roads, while Sordet's cavalry corps was marching from Avesnes towards Cambrai at right angles to the retreat. Sordet's men had been on the move since 5 August, and Frederic Coleman, whose position behind the wheel of his Bentley gave him no feel for the innate grubbiness of the cavalryman's life on active service, thought that: 'From their yellow helmets and blue tunics to their red breeches they appeared more campaign-soiled than one would have thought likely at such an early stage in proceedings'. One of Sordet's squadron leaders gave a graphic description of the miseries of the march:

> the temperature was very high; the roads very dusty. Although we were operating in a country rich in streams and springs, we were forbidden to water the horses to avoid lengthening the divisions, interminably. It

often was necessary to take steps against the efforts of some good cavalry-men to relieve their thirsty steeds. It was so tempting, this clear water, and the poor animals, with such insistence, stretched their dust-whitened noses towards it . . .

French cavalry, whose uniforms had changed little since the Second Empire, looked strange to the British. Sally Home thought that 'their weakness lay in the small attention that had been given to fighting on foot, and for this work the carbines they carried were an inferior weapon'. Sergeant Snelling cordially agreed, noting that 'they do not fight much dismounted and their carbines are very unreliable'. Kenneth Godsell found the cuirassiers of Sordet's division:

> easy to see at long distances, as the sun flashed in all directions from their shining breastplates. As the latter were not bullet-proof, it was difficult to understand their exact function. The French cavalryman was rarely seen off his horse. He had a rooted objection to dismounting. His animals were looking very thin and tired as a result of long and trying marches in this hot weather.

In contrast, British horsemen had already shown themselves masters of dismounted action, and as the retreat went on were to combine fire and shock in a way which emphasised the soundness of pre-war training.

The competition for road-space did not do much for inter-Allied relations. Paul Maze saw how:

> A tall French general, in a fever of agitation, was giving orders to officers arriving and departing . . . and then, looking at our transport in the middle of the reigning confusion, briskly turned towards us, a map in one hand, a crust of bread in the other, and said: 'Can't you see that you are congesting the whole of my retirement? You must get out of our way.'

A colonel did his best to reduce the tension by assuring Maze that '*La situation est sérieuse, mais pas grave.*' By now, too, the trickle of refugees was becoming a flood, and Alan Hanbury-Sparrow, march-ing east of the forest with the Royal Berkshires, was dismayed by 'this broken torrent of dusty misery. Wains drawn by great per-cherons, wagons tugged by oxen, tumbrils pulled by mules, pony-carts, donkey-carts, dog-carts, hand-carts, rusty victorias and lan-daus, perambulators, bicycles, tricycles, barrows and shandrydans, coagulate and concertina painfully along this via dolorosa.'

The retreat would have been increasingly painful had the roads been empty. Aubrey Herbert had already observed that even the Irish Guards were finding the marching hard. 'The men began to fall out a great deal on the road. The heat was very great. Many of the reservists were soft, and their feet found them out. Their rough clothes rubbed them. Tom carried rifles all day, and I carried rifles and kit on my horse, while the men hung onto the stirrups.'

Lieutenant Wernher of the 12th Lancers, displaying a touch of cavalryman's hauteur, thought that: 'The infantry were extraordinary to look at; all had beards, they had discarded a lot of their equipment, and cut off their sleeves above the elbow; very few were wearing puttees but all seemed in good heart.'

Haig set up his headquarters in Landrecies early on the afternoon of the 25th. He initially proposed to pause there very briefly, and expected to move westwards to join Smith-Dorrien at Le Cateau, but cancelled these orders when he received GHQ's instructions to fall back south-westwards on the 26th. His 1st Division, on the outer flank, went into billets in Marbaix and Dompierre, while 2nd Division was more widely spread, with 4th (Guards) Brigade at Landrecies, 6th Brigade at Maroilles, 5th Brigade at Noyelles sur Sambre and 5th Cavalry Brigade providing the rearguard at Leval. This deployment presupposed that Mormal and the Sambre formed a natural glacis protecting the corps' left front. Indeed, when Ma Jeffreys marched into Landrecies at 3.30 he asked a staff officer what he should do about outposts, only to be told that 'we were covered by other bodies of troops, and by the great Forêt de Mormal, through which there were no roads that could be used by troops'. But Mormal was, as we have seen, far from impassable, and the Sambre bridges had not been blown.

The British were saved from the worst consequences of misreading the ground by the fact that Kluck was still fighting blind. He was in firm contact with II Corps but did not realise that it formed only part of the BEF. His *IX Corps*, which would have met Haig's men had it moved southwards after Mons, had been retained by Bülow to mask Maubeuge — a decision which had done nothing to improve Kluck's regard for his more hesitant neighbour.

On the evening of 25 August, therefore, *First Army* behaved as if Smith-Dorrien's men, west of Le Cateau, were its only adversaries. The advanced guard of the *48th Infantry Regiment* of *III Corps* on Kluck's left — which had come through the forest on the Loquignol road, and had almost certainly passed the *auberge* where we had spent the night — collided with B Squadron 15th Hussars, 2nd

Division's cavalry, on Maroilles bridge, which is actually two miles north of the town. Ted Fowler recalled that: 'We dismounted and sent our horses back. We could see Germans creeping across the bridge and we fired away at them but they kept coming. Close enough for me to see a man with big Kaiser moustaches. He came running forward and I was sort of sorry when I shot him down. Then the Berkshires came up and we went back.' The Berkshires met the Germans on the long causeway which crosses the marshes south of the bridge and there was a raw mêlée, with bayonets freely used on both sides. The Berkshires had rather the better of it, pushing the Germans back onto the bridge, where they remained all night.

Meanwhile, *14th Infantry Regiment*, on the left of *IV Corps*, was marching along the Englefontaine road — within easy range of Le Rosembois, our lunch-stop — to Landrecies, where it was to spend the night before falling on II Corps' right flank at Le Cateau. There was a false alarm late in the afternoon when a German cavalry patrol rode unopposed into the northern outskirts of the town, causing panic amongst the inhabitants — and a certain amount of excitement amongst troopers of the North Irish Horse, the corps cavalry regiment, who rushed about shouting 'The Germans are on us'.

As a result of this disturbance, 3rd Coldstream Guards were posted north of the Sambre, just across the railway which, then as now, follows the line of the river. The Coldstream had scarcely reached their allocated position when they met a column coming in the other direction. An officer shouted 'Don't fire: we are French', and the NCO of the party covering the road hesitated. Captain the Hon. Charlie Monck gave the order to fire, and the Germans at once charged, some briefly grabbing a Coldstream machine-gun before they were felled by close-range musketry. The Grenadiers, billeted in the town, stood to their arms at once and moved up to the level crossing just behind the Coldstream, dropping a company off to hold the Sambre bridge and leaving another to watch the side-roads north of it. The Grenadier machine-guns were sent forward and assisted the Coldstream in repulsing the attack. The Germans then shelled the town, and in the process set light to some straw, by whose light they began to infiltrate men round the flanks of the Coldstream, though the Grenadiers at the level crossing — snap-shooting in very poor light — hit most of those who tried to cross the railway. German artillery had been brought up close, and a single 4.5 inch howitzer of 60th Battery RFA was manhandled forward to take it on. It scored a direct hit with its third round, and this effectively ended the action: there was sporadic firing until about 2.00 a.m., but no fresh attack.

The casualties of Landrecies were almost equal: 126 Coldstream, 7 Grenadiers and 127 Germans. What made the action more than just another unremarkable little skirmish was its effect on the British high command. Haig was not at his best. He had been constipated for days, and on the 24th his senior medical officer had, as Captain John Charteris of his staff tells us, 'dosed him with what must have been something designed for elephants, for the result was immediate and volcanic'. On the 25th he had improved, 'though very chewed up and ghastly to look at', but commanded from a staff-car rather than his charger's back that day. The attack found him off-balance, and Charteris remembered him declaiming: 'If we are caught, by God, we sell our lives dearly', which was not his style at all. Haig left by car at once — Brigadier-General Scott-Kerr of 4th Guards Brigade took over his old headquarters — and Charteris navigated through the misty valley to a village held by 1st Division.

Haig then telephoned GHQ, now at St Quentin, to report that his situation was 'very critical'. GHQ had already heard that the telephone operator at Le Cateau had been talking to his colleague at Landrecies when the latter exclaimed that the Germans had entered the town, so the news was not unexpected. But it was badly received, and GHQ was soon persuaded that, as Spears puts it, 'only a portion of the I Corps had been able to cut its way through the enemy'. Archie Murray, teetering on the edge of breakdown for days, collapsed. He was thus incommunicado when the curtain rose on the rest of that short night's drama, and French decided to send Smith-Dorrien to Haig's assistance.

If Haig had troubles, Smith-Dorrien had them in spades. On his right, 5th Division withdrew down the *Chaussée Brunehaut* almost unmolested, with 14th Brigade bringing up its rear. Count Gleichen, whose 15th Brigade headed the column, thought it 'a very long march that day, down the perfectly straight road skirting the Mormal forest and on to Le Cateau. It was, as a matter of fact, only twenty miles, but the hot day, with very little food, was most trying for the men.' There were the same heart-rending sights as on the other side of the forest, with 'pitiful crowds of women and old men and children, carrying bundles on their backs, or wheeling babies and more bundles in wheel-barrows, or perambulators, or broken-

down carts . . . children with their dolls or pet dogs, old women
and men hobbling along, already very tired although the sun had
not been up for more than an hour or two.' Gleichen rode on to
look at the chosen ground west of Le Cateau so as to be able to
apportion it to his battalions as they came in, and found that trenches
— shallow and exposed, but trenches nonetheless — had already
been dug by the inhabitants under French military supervision. 13th
Brigade arrived not long afterwards and formed up to Gleichen's
east, but 14th Brigade did not appear till nightfall.

On Smith-Dorrien's left, part of the Cavalry Division initially
swung wide to the eastern flank to support French troops falling
back from Valenciennes — Sally Home met a 'sporting colonel of
French Territorials who had fought the Germans till he had run out
of ammunition' — and shadow Marwitz's horsemen. Some of them
crossed the battlefield of Villers-en-Cauchies, where on 24 April
1794 two squadrons of the 15th Light Dragoons and two of Austrian
hussars had charged a six-battalion mass of Revolutionary infantry.
The squadron leaders swore on crossed swords to charge home,
'which agreement the men ratified by their cheers', and did precisely
that, although the British commander, Major William Aylett, was
bayoneted as he crashed into the square. The cavalry killed 800
French — neither side took prisoners that day — and chased the
fugitives to the gates of Bouchain. It was one of the finest examples
of shock action in the horse and musket era, although the 15th
Hussars, busy on the other side of Mormal, may have been forgiven
for not realising that they were so close to hallowed regimental
ground.

In some respects the fighting on 25 August 1914 looked more like
the action at Villers-en-Cauchies 120 years before than the battle at
Ypres only two months later. Captain Alfred Wirth, a German staff
officer, found it 'like being on manoeuvres; one could actually still
see the troops taking part. In the later fighting all that disappeared,
and, in the three day battle on the Marne especially, we experienced
the truth of the "emptiness of the battlefield".'

2nd Cavalry Brigade at first fell back between 3rd Division and
its pursuers. Arthur Osburn spent much of this busy day with
Lieutenant Pat Fitzgerald and the machine-gun section of the 4th
Dragoon Guards: at one moment they set up their guns on the
ramparts of Le Quesnoy — a gem of eighteenth-century fortification which lies a stranded starfish just west of the *chaussée* — to
support 3rd Division's rearguard. The next time Le Quesnoy smelt

powder was in October 1918, when the Canadians took it by storm, assaulting across its ditch and over its ramparts more like an eighteenth-century forlorn hope than seasoned veterans of a war of flamethrowers and poison-gas.

Mid-afternoon saw the cavalry drawn up near Vertain, north-east of Solesmes. Osburn saw how:

> over a wide open plain of stubble dotted with dark wheat-stacks our Brigades and regiments wheeled and galloped, formed and reformed in column of squadrons, the German horse artillery making ineffectual attempts to drive us back. Over the brown masses of horsemen charging across that rather dreary plain beneath a lowering sky on that sultry afternoon came white feathery bursts of shrapnel. The threatening sky, the restless symmetrical movements, the whole scene reminded me in some strange way of Milton's description of the legions of the dark angels practising for giant warfare with St. Michael on the plains of hell.

The 4th Hussars' account put it more succinctly: 'From the point of view of the regimental observer most of the day seemed to be spent in moving to form a target for enemy artillery, being scattered, and then forming up again.'

Such was the congestion on the roads, jammed with British troops, refugees and 'long trains of French wounded in rough country carts without covers or medical orderlies', that Allenby had little chance of moving his division as a formed body. Moreover, as he admitted some weeks later in a formal letter to Smith-Dorrien, 'a gap was opened between the flank and rear guards' and only the timely assistance of Brigadier-General McCracken of 7th Brigade prevented the Germans from exploiting it. Much of 2nd and 3rd Cavalry Brigades slid off south-westwards. The Official History suggests that they had been ordered to gain touch with I Corps, but Home, who was in a position to know the truth, acknowledged that they were 'driven south-east'. 1st Cavalry Brigade fell back south of Solesmes, where 4th Cavalry Brigade remained with divisional headquarters. By nightfall on the 25th, the Cavalry Division was a division in name only: its brigades marched and fought separated, and there was much dispersion within brigades and even regiments. Some units found the relaxation of control not unwelcome: the 18th Hussars fell in with a supply column at Inchy at 5.00 on the morning of the 26th, and 'had a good meal and filled our nosebags for the first time since Thulin' — the regiment's bivouac on the night of 22/23 August.

In the centre, between the flanking cavalry and the solid column of 5th Division at the forest's edge, came 3rd Division, with 7th Brigade covering its rear. By 6.00 the brigade had reached Solesmes, where it stood its pursuers off while the traffic-jam behind it gradually thinned out. Also south of Solesmes was 4th Division, which had handed over its coast defence duties in England to Territorials and Yeomanry, and detrained at Le Cateau and nearby stations on the 24th. Major-General Snow, the divisional commander, had been ordered to secure the high ground south of Solesmes to assist II Corps in its retirement, and was subsequently told to peel back onto Smith-Dorrien's left in the Le Cateau position. It was not until midnight that his last battalions left their blocking position and marched off south-westwards under pelting rain.

Behind them the horizon was aglow with the flames of burning villages. Some British officers had strong personal or regimental contacts with the Germans: Sir John French himself held the Order of the Red Eagle and wrote, almost affectionately, of 'the Emperor William' in his diary. Lieutenant-Colonel Willcox of the 3rd Hussars was to find himself in action against the 3rd German Hussars, 'a Prussian regiment to which the writer had been attached in the German manoeuvres of 1909 and with which the 3rd had exchanged Christmas cards for some years'. But the refugees and flame-dyed skyline forced many to change their opinions. Captain John Norwood of the 5th Dragoon Guards told his wife that:

> I have a very fond spot for the Germans whom I regard as our natural allies and I dislike the French — more so since I have known them than before. I must say the way the Germans have burnt whole villages and turned out the women has made me quite sick. I have time after time stayed in a perfect little village, with good hospitable souls . . . and before the day was over have seen the whole valley and plain burning for miles.

The dreadful fate of civilians caught up in war reinforced the inherent insularity of so many of all ranks of the BEF: Europe was, in a deep and profound sense, not vital to British interests. Aubrey Herbert's comrades thought that 'as far as our army in France was concerned, disaster, in the face of the numbers that we had to fight, was inevitable, but that this disaster was not vital as long as the Navy was safe'. An unnamed sergeant in the Essex regiment said much the same to the journalist Philip Gibbs. The Germans were 'a blighted nation on the move. You can't mow that down. We kill 'em and kill 'em and still they come on. They seem to have an endless line of fresh men.' Lieutenant Martin, who, as a medical officer, came closer to his enemy than many combatants, was favourably impressed by what he saw. 'The Germans were sturdy young men, strong-jawed and wiry,' he wrote. 'This was no canaille we were fighting, but a trained, determined soldiery who would fight hard and die gamely.'

Not all Smith-Dorrien's commanders were aware of the arrival of 4th Division. As the 4th Hussars were trotting back through Solesmes: 'there came the order "Draw swords!" Going up the hill out of the town, "Line on the left!" "Gosh, we're in for a charge." And sure enough there was infantry on top . . . ' The infantry was British and an accident was averted. But there had already been a number of incidents of what modern jargon terms 'blue on blue', and there were to be many more before the retreat was over. Cavalry was especially vulnerable as it came in sharpish through infantry pickets, often with the Germans close behind. Frank Richards fired his first shot in anger at 'a body of horsemen galloping towards us' who turned out to be the 19th Hussars. Lieutenant-Colonel Edwards of the 20th Hussars described a tragic misunderstanding in his field service notebook: 'On B Squadron leaving the farm they were mistaken by the machine-gun officer for Germans and he opened on them. Amongst the casualties thus caused was Captain Auty [?] who was reported killed by the squadron leader. A most stupid blunder on the part of the MGs.'

The night of 25/26 August, enlivened by alarms for I Corps, was almost universally wretched for II Corps. Most of the 3rd and 4th Divisions did not reach the Le Cateau position till well after dark. Few had eaten that day, and most were soaked to the skin by the persistent rain which had followed a spectacular storm in the late afternoon. Lieutenant C. L. Brereton of 39th Field Battery had detrained at Fresnoy le Grand to be told of a 'strategical retirement' by the Railway Transport Officer. His battery marched to Ligny, on the eastern edge of the position and: 'Eventually moved into boggy field in pitch dark, attempted some supper and lay down for the night extremely wet and uncomfortable'. Henry Owens had been told the 'strategical retirement' story in a more elaborate form: 'Official news — we are ordered not to take the offensive and are awaiting the arrival of our allies. Germans are said to have received a reverse on the Russian frontier: Austrians said to be defeated by the Serbians. Major Irwin full of great wit: most cheery soul. Pat the regimental terrier in great form.' Even his enthusiasm was blunted by the night move from Solesmes to Reumont, where he spent the night: 'Lay down in a straw shed, but slept very little as there was too much row from transport etc passing and I had a sort of feeling we might be left behind and ordered to go at any minute . . . ' Only a few hundred yards away, Corporal Watson passed the night in relative comfort in a barn. 'We were all very confident that evening,' he wrote.

> We heard that we were holding a fully entrenched position, and the General made a speech — I did not hear it — in which he told us that there had been a great Russian success, and that in the battle of the morrow a victory for us would smash the Germans once and for all. But our Captain was more pessimistic. He thought we should suffer a great disaster.

But why did Major-General Fergusson believe that there would be a battle on the 26th? At 7.30 on the evening of the 25th GHQ issued orders for a continuation of the retreat the following day, and Smith-Dorrien embodied these in his own instructions, issued from his headquarters at Bertry, south-west of Le Cateau, at 10.15 that night. Transport was to move off at 3.00 in the morning with infantry main bodies three hours behind. Allenby had not been allocated billets by GHQ, and decided to establish his headquarters in Beaumont, on the main Le Cateau–Cambrai road just north of Bertry. Their circumstances were far from luxurious. 'No food tonight for men or horses,' wrote Sally Home. 'Slept for two hours on a mattress in a small pub, but was woken up every half hour.' It was not till after 11.00 that GHQ's withdrawal orders found their way to Allenby's exhausted staff, and shortly afterwards Lieutenant-Colonel Ansell of the 5th Dragoon Guards rode in to report that his regiment and the 4th Division were now safely off the high ground north of the road.

Allenby saw at once that he was in real trouble. GHQ had ordered him to cover the Le Cateau position till II Corps and 4th Division were clear, but with the ridge abandoned and too few troops under his hand to recover it he could not hope to protect Smith-Dorrien and Snow. He went at once to Bertry and warned Smith-Dorrien that unless II Corps was away by daylight the Germans would be on it. Sir Horace summoned Hubert Hamilton of 3rd Division, whose headquarters were, fortuitously, also in Bertry, and asked him if his men could move whilst it was still dark. Hamilton's reply

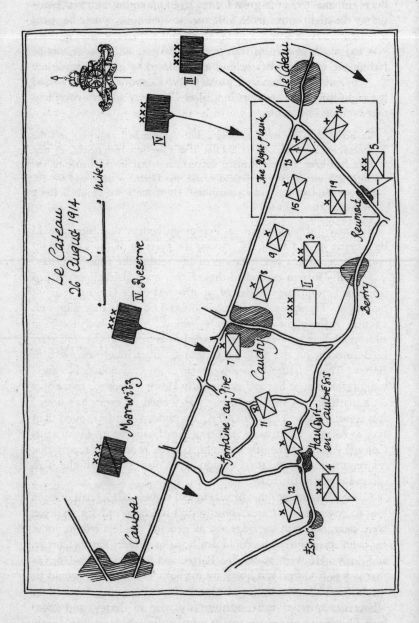

was emphatic. His rearguards were still coming in, and he doubted if the division could start before 9.00 in the morning. Allenby added — and we must wonder quite what the Bull made of the admission — that his own division was 'too much scattered and exhausted to be able to give useful assistance in covering the retreat next day'.

'This was the moment to which the whole of Smith-Dorrien's previous life had been directed,' declares his biographer, A J Smithers, 'and the decision now to be taken must be his alone.' If he retreated as ordered, his corps would be caught in a broken-backed battle south-west of Le Cateau, with Kluck's *IV* and *IV Reserve Corps* surging down from the north, *III Corps* flowing in from the north-east and Marwitz lapping in from the west to unleash cavalry and lorried *jäger* onto columns of exhausted infantry. With II Corps swamped, Haig's flank would be laid bare and the entire Allied left wing would risk being rolled up.

If he stood and fought the danger was scarcely less great. Although Smith-Dorrien could not know how badly the Germans had misjudged the BEF's deployment — Kluck now thought that it was all in line west of Le Cateau, facing east with a view to falling back on the Channel ports — the specific warnings of *Field Service Regulations*, his reading of military history, and the experience of the past few days all left him in no doubt that he risked being the victim of a small-scale Cannae. He would not have been surprised to read Kluck's operation order, written on the evening of the 24th, which proclaimed that 'the envelopment of the British Army, provided it stood, seemed certain'. His acrimonious relationship with Sir John French made decision even harder, for he knew that the field-marshal would not forgive him if things went wrong. *Field Service Regulations* had envisaged exactly this eventuality, but left the burden heavy on the local commander's back. Not only was he authorised to violate letter and spirit of formal orders if 'unexpected local circumstances' arose, but if a subordinate 'neglects to depart from the letter of his orders, when such departure is clearly demanded by circumstances, and failure ensues, he will be held responsible for such failure'.

Smith-Dorrien took his wife's photograph, which had been propped up by his bedside, and tucked it into his tunic, for he was in for a busy night. He announced that he would stand his ground in the hope of administering what he called 'a stopping blow' to the Germans. Allenby, technically under the direct command of GHQ, agreed to fight under his orders, and Snow, who was in the same position, also agreed to do so when one of Smith-Dorrien's staff found him shortly after 5.00 that morning. It was not easy to get orders out from divisional headquarters to brigades. Snow's infantry was 'at it hammer and tongs' not long after Smith-Dorrien's messenger reached him, while two battalions of 14th Brigade east of Le Cateau never heard of the change of plan. Sir Horace could also expect some help from Sordet's corps which was on the last leg of its march round to his eastern flank, and at first hoped for assistance from I Corps. However, at 3.30 he learnt that I Corps was itself under pressure and was himself bidden to march to its support. As French recorded crossly in his diary Smith-Dorrien refused to do so, and 'professed himself unable to move a man'.

Sir Horace sent a message by car to GHQ, where it arrived at 5.00, announcing his decision to fight. Murray was dead to the world, and French was woken to deal with it himself. His reply, the first fragmentary thoughts of an elderly man woken from a short sleep after a series of long and puzzling days, was not unhelpful.

> If you can hold your ground the situation appears likely to improve . . . Although you are given a free hand as to method this telegram is not intended to convey the impression that I am not anxious for you to carry out the retirement, and you must make every endeavour to do so.

At 6.30, having thought more deeply about the situation, French told Henry Wilson to phone Smith-Dorrien, and Sir Horace was duly summoned to the railway telephone in Bertry. Wilson urged him to break off the action as soon as possible and warned him of the danger of 'another Sedan', but when it was apparent that Smith-Dorrien could not be budged — his guns were already in action — Wilson ended by saying: 'good luck to you: yours is the first cheerful voice I have heard for three days'.

We were all decidedly cheerful when the lunch party broke up in a haze of bonhomie and Beaujolais. Having seen Evelyn and Clive safely mounted, I set off through Landrecies with John grinding along in the horse-box behind me, through the Faubourg du Quesnoy where the Coldstream had held off the Germans, over the level crossing and over the Sambre bridge into Landrecies proper. A house north of the bridge still shows the scars of the German shelling, and as we drove slowly down the main street it was not hard to imagine the Grenadier bugles spitting out the 'baba baba baba baa' of the alarm. *Trumpet and Bugle Sounds for the Army* gives its words as ''Larm is sounding, what's up now? Fire or fight, or jolly row? Into togs and off we go,' and Ma Jeffreys might have managed a taut smile because he 'was stark naked having a bath' when the bugles sounded. Alas, most of the guardsmen who tumbled out of these little houses and offices probably remembered the call by its politically incorrect words: 'There's a nigger on the wall! There's a nigger on the wall! There's a nigger on the wall!'

We turned right to leave Landrecies on the tiny D160 which follows the Sambre, and crossed the river again at Ors, on the edge of the forest of Bois L'Evêque, which seems to have been chipped off Mormal by some celestial mason. In the communal cemetery at Ors the poet Wilfred Owen lies alongside two VC winners, Second-Lieutenant James Kirk and Lieutenant-Colonel John Marshall, all killed in the war's final days: the dreadful 'official intimation' of Owen's death did not reach his home until the bells were ringing to celebrate the armistice on 11 November 1918. As we were tracing the route of the British Army of 1914, we might have been forgiven for imagining that most of the white Portland headstones we passed, either in communal cemeteries or in the generally larger Commonwealth War Graves Commission Cemeteries, marked the passage of the original BEF. But most date from 1918, and bear stark witness to the fact that British and Dominion forces in France lost 298,125 officers and men in the last three months of the war, a figure three times greater than the entire BEF which passed this way four years before, or well over twice the size of the Regular Army as I write.

The overwhelming impression is of very young private soldiers — one family, in its anguish and bitterness, has inscribed 'School, War, Death' on their eighteen-year-old son's headstone — and much-decorated NCOs and officers, here present in disproportionate numbers. As the war struck what was all too literally its dying fall, only the charismatic leadership of these lieutenant-colonels in their twenties (subalterns, so many of them, in 1914) and corporals with DCMs and MMs could hold an army of boys to a grindstone which showered young lives like sparks.

The British soldier has a knack of misunderstanding French. At the siege of Badajoz in 1812 the mutually-encouraging calls of French sentries — 'Sentinelle, garde à vous' — were translated as 'all's well in Badahoo'. The spine-tingling rattle of the *pas de charge* (one officer described it as 'the rum dum, the rum dum, the rum dum dummadum dum dum') was known, for reasons I cannot fathom, as 'old trousers', and pickets would look to their priming as the word went out 'look sharp, for here comes old trousers'. The faintly incongruous onion-dome impaled by the spire of St Martin's church rises briskly while the rest of Le Cateau-Cambrésis still yawns in the valley of the little Selle. The town's name was too much of a mouthful for the footsore warriors of the BEF, who pronounced it Leacatoo as if to rhyme with Waterloo.

The occasional Wykehamist or Etonian amongst the officer corps might have remembered something about the Treaty of Cateau-Cambrésis, signed there between the French and Spaniards in 1559, which ended the Italian wars and gave France the three strategically-important Lorraine bishoprics of Metz, Toul and Verdun. It would have taken a very sharp young officer to have known that it was also the birthplace of the painter Matisse, but the fact that it was also the home of Napoleon's Marshal Adolphe Mortier, Duke of Treviso, was more obvious, for the great man's statue glares sternly down the narrow square towards the attractive seventeenth-century town hall.

Old Mortier cannot have been favourably impressed by the sudden departure of GHQ from the old school at the far end of the square. No more was James Jack, taken from regimental duty to act as Staff Captain when 19th Brigade had formed. He had reported to GHQ on the afternoon of the 25th to find:

> the staff, clerks and typewriters are all 'in full swing', apparently free from any anxiety whatsoever. Tea cups and the remains of cakes lie on the tables. A charming, well-dressed, easy-mannered young staff officer hears the little I know of the day's operations, says that the 19th Brigade will billet here tonight and that orders will be sent to it. Finally, he remarks sympathetically 'You must be famished; go and have a good feed in an estaminet and come back in an hour'.

Jack duly sloped away and ate a large omelette and as many buttered rolls as he could hold and returned to find that: 'There is not a soul in the building, not a pen, all have "flown" with every stitch they possess'.

We wound through the Faubourg de Landrecies and then turned back on ourselves through the shuttered redbrick of the Rue de Fesmy into the Rue de Marche aux Chevaux, to reach the Centre Equestre du Cateau, where the horses were to spend the night. John's arched eyebrows announced that it was not exactly Hyde Park Barracks, but everyone was extraordinarily helpful — they had no hay but some soon materialised in the characteristically beat-up Renault van — and we had Jeopardy and Thatch stabled, and their tack cleaned, long before Evelyn and Clive arrived. So long, indeed, that we had drunk several cups of coffee in the rather threadbare clubhouse and were all privately wondering what on earth could have happened when they appeared. It transpired that if Jacques Decool was monarch of Mormal his writ ran less confidently outside: they had got lost near Ors and Evelyn had map-read them safely into Le Cateau.

We spent the night at the Hotel Florida, where the Guise road climbs out of the town. It was hard to imagine anything less like Florida. The blank house-fronts were broken by an archway with the hotel on one side and its café on another. The *patron* — an ex-soldier whose parachuting certificate hung beside his wife's English diplomas in the tiny lobby — was a pleasant but uncommunicative northerner married to a Spaniard, an appropriate union in view of Le Cateau's past. The Duke of Parma's men had trailed their pikes over its cobbles on their long journey up the 'Spanish road' that took them up through Burgundy, along the chain of Spanish garrisons in Lorraine, to Flanders and the Netherlands. On our own for the first time since leaving England, which was something of a relief, we ate at the hotel and then turned in. I made the mistake of switching on the television, and saw a snowstorm through which an exceedingly rude film could just be discerned. I did not even bother to adjust the set but fell into a dreamless sleep.

Early starts were beginning to lose their shock effect, and morning stables went quicker each day as the team shook down. We had the horses boxed by 9.00 a.m. and were on our way through Le Cateau along the Roman road which leads to Cambrai. Marshal Mortier was there on his pedestal, surveying the square full of Thursday-morning bustle. The centre of Le Cateau has changed so little that Frank Richards, who reached it at midnight on the 25/26th, would have recognised it at once.

The Royal Welch camped on the square in the centre of the town. We were told to get as much rest as we could. The majority sank down where they were and fell straight asleep. Although dead beat, Billy, Stevens and I went on a scrounge for food and drink. We entered a café, where there were lots of officers of other battalions, besides a couple of staff officers, mixed up with ordinary troops, all buying food and drink . . . I slept the sleep of the just that night, for about three hours. I could have done with forty-three, but we were roused up at 4 a.m. and ordered to leave our packs and greatcoats on the square . . . At dawn we marched out of Le Cateau with fixed bayonets. Duffy said: 'We'll have a bang at the bastards to-day.'

Nobby Clarke of the Bays must have passed Richards very early that morning as 1st Cavalry Brigade rode through the town to pick up the Guise road. He found it 'all very confused . . . as there was a lot of blokes just lying around in the streets. They looked as tired and browned off as any of us and probably hadn't had any food or drink either.'

The Cambrai road leaves Le Cateau through a cutting and crosses our familiar *Chaussée Brunehaut* just beyond it. It then runs, straight as a die, on towards Cambrai twelve miles away. On leaving Mormal we had crossed one of the major geographical frontiers on our route, as the sedimentary rock beneath Hainault gives way to the chalk of the Cambrésis. We had escaped from the 'close, blind country' of Mons and the sprawling villages to its south into a new landscape of long, rolling ridges dotted with small woods and tight, nucleated villages, each a mile or two apart so that plough-horses could plod out to a village's furthest fields and do a day's work. To the north of the road the ground rose into the broad, irregular ridge from which 4th Division had covered II Corps' retreat on the 25th, and to the south another gentle ridge, with the spire of Bertry just visible above it, marked the front of II Corps' position.

Hard on our left as we crossed the *Chaussée Brunehaut* was a knuckle of high ground held by the Suffolks of the exhausted 14th Brigade. The other two brigades of 5th Division, 13th and 15th, stood south of the road as far as the village of Troisvilles, where 3rd Division took the line on to Caudry with 9th Brigade behind Beaumont, 8th around Audencourt and 7th at Caudry. 4th Division, which still lacked its heavy battery, divisional cavalry and supporting services, buttressed Smith-Dorrien's left, with its three brigades stretching from Fontaine-au-Pire to Esnes.

We unboxed all four horses beside the church in Audencourt, right in the centre of Smith-Dorrien's position, and rode eastwards along a track which runs parallel with the main road and about 1000 yards from it. The infantry brigades facing the road had deployed in two rough lines, one 200–500 yards from the road and the other level with our track. Some battalions availed themselves of the trenches dug by the French, but others had to do their best with their entrenching tools, scratching out what Lieutenant E. H. W. Backhouse of the Suffolks called 'lying trenches', six feet long

1 Officers of 2nd Scottish Rifles at Le Cateau, 26 August 1914.

2 Le Cateau: 122nd Battery's gun-line was just to the left of the sunken lane, engaging Germans attacking from left to right. Lieutenant Lutyens and his fellow section commanders were in the road itself. The spire of Le Cateau church breaks the horizon on the right: the water tower in the centre stands above the cutting that takes the Cambrai road through the Montay spur.

3 Cerizy, looking up the valley with the San Quentin road, lined with low trees, crossing its head in the distance. Puisieux Farm is in the trees above Jeopardy's right ear, and *2nd Guard Dragoons* were on the slope where his left ear meets a patch of light stubble. Major Swetenham's squadron of the Greys fired from the forward edge of the wood on the extreme left, and the Lancers made their covered approach up the re-entrant immediately in front of us to charge on the axis that we now face.

4 Patrol of the 18th Hussars talking to Belgian civilians on the outskirts of Mons, 21 August 1914. It is a scorching day: the horses have fringes to keep the flies from their eyes and one of the troopers has rolled down his neck-cover.

5 'This broken torrent of dusty misery...' French refugees pass through a control point manned by British staff officers.

6 Néry: Captain Bradbury's grave.

7 Death on the uplands: a roadside grave near Nampcel.

8 'The 4th Hussars had been ordered to hold the forest edge...'
A German view of the Forest of Retz.

9 Cavalry on the Retreat.

10 The long slog: infantry on the Retreat.

11 Old Bill: British infantryman in
field service marching order,
August 1914.

12 Lieutenant Frederick Arkwright,
11th Hussars, in bivouac on the last day
of the retreat. He had fought at Néry
but was to die outside Ypres
in October 1914.

13 Unsung heroes: Horses of the German *4th Cavalry Division* buried at Haelen,
where the Belgians fought a successful delaying action.

14 Mons: Ollie, Evelyn, Clive and John in the Grande Place.

15 Men of A Company, 4th Battalion Royal Fusiliers, some of them with less than a day to live, in the Grande Place at Mons on 23 August 1914.

16 Alfresco lunch in the drizzle on the field of Le Cateau. The track behind us
winds up onto the knoll so bravely held by the Suffolks
and their supporting gunners on 26 August 1914.

17 Mortefontaine: leaving the Commandery.

and nine inches deep with the spoil piled up at the end facing the enemy.

Both the artillery commanders of the forward divisions — Brigadier-General Wing for 3rd Division and Brigadier-General Headlam for 5th Division — were convinced that the infantry would only stand the imminent shock if intimately supported by their gunner brothers. Batteries were accordingly pushed well forward: on our left as we rode were the gun-lines XXIII Brigade RFA, with two sections dug right into the infantry firing-line with orders not to fire until the final assault. Thatch fell comfortably into his stride, cunningly waiting until I was busy with map or binoculars to snatch at maize-leaves, and historical theory and the realities of the ground meshed inseparably. As we approached Troisvilles, Clive asked me where a battery commander would place his guns. I explained that he would try to tuck them into one of the tiny folds in the ground — 'like that one, with the cattle-trough in it' — and, sure enough, when I consulted the map, giving Thatch, now warming to his task, another light snack, there was a section of 121st Battery RFA, covered from frontal fire and enjoying an enfilade shoot across the front of 1st Northumberland Fusiliers south of Inchy.

We zig-zagged through Troisvilles, passing the church and the presbytery. George Barrow spent the night before the battle in the building: oddly enough he had been there to learn French as a boy, and had the same bed that he had slept in thirty years before. The village was held by 1st Dorset of Gleichen's brigade, with 1st Bedford in trenches on their right, just on the other side of the road that joins Troisvilles with the Cambrai road. The remnants of 1st Cheshire were in support, in a dip just north of the village cemetery, a section of 120th Battery RFA nestling into a covered position beside them. Gleichen himself was in a 'hollow sandy road' behind the Bedfords.

The ground had changed so little that the personal accounts which I carried with me, stuffed into the pockets of my lumberjack shirt (today, thank goodness, there were no appearances to keep up), might have been written the day before. In 1914 there was a superb field of fire stretching out towards the main road: in 1993 we watched a Norbert Dentressangle lorry sailing calmly through the beaten zone of the Bedfords' musketry. In 1914 the corn had been cut and stooked, and there were patches of sugar-beet: there was stubble and beet there in 1993.

The differences were tiny. The shoulder-high corn of 1914 was piled in stooks which were big enough to hide a man. Walter Bloem later watched the *Rathenow Hussars* quarter these very fields, rooting out stragglers from corn-stooks: 'The Hussars did not trouble to ransack every stook, but found that simply by galloping in threes or fours through a field shouting, and with lowered lances spiking a stook here and there, anyone hiding in them anywhere in the field surrendered'. In 1993 the corn was in more prosaic bales, and we trotted on deep into the sunken road to avoid a tractor towing a bail-laden trailer. Our weather was certainly warmer. Gleichen remembered that he wore a pullover under his tunic till 11.00 a.m., which was about the time that I rolled up my shirtsleeves. But at lunchtime even the weather took its cue from history's script, and a shower had us in waterproofs and the horses in New Zealand rugs.

Gleichen's right rear battalion, 1st Norfolk, was in our sunken road, the men in fire positions on the steep bank and the officers able to walk — or even ride — along the track without being engaged. However, the only tree in the landscape, so distinctive that it was marked on the 1914 map as *L'Arbre Rond*, gave German observation officers away on the slope across the main road a convenient aiming-mark. Lieutenant-Colonel Ballard told his pioneer sergeant to take it down, but as soon as the tree was half-cut the wind swung in from the south and threatened to blow it into the road: for Gleichen, anxious to preserve this covered lateral route, this would have been 'a real disaster'. The pioneers had to guy the tree up with ropes until eventually it was hauled down in the right direction. We stopped by a replacement, standing on the same spot as the old tree, and still shown as *L'Arbre Rond* by the Institut Géographique National. I scrambled up the bank to take photographs. The spire of Le Cateau church was in sight, two and a half miles away to the east, and a small clump of trees a mile closer marked the position of the Suffolks, the right-hand forward battalion of 5th Division.

We rode on down the track, looking for another track to our right which would take us to Reumont past the little Bois des Dix-Sept. There was no sign of it, and by the time we had realised that it was not going to appear as scheduled we had almost reached the *Chaussée Brunehaut*. I recognised the spot from one of the best descriptions of the battle, its images so striking that the Official History lifted them wholesale. It was the gun-line of XXVIII Brigade RFA, its three batteries — 122nd, 123rd and 124th — deployed

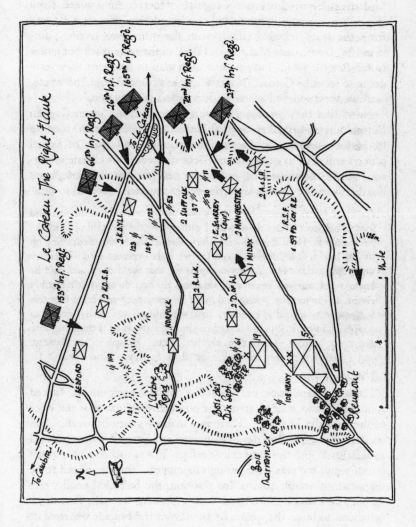

in numerical order from the road. 122nd Battery had been designated to support the original retirement and was well-sited with its guns partly dug in, but the other two batteries were more exposed. Lieutenant Lionel Lutyens, a regular officer commissioned from Woolwich in 1909, commanded the left section of 122nd Battery from the track where I stood, with the other two section commanders, Lieutenants McLeod and Peel, in the same track but closer to the Roman Road. Lutyens had been glad to hear that they were going to leave Le Cateau. 'It was a hopeless place to hold,' he wrote, 'and we were relieved when we had orders to move on.'

News that they were not moving after all came when Captain Bartholomew, Brigadier-General Headlam's Staff Captain, rode up to Major Stevens, the battery commander, and then beckoned officers and men to gather round. Second-Lieutenant Clarrie Hodgson, newly-commissioned and responsible for the field telephone link between the battery and brigade headquarters, listened to him.

He came over, dismounted, and stood up on one of the limbers and looked out over all the chaps who'd gathered round and told us what the situation was. He said it was very, very, serious and he was depending on us. He left us in no doubt as to what we were expected to do when we went into action. He said it was up to us, that we'd done well and he knew we'd do well again and wouldn't let him down. I felt terribly elated. I was terribly young and quite inexperienced and I felt that this was something really exciting, that something was really going to happen in my life. I wasn't scared or apprehensive at all. I thought more about my brother — my twin brother, Victor. He was in 124 Battery, and I hadn't seen him at all though their battery position wasn't far away.

Having taken stock of XXVIII Brigade's position we turned southwards and walked across the stubble to the track at the edge of the Bois des Dix-Sept. There is a shallow valley between it and the next copse, the Bois des Maronniers, and Smith-Dorrien ordered 19th Brigade into this convenient refuge. It was tucked neatly away out of view, but was close enough to support what he judged to be the most vulnerable part of his position, the Suffolks' knoll overlooking Le Cateau. The Royal Welch Fusiliers were the first of its battalions to leave the town. As the last of the brigade departed at about 6.00 p.m. there were shouts of 'The Uhlans are in the town,' and both 1st Middlesex and 1st Cameronians made what a Middlesex officer called 'a lively exit' covered by the Cameronians' pickets and machine-guns. The brigade turned left at the cross-roads where the

Roman roads meet and marched up the hill towards Reumont, through 2nd King's Own Yorkshire Light Infantry, 13th Brigade's right-hand battalion, covering the intersection. Lieutenant Robert Money, the Cameronians' machine-gun officer who had already earned James Jack's approval for the way he had handled his weapons that morning, wrote: 'see no one I know. Trenches rather pathetic as only entrenching tools used — better than nothing.' Lieutenant Godsell saw the infantry 'digging like beavers with any tool they could find but there was a great lack of tools, some of the infantry had their entrenching tools but they were not very efficient, some were using their bayonets, anything to get down a little deeper'.

19th Brigade turned off the road in Reumont and made its way down a farm track to reach its new position. We tied up one of our journey's loose ends as we trotted along the same track. Smith-Dorrien had commanded 19th Brigade in the Boer War and Evelyn commanded it now, from a building called Smith-Dorrien House. I tried to photograph him as he sat Jeopardy almost precisely on the spot occupied by his predecessor, Major-General Drummond, on 26th August 1914, but Thatch is the sworn enemy of steady camera-work, and I ended up with half a reel of stubble and grey ears.

Corporal Watson had seen 5th Division's heavy battery on the move a day or two previously. 'The old 108th passed by,' he wrote, 'huge good-natured guns, each drawn by eight gigantic plough-horses.' Bad jokes about 'gambardiers' would have been out of place, for its commander, Major Christopher de Sausmarez, was a peer's nephew and a baronet commanded one of his sections. De Sausmarez was one of the first to hear that the corps would be making a stand, and in the thick mist the big Clydesdales hauled their 60-pounders off the *chaussée* and down the track that leads to the Bois Maronnier while the major went on to set up his 'observing station' on the crest to his front, looking across the sunken road a mile away.

We crossed 108th Battery's gun-line and on the northern edge of Reumont turned right onto the road. Fergusson's headquarters was in the second house in the village, now on our immediate left. It once bore a plaque announcing the fact but this has long since gone, although there are still tell-tale holes in the wall. Fergusson's staff had built a wooden platform on the roof of the house, reached by a ladder from the back garden, and the general, his chief of staff and the commander of his signal company spent most of the day up there. Telephone operators manned lines to brigades from trenches on either side of the road, and a signals clerk sat at a table in the garden with cyclists and motor cyclists — Corporal Watson amongst them — lurking expectantly.

We did not stay on the main road for long, and crossed it to head north-east towards Le Cateau and approach 14th Brigade's position from the rear. Time was not on our side and we trotted down a long track with maize on our right and open downland on our left. The temptation was too much for Thatch, who nearly succeeded in decanting me when he made a determined lunge at the maize, and we reached the obelisk in the centre of the Suffolks' position with much badinage about my risk of becoming the last casualty of Le Cateau.

It is not hard to see why Lieutenant-Colonel Brett's battalion was posted up here. A long spur points north-eastwards from the main Reumont ridge, ending in the village of Montay, the other side of the Cambrai road: the cutting just outside Le Cateau takes the road through this spur. The town lies a mile to the north-east, and that strange spire — which peers omnisciently over the horizon from so many viewpoints in 5th Division's sector — is clearly visible. But why was such vital ground held by a single battalion? 1st Duke of Cornwall's Light Infantry and two companies of 2nd East Surrey had been bivouacked east of Le Cateau and did not get word of the change of plan, leaving Brigadier-General Rolt with only half his brigade: he decided, not unreasonably, to place his only other intact battalion, 1st Manchester, in support of the Suffolks.

If infantry was thin on the ground, the position was thick with gunners. Lieutenant-Colonel Stevens of XV Brigade had brought 52nd, 37th Howitzer, 80th and 11th Batteries right up onto the spur. Mindful of Headlam's insistence on providing really intimate support, and under the impression his brigade would be fought to the finish, he had the guns of 80th Battery, initially in covered positions, worked right forward by hand. Lieutenant Rory Macleod of 80th Battery was called forward to his battery observation post to be told that the corps was standing its ground. 'A hundred yards ahead of us on top of the ridge the Suffolks were hastily digging themselves in with their entrenching tools. This was the front line! As the mist began to clear we could see the high ground across the River Selle on our right flank. I heard Major Birley ask the Colonel, "Who is occupying it?" and the Colonel replied, "First Corps".'

Given the primitive nature of communications and their desire to hearten the infantry with their physical presence the gunners had some cause to deploy so close to the firing-line, but, on balance, they would have been wiser staying further back, dominating ground with fire: this was indeed the policy adopted by Brigadier-General Milne of 4th Division. When the battle began German counter-battery fire not only did cruel damage to the guns but also fell amongst the very infantry they were meant to aid. John Lucy, away to the left in Caudry, was at first heartened to hear a battery come into action just behind him, but gratitude turned to dismay as 'blinding flashes of concentrated explosions licked all about our single gallant field battery, which had been quickly marked down by the enemy, and which gradually slackened fire until it was ultimately smashed into silence'.

More serious for 14th Brigade was the problem identified by Birley. As we now know, the heights across the Selle were unoccupied and I Corps was in full retreat. 1st Cavalry Brigade and the detached elements of 14th Brigade, which fell back southwards, at first prevented the Germans from exploiting the valley of the Selle, but as the day wore on the Germans seeped inexorably down this natural conduit round 5th Division's right flank. We rode off the Suffolks' position down one of the re-entrants reaching up into the spur from the valley, and it was evident that however gallantly the Suffolks defended their front they could do nothing about Germans trickling round into their rear.

The first shots were fired in Le Cateau itself, when 19th Brigade held off German cavalry at the same time as the Duke of Cornwall's and the East Surreys, formed up ready to move by the railway bridge in the Faubourg de Landrecies, were surprised by elements of the German *7th Infantry Division*, who had spent the night on the south-west edge of Mormal and crept into Le Cateau under cover of the mist. Most of the British infantry fell back southwards, assisted by 1st and 3rd Cavalry Brigades, which were taking the Guise road, and eventually struck west across the Selle to rejoin 5th Division.

On the left flank, too, the battle began with a costly surprise. 1st King's Own of 12th Brigade was formed up ready to begin entrenching when it was caught by accurate long-range machine-gun fire and then shelled: it lost 400 men in a matter of minutes. Continued pressure on 12th Brigade, assailed by *2nd Cavalry Division* and two *jäger* battalions, persuaded Brigadier-General Wilson to pull back behind the Warnelle ravine. Lieutenant Brereton, whose battery came into action near Ligny-Haucourt to support the retirement recalled how: 'Infantry were coming hurriedly down the slopes towards us and through us. Most of them looked quite exhausted and it was evident that they had been badly cut up . . . Wounded were being hastily dressed by the side of the road, but it was obvious that there were no ambulances, and practically no medical arrangements.' By 11.00 a.m. the British left was secure for the moment, and even 11th Brigade, somewhat forward of the main line, was holding its ground south-west of Caudry with great tenacity.

From early morning onwards the battle followed a consistent pattern, with the flanks most heavily engaged and the centre — which enjoyed those superb shoots across the Cambrai road — treated with more circumspection. But all this time German artillery pounded British positions with a fire to which Smith-Dorrien's guns could make little effective response. There was one notable exception. At about noon, as the light improved, 108th Battery took a group of guns at Croix-Caluyau on the *Chaussée Brunehaut* due north of Le Cateau, and as Major de Sausmarez observed, 'the guns . . . appeared to cease firing soon after the battery had found their range, whilst those closer began to sweep and search for the battery, whose position, however, was so well concealed that they never brought really effective fire to bear on it'.

The right flank crumbled first. The Suffolks were not only pelted by shrapnel and high explosive but were machine-gunned from the spire of St Martin's church. Lieutenant-Colonel Brett was shot through the head early on, and his second-in-command, Major Doughty, took over. As casualties mounted amongst the Suffolks, 1st Argyll and Sutherland Highlanders of 19th Brigade went up to help them: two companies came into line on the Suffolks' right, just in time to face the first major infantry attack in this quarter as *7th Division* came on in solid masses. By now — it was mid-morning — the batteries on the spur were badly knocked about: 11th Battery had lost all its officers and retained only enough men to serve a single gun.

Things were no better down by the cross-roads, where Lieutenant Tom Butt of the King's Own Yorkshire Light Infantry had been told quite firmly that his battalion was to stay put. He was encouraged by the loyal support furnished by 122nd and 123rd Batteries — he watched a battery commander and his sergeant-major serve one gun till it ran out of ammunition — but reflected that it was 'shocking seeing one's friends of all ranks lying dead. Somehow the sight of dead horses sickened us even more. They were not free men like us.' Just behind him, Lionel Lutyens was also under pressure. One of his gunners was shot dead by a sniper within the first half hour, and later the gun-line was raked by a machine-gun that the Germans had worked up onto the spur.

The plight of the Suffolks worsened by the minute. The Manchesters sent a company and a machine-gun to prolong their line southwards and hold off German infantry coming up out of the valley, and soon two more Manchester companies went up, with the remainder of the Argylls. Both battalions lost heavily before they even reached the knoll and, once there, were subjected to the same hurricane of fire that winnowed the Suffolks. The Germans had already dragged machine-guns onto the lip of the cutting on the Cambrai road — it was probably one of these that hit 122nd Battery — and followed them with two field howitzers which silenced the last of 11th Battery's guns with direct fire.

Smith-Dorrien was no mean horseman and he needed all his skill that day. At midday he galloped under the shrapnel-puffs to see Fergusson in Reumont. He thought that as the Germans were so close he would have to counter-attack before he could disengage, but postponed his decision for the moment. No sooner had Smith-Dorrien gone than Fergusson saw that, as the Official History gently puts it, 'the right of his division was shaken and might give way'. Soon afterwards he warned the corps commander that a German division was well round his right flank — it was in fact his opposite number, the German *5th Division*, part of *III Corps* — and ten minutes later he suggested that unless he was sent assistance he ought to withdraw. This delicacy shrouds the unmistakable fact that some units were beginning to drift backwards out of the shells. De Sausmarez saw how 'one line retired slowly past the battery's observing station, there were no officers with it'. Another gunner officer was ashamed to see some of the infantry 'run like rabbits'. Watson, standing by the roadside in Reumont, knew that things were bad when broken batteries began to come back: 'There were teams with only a limber and without a gun . . . There were bits of teams and teams with only a couple of drivers. The faces of the men were awful, I smiled at one or two, but they shook their heads and turned away.'

It was evident to all observers that the Suffolks and King's Own Yorkshire Light Infantry could not last much longer, and Fergusson's gunners began to profit from a brief lull to start extracting their guns. The hours between 1.00 and 3.00 p.m. were a gunner's nightmare. The Royal Regiment of Artillery carries no colours. On parade, its guns are treated with the respect accorded to regimental colours, and their loss in action has always been a deeply painful matter. But as battery captains began to lead teams forwards out of the dead ground around Reumont we may doubt whether any abstract sense of honour or fear of disgrace nerved men to undertake a task which killed so many of them. There was the absurd disciplined familiarity of it all: Captain Jones walking on at the head of the column as if he was bringing the battery back up the Packway after a day on the ranges at Larkhill; Charlie, C subsection's off-lead baring his teeth at his stablemate Cuthbert, and drivers giving an 'eyes right' to Brigadier-General Headlam on his reeking charger. Then there was the knowledge that their comrades had been in action for six long hours under a fire so heavy that it had been difficult to get ammunition up to them: 37th (Howitzer) Battery had expended all its ammunition and 52nd Battery had fired 1,100 rounds. Drivers knew that only the arrival of the teams could save guns and mates alike, and when some battery captains called for volunteers, sadly aware that they would not need all their teams because guns had already been destroyed, there was no shortage of takers.

Teams broke into a gallop as they crossed the crest-line — 2nd Royal West Kents rose to their feet to cheer 122nd Battery's teams as they bucketed past — and made for their battery positions. We will let the fate of two of 5th Division's batteries speak for all. German infantry was so close to 122nd Battery, down there in front of the sunken road where it joins the _chaussée_, that gunners were crumpling to rifle-fire when, as Clarrie Hodgson heard,

> the order came down — _Save the guns!_ And the gun teams came dashing down, over the hill, right through the middle of all this carnage. And then the Hun opened up on them — artillery, machine-guns, everything! The horses were silhouetted against the skyline and made a perfect target. It was _absolute slaughter_! Men and horses were just blown to pieces.

'One of my teams was the only one that escaped unscathed,' recorded Lionel Lutyens.

> They drove straight up the road, limbered up and galloped away. It was very smart and good . . . My second team wasn't so lucky. They got as far as the sunken road and the leaders jibbed. The driver flogged them

onto the road and then one leader fell. A sergeant of mine and myself had just pulled him out of the way when the other leader fell, and then the driver. We were busy at the second horse when down came the near centre, and down came the off centre, and the driver. The horses fell so quietly it was hard to realise they were shot.

'We were still in position, doing what we could, although we were practically cut off by the Hun and realised our position was hopeless,' remembered Second-Lieutenant Hodgson. 'Our Colonel, the adjutant and two battery commanders had been killed, and the place was a shambles. Then, to our intense relief, came the order — *Every man for himself. Destroy the guns.*' Hodgson raced over to one of the guns and smashed its sight, then ran up the hill with a gunner carrying its breech-block. Lutyens was the last man off the position.

My groom had been standing waiting all the time with my two horses on the bank behind . . . I was so trembling with excitement and funk by now that I couldn't get my foot in the stirrup. I ran backwards trying to reach it, and expecting Bronco to be hit at any moment. However he was not, and I got up and let him go down the road as fast as he could gallop. We were bent over our horses' necks all the way down the road, as bullets were still flying pretty thick . . . it was an extraordinary sight, a wild short scene of galloping and falling horses, and then everyone gone, dead horses and dead men everywhere, four guns left solitary on the position, a few wagon limbers lying about, and one standing on the skyline with its pole straight up in the air. *Voilà tout.*

Up on the Suffolks' knoll, Rory Macleod was busy on one of 80th Battery's two surviving guns when he turned to see 'all the brigade teams racing up at a gallop led by Major Tailyour the Brigade Major . . . Shells were bursting all round them. It was a magnificent sight! Now and then a man or a horse or a whole team would go down. It was like Balaklava all over again!' Captain Douglas Reynolds led 37th (Howitzer) Battery's teams up its gun-line astride a sunken track just to the Suffolks' left front: he got four guns away but could not find teams to save the other two, so disabled them and returned to Reumont. There he appealed for volunteers to make a second attempt, and with Lieutenant Earle, who had already been wounded, he took the teams back up the spur. German infantrymen were already on the position and, to their great credit, they waved their arms at the oncoming teams and told the drivers to surrender. A month or two later, soldiers on either side, sensibilities blunted by suffering and enthusiasm rusted by dashed hopes of quick victory, would have shot the teams down with little remorse. But in August 1914, men still had illusions, and it came hard, especially for the 'tough, healthy countrymen' who made up the bulk of German infantry, to fire on those quiet bays coming steadily up the stubbled slope as if they were hauling a hay wain in Anhalt or Thuringia.

The teams walked till the last 300 yards and then broke into a gallop. The first galloped up to F subsection, and the wheel driver, Fred Luke, swung the limber so smartly that its hook was right over the trail eye, enabling Sergeant Butterworth and two surviving gunners (one of them a volunteer from D subsection) to limber up. They made for the track where Earle and Reynolds were waiting, but as they reached it Driver Coby of the centre pair was shot dead. As he fell backwards his whip spun into the air; Reynolds grabbed it and rode alongside the horses, keeping them at their work.

E subsection's team lost a leader, and Earle was helping Sergeant Bower — hit four times already — to unhook the wheelers to give them a chance to get the gun away when both wheelers fell and he himself was shot through the arm. He grabbed the wounded limb with his sound hand and shouted 'It's no good, you'll have to clear out'. The men took him at his word but, as Earle later wrote, describing the episode in the third person: 'That true Scot, Gunner Frazer, did not mean to lose his greatcoat and ran back to the limber to get it. Amazed, Earle turned his head to watch him and so the shot he received was only a glancing one through forehead and eye.' Sergeant Bower rode back and found him reeling along: Bower threw the wounded officer onto his horse but that too was shot, so he helped Earle all the way back to Reumont, and put him aboard one of 108th Battery's spare horses. It was 'not much fun on the bareback of a Clydesdale at the best of times', complained Earle.

Douglas Reynolds, Fred Luke and E subsection's lead driver, Job Drain, received the VC for their exploit; Bower and Trumpeter Waldron received the DCM. Reynolds wrote to Earle's mother to point out that he had actually recommended her son for the VC, and considered that he was especially deserving because his own section was already safe and it was not his duty to go back. Young Earle was eventually awarded the DSO, and made a good recovery from his wounds: the loss of an eye did not prevent him from becoming a brigadier in the next war. Like all mounted officers he had worn his sword that day, but jettisoned it after he was wounded.

It was picked up by a German officer who returned it to the Earle family — who have it still.

Lieutenant-Colonel Stevens of XXVIII Brigade had been wounded in the spine at the start of the battle but had stayed in his observation post on the Suffolks' position, and although Major Tailyour told him that some of the guns were now safe Stevens refused to withdraw without a direct order. By now the German infantry were almost on the knoll. Major Doughty of the Suffolks had been wounded while taking ammunition to his machine-guns, and command devolved on Major Peebles. Between 2.30 and 2.45 p.m. the Germans boiled in from front, right flank and rear. The Suffolks had little ammunition left, but the Argyll companies made good practice, two officers bringing down man after man and counting their scores aloud as if at a competition.

Major Peebles found himself in the same ghastly situation as Major Chetwynd-Stapylton of the Cheshires at Audregnies. If there was to be anything like a formal surrender it must occur before widespread hand-to-hand fighting, in which the officers on both sides would lose control and which the exhausted and outnumbered British could not hope to win. He stood up and ordered his men to cease firing. Lieutenant Backhouse thought that the surrender opened 'a black page in my life', for he did not return to England till 1919, but thought that Peebles was right. As it was, 2nd Battalion The Suffolk Regiment was effectively destroyed as a fighting force, with only two officers (quartermaster and transport officer) and 250 men left at the end of the day. XXVIII Brigade's nearby observation post was also overrun: Lieutenant-Colonel Stevens and his staff were captured, as was Major Jones, commander of 37th (Howitzer) Battery.

By now the sorely-tried 5th Division had at last been given permission to withdraw. At 1.40 p.m. Smith-Dorrien put the remaining battalions of 19th Brigade at Fergusson's disposal, told him to hold his ground a little longer to permit preliminary moves to be carried out, but to move when he saw fit: 3rd and 5th Divisions would follow his lead. It was not a moment too soon. Reumont was now like an antechamber of hell. Corporal Watson saw 'a big waggon drawn by two maddened horses come dashing down into the main street. They could not turn, but went straight into the wall of a house opposite. There was a dull crash and a squirming heap piled at the edge of the road.' The divisional signals wagon was obliterated by a direct hit (making it impossible to trace the details of

Fergusson's conduct of the battle), HE shells, bursting on rooftops, filled the air with splintered tiles, and houses caught fire.

James Jack had spent the day at 19th Brigade's command post on the crest just north-east of Reumont — just where we had crossed it — under sporadic fire:

> one shell burst so close to Turner (ADC) sitting on his horse that I momentarily thought both of them must be blown to bits. Neither of them was touched, and the only notice taken of the explosion by the Brigadier was an indignant glance; perhaps it had wakened him from a 'nap.' . . . When not busy we slept, except one on watch; the corn sheaves were so comfortable, the day so warm, and we were *so tired*.

He had just delivered a message to 108th Battery when the brigade commander returned from Fergusson's headquarters with news of the withdrawal, and told him to 'get some infantry on our particular front to hold their ground long enough to cover it'.

This was easier said than done. Jack — who, let us remember, had been junior captain in his battalion, commanding a platoon only a week before — had to persuade a commanding officer whose men had spent the day in mortal danger to turn back and prop up a position which was all too evidently collapsing. He walked forward — his groom had been wounded and his horses were missing — and met part of a battalion 'leisurely retiring in extended order'. His suggestion that it might stand 'was received with an incredulous stare, as if it were a demand for a money subscription . . . it passed on without stopping, I feeling rather daunted'. He had better luck with the two surviving Argyll companies 'marching quietly back in open order with tall, handsome Colonel Moulton-Barrett at their head. He answered the invitation to oppose the enemy a little longer by calling out "93rd (their old regimental number), about turn", the movement being executed on the spot with almost parade exactitude; his Highlanders were then again led forward to a suitable crest nearby.'

108th Battery began to thin out at about this time. One section was ordered away by Brigadier-General Headlam, but a gun came to grief in a ditch — Godsell observed that 'if language could effect a cure it would have been jog-trotting down the road some time ago' — and had to be abandoned. The remaining section took on infantry on the Suffolks' old position: 'Somewhat indiscreetly, they massed within a range of about 3200 [yards] from our two heavy guns. A Lyddite shell, bursting apparently in the middle of the mass, dispersed it again to the far side of the crest.' The guns kept up a continuous fire until ordered to retire, when 'they never checked their pace, a trot, until they were well clear of German artillery fire'. Lieutenant Pennycuick, his sappers in a firing line on a crest looking out towards the Suffolks' knoll, thought that the battery had done wonders: 'We could hear it fire and listened as the salvos passed over to watch eagerly for the burst. Time after time a huge gap would be mown in an enemy line of men; the fine shooting of these few remaining guns acted as a tonic to our morale.'

The withdrawal of 5th Division went better than might have been expected. Its artillery had suffered very severely, and the Suffolks and associated troops had been lost. The King's Own Yorkshire Light Infantry, down at the junction of the two Roman roads, was overwhelmed at about 3.30 p.m. Tom Butt was lying wounded beside his company commander Charlie Luther, a county cricketer. A German officer approached and recognised Luther, with whom he had played cricket; he took both British officers to a field hospital in Le Cateau. Further to the left, Gleichen watched 'lines of troops belonging to different battalions and even different brigades . . . retiring slowly over the open ground and under a heavy fire of shrapnel which seemed to do extraordinarily little damage'. The Germans nearly succeeded in hooking in across the Selle to cut the *chaussée*, the division's main line of retreat, but the two Argyll companies, lining a road-bank at the south-eastern corner of Reumont, kept them off: at about 5.00 Jack managed to sprint down to pass the Highlanders the order to withdraw.

Elsewhere the retirement went relatively well. Most units of the right two brigades of 3rd Division came back in good order, but 7th Brigade, near Caudry on its left, was close to being cut off. John Lucy was favourably impressed by Major-General Hamilton — 'a brave man who always came up to see things for himself' — but was shocked to see a nearby battalion panic.

Infantrymen mounted every vehicle in sight, while others ran alongside. Some of their wounded were slung on the gun limbers.

A staff officer, his face hot with the shame of it, diverted the fleeing men into a side street in the first village we came to [Montigny-en-Cambrésis], shouting frantically at them: 'For God's sake, men, be British soldiers' . . .

The sight of these soldiers of a regular battalion, stampeding, grumbling and looking about while they were being reformed was an unforgettable and disgraceful scene.

Lieutenant-Colonel W. D. Bird, John Lucy's commanding officer, took over the brigade when its commander was disabled by a shell and brought it out of action safely.

Audencourt, where we had unboxed our horses, was the only really black spot for 3rd Division. Its defenders — 1st Gordon Highlanders, with elements of 2nd Royal Scots and 2nd Royal Irish, all of whom had been engaged at Mons on 23 August — did not receive orders to withdraw, but stood fast on the northern edge of the village, shooting down hundreds of the German infantry who toiled through the knee-high beet towards them. At 8.30 that night German artillery redoubled its fire on Audencourt, and the flashes and bangs of this bombardment caused surprise and satisfaction to the troops of 3rd Division, now six miles away to the south. The second-in-command of the Gordons held the brevet rank of full colonel, which gave him that rank in the army but not in his own regiment: as senior officer in army rank, he assumed command of the entire detachment once it was obvious that it was cut off. The little force managed to get as far as Berty, deep amongst tired Germans, where, at about 3.00 on the morning of the 27th, it was overwhelmed by two of the regiments of *IV Corps.*

Although 4th Division did not begin to fall back till after 5.00, it had little difficulty in breaking clear, in part because Sordet's corps was now up on its left. Whatever the value of dismounted French cavalry there could be no gainsaying the effect of the 75mms of their horse artillery batteries, which were whupping away with typical panache beyond the British left by 4.30. As Smith-Dorrien was riding back from Bertry to his new headquarters at St Quentin he heard the din from his flank and galloped up a hill to ascertain that it was indeed Sordet's gunners and not something more sinister. Sally Home, who had spent the day with 4th Cavalry Brigade near Ligny-Haucourt, thought that Sordet's timely assistance 'saved us a lot of trouble in the evening'.

All three divisions left isolated parties of men on the battlefield. About half those left behind were eventually captured, but many escaped; one little band, based on a nucleus of Dublin Fusiliers but including stragglers from all three Le Cateau divisions and even two badly-lost men from 1st Division, made its way to safety in Boulogne. The future Field-Marshal Montgomery found himself cut off with two companies of Royal Warwicks: 'for three days we marched between the German cavalry screen and their main columns following behind, moving mostly by night and hiding by day. In command of our party was a first-class regimental officer, Major A J Poole, and it was entirely due to him that we finally got back to the British Expeditionary Force . . . '

The fate of some fugitives was not revealed until the end of the war. On 9 October 1918 Major F V Drake of the 11th Hussars was riding through Honnechy, just south of Reumont, when he was greeted by a wild-looking man under British escort with a cry of: 'That's my troop officer, Mr Drake'. It was in fact Private P. Fowler of A Squadron, who had been cut off on 26 August 1914 and had been sheltered by Madame Belmont-Gobert and her daughter in Bertry ever since. Corporal Hull of the same regiment had been hidden by another family, but was betrayed and — in civilian clothes at the time of his capture — shot as a spy. When the story was known, Madame Belmont-Gobert and her daughter were both awarded the OBE and given a small cash grant by the British government. It was, alas, too small, and when the ladies failed to make ends meet enough money was raised by public subscription in Britain to enable them to live in comfort. Private Fowler immediately rejoined the 11th Hussars at his own request and became a steward in the officers' mess, out of harm's way but still part of the regimental family.

Total British casualties at Le Cateau, once stragglers had come in, were 7,812 men and thirty-eight guns. Most of the lost guns were from 5th Division, while 4th Division's lack of ambulances ensured that a disproportionate amount of its wounded fell into German hands. We cannot do more than estimate German losses at around 5,000. Kluck had fought the whole battle under the impression that he was dealing with what he reported in his dispatch to Moltke as: 'The whole British Expeditionary Corps, six divisions, a cavalry division and several French Territorial Divisions'. He remained convinced that it was facing east, and orders issued on the evening of the 26th sent Marwitz's cavalry and *II Corps* off west of Cambrai in an effort to intercept it. The remainder of *First Army* was given a night's rest, and when it marched at dawn on the 27th it headed south-west, taking it away from the main British line of retreat.

Lack of immediate pursuit both puzzled and gratified the British. Opinions varied as to the real state of II Corps. Smith-Dorrien thought that the survivors were 'a wonderful sight: men smoking their pipes, apparently quite unconcerned, and walking steadily down the road — no formation of any sort, and men of all units mixed up together. I likened it at the time to a crowd coming away from a race meeting.' Lieutenant Pennycuick was attracted by the comparable simile of 'a crowd coming away from a football match . . . the scene was quite cheerful, few seemed downhearted'.

Lieutenant Godsell was not so sure. He thought the retreat 'looked like a perfect débâcle and every moment we expected to see Bosch cavalry appear over the crest'. 5th Division's column was 'an unthought-of confusion of men, guns, horses and wagons. All dead beat, many wounded, all foot sore. In this sorry state we jumbled rather than marched on to Estrées.' John Lucy contrasted his own men's disciplined behaviour to that of the 'undisciplined mob' around them. Frank Richards admitted that the strain of another forced march was terrible.

> We retired all night with fixed bayonets, many sleeping as they were marching along. If any angels were seen on the Retirement, as the newspaper accounts said they were, they were seen that night. March, march, for hour after hour, without no halt: we were now breaking into the fifth day of continuous marching with practically no sleep in between . . . Stevens said: 'There's a fine castle there, see?' pointing to one side of the road, But there was nothing there. Very nearly everyone was seeing things, we were all so dead-beat.

So too was Lieutenant Brereton. 'We . . . lost the whole of the Division,' he wrote, 'got blocked by cavalry on the road, wandered all round the place, lost our way sometimes, and half the battery at others. A perfectly miserable night. I was dead beat having done all the shooting all day, and had no rest and practically no food. At any halt I always went off to sleep and don't know how we ever reached Vendhuille.'

Lieutenant Horn, who had ridden down the Selle with 3rd Cavalry Brigade, saw 'a lot of infantry stragglers who looked dead-beat and did not seem to know which way to go, but most of them said they were the only ones left in their platoon or battalion'. Arthur Osburn, for whom the war looked increasingly like a gigantic establishment conspiracy, believed that some of these men

> were evidently not unwilling to be 'found' by the Germans. Once taken prisoner under circumstances for which they could not very strictly be blamed, they would naturally think themselves safe; at least safe from being roused at three o'clock in the morning; safe from forced marches with an eighty-pound pack on their backs; safe from any more pitched battles with the possibility of death and mutilation . . . Suddenly

released from all discipline, with no adjutant or sergeant-major to shout or threaten . . . they could hurl their burdensome packs into the nearest ditch and wait until the German advance patrols . . . would arrive and they could comfortably surrender.

GHQ took a gloomy view of the battle. Although French's official dispatch was later to pay fulsome tribute to Smith-Dorrien's 'rare and unusual coolness, intrepidity, and determination', when the two men met early on the 27th, in an interview made more than usually acrimonious by the fact that GHQ had been economical with the news that it had fallen back to Noyon, French accused Smith-Dorrien of being unrealistically optimistic. Indeed, French never quite allowed the real statistics to dull his original conviction that the battle had finished II Corps. When the field-marshal wrote *1914*, his less than reliable account of the campaign, he reported its losses as 14,000 men and eighty guns. In April 1915 he confided to Haig that he regretted not court-martialling Smith-Dorrien for giving battle, and even Archie Murray, an admirer of Smith-Dorrien's, thought that 'he did wrong to fight other than a strong rear-guard action'. Most tellingly, Colonel Huguet thought that the BEF had been beaten and had 'lost all cohesion' and his gloomy reports further increased Joffre's anxiety about the state of the Allied left. However, with the clarity of hindsight there can be no question that Smith-Dorrien was right to give battle. Although II Corps was badly mauled — and might have paid more dearly for its stand had Kluck had a better idea of its dispositions and intentions — it would have been in an infinitely worse state if Smith-Dorrien had simply withdrawn as ordered.

While II Corps was fighting for its life, I Corps marched back to Etreux, on the Oise due south of Landrecies, with the costly ambush of 2nd Connaught Rangers at Le Grand Fayt its only serious contact with the Germans. French had spent much of the day at St Quentin, where he met Joffre and Lanrezac in another of those conferences that threw added strain on Anglo-French relations. All Wilson's bowdlerising translation could not obscure the fact that, as Spears put it, Sir John believed that 'he had been ceaselessly attacked by overwhelming numbers, whereas the 5th Army, attacked by an enemy inferior in strength, had continuously held back behind his own, and had then retired without warning or explanation'. Lanrezac made no direct reply — he might with justice have pointed to the very real risks his army had run on the Meuse — but proceeded to exasperate French by talking 'vaguely of the retreat as if it was an academic question'.

After an embarrassing silence, Joffre, in his toneless voice, set about explaining the concept of his new *Instruction Générale No. 2*. He now saw clearly what was afoot, and proposed to constitute a mass of manoeuvre on his left by adding forces from the east to the BEF and 5th Army which, in the meantime, should fall back in concert onto strong natural positions, on the valley of the Somme and the high ground around Laon and the Forest of St Gobain, delaying the Germans with sharp rearguard actions. It transpired that although GHQ had received a copy of the instruction, French had not seen it, and the only useful result of the meeting was to arrange that Lanrezac should fall back on La Fère rather than St Quentin. However, if the detail of *Instruction Générale No. 2* was to prove irrelevant, in its underlying concept — a radical change in the balance of Allied deployment by shifting French troops to the western flank — lay the kernel of eventual success.

VI

TREKKING ON

By selecting rallying positions, organizing a covering force, and arranging for an early withdrawal of all transport, a defeated army may to some extent be saved the demoralization which usually accompanies a retreat. It is of great importance to clear the roads chosen for the withdrawal of all vehicles which are not essential to the fighting troops, and in order to restore the *moral* and efficiency of the fighting troops supplies of ammunition and food should be deposited alongside these roads.

Field Service Regulations

We had spent so long wandering about the battlefield of Le Cateau that our only hope of reaching Ribemont, on the Oise east-south-east of St Quentin, where we were to spend the night, was to box on for part of our way and ride the last leg. A less than leisurely lunch where the track to the Suffolk Memorial enters Le Cateau, under drizzle which soon turned to rain, was enlivened by misfired Grenadier politeness. Evelyn, assaulting the Maroilles with an enthusiasm undampened by the weather, had only half an eye on the track beside us when a trim, leather-clad figure with long, raven-black hair tripped past. He exclaimed 'Bonjour, mademoiselle' with more courtesy than accuracy, and received a frozen and moustachi-oed glare from the gentleman in question. I was quite glad to be off the position before he arrived with reinforcements.

We drove through Wassigny to cross the Oise at Hannapes, and then turned right onto the D946, I Corps' withdrawal route, which took us into Guise behind what seemed like an endless succession of tractors. The town might have had a forlorn look even in good weather. Its castle, improved by Francis, Duke of Guise (1519–1563) — who earned his niche in history by holding Metz against the

Emperor Charles V and recovering Calais from the English — was badly damaged during the First World War. It has been well restored, but the surrounding heavy industry takes the edge off quiet enjoyment. Local route-signing seemed to have been masterminded by somebody with a lateral sense of humour, and we managed to get off what seemed from the map an unmissable major road system into a succession of narrow streets.

John was nudged off to a flank by a *poids lourds* sign, and I stopped at a garage, wedged into the hillside on the edge of town, to fill up with diesel and give him time to catch up. I could either wait for a car ahead of me to move on or swing to the right of the diesel pump and, thinking as I did so that I might be taking my new-found mastery of towing onto its outer limits, I took the quicker option. Taking infinite care to line up the nozzle with the back of the Trooper I forgot about the trailer long enough for its mudguard to hook the pipe from one of the petrol pumps. The cashier erupted onto the forecourt like an infantry picket turning out to meet uhlans, and there was a certain degree of tension until it was established that no damage had been done. There was still no sign of John, so I drove on to the rendezvous on the Guise–St Quentin road and found him already there, atop a ridge of which bare-arsed is the only fit description, with a strong wind driving the last of the day's rain southwards. The country was like the downland around Le Cateau but on an even larger scale. There were few villages this side of the Oise, but several big farms, set four-square like fortresses on the chalk. Evelyn and I saddled Thatch and Jeopardy and, buttoned up to the chin in our waterproofs, set off down a track on our way to Ribemont.

On 27 August 1914 the Oise divided the BEF, with I Corps moving down its right bank and II Corps on its left. Lanrezac had agreed that Haig would have priority on the Etreux–Guise road — the tractor-encumbered route which took us into Guise — and over the next few days the BEF moved faster than the 5th Army, so that this road was used by two distinct bodies of retreating troops: the British I Corps on the 27th and Lanrezac's left-hand corps on the 28th.

Signs of the retreat are still there. On one of those windswept crests just south of Guise stands a farm whose name embodies the spirit of the place: Desolation. Across the road is a large military cemetery with dead from all three armies. There are a few British, some of them wounded in rearguard actions who died in ambulances or dressing stations and were buried here. On the 27th the pith-helmeted Major Charrier and his Munster Fusiliers, with the selfless support of a section of 118th Battery RFA and two troops of the 15th Hussars, had manned a blocking position on the Sambre Canal just north of Etreux while the remainder of the Corps got clear. Little Charrier held off a good chunk of *X Reserve Corps* of Bülow's *Second Army* from mid-morning to mid-afternoon. He fought his way back to Etreux and was eventually killed beside the last 18-pdr — its detachment dead around it — in the town. A subaltern took command of the tatters of the battalion, which held out in an orchard until the Germans overran it at nightfall, and 2nd Royal Munster Fusiliers joined the Cheshires, Suffolks and King's Own Yorkshire Light Infantry in that growing list of battalions which had remained faithful unto death.

There are dead Germans at Desolation Farm, lying under teutonic crosses of sombre granite. But the lasting impression is of the sacrifice made by Lanrezac's men. Such was the scale of the catastrophe which overwhelmed the French armies in August 1914 that it was impossible to give their dead honoured burial. By the end of August Joffre had lost 212,000 men, about twenty per cent of his mobilised strength and a horrifying forty per cent of his regular officers.

Although 5th Army was by no means as hard hit as those formations on Joffre's right, which had strewn the bare uplands of Lorraine with windrows of red-trousered infantry, it was stumbling back in agony. One of Lanrezac's corps — Franchet d'Esperey's I — was still in good order, but modern analysts would have muttered darkly about 'imminent combat ineffectiveness' when they surveyed the other three. III Corps had lost 10,000 men: its commander was about to be dismissed and two of its divisional commanders had vanished. An energetic gunner officer had taken charge of one of the leaderless divisions: we would have seen him on these very slopes on the 29th, moving between positions at a breakneck gallop with shrapnel whipping the sky over his head and his old-style *caban* — an officer's caped greatcoat — stiff in the air behind him. The two remaining corps had lost 6,000 men apiece.

Officers had paid the penalty for leading their men into battle with white gloves and drawn swords: battalions were now commanded by captains and companies by lieutenants. Staffs at divisional and brigade level were utterly worn out. There had been no provision for the twenty-four-hour manning of headquarters, and staff officers spent their days on horseback and their nights writing orders. The men had been marching and fighting all the way from Charleroi, with 'the furrow for mattress and the pack for pillow', and passing 75mm guns and limbers were 'garnished with soldiers'. Many had thrown away their *Azors*, their cumbersome old-fashioned packs — 'seldom has any army been given a piece of equipment so badly designed' — and were living on the army-issue loaf which looked like a massively-inflated bagel, its central hole facilitating the handy if inelegant practice of hanging it from the slung rifle. And even when the unwieldy cooking-pots had survived and there was something to put in them, as like as not the order to move came before the *soupe* — that all-in stew that formed the staple diet of French soldiers — was ready, and pots were up-ended to quench fires as the regiment prepared to move off.

It was the old story of the mercurial armies of France, flowing rather than marching, shoals of little peasants ostensibly at their last gasp but still — the Lord knows how — harbouring reserves of moral strength which could yet be conjured up. Perhaps by the sight of a tattered colour — there it goes, carried by a haunted young officer with big, quiet sergeants at his elbow — or the brassy appeal of the bugle summoning men to the charge with words which were both mundane and symbolic: 'There's a drop to be drunk up there, there's a drop to be drunk'. By now there was a sharp edge to the maintenance of fighting spirit, for Joffre had issued general orders telling officers that they must keep their men in line by whatever means were necessary. Not a few stragglers were encouraged by an officer's pistol, and in some cases Frenchmen died under French bullets as exasperated officers took on surly or drunken men who had had enough of the war.

So many of Lanrezac's men lie up here at Desolation Farm, in common graves whose markers make a paltry attempt to list the names of some of those beneath. Most have a surname only, and here is one, 'Lemoine, *officier*', perhaps recognisable only by a rag of superfine cloth or the tarnished curl of a *galon* round a mouldering wrist as the poor remnant of a man who once sported the white plume of St-Cyr or the fore-and-aft cap of the Ecole Polytechnique.

I was glad to get off these charnel downs and walk the last mile into Ribemont, a pile of red brick stacked in the broad, marshy valley of the Oise. All of us — men and horses — were spending the night at the Club Equestre de Ribemont. Its buildings, which seemed to have started life as a livery stable, would have been new when Lanrezac's 38th Division crossed the river there on the morning of 29 August 1914. A sturdy iron gate opened from the main road onto a courtyard with stables on the right and at the far end, and a barn and the house on the left. As I led Thatch down the cobbles past a long row of stalls I wondered who they had tenanted over the years: safe hacks for small-town lawyers, knowing carriage-horses who could do the ten miles back from St Quentin with a fuddled driver up on the box, and Max, Otto and Donna, German officers' chargers during the long stalemate of trench warfare when the front line ran just the other side of St Quentin.

Everything had seen better times, but there were signs that the tide of dilapidation was turning. Our horses were stabled at the end of the yard in stalls whose refurbishment was in progress as we arrived. Laurent and Bernadette, our hosts, were down-to-earth folk, keen on horses and dogs, and inordinately proud of their town. Did I know that the Marquis de Condorcet, the mathematician and philosopher who died in prison during the Revolution, had been born in Ribemont? I did not. And what about Napoleon's general, Louis de St. Hilaire, who had also had the good fortune to be born there? I confessed to knowing a good deal more about St. Hilaire than I did about Condorcet, and managed to do something for my reputation as the party's historian by remembering that St. Hilaire was one of Napoleon's salamanders, happiest where the fire was hottest. His division had helped break the Austro-Russian centre at Austerlitz in 1805, and Napoleon promised him promotion after distinguished conduct at Eckmühl in 1809: 'Well, you have earned your marshal's baton and you shall have it.' Sadly, he was killed at Aspern-Essling a month later, before the baton, crisp in velvet and gilt, had arrived from Paris.

It had always been made clear that this was not exactly the Ritz, but we had felt that it was better to stay at the stables than to leave the horses there and seek out a hotel in St Quentin. The accommodation was spartan. Evelyn and Clive shared one room, and Ollie, John and I another in what was to all intents and purposes a private house: it was exactly like the billets described in so many accounts. I thought of Count Gleichen's description of his brigade headquarters' billet at Ollizy, on the other side of the Oise, on 27 August 1914.

The farm was quite a good one of the usual form — i.e., the living-house forming one end of a big oblong courtyard, whilst barns and lofts and cowsheds filled up the other three sides . . . The people were most friendly, and supplied us with eggs and straw and a kitchen fire . . . I had a bed to lie on, and actually enjoyed a wash in a real basin, but the little bedroom was not very sweet or clean, and I'd as soon have slept with the others on straw in the kitchen and living-room.

Things were more salubrious at Ribemont, for upstairs was politely but firmly a 'no boots' zone, a wise precaution in view of the state of our footwear after evening stables. We drove into Origny St Benoit, the next town to the north, for dinner, returned to drink coffee with the hospitable Laurent and Bernadette in their kitchen, and retired to bed. Or at least retired to our rooms. I had the one bed, Ollie a sofa which was not quite of Welsh Guards proportions, and John unrolled his sleeping-bag on a camp bed under the window. There was a certain amount of snoring in our billet, and I began to doubt the wisdom of eating *choucroute* before spending a night in such circumstances. One must suffer for the sake of historical accuracy, and I only hope that my companions saw things the same way.

The 27th of August 1914 took I Corps to the high ground south of Guise — that sinister crest-line we had ridden over on our way to Ribemont — and II Corps to the west and south-west of St Quentin. For I Corps the retreat was marred by the loss of Charrier's gallant band at Etreux. But for II Corps and the 4th Division the twenty-four hours following the battle of Le Cateau was a painful odyssey. Smith-Dorrien had got the heavy transport of his divisional trains away in good time so as to leave the roads clear for the fighting troops, and his logisticians, following the orders of the BEF's eminently sensible Quartermaster-General, Wully Robertson, began dumping food at likely junctions so that the troops could help themselves as they passed.

Most of 5th Division and 19th Brigade reached the road-junction south of Estrées (fifteen miles from the battlefield) between 9.00 p.m. and midnight, soaked and exhausted. At the cross-roads staff officers shouted 'transport and mounted troops straight on, 3rd Division infantry to the right, 5th Division infantry to the left'. As small groups — often confidently believing themselves to be the sole survivors of their battalions — gathered in the rainy darkness, regimental and staff officers began to reassemble battalions and brigades, and at 4.00 in the morning a start of sorts was made.

Frank Richards, who been left behind trying to rouse men comatose with exhaustion, remembered that march all too well: 'Along the road we took were broken-down motor lorries, motor-cycles, dead horses and broken wagons. In a field were dumped a lot of rations. We had a feed, crammed some biscuits into our haversacks and moved off again. After a few minutes, by picking up more stragglers, we were twenty strong, men of several different battalions.' John Lucy watched exhaustion rob his comrades of their pride: 'That pained look in the troubled eyes of those who fell by the way will not easily be forgotten by those who saw it. That look imposed by circumstances on spent men seemed to demand all forgiveness from officers and comrades alike, as it conveyed a helpless and dumb farewell to arms.'

Henry Owens saw 'infantry chaps lying about all along the roadside absolutely dead beat. No greatcoats or anything; soaking wet and dead asleep.' Lieutenent Brereton was told that as the infantry were:

> quite done, we were to commandeer carts and horse them with horses out of our teams, and put as many infantrymen as possible on wagons and limbers. This was an awful march, not more than two horses in any team, about six infantrymen on each limber or wagon body, and everybody going to sleep and falling off limbers and horses the whole time. Halts, of which there were many, were perfect hell, because it was impossible to start off again.

As daylight came, Robert Money passed 'abandoned lorries (motor) here and there, sides of bacon, motor bikes, great coats, etc; . . . everywhere were men by ones and twos every sort of unit trekking on'.

Corporal Watson reached St Quentin 'wet, miserable and angry' just as dawn was breaking. In the centre of the town, through which much of this flotsam poured, Henry Owens watched 'staff officers at the roads entering the square sorting out parties of infantry, stray transport etc and directing them to their units'. By the time Arthur Osburn reached St Quentin in mid-afternoon with the cavalry rearguard, the remnants of de Lisle's brigade, there were no formed bodies of troops left in the town. However,

> the whole square was thronged with British infantrymen standing in groups or wandering about in an aimless fashion, most of them without either packs or rifles. Scores had gone to sleep sitting on the pavement, their backs against the fronts of the shops. Many exhausted lay at full length on the pavement. Some few, obviously intoxicated, wandered about firing in the air at real or imaginary aeroplanes.

Osburn watched the irrepressible Tom Bridges haranguing 'this disorganised mob that only a few hours before had represented at least two famous regiments of the 4th Division'. Bridges had evidently misjudged his audience, for one man shouted: 'Our old man (his Colonel) has surrendered to the Germans, and we'll stick to him. *We don't want any bloody cavalry interfering!*' With that, he aimed his rifle at Bridges. Osburn, so tired and hungry that he no longer cared what happened, went off in search of food and rest, surmising that 'the events of the last three or four days had evidently diminished the prestige of the officer caste' and wondering if Bridges would actually be shot.

John O'Flaherty knew a farrier sergeant-major who looked as if he kept a hedgehog under each arm and could crack coconuts between his buttocks. There were a few burly farriers available to Bridges at St Quentin, and, under a subaltern's direction, they managed to get many somnolent or drunken men out of shops and houses and into the square. But Bridges could see that some were in a such a poor state that they could march no further even if they wanted to, and set off for the *mairie* in the hope of commandeering transport to carry them to safety. The mayor indignantly refused and told Bridges he was too late: the men had already surrendered, and he had a document, signed by their commanding officers, to prove it.

St Quentin, sitting on a chalky hillock overlooking the Somme, is a comely town, built around a soaring Gothic basilica which smiles out across the downland for miles around. In 1557 it was besieged by the Spaniards, and the Constable Montmorency, marching to its relief, suffered a defeat so crushing that it inspired Philip II of Spain to build the Escorial. The town was no stranger to war: the basilica had been damaged in the siege of 1557 and was badly scarred by fire a century later.

The mayor may be forgiven for feeling that his fellow-citizens had much to lose from a battle in their prosperous streets. Hearing that the Germans were at Gricourt, only four miles from the centre of the town, he begged the commanding officers of the two battalions in it — 1st Royal Warwickshire and 2nd Royal Dublin Fusiliers of 4th Division's 10th Brigade — to fight the Germans outside. Both COs, Lieutenant-Colonel Arthur Mainwaring of the Warwicks and Lieutenant-Colonel John Elkington of the Dublins, made it clear that they could not fight. They had no artillery, their men were in disorder, and the very public departure of GHQ from

St Quentin station had not helped matters. The mayor then asked them to leave the town, so that their presence did not encourage the Germans to bombard it. This too was impossible: the men were at their last gasp and needed food and rest. In this case, said the mayor, they must surrender. Both officers agreed, and duly signed a document (how they must have regretted those groggy self-convicting signatures later) which the mayor intended to deliver to the Germans, just outside the town: their men piled arms and waited around the station.

Arthur Osburn, who knew just what it was like to ride exhausted into St Quentin after the march of a nightmare, felt that:

there was every excuse for the two colonels and the one or two pale-looking subalterns whom I had noticed mingling in the crowd down at the station. Without Staff, without maps or orders, without support from artillery or cavalry, what *could* the remnants of broken infantry do before the advance of a victorious army, whose cavalry could have mopped them up in an hour? Probably, looking back on it now, the two colonels did the only feasible and the brave thing. Middle-aged men, both of them looked utterly exhausted. From their appearance they were suffering severely from the sun; that alone might account for their not having thought of making use of the mayor as a collector of country carts.

Although Bridges was still suffering from the effects of his fall at Elouges — Osburn took him into Paris for a X-Ray a few days later — he rose to the occasion, told the mayor to assemble as many carts as possible, and provided them to the two battalions at the station, 'letting them know that I would leave no British soldier alive in St Quentin. Upon this they emerged from the station and gave no more trouble.' The remainder, about 500 strong, lay about the square, deaf to his entreaties. 'If one only had a band', he thought. At that moment he noticed a toy shop whose proprietor had not deserted it, and bought a drum and a penny whistle. His trumpeter marched round the square playing 'The British Grena-diers' on the whistle while Bridges accompanied him as best he could on the drum. Gradually, men stood up and formed fours, and a few, who had mouth-organs or Jew's harps in their haversacks, formed what Osburn called 'a sort of band'. One of the COs was persuaded to march in front of his men. 'My recollection', wrote Osburn, 'is that he looked very pale, entirely dazed, and had no Sam Browne belt, and leant heavily on his stick, apparently so exhausted with fatigue and heat that he could scarcely have known what he was doing.'

The tattered little company left St Quentin just after midnight, led by Bridges, one of the COs and the improvised band, with a few mounted men bringing up the rear. Both lieutenant-colonels were relieved of their commands later that day and charged with 'shamefully delivering up a garrison to the enemy'. They were tried in early September, and their courts-martial did not share Osburn's conviction that they had shown 'a more soldierly idea of comradeship in difficulty and danger' in sticking to their men rather than making their escape with a few of the fittest. Both were cashiered. The expression has nothing to do with accountancy, but is an echo of the French *casser*, to break. A cashiered officer is stripped of his commission — it is infinitely more serious than simply being required to resign — and its effect goes far beyond depriving him of pay, allowances and pension rights. In 1914, cashiering turned a man into a leper, liable to be rejected by family and friends and compelled to stand idly by while the others fought: it is hard to think of a worse fate for a regular officer.

Arthur Mainwaring sought to explain his conduct and had his own account of events printed privately: he then vanished into obscurity. John Elkington took a more extreme step. He returned to France, joined the Foreign Legion as a private soldier under an assumed name, fought with courage remarkable even in that band of brave men, reached the rank of sergeant, was decorated and terribly wounded. Most unusually, he was awarded the Distinguished Service Order and restored to his rank in the British Army by special command of the King. But his story does not really have a happy ending, for both his son and son-in-law were killed in the Second World War. Were they trying to lay the ghosts of St Quentin? We shall never know.

And as for the town itself, all the mayor's ingenuity could not save it from what was to come. It was just behind the German lines for most of the war, and that marvellous basilica, spared by German guns in 1914, was battered first by French and then by British artillery. When the Germans attacked on 21 March 1918, in that gambler's throw of an offensive that so nearly won the war, they poured through streets poisoned by British gas-shells. 'Here and there were men from other units who had been surprised by the gas,' recollected Pioneer Georg Zobel. 'They sat or lay and vomited pieces of their corroded lungs. Horrible, this death! And, much as they implored us, nobody dared to give them the *coup de grâce*. We were badly shaken by it all.'

The mood of GHQ continued gloomy on the 27th. Both corps were told to jettison all non-essential stores: the telegram to 4th Division put the order in true Wilsonian style: 'From Henry to Snowball. Throw overboard all ammunition and impedimenta not absolutely required, and load up your lame ducks on transport, horse and mechanical, and hustle along.' Haig's chief of staff tore the order up. Smith-Dorrien first heard of it when he saw Brigadier-General Aylmer Hunter-Weston ('Hunter-Bunter') of 11th Brigade looking unusually glum. Hunter-Weston complained that the order had 'a very damping effect on the troops, for it was clear that it would not have been issued unless we were in a very tight place'. Smith-Dorrien countermanded it at once, but was too late for 4th Division, whose officers 'sacrificed their spare clothes, boots etc at a time when they urgently needed them'.

GHQ's pessimism had by now thoroughly infected Huguet, who had been warned by French that there would be 'bitterness and regret' in England when news of the early battles arrived. Huguet telephoned Joffre at 8.15 that morning and told him that Sordet's corps must protect the BEF's retreat — and even attack if possible — adding ominously: 'If this co-operation is not very effective appreciation of ourselves (by the British) risks being very severe.' Joffre visited GHQ at Noyon at 11.00 a.m. and on returning to his headquarters sent French a fulsome congratulatory telegram, paying tribute to the BEF's 'devotion, energy and perseverence'. It was sound psychology. French was personally gratified by Joffre's thanks, and was able to use the message when he visited the troops the following day.

> I had the most agreeable surprise. I met the men and talked to them as they were lying about resting. I told them how much I appreciated the work and what the country thought of them. I told them also of Joffre's telegram and its publication in England. The wonderful spirit and bearing they showed was beyond all praise — ½ a million of them would walk over Europe!

Joffre already knew that fine words alone would not expunge the misunderstandings of the past week. Spears strove to be even-handed in his treatment of the British and the French, but believed that thus far the British had a right to feel aggrieved. 'Where they had looked for support,' he wrote, 'they had found only shadows;

schemes, plans, operations, everything had melted away, leaving only one reality — the enemy, who in overwhelming strength and with relentless purpose had driven home blow after blow.' In order to convince GHQ that he was serious, Joffre gave Lanrezac an unambiguous order to attack, concluding: 'Do not take into account what the English are doing on your left'. Lanrezac was infuriated by the order and his chief of staff quibbled over points of detail with GHQ, one of whose emissaries now arrived at 5th Army headquarters at Marle to make sure that there was no backsliding.

Encouraging assertions that Lanrezac was about to attack did not change the mood at GHQ, which had heard the tale before, and Huguet, never slow to send bad news, told Joffre that he thought it possible that the British might fall back on Le Havre to reorganise, exposing the 5th Army's flank as they did so. Joffre stepped up his pressure on Lanrezac, telling him to attack those elements of the German *Second Army* which were moving between the Oise and St Quentin. Lanrezac's staff were horrified. This meant swinging the whole army round by ninety degrees and then attacking across a river into the flank of an enemy of unknown strength. Colonel Alexandre, the GQG emissary, blithely waved his hand across the map to show how simple it was, provoking a distracted major to say: 'Oh, Colonel, don't talk nonsense'. 'You people can't be induced to do anything,' snapped Alexandre.

Lanrezac nearly refused to sign the final order, which went out at 8.00 on the evening of the 27th. The attack was to begin at dawn on the 29th. Two corps, XVIII and III, were to cross the Oise at Séry-les-Mézières, Ribemont and Origny respectively, while X Corps covered the movement by facing Guise. Lanrezac's freshest formation, I Corps, was to close up to Hérie-la-Viéville — on the main road four miles south of Desolation Farm — to throw its weight into the balance as required. A French liaison office had sought out Haig, finding him in the hamlet of Lucy, a stone's throw from Ribemont, and obtained provisional agreement that I Corps would join in the attack, an undertaking which seemed to be confirmed at another meeting at St Gobain that evening.

GHQ would have none of this. On the evening of the 27th it issued orders for a continuation of the retreat on the following day: the march would take I Corps to the Forest of St Gobain and II Corps well south of the Somme at Ham. When Sir John French heard that Haig had agreed to support Lanrezac he not only forbade him to do so, but irritably asked 'how it was that any confidential promise of support by First Corps was made to General Lanrezac or why any official exchange of ideas was initiated without authority from Headquarters'. This drew a brisk rejoinder from Haig, who begged French not to believe 'such allegations as the one under reference without first ascertaining whether it is true or not'. The news stunned 5th Army. 'For the first time I felt we were in the wrong,' wrote Spears. 'General Lanrezac's anger was terrific. He said terrible, unpardonable things concerning Sir John French and the British Army, but these I was careful not to hear; nor did I ever report what occurred that evening.'

Friday, 13 August 1993 was an inauspicious date for riding part of I Corps' route on 28 August 1914. At about 6.30 a.m. thuds and muffled cries from the room next door announced that Evelyn had adopted the Patent Method of waking Clive. Its alternative, the Patient Method, was to rouse him every ten minutes for an hour or so, but there was no time for that this morning. So the Patent Method it was: shoes, radio batteries and other handy objects were lobbed at the recumbent form which responded to direct hits by rolling from its sleeping-bag with commendable alacrity. We fed the horses before having our own breakfast — enamel-dissolving coffee and the freshest of *baguettes* — loaded our kit, and then began to groom and tack up. I was picking out Thatch's soup-plate hooves when there was a shout behind me, and I turned to see Jeopardy walking steadily away from the massive sliding doors of the stable-block at the end of the courtyard. A second desperate glance confirmed that he was walking away *with* one of them. Because someone had tethered him to its handle without benefit of bailer twine the door came down with a crash (there was an answering bang somewhere off-stage) and Jeopardy dragged it inexorably towards the conservatory. John caught him before more harm was done, but the existing damage seemed serious enough: a ten by twelve foot door was lying on the cobbles with a length of electric cable underneath it. It took all four of us, with the assistance of one valiant Frenchman up a ladder, to put the door back on its rails, and once there it seemed to work well enough. Which was more than could be said of the electricity. The sympathetic thump had been the explosion of a fuse-box, and when John and I left on Thatch and Jeopardy, Evelyn and Bernadette were engaged in discussions whose outcome seemed likely to be costly.

The previous night a considerate Frenchman had shown me the best way of getting out of Ribemont onto a track which follows the railway east of the Oise. John regarded the morning's mishap as the consequence of thoroughly unhorsemanlike behaviour on Someone's part and was in a black mood, so I was anxious not to add insult to injury by getting lost. However, what had seemed quite obvious from the front of a Peugeot was more obscure from horseback, and there was a certain degree of circumnavigation before we crossed the main road in what I was sure was the right place. 'Are we meant to ride through a garden centre?' asked John with sweet reasonableness, and I was about to admit that I was lost when I saw a rusty sign saying 'Poilu's Allotments'. It was not a garden centre at all, but strips of vegetable garden which had been given to ex-servicemen after the First World War, and the track between them was passable.

We rode between river and railway as far as Séry-les-Mézières. The day warmed up fast, and we were glad of the shade of the trees alongside the track. The valley floor, on our right, was about a mile wide, with the Oise itself meandering through lakes and marshes and the Oise canal cutting a straighter path. There were occasional tiny buildings — weekend 'cottages', perhaps — which were more than huts but definitely not bungalows, with patches of well-tended garden and a fine row of sunflowers level with the mighty muzzle. After Thatch's attempt to defoliate the battlefield of Le Cateau I was riding with a whip, but the old ruffian had seen it go aboard and was too shrewd to risk a clout for all the sunflowers in the world, though I could sense his regret as we plodded on past them.

In Séry-les-Mézières we rode out of the valley and through the town before dropping down once more to cross river and canal. I had not taken Thatch over a bridge before, and was pleased to see that he was not in the least concerned by them: dustbins are another matter, but then, there is no fathoming the equine mind. In Alaincourt, on the west bank, we headed south-west, making for the northern edge of Möy de l'Aisne.

As the British withdrew on 28 August there was a fifteen-mile fissure between the two corps. The German *Guard Cavalry Division*, moving ahead of Bülow's *Second Army*, pushed on south of St Quentin in two columns and threatened to exploit this gap. The westerly column was easily checked. Allenby sent 3rd Cavalry Brigade over towards the Oise, and early in the afternoon the 4th Hussars ambushed a party of uhlans near Benay, three miles west of Möy, and when the Germans attempted to work round the ambush the guns of E Battery stopped them easily.

The eastern column, led by *2nd Guard Dragoons*, was moving down the Roman road which runs from St Quentin to La Fère. Haig had given his chief gunner, Brigadier-General H. S. Horne, command of a flank guard consisting of 5th Cavalry Brigade, 5th Infantry Brigade and XXXVI Brigade RFA, and Horne had posted the cavalry on the west bank of the Oise. Between Möy and Alaincourt a long, irregular valley stretches westwards towards the village of Cerizy, with the St Quentin road cutting across its upper end. The Möy–Cerizy road runs about 300 yards south of the crest which forms the southern edge of the valley, and the valley is about a mile across at its widest. One British cavalry officer thought the ground was just like Salisbury Plain: there were a few small woods, and big open fields grew corn — now cut and stooked — or sugar-beet.

Sir Philip Chetwode reached Cerizy at 10.30 on the morning of 28 August, and posted a troop of the Royal Scots Greys to cover the main road on the northern edge of the valley, leaving C Squadron and the machine-guns lining the edge of a copse off the road on the valley's southern side, just north of the hamlet of La Guingette, where the Möy–Cerizy road crosses the main road. The remaining two squadrons of the Greys were in dead ground near the Möy–Cerizy road, the 20th Hussars were in Cerizy, the 12th Lancers in reserve in Möy, and brigade headquarters was in La Guingette.

The 12th Lancers were glad to hear that they would be in reserve as it was a scorching day: men and horses needed rest. They arrived in Möy at about midday, watered the horses in the Oise and then off-saddled and fed them in the château grounds. Officers and men washed and shaved — it was the first chance for several days — and then dozed or ate peaches which grew against the garden walls. In mid-afternoon they were aroused by the sound of firing from the Greys' outposts, and cognoscenti detected the 'toc' of Mauser carbines answering the sharper crack of Lee-Enfields. Lieutenant-Colonel Wormald ordered the regiment to saddle up, and set off at once with a small party from Regimental Headquarters, with Captain J. C. Michell's C Squadron and the machine-gun section not far behind him.

The German advanced guard had appeared on the scene at about 11.30 a.m., occupying La Folie Farm on the main road, and driving in the Greys' outpost but making no real progress. In early afternoon the Germans determined to force the issue, and two squadrons of *2nd Guard Dragoons* advanced east of the road towards the Greys' C Squadron. When they reached the valley floor the squadron and

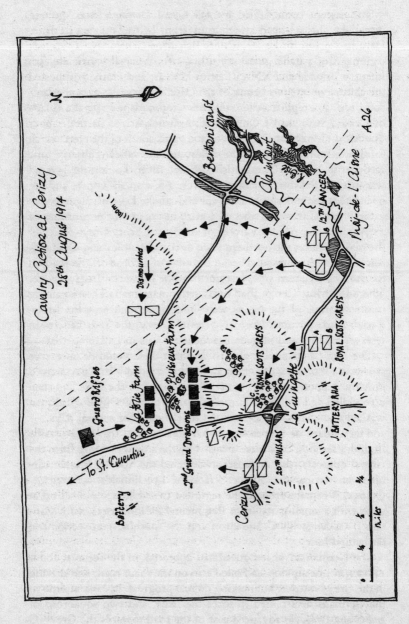

Cavalry Action at Cerizy
28th August 1914

machine-guns opened fire, and at exactly the same time Michell's squadron of the lancers, moving up from Möy, saw a squadron of cavalry in close order — a third squadron of *2nd Guard Dragoons* — moving parallel with the other two. Michell's men engaged them at once: the combined fire of both C Squadrons and the two machine-gun sections compelled the Germans to dismount in a beet-field just downhill from the big farm complex of Puisieux. At this juncture a section of J Battery galloped forward — Jasper, Jabber, Joubert and Jones reaching into their harness — to the southern lip of the valley and fired over open sights: the first few rounds stampeded the German horses, leaving the dragoons exposed on the forward slope below the farm.

John and I picked up Lieutenant-Colonel Wormald's route just north-west of Möy, and rode forward to follow the progress of the battle. Möy lay off to our left, and the valley began to open up in front of us. John's good humour had returned, but I was consulting the map with unusual frequency because there was a large road crossing the valley where none was shown on the map. At this juncture, Evelyn hove into sight in the Trooper. He had seen the problem — nothing less than the A26 autoroute — when buying the makings of lunch in Möy, and had already discovered that it was crossed by a bridge between Alaincourt and Puisieux. Thatch proved as imperturbable on road bridges as he was on bridges over water, and as we crossed the motorway we could see Puisieux, to our right front, and the copse occupied by the Greys' C Squadron to our left front. Michell's squadron, dismounted with the lancer machine-guns, was in the valley hard on our left.

Chetwode had been away at a conference with Haig when the fighting started. So far his subordinates had taken purposeful action without direct orders from brigade headquarters, and it is interesting to note that none of them had irrevocably committed him to a particular course of action. Chetwode saw the potential of the situation as soon as he galloped up. He ordered Wormald to take his two remaining squadrons on a wide outflanking movement along the northern lip of the valley and engage the Germans dismounted, and told J Battery to bring its remaining four guns into action. The Germans began to move slowly back up the slope, still shooting hard — Major Swetenham of the Greys was killed as he directed his squadron's fire.

Lieutenant-Colonel Wormald prepared to move C Squadron forward under cover of the fire of his other two squadrons, and sent his adjutant, Captain Bryant, to establish contact with them. The adjutant was back at the gallop almost at once. He had found so much dead ground in front of the German position that he was sure C Squadron could work its way closer to charge. Wormald advanced up a sharp gash in the valley side, holding the squadron to a walk to keep the horses fresh. John and I had been able to get a good feel for the land as we crossed the bridge — the gully is just visible amongst the folds of ground — and we rode across the stubble up it until I thought we were opposite the German position.

Wormald would have had the sound of carbine-fire to guide him. He ordered 'Line of Troop Column' as the squadron began to climb the steep slope, for the ground was rougher then than it is now. It slipped into line at the top, and Wormald shouted 'Gallop' and 'Charge'. C Squadron's trumpeter sounded the charge — 'Let 'em go, at 'em boys, now for a charge!' and the the colonel, adjutant, trumpet-major and two orderlies hurtled over the crest well ahead of the line. The 12th Lancers' War Diary reckons that it was a mere fifty yards from the crest to the German position. John and I rode it, and I can testify that even if the Germans had fallen back as far as Puisieux — and they were probably still well downhill from the farm — it would take a mere thirty seconds for the lancers to reach them. The line moved fast — far faster than sedate historians on sturdy greys — well-mounted officers setting a brave example, troopers determined not to let their mates get ahead of them, and front-rank men well aware that there was a lot of steel-tipped bamboo close behind them.

The *2nd Guard Dragoons (Queen Victoria's Own)* was a prestigious regiment and a good one. But as the Lancers' regimental history records: 'The surprise was complete and terrible. As the lance-points and the fluttering pennons bore down upon them a few Germans, shaken by the sight, cowered among the roots amongst which they were lying, but most rose to fight it out.' The Lancers' war diarist (almost certainly Captain Bryant) thought that the dragoons 'fought exceedingly gallantly, though some put up their hands or lay down in the roots'.

Wormald's command group was a natural target for the few rounds that the Germans managed to get off before the Lancers were upon them, and most of the Lancers' four killed and six wounded were suffered in the first few seconds. The colonel ran one dragoon through 'so thoroughly that his sword buckled and remained firmly embedded in the German's body' but was wounded and had his horse killed almost immediately. One orderly was killed and the other unhorsed, while Trumpet-Major Mowlam was badly wounded. Captain Michell's little headquarters was also hard hit: Michell was shot through the head and his squadron quartermaster-sergeant fell dead at his side.

Thereafter it was an unequal contest. The Germans had already had the worst of a lengthy firefight and were probably short of ammunition: it was one of the few occasions in the war when the steel had the edge over fire. Captain Bryant recorded cheerfully that he eschewed the new-fangled 1912 pattern but was using 'the old cutting sword, well sharpened, which went in and out of the Germans like a pat of butter'. He cut down five Germans, and another officer killed three with his sword and another with his revolver. Sergeant Percy Snelling was in C Squadron, but lost his horse early on. 'The Knut was shot through the leg when I went to mount,' he wrote, 'so I had to walk while the squadron galloped and charged them. Most of them threw down their arms but some picked them up again and fired after our chaps had spared them. About ninety were lanced and lots surrendered.'

Captain Bryant rallied the squadron after it had passed right through the dragoons and led it back again. Then, rallying it once more, he took it across the position a third time, but 'the enemy were vanquished and killed except for four unwounded men who were found hiding among the roots and taken prisoners'. The Greys' mounted squadrons now joined in, the regimental historian maintaining that 'though the charge was sounded by the trumpet-major there were practically no enemy left, as the 12th Lancers had done their work so thoroughly'. Paul Maze saw the action's crueller side: 'As a few Germans were hiding in the corn-stooks lances and swords were thrust through the hay and I heard fearful yells. The horses were very excited, as were the men, who were showing to one another the blood dripping off their sword-blades. Others were picking up souvenirs.'

There are glaring inconsistencies in the few eyewitness accounts of the charge. Both Bryant and Snelling describe Germans attempting to surrender, but there were only four unwounded prisoners. The Lancers' historian tells us that the death of Michell 'angered rather than dismayed' the squadron, and the fact that some Germans had thrown down their arms and picked them up again also caused irritation. The Reverend Dr Vogel, chaplain of the *Guard Cavalry*

Division, wrote that amongst the wounded 'were men with six or seven lance wounds, and several bullet wounds'.

I fear that trying to surrender to a horseman whose blood is up must rank high on any list of fruitless endeavours. The 1914 edition of *The Manual of Military Law* declares: 'It is forbidden to kill or wound an enemy who having laid down his arms . . . has surrendered at discretion'. Yet to expect respect for the letter of the law from a man who has passed through the beaten zone of his enemy's fire, seen a popular officer have his brains blown out, and watched men who have apparently surrendered become combatants once more, is to hope for more than flesh and blood can deliver. The question of whether failure to take prisoners under such circumstances constitutes a war crime arises after almost any war, and there is no shortage of stern letters to *The Times* to point out, perfectly correctly, that it does.

But the light of pure reason glows darkly through the smoke of war. The British soldier of 1914 thought it wrong to kill men who had patently surrendered. On 10 September 1914, Percy Snelling watched his comrades flush broken infantry out of some woods. 'One of our troops lanced all the Germans they saw until the NCOs stopped them. I could hardly believe it as it was a cowardly thing to do.' A month later, R. A. Lloyd saw an officer and a couple of troopers chase a single uhlan.

> Soon he stopped, raised his carbine, and aimed straight at the officer. As the latter rode direct at him, he changed his mind, threw the gun down, and put up his hands. A wild fellow named Bellingham, of the 'Skins', galloped at him and ran him through the body with his sword . . . Those present were shocked at the coldbloodedness of the deed.

Frank Richards, who spent the whole war on the Western Front, could vouch for only one case of prisoners being killed by their escort, and in this instance the murderer could plead some mitigation: the loss of his 'best pal' had, in Richards' view, 'upset him very much'. Killing in the heat of the moment, whatever the legal niceties, was another matter altogether. Ernst Junger, a highly-decorated German infantry officer, summed up the opinion of most experienced soldiers when he asserted that: 'the defending force, after driving their bullets into the attacking one at five paces' distance, must take the consequences. A man cannot change his feelings again during the last rush with a veil of blood before his eyes. He does not want to take prisoners but to kill.'

While the mêlée was going on, the Lancers' dismounted squadrons had prevented the two remaining dragoon squadrons from getting forward to assist their comrades. J Battery had lengthened its range as the charge went in — so that there were shells still whistling over the Germans' heads — and fortuitously caught infantry of the *Guard Rifles* in a wood near La Folie. The 20th Hussars, only two squadrons strong, advanced west of the main road and got close to a German battery but refrained from charging it because they were 'unavoidably somewhat out of touch with the remainder of the brigade'.

The action at Cerizy — obstinately called Möy by the 12th Lancers — 'very effectively damped the ardour of the German cavalry' and discouraged the *Guard Cavalry Division* from driving deeper into the gap between the two British corps. Lieutenant-General von Poseck suggests that the British crowed too loudly over it. 'On this day and the following day,' he wrote, 'The English cavalry covered, with remarkable gallantry, the English retreat. While this must be recognised without reserve, the success recorded in the report of General French and also the great losses which this cavalry is alleged to have inflicted on the advance guard regiments of the Richthofen Cavalry Corps are nevertheless greatly exaggerated.'

The exaggeration started early. In the second week of September 1914 the *Illustrated London News* carried a picture by Richard Caton Woodville (we have already seen him inventing history at Elouges) showing the Scots Greys charging with kilted Highlanders hanging onto their stirrups: this 'incident at the Battle of St Quentin' consciously harked back to the famous (and almost equally ill-founded) 'stirrup-charge' by the Greys and the Gordons at Waterloo. Countess Feodora Gleichen (sister of the commander of 15th Brigade) was inspired by Caton Woodville's work and press reports to create a bronze group of a charging trooper of the Greys with a Highlander clinging to his stirrup. Not only were there no Highlanders at Cerizy, but clinging one-handed to stirrup-leather and bounding along to keep pace with a galloping horse would tax the athletic ability of the sturdiest Jock. The bronze is now in the National Army Museum, and must be reckoned better art than history.

John and I rode off the battlefield onto the Möy–Cerizy road, where we met the road party and ate lunch. During our earlier meeting north of Möy I had not had much chance to ask how Evelyn had left things in Ribemont. It transpired that we had quickly been forgiven. 'That's horses for you' had been Bernadette's attitude.

She would accept no money for the repair of the damaged electrics, and Evelyn's present of a bottle of Scotch (we kept a reserve for just such eventualities) had brought an answering shower of Club Equestre de Ribemont badges. We christened them the Jeopardy Architectural Award, and wore them pinned to our shirts for the remainder of the trip.

Clive had spotted a Commonwealth War Graves Commission plate on the wall of Möy cemetery, just down the hill, and we drove there after lunch. Sure enough, there was a row of Portland headstones in the middle of the cemetery. To my surprise these turned out to have nothing to do with the First World War, but were the graves of the Australian crew of a bomber which had come down nearby in 1943. For the remainder of our ride we were to find that isolated graves in civilian cemeteries were more likely to be Second World War aircrew than anything else, and Bomber Command's losses were underlined by all too frequent discoveries of the crews of Lancasters, Halifaxes and Stirlings in a score of village cemeteries. Up against the back wall of Möy cemetery lie Major Swetenham, Captain Michell, his Squadron Quartermaster-Sergeant, and a private in the 20th Hussars. Michell, at forty-three, was not in the first flush of youth but his gravestone bears his family's proud inscription that he fell while gallantly leading his squadron. It seemed to me, as the sunlight bounced back from the bone-white stone, that there are far worse ways to go.

It was very much a dragoon day for us, for, having charted the misfortunes of the German *2nd Guard Dragoons*, we were to spend the night with the French 2nd Dragoons in their barracks at Couvron. To reach it we had to retrace our steps, crossing the Oise once more and traversing I Corps' 28th August withdrawal route. Evelyn and Clive rode, and I led the vehicles on to Couvron. The ground began to change as we approached, leaving the chalk downlands of the Vermandois for the high limestone north of the Aisne. To the south-west, the Forest of St Gobain swelled up out of the plain, and, to the south-east, rose the 'crowned mountain' of Laon — Lanrezac's headquarters on the 29th — built on a limestone mass which has become detached, over the millennia, from the sharp ridge which marks the beginning of the Ile de France.

I had secretly hoped for a textbook Second Empire cavalry barracks, with stables on the ground floor and barrack-rooms (in the nature of things both warm and smelly) above. But Couvron was an airfield, manned by the Americans after the Second World War and handed over on France's withdrawal from NATO's integrated command structure in 1962. It housed an artillery regiment as well as the 2nd Dragoons, whose commanding officer, Colonel de Noirmont, had generously offered to put us up. I already knew the dragoons by repute, for they are the only French regiment that can justly claim an unbroken history since their formation in 1635; when the Germans moved into the Unoccupied Zone of France in 1943 the regiment's standard was sent to safety in a submarine. The regiment had a fine fighting record. In 1815 it had formed a part of Kellermann's cavalry corps, and the ancestors of the officers who entertained us so generously had pounded through the trampled corn at Waterloo to swirl furiously between the squares in Wellington's centre. The French Army is currently engaged in what might best be described as the rediscovery of regimental tradition, and the 2nd Dragoons have revived their ancient title of *Condé Dragons*, and their badge bears a dragon (a pun which recalls that dragoons were named from the fire-spitting musket they carried) and the Great Condé's coat of arms and motto, '*Da Materiam Splendescam*'.

I am not sure that the Jacqueses and the de Rougemonts would have approved of their descendents, Holmes and Richardson, associating with French dragoons, for they had been an instrument of religious intolerance in the seventeenth century. In the process known as the *dragonnades* they were quartered on Huguenot households with orders to make themselves as unpleasant as possible: hence the verb to dragoon.

As we drove up to the barrack gates it was evident that this was a conscript army on Friday afternoon. Short-haired young men in civvies flooded out, many to be met by fond parents in the family car or by girlfriends whose enthusiastic greeting gave fragrant promise of a good weekend. The sentries at the gate were gunners and knew nothing of any arrangement between the British and the dragoons, but kept an eye on us, with amused correctness, while they phoned to find out what to do. All was evidently well, for we were told to follow signs to the dragoons' headquarters and saluted on our way. Finding the headquarters was not easy. The barracks was like Illinois transposed to France, with identical blocks of buildings arranged on gridiron streets. Eventually, I struck lucky and found regimental headquarters, where the second-in-command, standing in for the commanding officer, who was on leave, was waiting for us.

I doubt if even a British regiment which knew us well would

have arranged things better. Evelyn was to stay in the commanding officer's flat in RHQ, and the remainder of us would be housed in officers' flats in an accommodation block. The captain whose flat I borrowed had left a note begging me to 'use all you need in the room, the kitchen and the bathroom — towel, soap, cold or hot drinks, TV, radio' and had enclosed a regimental cap-badge and his squadron badge, a dragoon helmet superimposed on a dragon.

The stables were evidently expecting us. I recall a description of Union cavalry at the close of the American Civil War, looking, with their tight little shell-jackets and stubby carbines, as if they were designed to crawl through knot-holes. *Maréchal des logis chef* Olivier, the regiment's senior riding instructor, had exactly this workmanlike look in his light blue kepi, buff *terre de France* shirt and breeches, and black boots. He suspected that our horseshoes might need attention, so a corporal-farrier was ready. A vet — who had gained his professional qualification before doing his national service, and would serve his time as veterinary *aspirant* (an untranslatable rank best described as an officer cadet with power of command) — was also on hand. The stables — stalls in a building which had probably started life as an aircraft engine store — were light, airy and immaculately clean, and the grooms — their name in French, *palefreniers*, conjuring up visions of ambling medieval palfreys — may have been conscripts, but they took pride in their work and evidently loved horses. John was back on home ground and came close to forgiving us for the Ribemont incident.

We got Thatch and Jeopardy squared away quickly, cleaned the tack, sorted out the vehicles and waited for Evelyn and Clive. They arrived at 6.00 p.m. after a hot and tiring journey made worse by the fact that they had decided to walk in from the main gate without realising that it was another two miles to the stables. Evelyn was glad to see both farrier and vet, for Thomas's front shoes were worryingly loose, and he had managed to rub a raw patch under his tail. There was much discussion as to what should be done about the shoes: eventually the farrier put on a good broad pair which lasted well for the rest of the journey. The vet produced some ointment for Thomas's backside, and the wound was to heal very quickly.

All this took time, and we were in the familiar plight of having five minutes to change before joining a small party of officers for dinner in their mess. The mess — really an officers' club rather than a mess in the British sense — was of the style best termed

USAF utilitarian, and would not have won any architectural awards. We sat in the commanding officer's dining room, attractively decorated with dragoon memorabilia, and ate a seriously good dinner: asparagus, *Tournedos Rossini* and cholesterol-rich pudding. Afterwards we walked across to the *salle d'honneur*, a well set up regimental museum. Most British regimental collections are larger, but few (amongst the honourable exceptions are the Gloucesters' and Green Howards' museums) tell the regimental story as well or are as strong in early exhibits. I have collected French cavalry swords for thirty years and could cheerfully have stayed there for most of the night, but a degree of foot-shuffling from my companions suggested that I might be having too much of a good thing.

During the war, the Germans had bombarded the French capital with a long-range gun officially called the 21cm *Kaiser Wilhelm Geschütz*, but usually known simply as the Paris Gun. It is often confused with both the 38cm railway gun Long Max and the 42cm siege howitzer Big Bertha; IGN maps mark its emplacements, liberally strewn around the Forest of St Gobain, as *Ancienne Plateforme d'artillerie de la Bertha*. Outline plans for this formidable weapon were drawn up in 1916, but it was not until March 1918 that it opened fire at last. Barrels were based on Long Max's — themselves reserve stock for the battleship *Bremen* — with sleeves inserted to narrow the bore to 21cm. After fifty rounds the liner was so eroded that 24cm shells were fired: the liner lasted another fifty rounds at this calibre and 26cm shells were used for a final fifty rounds, after which the barrel required completely re-lining. Seven guns were built, and one was totally destroyed by a premature explosion, probably because a 26cm shell was inadvertently fired through a new 21cm liner. The shell weighed 236.5 lbs, and had a maximum range of 71.5 miles: at the zenith of its trajectory, ninety seconds after firing, it was 12,500 feet above the ground.

The Paris gun weighed in at 297 tons and could only be transported by railway. Its emplacements were reached by short spurs leading off main lines. A concrete bed 35 feet in diameter and 15 feet deep had a 28-foot metal turntable on top. The gun was run onto the emplacement between two bogies, and was then jacked onto the turntable and the bogies were removed. There are several emplacements near Couvron, and the dragoons suggested that we should hack off to see one. They would lend us three horses so that we could all ride out, leaving the morning pair — Ollie on Thatch and Clive on Jeopardy — to go on to the lunch rendezvous while the rest of us rode back to Couvron, boxed up Thomas and Magoo, and drove off to meet them.

We mounted under *Chef* Olivier's watchful eye. I made a less than elegant job of clambering aboard Kirsch, my borrowed *Selle Français* mare — how I yearned for the Colonel's Trivia — and I could see John and the *chef* exchange knowing looks. The *cheval de Selle Français* (French saddle horse) originated in a fast harness horse produced when Norman breeders crossed imported English thoroughbred stallions with tough general-purpose local mares. They have a good deal of the French Trotter in them, and once we were out of barracks Kirsch picked up a snip-snap trot that had us out at the emplacement an hour later.

There was not much to see, but as the site is on an army training area it had not been interfered with, and it was not hard to work out what was what. The metal turntable has gone — none of the guns were captured in France or found in Germany by the armistice commission — but the concrete emplacement is still there, the hole in its centre now filled with sinister black water. Well-preserved bunkers alongside a low embankment leading onto the main line sheltered the detachment and housed ammunition. The emplacement is folded neatly into the lower slopes of the forest, and was difficult to hit; the French did not manage to silence any of the Paris guns with counter-battery fire.

Shells fired from this position spun high above Crépy-en-Valois to fall in the north-eastern suburbs of Paris. To reach the city centre the Germans had other emplacements — we were to ride past one south of St Gobain that afternoon — which gave them the precious extra miles. Between 23 March and 9 August 1918 these guns hit Paris with 303 shells, killing 256 citizens and wounding another 620. This did not break French civilian morale, but was regarded as yet another example of hunnish frightfulness. As we wandered around the emplacement I thought of Saddam Hussein's supergun and Iraqi use of Scud missiles against urban targets during the Gulf War. Bombardment of civilians rarely produces the hoped-for result: its more likely consequence is to encourage reprisal and deepen the ravine of bitterness which divides the combatants.

We saw Ollie and Clive on their way and rode back to barracks. The dragoons had done so much for us that we distributed our thank-you presents — specially-made models of a 16th Lancer in 1914 field service marching order — in greater than usual profusion, and I left their barracks with a renewed respect for these ancient adversaries. Their *salle d'honneur* helped keep the regimental tradition alive, and it was easy to see that *Chef* Olivier and his team did much to foster the cavalry spirit. I had chatted to him about riding in the French army as we trotted back. He had joined as a simple *palefrenier* and worked his way up, with equitation courses alternating with spells of duty with a number of cavalry regiments. There was a close connection between military and civilian riding, and some of his horses were provided by the *Fédération Française d'Equitation* on condition that they could be used by civilians, and we certainly saw plenty of activity in stables and manège that Saturday. It struck me as another example of working consensus overriding departmental boundaries. Riding has a useful morale-building function in the cavalry, and is a popular civilian sport, argue the French; very well, let us bring the two together so that the one can help subsidise the other.

We had chosen the Carrefour de la Croix des Tables, deep in the forest two miles south-east of St Gobain, as our lunchtime rendezvous, and Ollie and Clive appeared, leading their horses down a long, straight ride, just as we arrived. It began to rain during lunch, but we had set the table up beneath massive pines so were not unduly inconvenienced. By the time I mounted Magoo and set off with Evelyn on Thomas, however, the rain was beating down steadily, and as we crossed the Laon–La Fère road to pick up the first of our forest tracks I was sure we were in for a wet afternoon. Within twenty minutes the rain had gone, and in another twenty we were unpleasantly hot in our macs. They came off somewhere north of Septvaux; we did not wear them again for the remainder of the retreat.

I was glad that the weather had picked up its cue, for on Sunday 30 August — only a week after Mons — I Corps found its march through the Forest of St Gobain unpleasantly hot. 'Marched off 3 a.m. through the Forest of St Gobain,' wrote Ma Jeffreys.

When the sun got up it became frightfully hot. We went on through the Forêt de Coucy and passed Coucy le Château, which seemed a wonderful old place. At one place in the forest a lot of pheasants were being reared in rows of coops. At a halt I had a talk with [Lieutenant-Colonel the Hon.] George Morris. He was very gloomy: said it was the old story of Allies failing to get on together and that everything was going wrong. He finished up by saying we should be re-embarking for England in a fortnight!

Chetwode's men were not far behind. 'Started for Brigade Rendez-vous at Armigny [just south of the Oise] at 4.00 a.m.,' recorded Lieutenant-Colonel Edwards of the 20th Hussars. 'Brigade marched to Deuillet [south of La Fère] and retired to successive positions at St Gobain and Coucy le Château to billets at Vauxaillon. Very hot day marching through woods.' Paul Maze, riding with the Greys in the same brigade, was more favourably impressed. He found the forest a 'haven of peace. We rode for miles over a carpet of moss cooled by the shade of high trees that met over our heads like the arches of cathedrals — the drive was like an endless aisle.' Aubrey Herbert's battalion had seen an aeroplane early that morning, and 'everybody fired at it at once; thousands of rounds must have been fired, and I found it useful in teaching Moonshine to stand fire. She took her first lesson well, although she broke up the formation of half a company. We often saw aeroplanes, and they were nearly always shot at, whether they belonged to friend or foe.'

While I Corps was trudging along those stifling forest rides, Lanrezac's men were pulling back from the slopes around Desolation Farm away to the north. They had attacked on the foggy morning of 29 August, and although Lanrezac's two attacking divisions got safely across the Oise — the long blue columns of the 38th Division would have swept right past our billet in Ribemont — they did not plunge rapier-like into the open flank of Bülow's right-hand corps, but were fought to a standstill west of the river, with the spire of St Quentin's basilica tantalisingly visible over the distant crests. By 1.00 p.m. the attack had palpably failed. It was then that the fussy, irascible and pessimistic Lanrezac proved that he had the opportunist eye of a shrewd tactician and deeper reserves of moral courage than his Allies could ever have guessed. He swung his main effort through ninety degrees, giving Franchet d'Esperey of I Corps operational control over III and X Corps and telling him to attack northwards towards Guise.

D'Esperey had already moved his headquarters up to Hérie-la-Viéville and had turned a blind eye to an order directing him to send a division off by rail to cover the left rear, so was well-placed to carry out these new instructions. He concentrated fifteen artillery regiments on a three-mile front and then threw his weight straight up the main Guise road. Too many times that summer had French infantry stepped off shoulder to shoulder, thin bayonets glinting on their long Lebel rifles, officers capering ahead of the line, only to be mown down — for once that cliché is the only appropriate phrase

— like corn before the scythe. But this time French shrapnel scoured those bald slopes like a giant sand-blaster and Bülow, his attention bent to the battle on his right, was caught flat-footed.

It was one of the month's few glorious moments. As his infantry boiled over the crest-line, d'Esperey ordered his staff to mount and rode forward, shouting to Colonel Pétain — a big, chilly-mannered infantryman commanding a brigade in his 1st Division, going on astride the road — 'Well, Mr Staff College Professor, what do you think of this movement?' Pétain's reply is not recorded, but it is clear that many of those present thought a great deal of the change from a long and dispiriting retirement to a sharp and well-executed counter-attack. 'Everyone was full of enthusiasm and wanted to press forward,' recalled one officer. 'We saw, we felt the will of the high command which had decided to be strongest there,' wrote another.

Although d'Esperey's attack did not reach Guise, it cleared the ground as far as Desolation Farm and sent disheartened Germans reeling down the hill into the town. Bülow, not the most resolute of the German army commanders, called for help from Kluck who promptly replied that he would change direction the following day, making for the Oise in the sector Compiègne–Chauny. In fact this was entirely unnecessary. Lanrezac's success was purely transient — the ground taken was relinquished on the orders of GQG on the 30th — and even Bülow soon got over the shock, telling Moltke on the 30th: 'Enemy decisively beaten today; strong forces retiring on La Fère. The British, who were barring the Oise south-west of La Fére, are also retreating in a southerly, and some in a south-easterly direction.' But instead of telling Kluck to resume his march south-westwards, Bülow directed him to maintain his south-easterly line in an effort to consummate *Second Army*'s supposed victory by cutting off Lanrezac.

The effects of this order were far-reaching. Kluck had already made contact with Manoury's 6th Army, currently forming up on the Allied left as Joffre shuttled troops across from Alsace-Lorraine. Had he churned on south-westwards he would not only have done such serious damage to Manoury's fragile little force as to render it incapable of carrying out the role assigned it, but might even have curled west and south of Paris as Schlieffen had intended. The change of direction gave Manoury a breathing-space, and though it brought *First Army* back into contact with the British, it began the process which would take Kluck east of Paris, offering a flank which the Allies could attack.

The attentive reader will have noticed that there has not been much mention of Moltke of late. This is because, during these breathless days of late August, he was not controlling events on the Western Front: events, increasingly, were controlling him. Although German Headquarters (OHL) moved from Koblenz to Luxembourg on the 29th, it was still too far away from the marching armies on the right wing to control their movements on a day-to-day basis. When Kluck swung in to assist Bülow, Moltke weakly assented to what was in effect a significant change of plan, agreeing that: 'The movements carried out by First Army conform to the intentions of OHL'.

If they did, it was only because OHL's vision was blurred by the fog of battle. Before the move to Luxembourg Moltke had briefly allowed himself the luxury of thinking that the Germans had won the war on the Western Front. But if the news from the west was generally good, that from the *Eighth Army* on the Eastern Front was emphatically bad. The Russians had won an early victory at Gumbinnen, persuading Moltke to replace the *Eighth Army*'s pessimistic commander with General von Hindenburg, brought out of retirement; Major-General Erich von Ludendorff, who had been instrumental in the capture of Liège, was dispatched to act as his chief of staff. This formidable duo was to inflict a shattering defeat on the Russians between 26–30 August. But Moltke, with no gambler's nerve, had already sent two corps from the Western Front to assist them. Two more had been sent to mask Antwerp and another invested Maubeuge; this latest dilution left the German right wing a total of five corps weaker with the decisive battle yet to come. And now, oblivious to his predecessor's emphasis on swinging round Paris, Moltke was prepared to allow his army commanders to chase a fleeting local advantage by beginning to turn in front of the French capital. Somewhere beneath the sandy soil of Pomerania old Schlieffen must have been spinning in his grave.

Not all Moltke's problems stemmed from primitive communications. He himself was finding the exercise of command an almost unbearable strain. The Kaiser 'positively revelled in blood', and Moltke found the Supreme War Lord's exuberant hand-rubbing increasingly hard to bear. There was plenty for the Kaiser to gloat about, for across the whole of the Western Front it was evident that the Germans were setting the pace. The French offensive into Alsace-

Lorraine had ended in disaster. Far from recovering the lost provinces, they had been bundled bloodily back onto their own territory — here again Moltke's instincts were flawed, for he allowed his armies there to counter-attack, thus driving the French back out of Schlieffen's trap — and were clinging to a line Verdun–Nancy–Belfort only with difficulty. The weary young men who made up the sweating mass of all combatant armies in those scorching weeks of late August and early September had long since lost any sense of perspective; the only realities were raw feet on dusty cobbles, the numbing weight of rifle and pack, and exhaustion so profound that many were sleep-walking. But even they could glimpse signposts and see that Paris was getting closer; the Germans were winning, and everybody knew it.

Yet they had not won, and, occasional flashes of optimism aside, Moltke knew that. There had been battles, but none which could be deemed decisive. There were prisoners, but not the sea of broken humanity left when an army disintegrated. There were captured guns, but not the abandoned batteries that betokened terminal loss of self-respect. Joffre knew all this too. Suddenly his bland stolidity, his insistence on a good lunch eaten in reverent silence, and his ability to nap in the back of a car while his chauffeur — a racing driver conscripted for just that purpose — hurtled him between headquarters at a dry-mouthed seventy, were qualities priced beyond rubies as the campaign teetered in the balance. For although the Allied armies had suffered appalling damage — moral no less than material — their central nervous system was still intact, and there were as yet no serious symptoms of that progressive sclerosis which presages collapse.

But behind Joffre's impassive mask lurked the realisation that his armies' spinal cord was close to snapping. On 1 September he ordered withdrawal to the line Verdun–Bar-le-Duc–Vitry-le-François–Arcis-sur-Aube and Nogent, with the British at Melun. As Correlli Barnett has emphasised in his study of the campaign, this left only three lateral railways from Paris to the armies of the centre and right, and a French railway expert acknowledged that: 'In a short time we should have been placed in the impossibility of keeping our armies alive and giving them the means to fight'.

Joffre's new orders made no difference to what, for tens of thousands of British and French soldiers, was the exhausting and dispiriting reality of the retreat. Douglas Haig's corps fell back through the Forest of St Gobain on 30 August 1914. As we rode through the forest seventy-nine years later I became aware, for the first time, of how tired I was. The succession of late nights, early starts, and the relentless drudgery of looking after horses had left me feeling more brittle than I would have expected. I wanted a bath, eight hours' uninterrupted sleep and the chance to sort out my kit — now an untidy bundle of questionable socks and shirts that made even Thatch roll his eyes. I had been fit when we started and none of the riding had caused me any difficulties until that day, when a combination of Kirsch's jerky little trot and leathers a hole too short had left me with a sore leg. Magoo was a good deal less comfortable than Thatch, and as the afternoon glowed on he needed more and more encouragement.

We had over fifteen miles to do and Evelyn set a good pace, walk and trot in equal portions and a good, mind-clearing canter over an open shoulder of hill north of Septvaux. The day got hotter and hotter, and there seemed nobody alive in the heat-haze apart from three walkers in the depth of the forest. A little girl scampered up to us and asked if we were Indians. I told her that alas we were not, just Englishmen riding from Mons to the Marne in our grandfathers' footsteps. Her parents were fascinated. When had we started? Where did we stay? How far did we ride each day? The little girl was unimpressed, and as she tripped away she told her mother that Englishmen were fine but Indians would have been more fun.

In mid-afternoon we dropped down a long valley towards the valley of the Ailette and the forest fell away on both flanks. Evelyn pointed at a spur on our left. 'Coucy-le-Château is up there,' he said. 'I know it was flattened during the First World War, but I'm surprised it's *that* flattened.' My morale took a nasty jolt. I had been to Coucy-le-Château before, and knew perfectly well that this was not it. The puzzle solved itself very quickly as we rode into a village which announced itself as Coucy-la-Ville: we had come out of the forest on a track just on the wrong side of the Renault brook, and were still a mile or two north of the castle. The horses stamped through the village's one long street, whose house-fronts seemed to reflect the heat like the bars of an electric fire, and as we emerged at the far end there, up on our left, was the castle on its hill.

The sight of Coucy never fails to move me. It is the greatest medieval castle in France, capital of a family more powerful than many monarchs, who scorned high-sounding titles and took as their motto a couplet of mock humility:

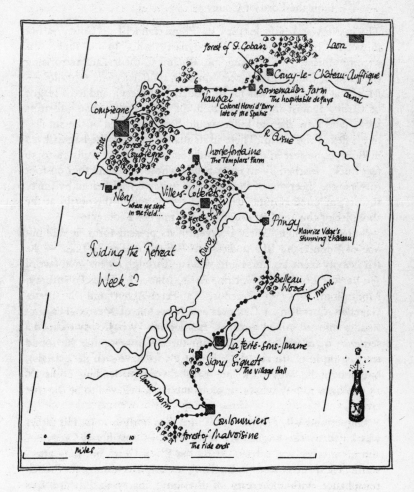

forest of St Gobain

Laon

Concy-le-Château-Auffrique

5 Bonnemaison farm
The hospitable de fays

6 Naupal
Colonel Henri d'Evry
late of the Spahis

Compiègne

R. Oise

forest of
Compiègne

R. Aisne

canal

8 Montefontaine
The Templars' farm

7 Néry
when we slept
in the field...

Villers-Cotterêts

forest of
Villers-Cotterêts

9 Pringy
Maurice Vidge's
stunning château

Riding the Retreat

Week 2

R. Ourcq

Belleau
Wood

R. Marne

La ferté-sous-Jouarre

10 Signy Signets
The village hall

R. Grand Morin

Coulommiers

forest of Malvoisine
The ride ends

0   5   10
Miles

Roi ne suis, ne Prince, ne Duc, ne Comte aussi.
Je suis le Sire de Coucy.

(Not king nor prince, not Duke nor Count am I;
I am the Lord of Coucy.)

The castle was begun in 1223 by Enguerrand III de Coucy, a not unworthy representative of his dynasty who, in his time, was excommunicated for breaking into Rheims Cathedral and terrorising the canons, fought in a succession of wars (*Coucy à la merveille* — Marvel at Coucy — was his immodest battle-cry), and led a league of barons against the crown itself. In plan, Enguerrand's fortress looks (and how the old killer would have approved of the simile) like a flexed right arm. There in its mailed grip lay the largest keep in Europe, 90 feet in diameter and 180 feet high, its walls 18 to 30 feet thick, clenched by an inner bailey whose walls and four 90-foot towers rose sheer out of the valley. A massive wall braced by thirty towers surrounded outer bailey and town, and in the north, at the shoulder of this mighty limb, was the mighty Laon gate.

Stunning though Coucy is, even in its present form, it was but one of Enguerrand III's possessions. When he died in 1242 — he fell heavily from his horse and was run through by his own sword — he was Lord of St Gobain, Assis, Marle, La Fère, Folembray, Montmirail, Oisy, Crêvecour, La Ferté-Acoul and La Ferté-Gaucher, Castellan of Cambrai and Viscount of Meaux. His successors enjoyed mixed fortunes. Enguerrand IV narrowly escaped a sentence of death for stringing up three young squires he found trespassing in his forest (those bright glades have seen dark deeds), but bought his way back into royal favour by lending Louis IX 15,000 *livres* to buy what that pious monarch believed to be the true cross.

Enguerrand VII, greatest of his line, was born in 1340. His father was killed by the English six years later — possibly at Crécy — and his mother was carried off by the Black Death not long afterwards. He spent 1360–67 in England, initially as a hostage for French compliance with the treaty of Bretigny, marrying Edward III's daughter Isabella and being created Earl of Bedford. The king improved the bargain by agreeing to release the Count of Soissons, who had as yet been unable to buy his liberty, at the price of his county which was presented to Enguerrand. Coucy's life was dominated by war. He campaigned in Italy, Austria, Switzerland,

France and North Africa, and eventually perished in 1397 after being captured by the Turks at the disastrous Battle of Nicopolis. 'O St Lambert, Coucy, La Fère,' declaimed the poet Eustache Deschamps,

> Marle, Oisy and St Gobain,
> Weep for your lord, the good seigneur,
> Who served so well his sovereign
> With prowess great in many lands . . .

The Coucy inheritance dwindled after Enguerrand died. His daughter sold the barony to the Duke of Orleans (the good duke, alas, omitted to disgorge much of the purchase price), and it passed on to the Orleans branch of the royal house. Coucy itself was a centre of noble resistance to the regency of Cardinal Mazarin, and in 1652 the cardinal's sappers did their best to blow up the keep, but its stout masonry was too much for them. Forty years on, nature came close to succeeding where man had failed, and an earthquake left a great crack in its enormous wall. And there the castle stood for another two centuries, glaring out angrily over the Ailette and the Forest of St Gobain. It caught the eye of the parvenu emperor Napoleon III, who was on the lookout for a restorable ruin, but he eventually decided to renovate Louis of Orleans' castle at Pierrefonds, which was more accessible from Paris. The architect, Viollet-le-Duc, much given to over-medievalising the buildings he tinkered with, threw two broad belts of iron round the keep and took steps to prevent further deterioration.

With such a turbulent history behind it, Coucy might have expected that the worst was over. But in 1917 the Germans planned to shorten their line in France, and thus reduce the troops required for defensive purposes, by withdrawing from the great salient which bulged out to Noyon like some malignant growth. The land between their old position and the new Hindenburg Line was devastated with a thoroughness that dismayed even some of its perpetrators: not for nothing was the operation named after Alberich, the spiteful dwarf in the Nibelungen saga. Railways were ripped up, roads cratered and bridges dynamited. Unoffending avenues of trees were hewn down across the roads they had once shaded; even orchards were levelled. Slabs of explosive were tucked up chimneys to bring down the house when the fire was lit, and a huge mine, detonated by a delayed action fuse, destroyed Bapaume town hall, burying the Australian brigade headquarters which had taken refuge in it. One German, stunned at the destruction carried out by his countrymen, left a placard in the ruins of Péronne begging passers-by: 'Don't be angry: Only wonder'.

Crown Prince Rupprecht of Bavaria, the more than competent commander of the German army group in Picardy (it was he who gave the French such a pounding in Alsace-Lorraine in 1914) begged Ludendorff, the real power behind the German military machine, to spare Coucy — manifestly of no military value — whose destruction 'would only mean a blow to our own prestige quite uselessly'. It was never wise to appeal to Ludendorff's finer feelings: German engineers stuffed twenty-eight tons of explosives into the keep and blew it to pieces.

The towers of the inner bailey are sadly cropped, but much of the curtain wall and its round towers have survived, and the commanding ruins were in our sight for a good hour as we turned north of Coucy to cross the Ailette at Pont St Mard. We were making for Bonnemaison Farm, three miles south of the Ailette, not far from Vauxaillon, where 3rd and 5th Cavalry Brigades spent the night of 30 August, and between the halting-places of the two divisions of I Corps. By now the gap in the British centre was only six miles wide, and II Corps — together with the newly-formed III Corps, which comprised 4th Division and 19th Brigade — had reached the Aisne around Attichy. Allenby had at last regained control of a large part of his division, and had 1st, 2nd and 4th Cavalry Brigades on the BEF's left around Compiègne.

The oppressive heat forced Haig to curtail his march on the 30th, and as we emerged from the valley to climb onto the open limestone beyond it it was not hard to see why. We were at our hottest between 4.00 and 6.00 p.m. when the ground seemed to throw back the warmth it had absorbed all day. I must have looked disheartened, because Evelyn slipped into the brigadierish mode and told me, every half-mile or so, that it was only another mile. Eventually we caught sight of Bonnemaison, standing sturdily amongst its trees just over the watershed between the Ailette and the Hozien brook, a tributary of the Aisne.

When my feet hit the ground as we dismounted to walk the last mile I knew all was not well. I had been kicking the tired Magoo on so relentlessly that the insides of my calves were very sore indeed, and I suspected that something rather nasty lurked beneath my boots, now crusty-white with horse sweat. Magoo had had enough. He splayed his legs, lowered his head and would not move. I got him going by a mixture of tugging and cajoling, and we limped down a tiny road towards the farm. A stringy youth — pimples and *bleu de travail* in equal parts — on a small but noisy moped puttered slowly past us, turned round and puttered back. Then, sure enough, he repeated the process, revving exploratorily for good measure. If looks could kill, his bones would be whitening in the ditch. Our basilisk stares must have conveyed an unmistakable message, for he fizzled and banged his way across the crest and did not reappear. There was not a lot of chatter over the last few hundred yards. We agreed that it was as well that we would not be set a tactical problem on our arrival, and I began to understand, just a little, how the St Quentin colonels must have felt.

Bonnemaison was an instant restorative. We crunched down the drive into the yard, which would have housed an infantry battalion and effortlessly swallowed up our vehicles, with a long row of farm-buildings opposite and to the right, and the house — four stories of brick dovetailed with limestone, demonstrating that we were on the frontier between Picardy brick and Ile de France stone — on our left. The others were already there, and the stalls, with plenty of clean hay, had the O'Flaherty seal of approval. Our host, Monsieur de Fay, wandered down to welcome us, and suggested that we might care to join him for a drink on the lawn when we had finished with the horses. I left Magoo at his supper and walked up through a wicket-gate onto the lawn, where the de Fays were relaxing on garden furniture with the creeper-covered elevation providing the perfect backdrop. There was a dull murmur which I first took for a distant motorway, but which turned out to be a myriad of bees busy in the creeper. Madame de Fay, an attractive, stately lady, introduced me to her son, daughter and son-in-law who were down from Paris for the weekend, and the family and its fox-terrier (*un fox*) made me so welcome that I quite forgot how fed-up I had been only an hour before.

There was to be a small, informal drinks party followed by dinner for the family, and a shower beforehand was a real necessity. Evelyn, Ollie and I worried our suitcases up the winding staircase to our rooms at the top of the house; Clive and John were to sleep in a cottage across the yard. My room, sky-blue sprigged with white, was tucked away under the eaves with a view across the lawn and down towards the headwaters of the Hozien. The whole house was redolent of unlaboured good taste with the deep patina that few designers can imitate. There were good pictures, old hunting prints, nice furniture, and a fine rain of bibelots, not perched archly on highly-polished surfaces but scattered about with unconcern. And yet it was a working farm: I did not feel in the least out of place clumping upstairs in my dirty boots.

I am a chronic hypochondriac. Every year I am afflicted by terminal headcolds and incurable twinges, and I never travel without a wide selection of pills and potions to tackle everything from warts to amoebic dysentery. I was glad of them that evening. When my boots came off they brought a certain amount of skin from the inside of my calves with them, and I went downstairs in a mingled aura of cologne and antiseptic. Drinks were on the lawn, and the de Fays had kindly invited a selection of English-speaking neighbours to minimise the language problem. However, champagne is not only an admirable anaesthetic but a rich thesaurus, and I spoke French with unusual fluency!

At about 8.30 the neighbours slipped away and we went in to dinner. It was in the same style as everything else at Bonnemaison, delightful but unfussy. We started with port-filled melon, went on to pork and spinach (how ordinary that sounds, but how marvellous it tasted), made a brief raid on the Maroilles and finished with orange sorbet. The de Fays are an ancient family, part of this high limestone landscape. I could not help noticing the simple fleur-de-lys blazon on Monsieur de Fay's signet ring. 'Ah, that,' he said. 'My ancestor got it for saving the life of King Philip at the battle of Bouvines.' I remembered the story. At Bouvines, in 1214, Philip Augustus was unhorsed while fighting a mixed force of Flemings, Germans and English. A huddle of footsoldiers were fumbling for a gap in the king's armour through which they could slip a dagger when a party of French knights rescued the king: hence the de Fay arms.

I rashly recalled another de Fay: Godemars, bailiff of the Vermandois, who commanded the detachment which defended the Somme ford at Blanchetaque against the English during the Crécy campaign of 1346. From the French perspective this was a less than happy story. The little force had been riddled by archery and driven off by English knights: Godemars was wounded, lost his banner, and then heard that King Philip had announced his intention of hanging him for his failure to hold the crossing. Fortunately, so Monsieur de Fay assured me gravely, this was no slight on the family escutcheon, for the name was not uncommon and the unlucky Godemars was no relative of *his*.

There had been de Fays at Bonnemaison for many years, and it was not hard to imagine an ancestor of our kindly host riding away on that fatal expedition to Nicopolis behind Enguerrand de Coucy's red and white banner. I was surprised to hear that the house had been totally destroyed during the First World War, for it had certainly been sympathetically rebuilt. The feature on which it stands, dominating the ground for miles around, had been taken by the 5th Cuirassiers in May 1918. The younger de Fay had done his national service as an *aspirant* with the regiment, and found that one of its tanks was named *Bonnemaison* after the battle. Just as the 2nd Dragoons had delved into the *ancien régime* to rediscover Condé, so the 5th Cuirassiers had revived their old title, *Roi de Pologne*. The monarch in question was Stanislas Leszczynski, elected king of Poland in 1704 but driven out by Peter the Great in 1709. His son-in-law, Louis XV, had made him Duke of Lorraine, and Stanislas ended his days in his charming little capital at Nancy, whose famous square bears his name.

By the time that I sipped *eau de vie* in front of the fireplace it was hard to imagine that I had never been to Bonnemaison before — and harder still to think that, in the rough old way of the world, I would probably never be there again. I felt entirely at home with the de Fays, and the proximity of Coucy, our discussion of the Crécy campaign, and the fact that British horsemen had trotted back past the farm on 31 August 1914 — they might easily have watered their horses in this very yard — served only to emphasise our common history. So what *were* we going to do about Maastricht, asked de Fay *fils*. I thought it would be a close-run thing in Parliament (how right I was) and that if the question was put to a referendum it might be closer still. He hoped that we would ratify the treaty, for, whatever we might think about it, many Frenchmen saw Britain as a cultural counterweight to Germany, and a Europe without Britain would be a poorer place.

VII

MOST DISTRESSING SIGHTS

Success in war depends more on moral than physical qualities. Skill cannot compensate for want of courage, energy and determination; but even high moral qualities may not avail without careful preparation and skilful direction.

Field Service Regulations

Haig's corps had spent 29 August 1914 resting north of the Forest of St Gobain — we can understand Lanrezac's rage at British refusal to help him that day — and after nearly a week on the road we too needed rest. On 15 August 1993 we planned to take things quietly. We would travel due west to Nampcel, which would put us back on II Corps' route. It was only nine miles away as the crow flies, and Evelyn and Clive would ride Thomas and Jeopardy and lead Thatch and Magoo, so that all four horses would have some exercise. Although they were off to church that Sunday morning, for it was the feast of the Assumption of the Blessed Virgin Mary, the de Fays had been down into Pont St Mard to conjure up some fresh croissants, and we left Bonnemaison well-breakfasted and in high good humour.

I took the road party down to Epagny and then drove through Autreches to reach yet another *Chaussée Brunehaut* which runs along a stark re-entrant jabbing down towards Vic-sur-Aisne like a giant's finger. The critical reader will observe that there are quicker ways of getting from Bonnemaison to Nampcel, but Ollie's map-reading was not at its most incisive that morning. In any event, we had time on our side, and the villages north of the Aisne were at their best, with church-bells all along the valley and a smell of incense so penetrating that it briefly competed with the more pungent aura of boot and saddle which the Trooper had now taken on.

Nampcel lies at the head of a sharp slash in the limestone, and our destination, Pertron Farm, clung to the southern edge of the cut. Our host, Colonel Henri d'Evry, was waiting for us, dark and wiry in his Sunday best. He explained that he had to be off to church, but wanted to show us where we could put ourselves and the horses before he went. Pertron was quite unlike Bonnemaison but no less striking. We approached up a winding, tree-lined track with caves in the limestone on our right. The farm complex, all built from the same honey-coloured stone, was rectangular, with a cathedral-like barn on the right, a long two-storey run of buildings — stables below and hay-lofts above — on the left, and the d'Evrys' house hard on the left by the entrance. The good colonel was anxious to give us as many options as possible. We could put the horses here — or perhaps there. We could sleep in the loft — or in another barn. The horse-box could go in the courtyard; or, if we preferred, there was good hard standing higher up the hill. He was showing me yet another possible parking spot when Madame d'Evry, who had made several attempts to get her husband off to church, drove up from the house, shone me a knowing smile, and opened the passenger door. The colonel shrugged and got in; all good soldiers know when the odds are impossible.

We parked the box and the Trooper in the yard and set about preparing the stables, which had not been used as such for many a year. There was a car sideways-on in one of the stalls: it must have been carried in by brute strength. It took an hour or so to put down hay and fill buckets, and we then turned our attention to assembling camp beds in the loft above. It was another scorching day, and the opportunity to do some washing was too good to miss. I dealt with a week's accumulated socks and underwear in a stone trough next to the stables, cunningly fashioned a clothes-horse from a piece of old timber, and rigged it in one of the loft windows so that the clothes would be in the warm air but would not make the yard look like a dhobi-wallah's. Like so many of my good ideas, the clothes-horse lasted five minutes: a freak gust on that otherwise airless morning blew it down into the yard, and I was intimately supplied with chaff for the remainder of the trip.

Evelyn and Clive rode in at 2.00 p.m., slightly better in health than temper. I could see why, for the familiar grey muzzle bore the green badge of shame: Thatch, the menace of the stick removed, had snacked his way across the Berlinval plateau and was not the most popular horse in Christendom. We ate a leisurely lunch in the shade of the huge barn, and I was secretly glad not to be riding out under the polished dome of the sky that afternoon. Colonel d'Evry was eager to show us the battlefields around Nampcel, of which he had made a special study, and we set off in his car after lunch. When the Germans fell back from the Marne in September 1914, they dug in on the high ground overlooking the Aisne, and the French launched repeated attacks out of the valley against these great farm complexes — Escafaut, Quennevières, Touvent — that command the re-entrants like scaled-up limestone pillboxes. The fighting showed the French Army of 1915 at its worst and best. Plans were usually unimaginative and there was never enough artillery; in particular, there were too few heavy guns to deal with trench-systems which linked up with the caves honeycombing the limestone. Time and time again, French infantry answered the thin call of their bugles with an ardour worthy of a better plan, and monuments to their wasted valour dot this naked landscape.

On the edge of a field beside the road to Vic lies Second-Lieutenant Michel Desjardins of the 204th infantry, killed in action on 18 June 1918 — when the French stopped the last of Ludendorff's offensives on these slopes — at the age of twenty. An empty shrapnel shell had been filled with flowers and left at the foot of his cross. Further north was the *Butte des Zouaves*, a shell-pitted, grassy knoll where a memorial commemorates soldiers of a Zouave regiment — Europeans recruited in Algeria — who fell there in 1915, many of them entombed in the limestone. All around lay the debris of battle: here the trigger-guard of a Lebel, there the butt-plate of a Mauser 98. I even found a .303 cartridge, which can only have been dropped by one of Smith-Dorrien's men on his way to Attichy on 30 August.

The most striking piece of jetsam was an unexploded 210mm heavy shell. One of the problems confronting French and Germans alike in this limestone country was that conventional shells exploded on the ground or just beneath it. If a fuse on the shell's nose was set to give a long delay between impact and explosion in an effort to pierce the roof of a cave or deep dug-out — which might work well enough on soft ground — the fuse would be damaged as it penetrated the limestone and the shell would fail to explode. The answer was to use base-fused projectiles, and this monster lying beside the *butte* had a brass fuse still screwed securely into its base.

The iron harvest is garnered at almost every track-junction. The majority of shells are French 75mm or German 77mm, lying in rusty heaps to await the bomb disposal teams. They are still killers. 'I had some difficult moments when I was serving,' said Henri d'Evry, 'but have never been closer to death than during spring ploughing this year. A shell blew the back of the plough and spattered my tractor cab with shrapnel.'

On our way back into Nampcel we stopped at a bunker shown as *Abri du Kronprinz* on the *Institut Géographique National* map. It is wedged under the southern lip of the valley and reinforced by stone from the ruins of the village. German defences often reached a level of sophistication shunned by the Allies, who assumed that the next big push would get the Germans on the move. Why construct elaborate defences if you did not expect to stay in them for long? The bunker at Nampcel is a two-storey structure, the size of a decent three-bedroom house. The floors are neatly tiled, and rotting battens on the walls show where wooden panelling was fixed. A tunnel, now blocked, leads off towards the front trench system. There is a tendency to call all such command bunkers *Abri du Kronprinz*, but there is only the slimmest of chances that 'Little Willie' — far less of a success as an army commander than his fellow crown prince, Rupprecht — was over here. It is more likely that some monocled *oberst* commanded his regiment from these solidly-built rooms, looking out across Nampcel at the smoke from 155mm shells which could never quite drop in sharply enough over the valley edge to reach him.

If the *abri* was impressive, the caves were almost unbelievable. They were all around Nampcel, chamber after connecting chamber cut out by masons quarrying stone, used by the Germans between September 1914 and their withdrawal to the Hindenburg Line in April 1917, and again briefly in the early summer of 1918, and by the French in 1917 and late 1918. Multinational graffiti embosses their butter-soft walls. At the entrance to a big cave north of the village, an iron cross surmounts a signpost to *Stabs 7 Kompanie*, and further inside an elaborate script announces the *Poste Chirurgicale* of the 37th Division. Unofficial artists have made their own contributions, not always in the best of taste: the kindest thing that can be said for Gretchen, carved with much anatomical emphasis by a homesick German, is that she is a sturdy girl.

Henri d'Evry's mother had remained in Nampcel throughout the First World War. Her farmhouse, La Carrière, across the valley from Pertron, was flattened by shelling, but she stayed on in the caves behind it. When the Germans withdrew in 1918, they left behind one of their guns, and the advancing French presented it to madame. There it lies, amongst the nettles in a corner of the farmyard, a 77mm produced so late in the war that its barrel did not bear the usual royal cypher or inscription proclaiming it 'The King's Last Argument'.

Pertron farmhouse was full of d'Evrys that weekend. There was a daughter, across from Paris with her young sons — they had exhausted John's supply of sweets when he tried to bribe them away from the horses that afternoon — and a son, back from his regiment with a fellow subaltern. Henri regretted that he could not fit us all in to dinner, but would we join him for a drink before we went off to dine at the 'Croix d'Or' in Attichy, where he had booked us a table for 8.00? There was a fête in the village and, as he was mayor, he had to go and set off the fireworks, but would be back at 7.00. We kept an eye on his garage so that we did not arrive before him, but it was not until 8.00 that he reappeared, civic duty done. He assured us that there would be no problem over our table, phoned Attichy, and set about opening bottles.

As the champagne flowed, we chatted about our trip. He knew more than a little about the cavalry, for he had served with a mounted *spahi* regiment in Algeria during the war between the French and the *Front de Libération Nationale*. Horsed cavalry still had a role there even in the early 1960s, he assured us. The *spahis* rode tough little Barb stallions — 'good horses, mind, but a real handful' — said the colonel. They had been one of the sights of the campaign in 1914. 'We saw some of their Algerian cavalry for the first time,' wrote Sally Home on 7 September, 'mounted on tiny Barb ponies but all quite cheerful.' In the Algerian war the *spahis* carried American MI carbines, and there was a light machine-gun in each troop. The officers had pistols, and all ranks still carried the brass-hilted 1822 pattern light cavalry sabre tucked under their saddle flap on the nearside. A squadron would advance in open order with two of its four troops leading, an NCO and four men well ahead of each troop. When the point bumped guerrillas, the squadron would dismount and fight on foot. It was a good system, for the Barbs could cover ground impassible to vehicles, and the men were far fresher than infantry when the fighting started.

On one occasion in 1961, when he was leading one of the forward troops of a *spahi* squadron in the mountains, Henri d'Evry's unit ran into a position that was much too strong for it. 'It was a bad business,' he said.

> I had several men hit and it was hard to get the wounded away: you know what that meant. Then the squadron leader called the officers back to a gully 300 metres behind, where the led horses were. 'Gentlemen,' he said, 'I am going to charge.' We all looked very hard at him, then saluted, went back to our troops, and drew swords. He ordered *'En avant, chargez, galop.'* We troop leaders repeated it, and the troopers came out of the gully really fast, with a yell. The *fellagha* were taken completely by surprise. We must have killed twenty of them, and we didn't lose a man.

He brought some tack out of his study — red Morocco leather over a deep saddle, and a painfully severe bit — and we talked about the *spahis* and the 6th Hussars, which he had commanded (I fear that they had been at Yorktown when Cornwallis surrendered in 1781, but we will not hold that against them). Madame gave no hint of the fact that the combination of fireworks and light cavalry was not doing much for dinner, but I looked at my watch and saw that we were already an hour late for our table at Attichy.

We were an hour and a half late when we eventually arrived, and I was ready for squalls. There was not a cloud on the horizon. We were the Englishmen Monsieur d'Evry had phoned about? Late? Don't mention it. It was one of the best dinners of the fortnight — and there was fierce competition. I started with a chicken liver salad of such gargantuan proportions that I first thought that I had been served someone else's main course by mistake, then I ate sea-bass grilled with fennel, looked briefly at the cheese and finished, for I am boringly predictable where puddings are concerned, with *crème caramel*. Having ascertained that Ollie was driving back, I drank rather a lot of Sylvaner — as I glance at the bill to refresh my memory I see that some heavy metal fanatics preferred Côtes du Rhône, but I could not have done it justice on such a sticky night.

The 'Croix d'Or' had something in common with the de Fay household: stylish but unpretentious, self-assured without a hint of arrogance. And very kind. In 1914 it was less difficult than we might think for soldiers to communicate with their families. The Army's postal service continued to operate even during the retreat — letters took three or four days — and many officers dropped into French post offices and sent telegrams which arrived a good deal faster. Some of us, however, were finding communication ridiculously difficult. It went against the grain to make international calls from private houses, and if there was a phone box handy, and we had the right change, then there was nowhere convenient to park the horse. John was particularly anxious to phone home, and asked our waitress if there was a telephone in the restaurant. She looked puzzled. Of course there was: it was not a pay phone, but he was welcome to use it. He duly phoned Melton Mowbray and returned looking much more cheerful. How much was the call? A dismissive shrug. Now, were we going to risk a *pousse café*?

It was not a quiet night. By about 4.00 in the morning the clink of hooves on cobbles, coming up from the stables below, could no longer be ignored. At least one horse had broken out of its stall — there were no doors, so the horses had been tied by their head-collars — and would have to be put back in. I hauled on jeans and boots, and Evelyn saw me in the half-light and at once got up himself. Downstairs, we saw that Magoo had joined the greys in an escape committee at one end of the stable, where there was a variety of things that Thatch might have deemed edible. Fortunately, he seemed to have eaten nothing, so the spectre of colic did not raise its head. By the time we had tied the horses up again sleep was out of the question, and I walked up onto the plateau above the farm and watched the beginning of another baking day.

None of us was at our best that Monday as we boxed all the horses and drove to the *Rond-Pont de l'Armistice*, just east of Compi-ègne. There had been a knot of railway spurs there in 1918, built for shifting heavy guns between lines, and early on 7 November 1918 the German delegation arrived by train from La Capelle, south of Maubeuge. Foch — a corps commander in front of Nancy in August 1914 but Allied commander-in-chief in 1918 — received them for a wintry interview in his carriage at 9.00 a.m. At 10.00 on the evening of the 10th the German government authorised its delegation to accept the Allied conditions, and the armistice was signed at 5.15 a.m. on the 11th: it was to take effect at 11.00 that same morning.

The spot where Foch's carriage stood is marked by rails and sleepers with a commemorative stone between them, and nearby is a small museum which contained the carriage itself. In June 1940, Hitler's fine sense of historical irony encouraged him to bring the French delegation to the same carriage to sign the armistice which ended the 1940 campaign; it was then taken gleefully back to Ger-many and destroyed by the RAF in a bombing raid. The museum now houses an identical carriage from the same works as the original, but somehow the sense of place has evaporated.

John and Clive rode the first leg. We had picked a lunchtime rendezvous from the map, but when we attempted to drive to it found all approach tracks blocked by low wooden barriers. Eventually, we parked the box and the Trooper as close as we could get them to the selected *carrefour* and walked out to meet the riders. Confused by a profusion of identical-looking junctions, they were over an hour late, and lunch was unusually hurried. The horses were hitched to one side of the box — the other was hard against bushes on the other edge of the track — and as I crouched under their heads to get past I stumbled, put out a hand to support myself, and gave the startled Jeopardy cause to nip me. He caught my right index finger squarely in an unyielding bite. I walked straight into the woods to nurse my pain, but found it hard to tighten up the girth when it came time to mount.

I suppose that Compiègne is the most beautiful of the forests we rode through. Henry Owens had certainly liked it, and enthused about its 'beautiful old beeches, oaks etc' on 30 August. Its tracks, many of them laid out for hunting by Napoleon III, are wide and sandy, and most of the *carrefours* (with evocative names like Puits de Roi, Cheval Noir, Hamadryades, Sanglier and Grand Maréchal) have pretty white signposts which ought to make map-reading easy. But I was out of sorts as we tittupped through its sun-dappled glades. Sunday ought to have been a rest-day, but I had spent it rooting around the *Butte des Zouaves* and Touvent Farm, and had compounded the folly by doing much for the prosperity of the *vignerons* of Alsace. My head ached, my finger throbbed, and the nail had already turned a discouraging purple.

The afternoon went on, and on, and on, and we eventually emerged from the forest above Béthisy St Martin to see that our destination, Néry, was still separated from us by another aching limestone ridge just like those on the other side of the Aisne. The sweat ran from under my hat in rivulets which joined to form a quagmire where belt and breeches met shirt. I make a point of wearing a hard hat when riding, but for most of that afternoon it was more than I could bear, and hung from a D ring on my saddle. Those personal accounts of this stage in the campaign made such perfect sense. Alan Hanbury-Sparrow had looked at the weary column of his own battalion.

Walking at its head come the CO and his adjutant, and the old man is so weary that only his courage gets him along. Behind him creeps the battalion at the slow, lumbering pace of the agricultural labourer. Half the packs are missing, three-quarters of the greatcoats gone; woollen cap-comforters — absurd name — are the headgear of many, whilst not a few got rid of all their equipment and carry only a rifle and a cotton bandolier. Altogether it's a distressing and alarming sight, this column where no four are abreast and no two in step.

Sally Home thought the cavalry almost as exhausted. The last leg of the journey down to the Aisne had been 'a most trying march . . . men slept in saddles — they had been going for three days — little or no food, little or no sleep'. When he rode through Compiègne on the 30th he pitied

the poor inhabitants, they are terrified of Germans. You see old men, old and young women and children fleeing along the roads, it is terrible, who wants war? This retirement is a terrible strain, and the only thing that keeps one up is the knowledge that Russia is advancing and Germany must, must beat France before she can turn and cope with Russia. I know this but the men don't — they are wonderful really.

The rumour of Russian success — a broadening ripple from that scrambling little victory at Gumbinnen on 20 August — was widespread. On the 28th, Henry Owens heard 'great news about the war'. The Russians were about to bombard Berlin, and the Germans on the Western Front were cut off by a French army driving up through their lines of communication. Nobby Clarke of the Bays 'heard that the Germans had been asking for peace', and wondered 'if we'd won, drawn or lost!' Had the truth been known — that as tired troopers swayed in their saddles down these forest rides, thousands of dispirited Russians were already surrendering amongst the pine-trees of East Prussia — morale might have been a good deal worse.

Things were much the same for the Germans. 'Of the general situation, even of that of our own army,' thought Walter Bloem, 'the senior staff-officers one met appeared to know nothing. The so-called 'common herd' . . . had to be kept moving like a flock of sheep and given no why or wherefore.' His Brandenburgers had descended the Somme valley with Péronne in flames on their right, and in Mesnil-Bruntel, just south of the burning town, Captain

Bloem was billeted on a woman who, unlike so many of her neighbours, had stayed put. 'Why should I run away?' she asked him.

> In the year 1870, when I was quite a young woman, a German army-doctor was billeted here for twelve days, and, believe me, I looked after him properly. I did all his washing, mended his clothes. I did every mortal thing for him, *tout, tout, tout, monsieur*! and all for love . . . Oh what a handsome fellow he was!

On 28 August Hans Stegemann wrote enthusiastically about his unit's performance at Le Cateau, but concluded: 'I will write no more about the battlefield. It is difficult to see how anybody came out of it unscathed. One gets quite cold-blooded and indifferent.'

Already the BEF was looking different. Not only was uniform being worn anyhow, much of it with unofficial modifications like cut-off sleeves and trouser-legs, but officers and men alike had little chance to wash or shave and most were bearded. Count Gleichen managed to get two days' growth off on the 28th by moistening his brush in the dew on the grass but he was luckier than most. 'Bathing and shaving were out of the question,' admitted George Barrow. 'We all had beards.' Arthur Osburn spent that night in the village of Le Plessis Patte d'Oie, between Ham and Noyon, and at 7.00 the next morning was trying to remove the past week's grime, 'squatting on the floor with only a towel round my waist, trying to shave, before a piece of looking glass propped up on a chair' when the Germans arrived. In the ensuing panic he lost all his medical equipment, as well as his razor, toothbrush, water-bottle and field-glasses. 'The infantry stragglers look the utter limit,' thought Trevor Horn, 'unshaved or washed, clothes filthy, and a general sullen don't-care appearance to them.'

There were fewer swords in evidence than there had been a week before. 'Officers were able to get rid of their swords,' wrote James Pennycuick after Le Cateau. George Barrow was surprised at Verberie, just up the road from Béthisy, where we left the forest, and escaped in the nick of time, leaving his sword behind. He was not sorry, for it was 'a useless weapon'. Sometimes it was as well that so many swords had been jettisoned. Robert Money recalled a night move 'enlivened by Vandela threatening to spit the Regimental Sergeant Major with his sword. I don't know why, anyway he had no sword so it was alright.'

It was a hard retreat for horses as well as men. Lieutenant Brereton recorded that Major Eardley-Russell of 39th Field Battery 'collapsed from fatigue' on the 28th, and on the 29th 'two or three [horses] were quite exhausted, so had to be shot before we left . . . The question of horses was getting rather serious. We had lost quite a few at Le Cateau and a few more had since had to be shot. All horse shoes had been thrown away at Voyennes and some of our horses wanted shoeing badly.' Kenneth Godsell thought that: 'The horses are in a wretched state — at least the 1st Line transport horses — and I am afraid it is due to bad horsemanship and carelessness. One of the Manchesters' SAA [Small Arms Ammunition] horses was one of the most disgusting things I have ever seen through ignorance on the part of the transport officer. Our horses are prize winners by comparison.' 'We were often hungry,' remembered Nobby Clarke of the Bays, 'and so were the mules and horses and how those poor creatures suffered. I think they must have been more tired and out of condition than we were. Innocent victims of man-made madness. They broke your heart, especially when you passed the injured ones, left to die, in agony and screaming with pain and terror.'

We followed the German *4th Cavalry Division* to Néry. It had passed the *Rond-Pont de l'Armistice* at dusk on 31 August and reached Béthisy St Martin at 4.00 on the morning of 1 September. The division — three two-regiment brigades and a twelve gun horse artillery *Abteilung* — had lost 468 men at Haelen on 12 August, and had been clipped again at Le Cateau, when 4th Division's gunners had killed its artillery commander, Major Wagner. In order to make better speed in pursuit of II Corps, the division had abandoned its regimental transport and ammunition column on the Oise on 31 August, and that night Lieutenant-General von Garnier set a murderous pace down these sandy rides through the forest. Troopers slept in the saddle and awoke in a different squadron — or even a different regiment. His *3rd Brigade* relieved the *17th Brigade* on advanced guard at dawn, and scarcely had it done so when news came in that a British force was bivouacked at Néry.

Garnier at once issued orders for an attack. His guns, with the *Guards Machine-gun Battery* on their left, would be pushed forward onto a ridge 600 yards from the village. Under their cover, *3rd Brigade* would attack the British left flank from Béthisy St Pierre, while *17th Brigade* would leave its *17th Dragoons* in the big farm at Le Plessis Châtelain and attack the British right with the *18th Dragoons*. Garnier's remaining brigade, *18th*, was held back as divisional reserve.

The ground at first seemed to confirm the wisdom of the plan.

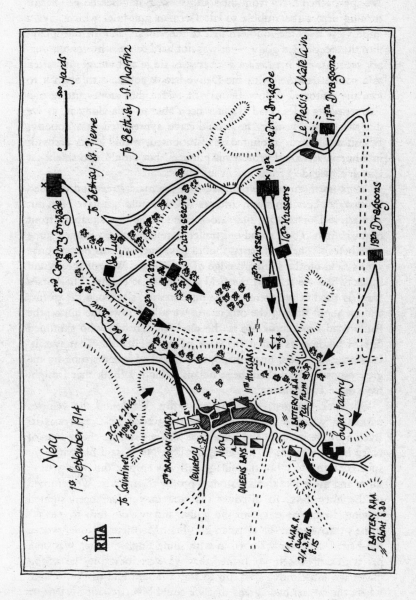

Néry
1st September 1914

We approached Néry from the south-west, riding behind Feu Farm, turning across the stubble to the German gun-line, which gave a good view over the southern part of the village, and then dropping into the steep-sided gully — it was not hard to see why contemporary accounts call it a ravine — between ridge and village. It started as a natural feature, with the Deuve brook coursing through it to join the Automne below Béthisy St Pierre, but stone-cutting had sharpened its sides. Had Garnier been able to ride along it, as we did that early evening, he would have appreciated that nobody, British or German, mounted or dismounted, would attack across it in a hurry. It would protect his gunners, but would also shield 1st Cavalry Brigade's front just as effectively.

At its northern end, we turned into the main street and plodded southwards between stone cottages which would not have been out of place in Dorset. Our first shock came in the tiny square in front of the church. There stood our trailer, carefully pre-positioned some time before. The road party should have moved it to our bivouac site, a field on the southern edge of the village. We got the second shock when we reached the field and found it empty. The horses were as tired as we were, so we dismounted, slackened the girths, and set about finding the others. As we toiled down the hill on the Rully road I got too close to the plodding Thatch, who skimmed one of his hooves down the back of my right calf. That was it. Headache, no sleep, bitten hand, no kit and now hamstrung by the grey monster. Had there been uhlans behind, I think that I might have done a Flashman.

Our luck changed, but only gradually. We found the vehicles parked in what seemed to us to be the wrong field. But was it? Evelyn drove me into the hamlet of Verines, where the mayor of Néry lived. He was at the village hall in Néry, said his wife. We sped back to Néry but the village hall was empty: this was getting more and more like the Keystone Cops by the minute. We returned to the horse-box, to discover that the mayor had been sighted driving down the track up the gully, and we ran him to earth a stone's throw from the German gun-line. Monsieur Claude, whose red-haired daughter weighed in with some English which was on a par with our French, confirmed that we were indeed in the wrong place: we must move back up to the southern end of the village, where the farmer had agreed that we could bivouac. For his part he was happy to give us the keys to the village hall so that we could use the showers, and he promised to return later to see how we were. I suspected that he was more anxious to see that we were actually in the right place after the evening's peregrinations.

We set up in a field occupied on the night of 31 August/1 September, 1914 by L Battery RHA. The remainder of 1st Cavalry Brigade was in the village to the north, with the Bays west of the main street, where the Villeneuve road enters Néry, the 11th Hussars in the centre of the village, around the church, and the 5th Dragoon Guards at its northern end, opposite the cemetery. Our preoccupations were much the same as those of Brigadier-General Briggs' tired horsemen. We had to water the horses, which meant filling jerry-cans in the village hall and bringing them down into the field, and feed them. It had been difficult to find hay in Nampcel, and although Henri d'Evry had tracked some down he had been the first to admit that it was not of the best, and even the omnivorous Thatch had his doubts about it. I am not certain that much tack-cleaning went on during the retreat, but we cleaned ours every night, and a fair division of labour gave me (an incompetent cook, and definitely in the infant class when it came to stable management) all four sets. Now I really understood William Nicholson's delight at his appointment as a signaller in H Battery RHA 'which put me into the battery staff and relieved me of my two sets of draught harness which was a great day for me'.

Monsieur Claude returned while I was up to my elbows in saddle-soap; John and Clive were rigging a picket line for the horses and Evelyn was finishing feeding them. Hard on his heels came a Renault van, driven by a weatherbeaten, stocky, dark-haired man built like the model for a John O'Flaherty farrier. It was the owner of the field. He was delighted to let us camp there, but would we not prefer a better site up in the village, closer to running water? We wanted to bivouac in L Battery's field? Very well, they were brave fellows and he quite understood. But what an earth was that in the haynets? Hay? Rubbish. It was terrible stuff, full of dust, and would make the horses cough. He was dead right. Thatch gave a wet snort almost exactly on cue: I could have killed the brute. Where had we got it? North of the Aisne? God knows what they fed horses there, but it would never do in Néry. 'You, young man,' he said (I am not called that much these days) 'you come along with me and we'll get these horses fixed up.'

The farmer — with my fatigue and his patois I never discovered his name — drove me to his house just inside the 11th Hussars' lines. An assortment of dogs bounded up to greet us as we entered;

there was a cat perched dangerously on the edge of the Aga, and a mynah somewhere audibly offstage. His wife, in build the female counterpart of the farmer himself, recognised me at once. 'I saw you ride in on that big grey,' she said. 'I've got one just like him: come and have a look.' But first we should have a drink. After two vision-blurring measures of Ricard, I swayed expansively down the yard to look at the horses. Madame undid the back gate: a Percheron and a butterball of a bay with palomino mane and tail — which turned out to be a Comtois — trotted happily over to their mistress's whistle. I could almost have mistaken the Percheron for my own long-faced chum. There was the same less than fashionable head, the same huge hooves, even the same dappled grey.

What with the Ricard and the discovery of Thatch's great-uncle I would have forgotten the hay, but the farmer remembered in time and we returned to the field with the van full of it. 'That's proper hay,' he announced proudly, jamming a handful of it under John's nose. 'Good and sweet, with lots of clover. Your horses will love it.' Corporal Watson had complained of finding hereabouts 'fierce middle-aged Frenchmen of the *bourgeois* class, hard as Scotsmen, close as Jews, and with feelings about as fine as those of a motor-bus'. His description struck no chord with us. The farmer positively refused payment for the hay, accepted a bottle of Scotch with genuine reluctance, and hoped that we might have time to drop in on him before we left.

By now Ollie had finished cooking. The meal, tinned steak and kidney pudding, peas and potatoes from army compo rations, could scarcely have been more of a contrast to the delights of the 'Croix d'Or'. But I was past caring. I fell on a massive portion with a hunger sharpened by the day's tribulations, and the fact that the Château Beauregard was not perhaps ideally *chambré* caused me no pain at all. We were finishing supper in the golden circle of an oil lamp when Thomas broke away from the picket line and strode purposefully over to join us, standing quietly with his head over the table, almost joining the conversation and certainly casting a wistful eye over the claret.

We slept in the open, heads on our saddles, posting one sentry to keep an eye on the horses. Evelyn, who took the first watch, woke me at 12.30 a.m., and I paced about under the brightest stars I can remember, thinking of L Battery seventy-nine years before, officers (two of them spending their last night on earth) in their bed-rolls under the hedge behind us, horse-lines near the road and the six 13-

pounders, dew dulling paint and brasswork, in line by the gate at the top of the field. The sounds were just the same. Magoo snored softly, Jeopardy paced about restlessly, and Thatch rasped away at an empty haynet: there were grunts from my sleeping companions, and a creak of leather as somebody strove to make more of a pillow of their saddle. I was just getting ready to rouse Ollie at 2.00 a.m. when Jeopardy broke loose. He had ingeniously contrived to unclip his lead-rope as well as pull it off the picket line, and Thatch — I would have thought better of him — slipped a hoof over it. It took me an age of scrabbling in stubble and dung by torchlight to find it, but eventually Jeopardy was secure again. I woke Ollie and was asleep in seconds.

17 August 1993 dawned misty, but visibility was much better than on the morning of 1 September 1914 when it was barely 100 yards. 1st Cavalry Brigade had been ordered to be ready to move at dawn. At 4.00 a.m. it stood to arms but as the mist was so thick the move was postponed and units were told that they could unsaddle and have breakfast. L Battery had been formed up in column of sections at the top of our field, and on hearing of the change of plan Major Sclater-Booth ordered the teams to be unhooked and taken off to be watered.

Brigadier-General Briggs, believing that he was in reserve and that there were other units between his brigade and the enemy, had taken no steps to screen the position, and units — each in theory responsible for its immediate front — did nothing till 4.15 a.m. when the 11th Hussars sent out Lieutenant G. W. A. Tailby with Corporal Parker and five picked men. Tailby's squadron leader had told him to reconnoitre the ground east and south-east of the village to see if there was any sign of hostile movement to the north. He found a zig-zag path which took him up the gully — it was a steep ride in broad daylight and cannot have been much fun in the mist — and then cast about the plateau.

He found nothing and was on his way back when, not far from the spot where the track leaves the gully, he spotted a column of dismounted cavalry to the east. 'By the appearance of their long cloaks and spiked helmets,' he reported, 'I knew they could be none other than the much heard-of uhlans.' They were actually the *2nd Cuirassiers* of *3rd Cavalry Brigade*, and when one of Tailby's men — who had not seen the bulk of the Germans — fired at their leading scouts, the cuirassiers mounted and charged Tailby. He galloped straight for the gully and found a cart track but his horse fell and would not get up, so he told the patrol to get away and scrambled into the bushes. The Germans wheeled off and Corporal Parker soon reappeared with Tailby's horse. They galloped into the northern end of the village, where a woman outside an *estaminet* produced a cloak and a rifle dropped by Germans who had been startled by the patrol's appearance. Tailby sent Parker to warn the 5th Dragoon Guards, and returned to his own regimental headquarters to announce that the enemy was close. He was not at first believed, but the cloak and rifle enabled him to carry the argument. Lieutenant-Colonel Pitman of the 11th was on his way to brigade headquarters when the German artillery opened fire: surprise was almost complete.

Lieutenant-General von Poseck was right to proclaim that: 'The security of the English troops, apparently worn out by the long retreat, failed completely.' There was chaos in the village as shells burst amongst L Battery's guns and the Bays' horses to the rear. Nobby Clarke thought that 'a lot of them were terribly injured and killed and many of them had stampeded off with fright. There were men hanging onto them but we couldn't stop the horses bolting. We had no idea of what was happening, just that we had been shelled. Then it seemed that everybody got into action. Gunners dragged their guns into action, troopers improvised a firing line.'

Major Sclater-Booth was knocked down and disabled by a shell-burst on his way back from brigade headquarters, and Captain Bradbury managed to swing three guns into action against the batteries only 600 yards away. One was immediately atomised by a direct hit, and soon Lieutenant Giffard's gun was also silenced, its detachment wiped out. Gunner Darbyshire was crouched in the layer's seat of the surviving gun, 'but so awful was the concussion of our own explosions [British shrapnel would have been set to burst almost at the gun's muzzle] and the bursting German shells that I could not bear it for long. I kept it up for about twenty minutes, then my nose and ears were bleeding because of the concussion . . .' Darbyshire stepped down to give a hand with ammunition and Lieutenant Campbell took over. He had fired only a couple of rounds when a shell burst under the gun-shield and hurled him, mortally wounded, six yards away.

Another HE shell burst just behind the gun, knocking Darbyshire down as he ran forward with an armful of ammunition and taking off both Bradbury's legs. 'Though the captain knew that death was very near,' wrote Darbyshire, 'he thought of his men to the last, and begged to be carried away, so that they should not be upset by seeing him, or hearing the cries which he could not restrain.' Battery Sergeant-Major Dorrell now took command of the gun, manned by Sergeant Nelson, Driver Osborne and Gunner Darbyshire. Nelson was wounded soon afterwards, and Osborne was hit in the ribs by a spoke ripped from a wagon-wheel, but they kept firing until I Battery unlimbered 2,000 yards behind them at about 8.00 a.m.

Briggs had been caught badly off-balance, and to make matters worse his brigade major, Stephen Cawley of the 20th Hussars, was hit early on. Lieutenant Arkwright of the 11th Hussars saw him sprawled in the main street 'with a ghastly wound in his head, obviously done for, poor chap, although he was still alive then. On the other side was a gunner corporal firing away with a rifle quite regardless of bullets all about him, and cursing the Germans all the time, saying they had wiped out his battery and praying they might all be killed themselves and so on.' Briggs was a hard man. He had commanded the Imperial Light Horse — 'filled up with tough frontiersmen, hunters, gold seekers and colonial boys' during the Boer War — and at Néry he rose to the occasion. He pulled A Squadron of the 11th Hussars into brigade reserve, and used it to barricade the southern end of the village, while the other two squadrons and the regiment's machine-guns lined the stone-built houses and garden walls on its eastern edge and engaged the guns on the ridge.

Lieutenant-Colonel Ansell of the 5th Dragoon Guards was ordered to turn the German right flank. His regiment had lost so many horses that it could only mount two squadrons, and he dropped one off on the northern end of the 11th Hussars' firing line and led the other across the gully and up onto the ridge. Because of the mist the Germans — *3rd Cuirassiers* and *9th Uhlans* — could not see that Ansell's force was so tiny, and his counter-attack effectively stopped their advance, securing the northern flank. But at a cost. 'We enlisted to be professional soldiers,' thought Richard Chant, 'and believe me Colonel Ansell made us just that.' 1 September was 'a sad day for the regiment,' he lamented, 'as Colonel Ansell was fatally wounded'. Captain Edward Balfour, his adjutant, thought that the CO's death actually inspired the men. 'When the Colonel was killed,' he wrote, 'they got a bit mutinous and were all for going back towards the Germans.'

On the southern flank, a handful of men from Major Ing's squadron of the Bays — led by Lieutenants de Crespigny and Misa, with the deft assistance of Sergeant-Major Fraser — worked their way close to the sugar-factory at the junction of the Béthisy St Pierre and Rully roads. They were unable to stop the *18th Dragoons* of *17th Cavalry Brigade* getting into the factory, but prevented any move across the road. 'We managed to stem the German advance for a while,' wrote Nobby Clarke, 'but due to casualties we had to withdraw. The Germans were machine-gunning us from the sugar-factory and I recall that the Germans were finally shelled out of the factory and outbuildings by I Battery of the Royal Horse Artillery.' De Crespigny was killed, and only three of the party were unwounded.

With both his flanking brigades stuck fast, Lieutenant-General von Garnier committed his reserve, *18th Cavalry Brigade*, at about 7.00 a.m. Its two regiments, *15th* and *16th Hussars*, made a mounted advance towards Feu Farm and L Battery's position, but although the *16th*, on the German left, actually got into the gully both regiments had to dismount and could make no progress in the face of the rifle and machine-gun fire from the village.

Briggs had sent gallopers off to ask for help as soon as the battle started. 4th Cavalry Brigade was at Verberie, three miles to the north-east, and because the mist made it hard for Brigadier-General Bingham to work out what was happening, he shunned a radical solution but dismounted two of his regiments, 3rd Hussars and 6th Dragoon Guards, just east of the village, and sent a squadron of the Household Cavalry to work round the German flank by the sugar-factory. Its leading troop, under Lieutenant 'Volley' Heath, rode for the guns, and Heath seems to have got right up onto the ridge before he fell.

Bingham's gunners made the decisive contribution. I Battery came into south-west of the sugar-factory at 8.00 a.m. and its shells made German COs, whose men were now fighting dismounted, fearful for their led horses. Worse still, British infantry was now coming up, part of the Middlesex from the north-west and the Warwicks and Dublin Fusiliers, much-recovered since St Quentin, from the west. Lieutenant-General von Garnier decided to break off the action. He had lost 188 officers and men and 232 horses. As far as his gunners were concerned, it was Le Cateau in reverse, for the ridge was now swept by British fire and only four of the guns could be got away. 1st Cavalry Brigade had lost 133 of all ranks and up to 390 horses, and L Battery was effectively a total loss; H Battery RHA came out from England later that month to replace it.

After breakfast on Tuesday 17 August we drove through Néry to the cemetery at its far end. The sleepy village gives no hint of its state after the fight. 'When the battle ended,' remembered Private Clarke,

> somewhere about 10.00 a.m., we helped collect the wounded and cleaned up, collecting bits and pieces of useful equipment. Many men and horses, both British and German dead and abandoned guns . . . I never saw my own horse again. She was called 'Daisy'. She was a lovely, docile, intelligent girl. I had a quick look for her but I suppose she'd either been blown to bits or stampeded and ended up as someone else's mount in another regiment.

James Jack came up with the advanced guard of 19th Brigade to find Briggs 'assisting to man a Vickers gun'. Robert Money arrived to find the 'ground littered with dead horses, wounded men etc. But the German guns were standing deserted. The comic thing is that the Middlesex claim to have captured 11 of them, whereas it was our gunners who actually killed the Germans . . . ' Colour-Sergeant E. M. Lyons of the Warwicks had asked an RAMC major if he could go ahead to help with the wounded.

> As we got near the village most distressing sights met us. On the roadside there were turned over limbers complete with teams of poor horses all killed trying to escape and just off the roadside were lying the bodies of the drivers. I felt very sad. In the village I assisted the RAMC men to load up the ambulances. After the last one went off I was still scouting around to make sure there were no more wounded. There was one we couldn't put in the ambulance he was so badly wounded so we borrowed a farm cart and packed it with straw and made him as comfortable as possible. He was the battery commander Capt Bradbury who I'm sorry to say died soon.

Captain Edward Kinder Bradbury VC RHA lies in the communal cemetery at Néry. His headstone also remembers the two other VCs of the action, Battery Sergeant-Major G. T. Dorrell and Sergeant D. Nelson. Dorrell became a lieutenant-colonel and survived the war. I already knew Nelson's fate, for while looking for the grave of Major-General Thompson Capper at Lillers in Flanders three years before I had passed the headstone of Major David Nelson VC RFA, killed in the spring of 1918.

There are another 16 RHA graves in the cemetery, and a small obelisk honours another seven members of L Battery. Against the back wall, by Bradbury's grave, a larger pillar commemorates

Bradbury, Campbell and Stephen Cawley, the brigade major. My knowledge of the Cawley family is consistent with my ability to recall historical details but to forget my own birthday. About ten years ago, my wife and I had been staying at Hope End, jewel among country house hotels, near Ledbury, and while pottering idly back from Ludlow we had called in to see the National Trust's Berrington Hall, near Leominster.

The war hit landed families so hard that a visit to a stately home all too often furnishes melancholy evidence of the lost generation. In a downstairs room at Berrington hangs a photograph of the house's owner, Sir Frederick Cawley, with his four sons, ready to hack out to a meet of the North Herefordshire Hounds in 1908. The photograph speaks louder than tomes of worthy demography. Stephen was killed at Néry. Harold let neither his age (he was thirty-six) nor his seat in the Commons dissuade him from volunteering. He died in Gallipoli on 23 September 1915 while serving with the Manchesters, and lies in Lancashire Landing Cemetery at Cape Helles. Oswald, the youngest brother, was killed at Merville, near Armentières, on 22 August 1918. His father, elevated to the peerage as Baron Cawley, had enough influence with the Imperial War Graves Commission to have him exhumed, and so Captain the Honourable Oswald Cawley, Shropshire Yeomanry, rests in Néry cemetery with Major John Stephen Cawley, 20th Hussars. *Noblesse oblige*, indeed.

I am wobbly about prayer, but it came easily enough that morning, with the dew on my boots and the brassy old sun sneaking out across the rooftops of Néry. Somehow, after the previous day's mishaps, I had crashed through a pain barrier. I was unquestionably filthy: when I stopped in Crépy-en-Valois to buy lunch later the queue wilted as I joined it. My sensibilities were so blunted that I found myself cleaning my teeth after sponging what is euphemistically termed Thatch's dock area without having washed my hands in the interim and the fact worried me not at all. One breeches pocket was full of bailer twine, and in the other I had a penknife and a few francs. I had slept for perhaps five hours for each of the past three nights, but thought that I could go on for ever.

That Tuesday we were to ride back across the BEF's line of retreat, get into I Corps territory again, and spend the following day looking at the action at Villers-Cotterêts, fought on the same day as Néry. We have seen that the continued withdrawal was having a steadily abrasive effect on the BEF. Many units which had not yet fired a shot in anger — much of I Corps, folded back behind the French 5th Army for the past week, came into this category — were leaving a tail of stragglers behind them. Battalions which had fought at Mons and Le Cateau, and now found the Germans close behind them again as Kluch's turn scraped *1st Army* right across the BEF, were often in a much worse state. Even John Lucy, so proud of his Irish Rifles, saw the warning signs.

> I rate Tymble for lurching out of his section of fours, and he tells me to go to bloody hell. I say: 'Shut up, cover over, and get the step.' He tells me that bastards like me ought to be shot for annoying the troops, and that it would not take him long to do it. I get annoyed, and moving close to him ask him gently what he would suppose I would be doing while he was loading up to shoot me. His comrade nudges him. He titters like a drunkard, wipes his mouth wearily with his sleeve, and says he is sorry.

The retreat was doing as much damage to Anglo-French relations. On the 29th, Joffre, disturbed by persistent rumours that GHQ was considering withdrawing from the line altogether, had driven over to Compiègne to see Sir John French. Joffre emphasised that it was vital for the BEF to stay up in the line, and assured him that the Russian offensive would soon force the Germans to curtail their operations in the west. French declared that his troops were at their last gasp and required forty-eight hours' rest, and Murray tugged at the skirts of his chief's tunic to prevent him yielding to Joffre's pleas.

First World War generals can no more win the historiographical battle than they could achieve clean breakthroughs on the Western Front. French and his successor, Haig, are repeatedly criticised for persisting with offensives — the deadly litany goes from Neuve Chapelle and Loos in 1915, through the Somme in 1916 to Third Ypres in 1917 — long after their subordinates had any confidence in success. Yet, in contrast, French is accused of lack of firmness because he over-identified with his men in early September 1914. He had become convinced that the BEF urgently needed to rest and refit, and this was an accurate reflection of the opinion of most of his officers and men. 'The real truth', declared Sally Home on 5 September, 'is that we must refit.' On 30 September French warned Joffre that:

> I feel it very necessary to impress upon you that the British army cannot under any circumstances take up a position in the front line for at least

ten days. I require men and guns to make good casualties which have not been properly estimated owing to continual retirement between fighting rearguards. You will thus understand that I cannot meet your wishes to fill the gap between the Fifth and Sixth Armies . . .

A horrified Joffre had no alternative but to agree, although he did persuade GHQ to move east of Paris to avoid becoming tangled in 6th Army's communications. Kitchener, in London, got wind of the plan when he heard that the BEF's main base was to be changed from Le Havre to St Nazaire, and Le Mans would replace Amiens as the forward base. He immediately asked French for more details, and Sir John replied with a general criticism of the French high command and the assurance that he did not propose 'a prolonged or definite retreat'. On the 31st, Sir John again told Kitchener that he could not stay in the line, and when Sir Francis Bertie, Ambassador in Paris, passed on an entreaty from President Poincaré, French responded gruffly: 'I cannot do anything until I can refit'.

French was wrong. The BEF was committed to a life-or-death struggle, and the idea that it could somehow slip out of the line, refit and appear when it felt better was at variance with the real character of the war. Sir John's badly-worded and often contradictory telegrams showed that he was not thinking clearly. However, his disquiet was not altogether unreasonable in view of the almost total disaster which had now overtaken Joffre's plan. And we should not censure French for having a rather British view of war. By the standards of his own experience (and GHQ was as consistently overestimating British casualties at this time as it was to overestimate German casualties for the remainder of the war) the BEF had lost very heavily. Whole units had disappeared. More guns had been lost than at any time since the American War of Independence. Old friends were visibly shattered. George Barrow saw even the rock-like Allenby crumble for a moment, when he 'sat on a chair, elbows on knees, and head on hands in the attitude of utter fatigue and dejection'. And nice youngsters, fresh-faced sons of brother officers, youthful reminders of his own time as a subaltern, were dying. French was wrong; but we should think hard before we turn the laser of hindsight on this tired old gentleman who was doing his best for the army he had spent his life in.

On 1 September, with Nobby Clarke still picking his way through the debris at Néry, Kitchener and French met at the British Embassy in Paris for what we would now call an interview without coffee.

Although there is no impartial account of the conversation, Kitchener's telegram to the cabinet said it all: 'French's troops are now engaged in the fighting line where he will remain conforming to the movements of the French army though at the same time acting with caution to avoid being in any way unsupported on his flanks'. French was not one to forgive and forget. He complained to Winston Churchill that the meeting had taken him away from GHQ on 'a very critical day', and was deeply hurt by the fact that the cabinet had chosen to 'send another FM out here to lecture me (he came in FM's uniform) . . . ' But there was no more talk of withdrawing from the line: Joffre and French would stand or fall together.

17 August 1993 was a textbook day. Clive and Ollie rode out to May Farm, north of Crépy-en-Valois. Once again we had selected the spot from the map, but unlike the barricaded *carrefour* in the Forest of Compiègne it was easy of access, and the farmer's wife was happy to let us set up our table in the forecourt of her substantial house on its windswept ridge. Our lunch was pleasantly interrupted by two English ladies, mother and daughter, friends of the family on whose property we were encamped. When Evelyn and I rode off on Jeopardy and Thatch they were still being entertained by the wheels party, glad of the opportunity of speaking English to a pretty girl.

We rode due east down a long track between two huge stubble-fields, and then edged north to pick up a disused railway track which runs through the oak and beech of the Forest of Retz. Thatch burst up its embankment through the underbrush in fine style, for once shaming the more circumspect Jeopardy. It was pleasantly cool in the forest, Mr Thatch was punching along happily, and by now I was so used to his rhythm that I felt positively centaur-like. Suddenly there was a crash in the undergrowth on my right, a flash of something feral and tawny, and Jeopardy was away at a gallop with Thatch flat out behind him. A huge stag, with a head like a hat-rack, was loping along almost parallel with us. We had roused him from his afternoon nap, and his unexpected appearance had spooked the horses. He turned away at right angles and stopped for a moment: Evelyn had Jeopardy under control and Thatch settled back into a walk.

The Forest of Retz cloaks the long ridge north of the River Automne, and its northern fringes creep down onto the limestone uplands stretching off to the Aisne. It was only ten miles or so as the crow flies from our encounter with the stag to Attichy, where we had eaten so well two nights before. In August 1914 this wooded feature was important because it gave I Corps' rearguard the opportunity to face Kluck's leading formations on not unfavourable terms.

As we neared the forest edge by Taillefontaine we crossed the scene of another bitter little action fought on 1 September. Hubert Gough's 3rd Cavalry Brigade was screening the gap between I Corps and 5th Division, around Crépy-en-Valois on the right of II Corps. Trevor Horn of the 16th Lancers was in the saddle at 3.00 that morning, and remembered falling back through Mortefontaine and Taillefontaine, to 'a big wood' — the Forest of Retz. The 4th Hussars formed the rearguard. Their commanding officer, Lieutenant-Colonel Ian Hogg, had been ordered to hold the forest edge till 12.30, and left A and C Squadrons forward, fighting dismounted, with B in reserve. German infantry — from the *5th Division*, which had faced British musketry a lifetime before at St Ghislain on the Condé Canal — fought its way up through dense undergrowth, and Lieutenant-Colonel Hogg was hit as he tried to bring C Squadron out of action. The regiment gave ground slowly, as Walter Bloem, who had just fallen foul of his brigade commander for allowing one of his men to go into action with a *baguette* stuck under his arm, saw. 'The march continued and was a harassing one,' he wrote. 'After a few minutes rifle bullets whistled out of the woods on our left and right. A Hussar from one of the cavalry patrols lay dying by the roadside close to his horse, also breathing its last.' He eventually reached Haramont, on the far side of the forest, where one of his men reported that an English colonel was dying with a doctor attending him. The doctor — it was Captain Wethered, medical officer of the 4th Hussars — was brought forward, 'a look of cool indifference on his clean-shaven face' and reported that Lieutenant-Colonel Hogg had just died.

We followed 3rd Cavalry Brigade's route in reverse, dismounting to walk down the steep slope into Taillefontaine, clinging to the hillside in the baking heat. With its warm stone, higgledy-piggledy houses and craggy church the village looked out of place in northern Europe, and there was a *méridional* tang to the air as we rode up the cobbled high street, our heads level with kitchen windows, all of which seemed to exude hot, herby smells. In the hamlet of Marival we crossed a bridge over the St Clothilde brook — with the Oise behind him Thatch scorned such obstacles — ambled up the last hill and then dismounted to walk into Mortefontaine.

The horses were to spend the night in a Commandery, a twelfth-century fortified farm built by the Knights Templar. The Templars were founded in the recently-captured Jerusalem in about 1118 (their guiding spirit was Hugues de Payens, a knight from these parts; we might have seen him spurring along the forest edge, hawk on his wrist) as a military order, at once martial and monastic. By the end of the century the Templars and their rival Hospitallers had waxed so powerful as to overshadow the secular church in Outremer. They provided a steady supply of tough professional soldiers and built great castles that no individual nobleman could afford to maintain. Their money came not only from gifts, legacies, and the profits from farms like this, but they also showed an unexpected aptitude for banking.

Yet the Military Orders were also quarrelsome (Templars and Hospitallers were at daggers drawn) and, because their only suzerain was the Pope, all but impossible for the rulers of eastern Christendom to control. The Templars' wealth and selfishness aroused smouldering hostility, and the loss of Outremer left them kicking their heels on Cyprus, anxious to undertake another Crusade. When their Grand Master, Jacques de Molay, visited Pope Clement V at Avignon in 1306 to discuss a planned expedition, he discovered that his Order was being accused of heretical and indecent practices.

Sir Steven Runciman has concluded that there 'was probably just enough substance' in these accusations to suggest a line along which the Templars could best be attacked. King Philip the Fair had much to gain from the suppression of the Templars. And because Pope Clement was not only his man (as Bertrand de Gouth, Archbishop of Bordeaux he had been on good terms with the king) but had taken refuge in Avignon from the disturbances in Rome, the knights were unlikely to find support from their suzerain. In 1306, Philip arrested all the Templars in France; they were condemned after trials marred by torture and false witness. The Order was at last suppressed by the Pope in 1312, and in March 1314 Jacques de Molay was burnt at the stake in Paris — at the tip of the Ile de la Cité where the Square Henri IV now stands. His last years had been a miserable catalogue of torture, imprisonment, confession and recantation, but he died with a courage that would not have shamed his fighting forebears, solemnly cursing Philip and his descendants from the flames. Some were to blame the misfortunes of Philip's line — the Accursed Kings — on the Grand Master's dying malediction.

Some of our night halts had drawn the First World War strongly to mind. But as we walked in under the turreted gate at

Mortefontaine, with a squat drum tower on our left, the image was nothing if not medieval. Ahead of us was the house, garnished with a spired tower that Viollet-le-Duc would have admired, and all around the yard were farm buildings of the same oaty stone as the rest of the village. Although this area was fought across in 1914, it was spared thereafter, and south of the Aisne we had ridden through villages that had not been flattened and rebuilt, as was the case with so many north of the river. The stunning Madame Ferté met us with a posse of pretty daughters, and our horses, unusually well fussed-over, were soon comfortably bedded down in stalls at the far end of the courtyard.

We were to spend the night in the Hôtel de l'Abbaye at Longpont, ten miles to the east. The tiny village lies under the shadow of the ruined church of the Cistercian monastery, consecrated in 1227 in the presence of the young Louis IX and his wife Blanche of Castile. The infantrymen of the *18th Division* of Kluck's *IX Corps* spent the night of 1 September 1914 there, but I fear that their interest in ecclesiastical architecture may have been subordinated to picking cautiously at raw feet and rubbing sore shoulders. The hotel, with its woodwork and antlers, has an Edwardian baronial feel to it, and we arrived, for once, in time for a bath and a snooze. If I do not remember dinner it is because it was unexceptional by comparison with some of our gastronomic pitched battles.

Wednesday 18 August was a Household Division benefit. We were to ride across the battlefield of Villers-Cotterêts, and some juggling with box and Trooper enabled us to mount all but Ollie. We clattered out of Mortefontaine in fine style to the sound of Evelyn's hunting horn. I had Lesson 1 on the horn just north of Longavesne — frenzied baying from a nearby farm suggested that my horn-blowing is passably bilingual — and as we rode into the forest near Vivières I had Lesson 2 and squeezed out a 'Gone Away' — woo, woo, woowoo, woo — which was close enough to the real thing to lead Thatch to believe that there was a fox about and give me an interesting moment or two.

I Corps moved off at 4.00 on the morning of 1 September, with both its divisions converging on Villers-Cotterêts, 1st Division from Soissons to the north-east and 2nd Division using the road which drops south from Vic-sur-Aisne and runs through Vivières to the Rond de la Reine, a cartwheel junction in the midst of the woods. We have seen how 3rd Cavalry Brigade screened the left flank around Mortefontaine and Taillefontaine, preventing Captain Bloem

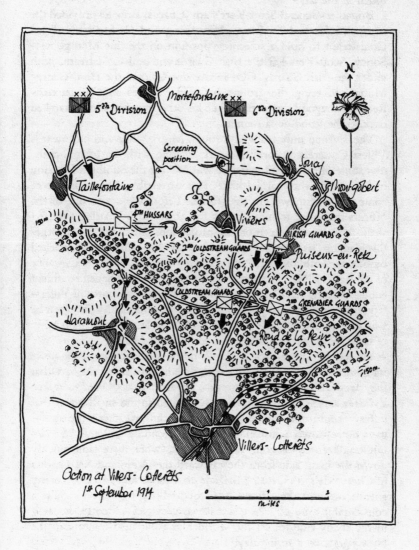

Action at Villers-Cotterêts
1st September 1914

and his comrades from getting through the forest to Haramont for much of the day.

Brigadier-General Scott-Kerr's 4th (Guards) Brigade provided the rearguard for 2nd Division. After using 2nd Grenadiers and 3rd Coldstream to hold a screening position on the line Montgobert–Soucy, Scott-Kerr left the Irish Guards and 2nd Coldstream, both under the Irish Guards' CO, Lieutenant-Colonel the Hon. George Morris, covering the ground between Vivières and Puisieux-en-Retz, just beyond the forest, while his other two battalions marched back to the Rond de la Reine.

The division duly trudged through Morris's line and on towards Villers-Cotterêts. Aubrey Herbert, waiting with the Irish Guards, met some of his constituents (he was MP for the Southern Division of Somerset) who warned him: 'This be terrible dangerous. Do'ee come along with we'. In the stillness before the attack one of the officers remarked to him: 'I may live to see many battles; I think I shall, for I am very keen on my profession, but I shall never forget this plain or this morning'. At about 10.00 a.m. Morris was attacked by Germans moving in from the north-west, but, with the assistance of 9th Battery RFA, he stopped them so sharply that he felt confident enough to send the Coldstream back to the railway north of Villers-Cotterêts. He was just preparing to follow with his Micks when he was told by the brigadier not to move too fast, as the main body of the division was to be given a long midday halt.

Ma Jeffreys, now back at the Rond de la Reine, heard the news with such incredulity that he underlined in his diary the fact that they were to hold 'till 1.00 *to enable the rest of the Divisions to halt and have dinners* . . . ' His CO — so tired in the small hours that Jeffreys could not rouse him to receive the brigadier's orders — gave Jeffreys two companies east of the Rond de la Reine. 'We had not long been in position,' wrote Jeffreys, 'when there came quickly down the main ride from the eastward the Greys and XII Lancers of Chetwode's 5th Cavalry Brigade . . . as we all had a good many friends amongst the officers, we stood talking together for quite a considerable time . . . As it was it was very pleasant coffee-housing in the shady ride for all the world like a big field hunting in the New Forest on a spring day.'

There was less chit-chat amongst the oaks a mile to the north. No sooner had Morris been told to fall back slowly than the Germans attacked again. A Grenadier company was sent forward to help him, but with the restricted field of fire in the wood the guardsmen did not enjoy the advantage conferred by their ferocious musketry in open country. 'There were bullets everywhere and men were falling,' wrote Herbert, 'but the fire was still too high. One bullet in about half a million must have hit a man . . . I carry in my mind a number of vivid pictures — Desmond [Fitzgerald] on his horse, Valentine [Castlerosse] and I discussing fatalism, the CO smoking cigarettes in the cinema holders that I had bought for him a few days before.'

Morris was killed — in his regiment's first serious engagement since its formation in 1900 — and though his companies fought their way back like islands of khaki in a sea of grey, the Germans managed to get round them and between the companies of 3rd Coldstream, on the Grenadiers' left to the west of the Rond de la Reine. Jeffreys, who could see few Germans to his front where the trees were bigger and the ground between them more open, found that 'a good many bullets began to come over from our left'. Lieutenant Neville Woodroffe of the Irish Guards, who managed to get back to the Coldstream line, thought that 'the wood was so thick that I fear many shot one's own men', and there was what Jeffreys called 'very confused fighting at point-blank range' as the tide lapped round the Grenadiers' left flank.

At this juncture the brigadier was hit — Jeffreys saw the brigade major leading him away 'badly wounded and obviously in great pain'. An orderly arrived from battalion headquarters telling Jeffreys that the battalion was going to withdraw, and with great presence of mind he realised that with the brigadier down the senior surviving CO — Noel Corry of his own 2nd Grenadiers — would take over, so he himself ought to take command of the battalion. The brigade's survivors withdrew into Villers-Cotterêts, with Jeffreys' men falling back by companies and keeping up a brisk fire. The Germans did not press the pursuit. Jeffreys thought that they had 'not only lost heavily but got very mixed up in the thick forest, and we could hear them shouting orders and blowing little horns apparently to rally their men'. The action cost 4th (Guards) Brigade over 360 officers and men, and 6th Brigade, which held the southern exits of the town while the guardsmen got clear, lost another 160.

We rode up to the Rond de la Reine across the ground swept by the musketry of Ma Jeffreys' two companies, and then turned to walk our horses in down the big ride used by Chetwode's horsemen. A floridly Gallic monument (surprisingly erected by Lieutenant George Cecil's grieving mother) stands south of the Vivières-

Villers-Cotterêts road as it hairpins up to the junction, and just down the hill to the south-east, slipped in beside the road, is the Guards Cemetery.

The dead guardsmen were initially buried on 2 September in a number of scattered graves. It was sometimes possible for well-connected relatives of those killed on the Western Front to obtain permission to visit the battle area: late in 1915 Rudyard Kipling searched fruitlessly for the grave of his son Jack, killed at Loos with the Irish Guards. When Lady Edward Cecil went out to search for her boy in September 1914, after the German withdrawal, she found several inadequately marked graves, but no sign of her son's; indeed, there was a rumour — to which she wisely paid little heed — that he had been wounded and captured. George Morris's brother, Lord Killanin, visited the battlefield in November, and found a mass grave just short of the Rond de la Reine. A cross, its inscription in French, testified to the presence of twenty British soldiers, but a nearby note on a tree, written in indelible pencil in German, suggested that the number was actually 200.

Lord Killanin's party set about the grim task of exhumation: 'in no case was it possible to identify a body by features — hair, teeth, as owing to the length of time (two and a half months) since burial and to the manner in which these dead had been treated, the faces were quite unrecognisable, often smashed, and were all thickly coated with clay and blood'. They managed to identify Geoffrey Lambton of the Coldstream and Charles Tisdall of the Irish Guards. Killanin thought that he recognised his brother's body from its general build, and clinched the matter by finding a wristwatch with his name on it. One officer's corpse was tentatively identified 'from the size of the boots', and then the initials GEC embroidered on the vest confirmed that it was indeed George Cecil. Lord Killanin arranged for the cemetery to be properly marked, and subsequently the Imperial War Graves Commission took it over. Despite its proximity to the road it is a quiet and lovely place, and while I stood there, trying to put it all into perspective, a shaft of midday sunlight picked out the Cross of Sacrifice.

That afternoon we were to go on to Pringy, to the south-west beyond I Corps' right flank. Evelyn and Ollie rode, and I took the vehicles out past Longpont and then down through Blanzy and Billy-sur-Ourcq. With John and Ollie in the box behind me, I pulled off a nifty piece of simultaneous driving and map-reading, cutting down sharply from the road onto a long unmarked drive which leads to Maurice Velge's château. Pride comes before a fall. As we drove up to the château from its southern end, I thought that the gates through its wrought-iron railings looked narrow, and so they were. I managed to get the Trooper through but the trailer, an inch or two wider, would not follow.

There was much local interest. A burly, open-faced young gardener appeared, followed by an older gentleman whose tum imposed serious structural strain on his T shirt. We were the English officers? Good. He was a warrant-officer of *gendarmerie*, now retired, who came to lend his son a hand in the garden from time to time. The gate? No problem. The trailer might just go through, and if it didn't, then Monsieur Velge, a good boss, wouldn't mind a bit of damage in a good cause. I was less confident, and asked if there was another way in. There was, and after much revving and shouting (with the long-suffering John eventually coming up to show me how a trailer really should be backed) we went back down the drive, onto the road and into the château grounds from the north.

If I had to design myself a perfect middle-sized château, just right for a house-party of a dozen or so, then Pringy would be the answer. Built of Camembert-coloured stone and rose-pink brick, its broad front, two confident rows of long windows with little dormers peeking from the roof, is finished off by end wings which embrace a pea-shingle courtyard. Steps lead down to a formal garden and a pond. The present house dates from the seventeenth century (were it in England we might suspect the influence, if not the hand, of Inigo Jones) but just behind it are the remains of something far older, with a medieval tower above stables cut into the rock.

Monsieur Velge's industrious groom Roseline (whose t-shirt was under as much strain as that of my *gendarme* friend, although the source of stress was a little higher) was working in a more recent stable-block just along from the tower. Her domain was in apple-pie order, and John became almost benevolent. We had Thatch and Jeopardy washed and stabled and their tack cleaned by the time Evelyn and Ollie stumped in, and we presented ourselves at the château's front door and rang the bell. We knew that Maurice Velge, who was driving down from Antwerp to meet us, would not be there yet, but his housekeeper was expecting us.

It was rather like being let loose in a stately home after the visitors have gone for the day. From the cool, flagstoned hall we went up the wide double staircase to a series of long saloons looking out across the front of the house. There were comfortable bedrooms behind, and the housekeeper invited us to take our pick and scuttled off to find some cold beer. We drank it gratefully in Maurice's study in the north wing. Our host purred up in a sleek black car at about 7.00 p.m. and at once put us at our ease. He spoke beautiful English of a slightly 1920s vintage; indeed, with his old-style courtesy it was not hard to compare him with some of those hospitable aristocrats who had welcomed our grandfathers. Arthur Osburn had spent the night of 30/31 August in the château at Vieux Moulin (close to our ill-starred lunch halt in the Forest of Compiègne) and the old *seigneur* showed him to 'a large chamber, the walls and ceiling lined with rusty brown leather, cracked and faded, and here and there faint traces of gilt fleur-de-lys stamped upon it'. George Barrow had spent a night in the Comte d'Anvers' magnificent Louis XIV château at Champs, and recalled that he had to mount three steps on a platform to reach his bed.

It was typical of Maurice's attentiveness that he had organised a dinner party that night, inviting the de Fays down from Bonnemaison, the Fertés across from Mortefontaine, and Antoinette and Christian de Laglande from Folembray. We drank champagne amongst the hunting prints and trophies in Maurice's smoking room, and then marched along the house to dinner. The meal started with a tasty Velge-designed dish of mushrooms and potted shrimps, and moved on through lamb the same rosy-pink as the brickwork to cheese and chocolate mousse. The housekeeper and her daughter waited with relaxed efficiency and plied magnums of claret which were a perfect match for the lamb. After dinner we went upstairs to the library for coffee, and I had a glass or three of Islay malt. My notes for the day end 'to bed at 1.30', and I am not surprised that my hand looks shaky.

The blacksmith was expected at 8.00 on Thursday morning, and I clumped down the stairs, feeling surprisingly good, in plenty of time to meet him. Dominique Gilis, who drove up in a well-fitted Landcruiser just as I reached the stables, was slight and wiry, not in the least like the O'Flaherty image of the grim farrier. Jeopardy's shoes were coming loose and his hooves had not been in the best of order when we started. I tried to referee between John and Dominique, but they managed to do quite well in equestrian *lingua franca* and Jeopardy was duly fitted with a new set of shoes.

After a breakfast of bacon and eggs, we discussed the day's ride. We were to cross the Marne and sleep in the village hall at Signy-Signets, south-east of La Ferté-sous-Jouarre. The first leg of the march would take us to Belleau, nine miles away as the crow flies, and Maurice intended to accompany us. His horses had only just come in from grass, so he would not set a ripping pace: it would take us two hours. Three at least, thought Evelyn. Maurice firmly replied that he felt that two would be about right, but we should have to see. We mounted all four of our horses for a photograph in front of the château. Maurice had an approving word for each of them; nothing was said about old Thatch's ancestry, but he was evidently 'a good strong chap'.

Maurice, Roseline, Evelyn and I left for Belleau, crossing the Ourcq on the edge of Pringy and then striking off cross country. It was a morning of delicate understatement. 'Do you think we might risk a gentle trot?' asked Maurice. We did — for a few hundred yards. Then a gentle trot became a steady canter, and we ate up the miles over the open stubble. I would not have risked it in England, but nobody seemed to mind our riding across their fields now that the corn was cut. Maurice would pause long enough to exchange a word with a farmer here and a woman busy with her clothes-line there, and then suggest that another light trot might be just the ticket. He set a straight line and a good pace. Somewhere east of Neuilly St Front we came up to a big, overgrown bank that would have done duty for one of Enguerrand de Coucy's ditches. I caught Evelyn's eye, and we agreed that Maurice would not risk it. What nonsense. He went straight up without so much as a pause. The heavy brigade was bringing up the rear, and I should have stopped until the way was clear before giving Thatch his head. I didn't, and was about half-way up when someone slid back past me. Thatch dropped onto his front knees, paused, then threw himself back onto his feet and bounded up the slope, launching me into the air. I came down with my stomach across the saddle, a vice-like grip on a stirrup leather and the tightest sphincter in the Ile de France. I managed, somehow or other, to recover my seat, and on we cantered.

We reached the hill above Belleau very close to the two-hour deadline, and got separated as we tried to find a route through an untidy warren on the edge of the Bois des Meules. I was at the rear as usual, and saw Maurice and his groom peel back from the wood and head for a re-entrant. Evelyn shouted, from somewhere in the wood, that he had found a path, but I decided to stick with the man I could see. Maurice was dressed informally that morning: a cotton print shirt, and grey cord riding trousers over jodhpur boots. The only suggestion that this was not just a middle-aged gentleman out for a quiet hack came from the unobtrusive spurs on his heels, and as we neared Belleau mere cantering became a thing of the past. I still had not understood the rules of the game. 'Er, Maurice,' I yelled breathlessly, 'we seem to have lost Evelyn.' We entered the village at a gallop, tore along the verge (I missed the village sign by an inch), pounded up the hill on the far side and then turned in to belt home to the rendezvous. I was far too excited to be scared, and have never been prouder of Thatch, who had no intention of being left behind by these dish-faced types. The *gendarme*'s son was there with both horse-boxes, and some chilled St Veran and silver goblets were to hand. John grabbed Thatch and covered him with a sweat-rug (I needed one myself), and Maurice looked at his watch. 'I rather fancy that we are a minute or two early,' he said, with a forgivable trace of satisfaction. The first glass had already slipped down when Evelyn rode up from the village. It is not often that the Grenadiers come second, and there are worse ways of doing it.

After saying goodbye to Maurice Velge — how much we had to thank him for, as it had been his seal of approval that had opened so many doors to us — we walked across to the American military cemetery on the edge of Belleau Wood. It is the last resting-place of 2,289 Americans, most of them killed when Pershing's men moved into the line here to check the progress of Ludendorff's spring offensive in 1918. The wood itself was the scene of fierce fighting in June, and the 2nd Division, which included a Marine brigade, played a distinguished part in it.

I was by now quite used to going on ahead to sort out accommodation, and after the morning's entertainment I was not sorry to take the road party over the Marne at La Ferté-sous-Jouarre and on to Signy-Signets. The BEF fell back across the river on 3 September, most of it crossing east of the town, but 5th Cavalry Brigade, whose steps we seemed to be dogging, actually going through it. At least part of the BEF seemed to have found its second wind by this time, much as I had after that brain-boiling ride to Néry. James Penny-cuick recalled that:

> The day's march started in the dark, perhaps between 2 and 4 am . . . There was a routine halt of ten minutes every clock hour and a longer halt to allow tea to be made and many unofficial pauses.
>
> About 2 pm the Company would be turned into a field and bivouacs set out, officers unrolling their valises under some hedge. Fires were lit and dinners cooked . . . The horses kept very fit, there were few sore backs although more often than not they stood with their harness all night.

After the main meal we were glad to turn in and take what sleep we could unless there were demolition jobs to be done.

There were such jobs aplenty. Pennycuick had already earned a DSO for blowing the Oise bridge at Pontoise right in the face of the German advanced guard. Godsell had been nearby in divisional headquarters while Lieutenant Smythe was working on two more. It was vital that he blew the railway bridge but left the adjoining road bridge intact until the troops had crossed.

> Suddenly the candles flickered and there was a big explosion. 'Ah,' said one, 'that's one of the bridges gone' — 'Good fellows, those sappers' — 'Yes, I think Smythe is in charge — you remember him at the Curragh — good to hounds — always near at the kill — had an awkward looking white horse [what *can* he have meant?] — believe he brought it out here with him — soaked it in coffee so it shouldn't show so — then the awkward beast shook it all off on board ship and is as white as ever now — saw it on the road yesterday — Ah yes, I believe he is an Irishman' . . . The candles flickered and there was another loud explosion. — 'Blast these sappers, they've blown the road bridge' — 'damn that fellow Smythe' — 'Never trust an Irishman' . . .

Smythe had in fact dealt with the correct bridge in two halves. The bridges over the languid Marne were blown after the BEF had crossed (although the one at La Ferté, which we used that Thursday, was only part-destroyed because of lack of explosives). Boats were smashed to make it difficult for the Germans to get reconnaissance parties across, and Kenneth Godsell hated it. 'I had to take my section and work up the river for three miles and destroy all boats,' he wrote. 'This was most unpleasant, as there were a large number of rowing boats all up the river and the owners hated seeing us shove a crowbar through them. One little motor boat was a beauty, and it went to my heart to sink it.'

The German advance was reaching its culminating point — Clausewitz would have seen it as an example of 'the diminishing power of the offensive' — although there were few on either side who recognised it. On 2 September Kluck edged south again in an effort to catch the BEF, but that night he received a signal from Moltke, ordering him to act as flank guard to *Second Army* which was to take part in an advance south-eastwards, in an effort to push the French away from Paris. As Kluck was already a day ahead of Bülow, this would involve him in pausing for two whole days, and he had no intention of complying, but drove in between the Grand

Morin and the Marne, hard on the heels of the French 5th Army. Walter Bloem's grenadiers were all in. 'It was no pleasure', he reflected, 'to look at the inflamed heels, soles and toes of my wretched young lads, whole patches of skin rubbed to the raw flesh.'

It was Moltke's nerve, not the exhausted bodies of his soldiers, that failed at this, the crucial moment of the campaign. On the evening of 4 September he sent a long memorandum to his army commanders, telling them that the attempt to force the French south-east had been rendered impracticable. On the right wing Kluck and Bülow were to hold their ground (though Moltke was uncertain as to quite where this was), while the armies of the left wing (already up against stiff resistance) were to attack.

Joffre's own plans hardened at precisely the same time. He knew, from the report of a pilot from the Paris garrison, that Kluck had turned in front of Paris and could be assailed in the flank, and by now the build-up on the Allied left had reached such a level that such an attack might possibly succeed. Despite the ephemeral success of Guise he could no longer rely on Lanrezac, so he replaced him with Franchet d'Esperey — 'Desperate Frankie' to his Allies — who lost no time in striking up a good relationship with Sir John French. On 4 September French spent the morning visiting his troops and returned to GHQ at Melun to discover that Murray had tentatively agreed to co-operate in a French attack on the German right wing.

Sir John was not quite sure what to do. Haig was 'much depressed about the state of his troops', and Smith-Dorrien feared that discipline had deteriorated because of heavy officer casualties. Major de Sausmarez caught the backwash of this mood, and on 5 September attended an address by Major-General Fergusson, who 'talked seriously about the maintenance of discipline, the prevention of straggling and falling out on the line of march, etc, also about the slackness that now obtains everywhere in the matter of saluting'. This soon worked its way down the chain of command, and the very next day de Sausmarez 'awarded 28 days Field Punishment No 2 and a fine of 10/- to Gnr W. Smith of the Battery Ammunition Column, who had been drunk and creating a disturbance at Tourneau the day before'.

Joffre judged his moment finely. On the morning of 5 September he drove across to see French in his quarters in the Château of Vaux le Pénil, thanked him for agreeing to help, and then, in what Spears called his 'low, toneless albino voice', explained the situation. All eyes were on the field-marshal. Several officers were ready to translate, but Sir John signed to show that he understood. Warming to his task, Joffre explained his scheme, declaring that he planned to throw his last company into battle to save France and begging for the wholehearted support of the BEF. He turned full on to Sir John, clasping his hands so tightly as to hurt them, and said: '*Monsieur le Maréchal, c'est la France qui vous supplie*'.

Emotional appeals were rarely wasted on Johnnie French. His face reddened: tears welled up in his eyes and coursed down his cheeks. He did his best to reply, but feelings and language were too much for him. 'Damn it, I can't explain,' he gasped, 'tell him that all men can do our fellows will do.' 'The Field-Marshal says "yes",' announced Wilson. Murray at once intervened to say that the BEF could not start its advance as early as the French hoped, but Joffre was drained and past caring. 'It cannot be helped,' he said. 'Let them start as soon as they can. I have the marshal's word, and that is enough for me.'

Signy-Signets, where we spent the night, was on the BEF's line of withdrawal on 4 September, the penultimate day of the retreat. Brigadier Johnnie Rickett, the military attaché in Paris, had arranged that we could spend the night in the village hall, with the horses turned out in a nearby field. We were expected at the *mairie*, and the mayor's secretary gave us the key to the hall. As we were letting ourselves in the *garde champêtre* appeared in order to show us how the lights and cookers worked. He was followed by a gruff old gentleman who told me that the gate at the corner of the maize field and the cemetery was open. I could not think that this had anything to do with us, and laboriously explained that we were Englishmen riding from Mons . . . 'I know all that,' he said. 'But if you put your horses in the field there, they'll cross the brook — *there* — be up that other field, round the corner and out of the gate. And then,' he swung an arm low, fist clenched, and clapped the other hand down on his bicep, 'they'll fuck off.' I dutifully toiled across the brook, up the other field, round the corner and shut the gate.

Evelyn and Clive were there when I got back. They had had an uneventful ride, though the combined efforts of Allied and German sappers had prevented them from finding a dignified old bridge on which they could persuade someone to photograph them, so there was to be no 'hoofbeats over the Marne' illustration for this book. Our next visitor then marched in. It was the sergeant of *gendarmerie*, who had just looked in to make sure that we were happy and to find out where we were eating. Of course we could go in to La Ferté-sous-Jouarre, but he rather liked Le Mouton Chop in Pierre Levée, and would happily book us a table if that suited us. It suited us very well, and he returned shortly afterwards to confirm that we were expected for 8.00 p.m. The last visitor of the afternoon was the deputy mayor, sleek, busy, dapper and trimly moustachioed. *Madame le Maire* regretted that she could not call herself, but she was away on holiday. Was everything all right? And where *were* we eating?

While I was waiting for the others to finish washing I chatted to the *garde champêtre*, a brown, shrunken old man who would be retiring next year. I was not sure just what a *garde champêtre* was, and made the mistake of asking if he was a sort of *gendarme*. 'Not at all, not at all,' he assured me, very much on his dignity. 'I'm more powerful than a *gendarme*, I am. I've taken an oath, not just been enlisted.' I tried another tack. Was he a sort of gamekeeper? There was a bit of that, he said, but it was not much to his taste: 'I like all creatures and it seems a shame to kill them'. In any case, the shooting round here was very social, in the hands of 'people from Paris, lawyers — that sort of thing. But fishing — fishing in the Marne — that was a different matter altogether . . . '

The conversation revealed just how far we had slipped under the shadow of Paris. For much of our journey our attempts to secure our belongings had been greeted with amused disbelief. Why bother? Who in the village would steal your saddles? But here, the *garde champêtre* said, it would be as well if we locked up. The local kids were fine, but sometimes, you understand, there were visitors from other villages . . .

Le Mouton Chop produced honest if unremarkable steaks, and we returned to the village hall for an uneventful night on our camp beds. Friday, 20 August was the last day of our ride, and it was to take us to a rendezvous just north of Rozoy, completing the march of the BEF on 5 September 1914, the last day of the retreat. We hoped to finish the ride in a long morning and then box on to Fontainebleau, where we were spending the night, but it was one of those mornings that went on and on and on. The fields were smaller, crimped in with hedges and ditches, and our cavalier habit of picking tracks from the map (just as the BEF had long since run off its maps, so we had run off our ANTE routes) was thwarted by a devilish selection of gates, barriers and warning signs. Only the Forest of Malvoisine offered the remotest echo of those big woods further north, and even then it had the last laugh with rides that always went obliquely to our line of march. It was early afternoon when I led Thatch down a long straight road to the box. I would like to claim that it was a *Chaussée Brunehaut*, but the map obstinately refuses to bear out my suspicions. Evelyn dug out the bottle of champagne given us by M. Claude at Néry, and gave us the toast: 'To the book'. Thatch, attending to his haynet, puckered those rubbery lips into what might pass for a grin.

EPILOGUE

Tom Bridges had been nearby when the first shots of the BEF's campaign were fired, and it was entirely fitting that he should watch the tide turn south of the Marne. On 6 September his squadron was advanced guard:

> and from the village of Pécy which was on a hill, we were able to see their infantry halted on the road. An Uhlan patrol which reconnoitred us was hotly dealt with. I sent back a frantic appeal for guns. A German battery barked at us and set fire to a house. Then the phenomenon occurred. Under our eyes the enemy column began to wheel round in the road and retire to the north. It was the peak of Von Kluck's advance.

News that the retreat was over delighted the BEF. 'The happiest day in my life; we marched towards the rising sun,' exulted Colonel Jack Seely, Liberal politician turned soldier. 'This totally unexpected news almost passed belief after the long depressing retreat,' agreed James Jack. 'This brigade is certainly in good form once more.'

'The colonel informs us that the German advance has been checked,' wrote Bombardier Tom Langston on 7 September, 'and they are now making a hurried retreat. As I have said before we are all fed up with the long retreat and everyone is eager to get a smack at the enemy.' William Edgington was equally delighted: 'Great joy in the change of direction after continually marching south.' It was characteristic of Henry Owens' fondness for descriptive asides that his diary entry for 7 September focuses on the breakfast menu: 'Entertained a French Captain of Cuirassiers to breakfast. Eggs & bacon, bread & butter, jam, tea & fresh milk. The French officer is a very nice chap. Very interesting. Discussed his steel helmet. Said he preferred it to our caps. Not very heavy and kept the sun and rain off.' Yet even our hunting doctor was not immune from the air of general excitement: 'Our army successful all along the line. Enemy retreating.'

In the second week of September the decisive battle of the campaign boiled up along the Marne valley. For one of the 'great battles of history' it was a confused and formless affair, with no cunning turning movements, decisive breakthroughs or sudden collapses. Joffre had set much store on his flank attack, but, in a remarkable display of clear-headed command and slick staff-work, Kluck managed to swing westwards to meet Manoury's 6th Army on the Ourcq and succeeded in driving it back with heavy losses. Bloem remembered the march which took him to the Ourcq as the worst of the war, and when he arrived at Noroy-le-Bourg he managed a quick bath. Accidentally catching sight of himself in a mirror: 'I nearly collapsed in astonishment. Lean as a skeleton, my skin covered in a regular crust of dust and sweat, my cheeks sunk in, my hair long and much greyer, my chin and jaw smothered with an untidy greyish beard: so that was me!'

Kluck's successful manoeuvre widened the gap between the German First and Second Armies. In theory the BEF might have been able to exploit this gap, but in practice it was already weary and had started its counter-attack a day later than the French: it made slow progress in the face of dogged resistance. 'The German troops fought well,' admitted Sally Home on 8 September, watching the crossing of the Morin at Sablonnières, 'and I spoke to several prisoners — they told me their orders were to defend the crossing until told to retire. Of course no one told them to retire and so they stayed until killed or captured — their discipline must be very good.' 'Soarer' Campbell managed to lead the 9th Lancers in another charge, and had just pistolled a German officer who was making a cut at him when he was wafted out of the saddle by a lance-thrust. Arthur Osburn found him sprawled in the clover: ' "I am sorry to find you like this, sir," I said, kneeling down to dress his wounds. "Not at all, my boy! Not at all! I've just had the best quarter of an hour I've ever had in my life." ' While the BEF threatened the junction between Kluck and Bülow, Franchet d'Esperey's 5th Army and Foch's newly-formed 9th Army took on Bülow himself. They had mixed fortunes, with the 5th Army making some progress but having to send support to the hard-pressed Foch on its right.

The weakest links in this chain of chaos strung along the Marne were not the fighting troops — though all were dead tired — but their leaders. Joffre had already dismissed Lanrezac, and in Franchet d'Esperey and Foch he had resolute army commanders who understood precisely what he wanted them to achieve and knew, all too well, that they were fighting at the very gates of Paris. He was a frequent visitor to army headquarters, and though he did not say much — sometimes he would arrive, listen to a briefing and depart without a word — he was as sensitive to the mood of the battle as a spider, poised on his web, is to the smallest intrusion.

Moltke was miles away in Luxembourg, in a state of growing mental exhaustion. News of the battle was slow to seep through to him, and lack of reserves meant that even when it arrived he could do little to influence the fighting. The leaden weight of command crushed the life out of him. On 7 September he told his wife:

> Today our armies are fighting all the way from Paris to upper Alsace. I would give my life, as thousands have done, for victory. How much blood has been spilled and how much misery has come upon numberless innocent people whose houses have been burned and razed to the ground.
>
> Terror overcomes me when I think about this, and the feeling I have is as if I must answer for this horror, and yet I could not act otherwise than as I have.

A more single-minded German commander could yet have won. Rupprecht had made good progress in Alsace-Lorraine, and although his attack had stalled in front of Nancy, the French were more badly shaken than Moltke realised. The fighting on the Marne was still inconclusive: if Bülow was making heavy weather of it, Kluck was pushing Manoury hard and might soon break the 6th Army altogether. Moltke's tragedy was that he could see so little of this. He was acutely sensitive to war, whose stresses weighed heavier by the minute, but lacked that fifth-finger sense which gives insight into battle.

On 8 September Moltke sent Lieutenant-Colonel Hentsch, chief of his foreign armies section and a level-headed, trusted staff officer, on his second visit to the front. Despite subsequent denials by the chief of OHL's operations section, it is evident that Hentsch had more than a watching brief. He himself believed that his masters hoped 'that the crisis would be mastered and that it would not be necessary to retreat. But in case such a retreat proved essential, they pointed out to me the line Ste Menehould–Reims–Fismes–Soissons as a general direction for the mass of the German army.'

Hentsch started his visit with *Fourth* and *Fifth Armies*, pushing confidently south-west towards Troyes. His fellow-Saxons of *Third Army* had taken Fère-Champenoise that day and were guardedly optimistic. But the end of a rattling, dusty journey brought him to Bülow's headquarters in the Château de Montmort, north-east of Montmirail. The rear areas of even winning armies are not comfortable places, and Hentsch's jolting drive had taken him across the path of supply columns and streams of wounded. It was a stark contrast to the neat arrows on situation maps in Luxembourg, and the combination of fatigue and visions of disorganisation left Hentsch dangerously receptive to Bülow's calm pessimism. They reached no conclusion that evening, but the following morning Hentsch was persuaded that Bülow was in real difficulties, with Kluck's departure for the Ourcq laying bare his right flank.

By the time that Hentsch reached Kluck's headquarters at Mareuil — it took him seven dusty hours to cover the sixty miles — he was even more pessimistic. Kluck shunned participation in a potentially painful discussion by not appearing at this crucial meeting, but General von Kuhl, his chief of staff, recognised that if *Second Army* was going to pull back, *First Army* could scarcely stay where it was. Kuhl was optimistic, but when Hentsch asked him if he was confident of beating Manoury that day and then of swinging south to rescue Bülow, Kuhl had to confess that he was not. Hentsch immediately 'gave the First Army the order to retreat, basing my action on the full powers given me, because it was only in this way one could bring it once more into cooperation with the Second Army'. Joffre may not have won the battle of the Marne; but Moltke had certainly lost it.

A few seconds' reflection on the geography of the British retreat from Mons will point the way ahead to the next phase of the war. The Germans fell back from the Marne to the next defensible line to the north. It is, of course, marked by our languid old friend the Aisne, sliding through the limestone below Nampcel and Bonnemaison. Even hastily-dug positions on those bare ridges to its north were all but impervious to the artillery at the Allies' disposal. Sir John French caught the battle's new mood more quickly than Henry Wilson, who told a crony at GQG that 'unless we make some serious blunder we ought to be at Elsenborn in four weeks . . .' French, however, wrote on 14 September that 'the enemy is making a determined stand on the Aisne', and later reported to the King that: 'the battle of the Aisne is very typical of what battles in the future are most likely to resemble. Siege operations will enter largely into the tactical problems — the *spade* will be as great a necessity as the rifle, and the heaviest calibres and types of artillery will be brought up in support on either side.' It was the beginning of trench warfare, and the end of the old world of sword-knot and bit-boss, lancer and dragoon. Enguerrand de Coucy might have understood the events that had unrolled over his fief over the past two weeks, but those of the next four long years would have been impossible for the old warrior to grasp.

The retreat from Mons had taken the BEF across 136 miles as the crow flies and at least 200 as the soldier plods. When Sir James Edmonds produced the first volume of the Official History he compared it favourably with the Army's three other notable retreats: Sir John Moore's to Corunna in 1808–9, Wellington's after Talavera in 1809 and from Burgos to Ciudad Rodrigo in 1812. Exactly twenty years after Edmonds wrote this, the British Army conducted the far longer retreat of some 900 miles through Burma, in the face of a remorseless enemy and in the most appalling conditions. Mons is not, therefore, the Army's longest retreat, although the speed with which it was conducted helped make it one of the most painful.

Survivors recalled the numbing lack of sleep. One officer thought that infantry averaged four hours' rest in twenty-four and mounted men only three. Stanley Maude, a middle-ranking member of III Corps' staff, thought that he averaged three hours' sleep a night while officers on divisional and brigade staffs had even less. 'I would never have believed that men could be so tired and so hungry and yet live,' affirmed another officer.

The fact that the BEF was retreating made tiredness weigh heavier. Its members squirmed when they tried to explain to French civilians that it was simply, as W. H. L. Watson put it: '*Mouvement stratégique pour attaquer le mieux*'. Arthur Osburn and his comrades were chastened by an old lady who told them, from her cottage window: 'You make a mistake! The enemy is *behind* you! Ah! Are you not riding in the wrong direction?' 'The bitter sarcasm in her voice as she watched us bolting from the haze of smoke and the rattle of artillery . . . was immeasurable,' confessed Osburn.

We have seen how men coped. Comradeship, self-respect and regimental pride — usually in that order — all played their part. The habit of obedience made its own contribution, and in Major-General Fergusson's by no means unique strictures on discipline we glimpse a worried recognition that this, like boot-heels or wagon-wheels, had been abraded by the retreat. Frank Richards and his mate Duffy were not best pleased to find themselves on saluting parades in the Aisne valley: 'Duffy said we didn't have a ghost of a chance under this sort of conditions and were bound to lose the war. I have often thought since then that our time would have been far better employed if we had learned something about a machine-gun.'

Draconian sanctions were applied to extreme cases of failure. Soldiers who disappeared on the retreat and were subsequently discovered when the BEF moved northwards had to give a careful account of themselves, and the Army dealt remorselessly with those it believed had intended not to rejoin the ranks. On 8 September, Count Gleichen recorded that: 'we had, before starting, the unpleasant duty to perform of detailing a firing-party to execute a deserter . . . He had cleared out and managed to get hold of some civilian clothes, and, having lost himself, had asked the way of a gamekeeper he met. The gamekeeper happened to be an Englishman, and what was more, an old soldier, and he promptly gave him up to the authorities as a deserter.' This unlucky soldier (the first of the 351 executed by the British during the war) was the eighteen-year-old Private T. J. Highgate of the Royal West Kent, a veteran of Mons and Le Cateau, convicted only two days previously and shot with a haste which testifies to the authorities' desire to re-knit the frayed bonds of discipline.

Darker forces helped men keep going. I am as fond of the British Army of 1914 as any man, but cannot avoid noticing that folded in its collective subconscious was a slice of the freebooting spirit which had helped take Henry V's men to Agincourt. When Frank Richards walked round Amiens cathedral one of his mates suggested that 'it would be a fine place to loot'. Trevor Horn thought that 'there's no compunction about looting an orchard or even seeing what's inside an empty house, as after all if we don't take food or wine the Germans will'. He had fired a good deal of machine-gun ammunition, so there was room in his limbers for plenty of the 'fizzy something Brut'. Sometimes horses and equipment were simply 'borrowed' from another unit. 'Picked up a decent looking horse in the dark,' admitted Horn, 'very badly girth galled, but should go into the team as it looks that stamp.' He was very pleased with his 'find', and reported that: 'New horse the "Pick up" a great success as "off lead".' Sometimes there was a darker side to all this. When the BEF moved up to the Aisne, Corporal Watson saw infantry moving through a field which had dead and wounded Germans scattered about it like poppies. 'Sometimes Tommy is not a pleasant animal,' he said, 'and I hated him that afternoon. One dead German had his pockets full of chocolate. They scrambled over him, pulling him about, until it was all divided.' On 7 September, Lieutenant-Colonel Edwards tried to put a stop to such behaviour, and paraded the 20th Hussars to warn them 'that men found looting would be tried and probably shot'.

Some survivors were ambivalent about the retreat. R. G. Garrod — who was probably in the audience when Lieutenant-Colonel Edwards read the riot act on 7 September — thought that it took some time for danger to sink in. 'It's queer that, being our first experience of war, we were not so much frightened as very excited,' he wrote, 'and it wasn't until after two or three weeks of constantly fighting rearguard actions, reconnaissance patrols, and seeing our mates killed and wounded that the real horror of it came home to us, and if everyone else was as frightened as I was, then we were all petrified.' Nobby Clarke of the Bays found it somehow easier than he had expected. 'Everything seemed to happen so quickly, events were out of our control,' he wrote of Néry. 'I know I felt frightened and excited at the same time. We were a very highly-trained and efficient regiment and we did as we were trained to do, responding quickly to a situation without question. And if you wanted to live you had to kill.'

Captain Edward Balfour of the 5th Dragoon Guards, who acted as brigade-major of 1st Cavalry Brigade after Stephen Cawley's death, remembered that:

> We marched and fought practically continuously for 6 days. The Colonel [Ansell] reckoned that he and I had only 10 hours sleep in 8 days, but then one had 30 years of full nights rest to draw upon. In addition for 5 or 6 days we got practically no supplies. The cavalry we were with lived more or less on fruit out of gardens and what we could get in the country, but we had a great time and it was worth having done it. It is something to be with a rearguard squadron and see a whole corps deployed against it.

George Barrow's conclusion was even more straightforward.

> I enjoyed every minute of the retreat — the excitement, the movement, the villages and fine old churches, the sight of French cavalry, cuirassiers wearing their cuirasses, dragoons with helmets and flowing plumes straight out of Detaille's and de Neuville's pictures . . . the absorbing

interest of one's work, the novelty of fighting alongside French troops, the feeling of relief and satisfaction that the clash with Germany had come, that clash which we soldiers knew was bound to come and which the politicians blamed us for knowing and spoke of as unthinkable.

And there were lighter moments, even in the chaos of St Quentin. Kenneth Godsell paused to join a crowd at the canal bridge there, and saw that:

> in the middle of the canal was quite the largest woman I have ever seen outside the famous travelling circus. She was floating as nature would not permit such a body to sink . . . On the bank were two friends of slighter proportions and two tommies. The latter were fishing for her with the butts of their rifles. The butt of one rifle caught in her fabric covering and she was gradually towed towards the shore. One indiscreet tug pulled the garment over her head, she had nothing on underneath. The shriek of joy — most lamented — from the onlookers could only have added to the woman's discomfort.

As far as the British Army's experience of war went, the retreat was certainly costly. On 5 September the BEF had 20,000 men fewer than its original strength of 100,000 or so, but many stragglers soon trooped in and the eventual loss was a little over 15,000 killed, wounded and missing. Wellington had lost about the same — albeit from a much smaller army — at Waterloo, and British battle casualties in the whole Crimean war were rather lighter.

As the months went on, survivors of Mons looked back, almost with nostalgia, to casualties on this scale. After the war hardened into trenchlock on the Aisne the BEF was moved up to Flanders in the vain quest for an open flank. The First Battle of Ypres cost it 58,000 men, and Sir James Edmonds affirmed that: 'In the British battalions which fought from Mons to Ypres there scarcely remained with the colours an average of one officer and thirty men of those who had landed in August, 1914. The old British Army was gone beyond recall.' The fruitless offensives in the spring of 1915 — Neuve Chapelle, Festubert and Aubers Ridge — finished off most of the surviving few who remembered that misty morning on the Mons–Condé canal or the shambling withdrawal from Le Cateau.

The officers and men through whose eyes we have watched the retreat met a variety of fates. Some were to die very soon. Captain John Norwood, who had thanked his wife for allowing him to go to war, fell on the Marne; Pat Fitzgerald, blithe machine-gun officer of the 4th Dragoon Guards, whose simple faith had him on his knees beside his bed before turning in, even in a crowded billet, died on the Aisne; and Frederick Arkwright of the 11th Hussars, who had seen 'poor Cawley' at the point of death at Néry, joined him in October at Ypres. We saw Neville Woodroffe fight his way back up the ridge at Villers-Cotterêts with his Micks. He too died at Ypres, and his batman's letter to his mother shows that rank was no barrier to genuine affection: 'But there is one I can never forget that is my late Master I shall never forget him. If it had been my own brother I would not feel so sorry as he was more like a brother to me than an officer i[n] c[harge] of me. I hope you will not be offended with this letter as I am but a Pte soldier.'

Others lived longer. William Edgington was commissioned in 1915 but was killed so soon afterwards that he never appears in the *Army List* in his new rank. The last entry in his diary, written on 2 May, concludes: 'When will it end?' Francis Grenfell of the 9th Lancers, awarded the VC for his gallantry at Elouges, died two weeks after Edgington. Douglas Reynolds, who had won the VC saving 37th Battery's guns at Le Cateau, was killed as a major in February 1916, the year of the Somme. Lionel Lutyens — who we last saw as a frightened subaltern at Le Cateau — won a Military Cross on the Somme and commanded 37th Battery. He was sniped in the Ypres salient in January 1918 and buried at Elverdinghe, with 'his dear horse Bronco that had been with him all the war, following behind the coffin'.

Then there were those who bore charmed lives. Frank Richards survived the war, obstinately refusing promotion, and was awarded both Distinguished Conduct Medal and Military Medal. Robert Graves, a wartime officer in his regiment, persuaded him to write *Old Soldiers Never Die*, one of the first and best private soldier's accounts of the war. Percy Snelling left the relative safety of the cavalry to become an officer in the Green Howards in 1917 and retire as a captain. Regimental Quartermaster-Sergeant Fitzpatrick of the Royal Irish received a DCM and a commission for his work at Mons, and was a lieutenant-colonel at the end of the war. John Lucy was commissioned in 1917 and terribly wounded in December that year. He stayed on in the Army after the war, and after retirement became a well-known radio commentator for Radio Eireann. In 1939 he rejoined the Army, and eventually commanded a Young Soldiers' battalion of the Royal Ulster Rifles. His brother Denis had died on the Aisne, and is commemorated on the Memorial to the Missing at La Ferté-sous-Jouarre, just where we crossed the river.

When John wrote *There's a Devil in the Drum* he froze his last frame of Denis, going steadily up the slope well out in front of his section: 'Forward he went, and out of my sight for ever'. Paul Maze survived to become a distinguished artist, but his commanding officer was less fortunate: Brigadier-General Bulkeley-Johnson was killed at Arras in April 1917, bustling up to the front line in red-banded cap and smart waterproof coat to see just where his cavalry brigade should go in. Muddy infantry officers warned him to watch his step, but a sniper felled him minutes later.

Arthur Osburn was, in a sense, as much of a victim of the war as the men whose wounds he tended, and *Unwilling Passenger* is a catalogue of a growing disillusionment which neither promotion to lieutenant-colonel nor award of the DSO could begin to expunge. Henry Owens, our cheery hunting doctor, survived the war.

> On Friday 17th January 1919 about 20 of us waited at the bottom of the Gressenhall coverts . . . Frank Crossby was out. I had last seen him just before he was wounded and captured at Messines in 1914. Hounds gave tongue in covert and a moment later a fox whisked out with a fine white tip to his brush. Somebody hollowed 'gone away'. Hounds came rattling out of covert and settled to his line. We shortened our reins for a really good gallop and I thought to myself that we really have reached The End Of The War.

He married in 1920 but died a year later: the war had so weakened his constitution that he fell easy prey to pneumonia. Alan Hanbury-Sparrow DSO MC rose to command a Royal Berkshire battalion in 1917 and was gassed outside Ypres. He admitted that: 'Passchendaele broke me. When I got out again in April, I only lasted three months, as I simply couldn't stand it any longer.'

Some had a good war. Tom Bridges was badly wounded as a divisional commander at Passchendaele — he characteristically set off across the mud while it was 'raining old iron' — but the loss of a leg did not prevent him from becoming Governor-General of South Australia. George Barrow commanded the Yeomanry division in Palestine and retired as a full general, which rank he happily exchanged for that of 'full private' in the Home Guard in the Second World War. Soarer Campbell made a good recovery from the wounds he suffered on the Marne: he too was a divisional commander at the war's end, and died, a full general, in 1936. Amongst our other cavalrymen, Sally Home became a brigadier-general in the First World War and Edward Balfour a brigadier in the Second.

Ma Jeffreys also prospered. He spent the whole of the war on the Western Front, apart from a period of convalescence in 1916, and was commanding 19th Division when the war ended. He retired as a general, became Conservative MP for Petersfield in 1951, and was ennobled as Baron Jeffreys the following year. Of our sapper subalterns, James Pennycuick became a brigadier and Kenneth Godsell a lieutenant-colonel. Our one Gambardier, Christopher de Sausmarez, retired as a brigadier-general and became *seigneur* of the family fief of Sausmarez on the island of Guernsey. He had won his DSO in the South African war, and died, in the age of Beatles and mini-skirts, in 1966.

The *Army List* could be very fickle. G. W. A. Tailby, a lieutenant at Néry in September 1914, was still a lieutenant four years later, while W. H. L. Watson, a hastily-appointed corporal RE in 1914, ended the war as a major in the Royal Tank Corps. Both our Cameronians had successful careers. James Jack commanded an infantry brigade at the close of the war and retired (his health damaged as much by hard riding as vigorous campaigning) in 1921. He lived in Leicestershire, where Tailby was a near neighbour. Robert Money, Jack's second-in-command at the Cameronian depot in 1920–21, went on to become a major-general.

Had this book dealt with cavalry later in the war I would have made more use of Rudolf Binding's *A Fatalist at War*. There were certainly times when I felt close to him. 'As a cavalryman,' he wrote, 'one asks Nature daily why man is not born with breeches on; for one never takes them off.' He had been comfortably off before the war, and after it made a good living as a popular novelist and poet, dying in 1938. Walter Bloem was not so lucky. Wounded on the Aisne, he served on both Eastern and Western fronts, was wounded twice more, and ended the war as a major on the General Staff. He became disillusioned with the Weimar republic after initially supporting it, and joined the Nazi Party in 1938. Although he was over seventy, he volunteered for active service in 1939 and contributed to the German war effort as a writer and speaker. He lost his son on the Eastern Front, survived imprisonment by the Russians, and died a forgotten and disappointed man in 1951.

Military dynasties have their own perils, and in war a father's pride often turns to ashes. Brigadier-General Cis Bingham lost his Coldstream son on the Aisne; Walter Congreve was a corps commander when his boy Billy died on the Somme, and even Allenby's resolution wavered when his only son Michael, a gunner officer, died of wounds at the age of nineteen. My own historical objectivity crumbles when I reflect on a letter of consolation he wrote to his wife, with his strong, careful script blotched by tears.

But we must get back to happier times on our own line of march. After our jubilant, if rather late, lunch on Friday, 20 August, we drove down to Fontainebleau where we had arranged accommodation for the horses with the *Centre Sportif d'Equitation Militaire*, tucked away in a wonderful stable complex behind the palace. There are five centuries of equestrian architecture there. Some traces of Francis I's stables remain, dwarfed by a huge indoor riding-school which looks like an inverted rowing-boat. The comparison is not inexact, for it was built by shipwrights during the Napoleonic wars. As one of our hosts generously explained, there was not much else for them to do after Trafalgar. The majority of the buildings date from the 'golden age' of the French Army after the Franco-Prussian War when the artillery school was at Fontainebleau. As we walked over the cobbles on yet another stiflingly hot afternoon it was not hard to imagine horse-gunners wheeling their teams under the plane-trees and thinking of that inevitable clash out to the east beneath the blue line of the Vosges.

We were looked after by the deputy commandant, Lieutenant-Colonel Tarneguy de Robien, and a charming young veterinary *aspirant*, Matthieu Ricard. Or perhaps I should say Matthew, for he has a French father and an English mother and is bilingual, a matter of no little importance, for we wanted to be sure that the veterinary documents were in the correct form for our return to Britain. Lieutenant-Colonel de Robien and his officers entertained us to a glass of champagne in their *popote* — a little officers' mess which might easily have been the ante-room to a British cavalry mess at Paderborn or Catterick. We drank the traditional toast to St George and the cavalry, and then departed unsteadily for the Hôtel Richelieu, in Fontainebleau itself. I made the mistake of lying down for a moment after my shower, and awoke, microwave-hot, to realise that I was almost late for dinner.

We had promised ourselves a gentle Saturday. At 9.00 a.m. Tarneguy de Robien and Matthieu Ricard took us out into the Forest of Fontainebleau to see the CSEM's practice racecourse and jumps. We went around the edge of the track at what was meant to be a gentle canter, but Thatch was less collected than he might have been and took me past Evelyn at some speed, provoking Tarneguy to ask if it was the custom, in the British Army, to accelerate past one's

commanding officer. I was saved from some untruthful explanation
by the sight of Matthieu's horse slipping and giving him a spectacular fall from which he emerged bruised in dignity but otherwise
intact. We went down a row of simple jumps, and the grey monster
enjoyed himself so much that he larrumphed on to leap a low
wall which was part of something entirely different, attracting not
altogether complimentary comments about 'the flying Percheron'.
He was revenged soon afterwards, for when we posed for photographs in the water-jump he beat the suspect element with a mighty
hoof, splashing the well-pressed buff uniforms around me with
muddy water.

Some of us made a half-hearted attempt to hoover up culture that
afternoon, and walked around the palace in the deadening heat. My
heart was not really in it, and I was not sorry to get back to my
room, strip off and collapse on the bed. We had originally intended
to drive into Paris for a celebratory dinner, but mercifully a doubt
over the name of the restaurant — I remembered it as *Au Tournant
de la Butte*, but the telephone directory revealed only a *Relais de la
Butte* — gave pause for thought, and we eventually settled for the
François I, just across the square from the palace and a short stumble
from the hotel. From our table on the pavement we enjoyed one of
the best views in France. Francis I's royal apartments stood floodlit
across that sweep of cobbles which has the alternative titles *Cour du
Cheval Blanc*, from an equestrian statue that once stood in the courtyard, and *Cour des Adieux* because Napoleon bade farewell to his
guard there, at the foot of the great double staircase, when he went
into exile on 20 April 1814. Either title suited us well: it was our
last night together; and our own trusty greys, now dreaming of oats
and green fields, were in the stables just behind the palace. It was
not an evening of self-restraint. We ate *foie gras*, bream cooked with
fennel and ginger, and a pudding of red fruits. A good deal of
Sylvaner slipped down — we had, after all, to replace all that fluid
sweated out over the jumps — and my last night in France had
much in common with my first for I cannot remember getting
home.

On Sunday morning we endured the worst start of the fortnight.
Up at 4.30 a.m., stables at 5.00, and off at 5.30 in pitch darkness
laced with drizzle. The connector between the trailer (now housing
Thatch again) and the Trooper had been suspect for days, and it
chose this moment to distribute itself, in several tiny parts, over the
stable-yard. As we set off for Paris in heavy traffic (it was the

weekend of the *rentrée des vacances*, and all Paris was churning home-wards) I kept wondering whether the combination of copper wire and silver paper would keep the lights on. We percolated through roadworks on the *périphérique*, with desperate glances into the wing-mirrors to make sure that John was still trundling along behind. By the time we reached the services near Compiègne on the A1 I was glad to stop, eat several currant-embedded croissants, and let Evelyn take over for the drive to Calais.

The freight office brought our long-expected bureaucratic glitch. Our documents made little sense to the girl behind the VDU. Who was travelling in which vehicle? Was the horse-box towing a trailer? Which of us was Monsieur Thatch? It went on and on until I thought that we would still be arguing the toss, debating whether Magoo or Jeopardy was going to drive the trailer, when the boat sailed. Eventually the manager weighed in. Our documents were fine, but we would need to sign an indemnity form in case the horses were injured because the sea was so rough. By now we would have signed almost anything, and we got on board for what was a remark-ably smooth crossing with minutes to spare.

We did some cross-decking at a service station just outside Dover, and went our separate ways. Ollie was picked up by his wife; Evelyn, Clive and John set off for Melton, and I headed back to Hampshire. I was sorry to see them go. We had all got on remark-ably well despite tussles with fences and stable-doors, and I knew that I would miss them. During the journey the drizzle promoted itself to rain, and I stopped to lower the flap between the trailer's roof and tail-board, a task which required a degree in mechanical engineering and had me cursing damply by the roadside for several minutes. As I perched insecurely on the mudguard, trying to undo a piece of the now-ubiquitous bailer twine, I looked across the broad grey back and realised just how fond I had become of Thatch.

Like R. A. Lloyd, an experienced Life Guards NCO, 'I have no great opinion of horses' intelligence'. However, Curly Birch, horse gunner and equitation expert, advises us that 'before . . . condemn-ing our horses as less intelligent than our dogs, we should remember that the former spend many hours out of the twenty-four tied up in front of a wall, a state of affairs which is not conducive to the development of the brain'. He believed that much could be done to develop the horse's intellect, and cited the example of Tommy, a charger of his acquaintance, which if turned loose would walk, trot, canter, jump and change legs at the canter simply on his master's

word of command. I fear that Thatch is not in this league. He
willingly lifts his hooves to have them picked and responds promptly
to all the aids, but harbours an unreasoning fear of dustbins. He
will pass tankers and juggernauts without alarm, but cannot abide
the tractor that he sees every day, and in his eagerness to grab his
haynet he will sometimes rap his nose smartly against the wall.

I had always intended to sell him on immediately the expedition
was over, but was soon to discover that I could not bring myself
to do so. He now lives at livery at Newton Valence, and my bank
statement unerringly demonstrates that he is the greatest single item
of expenditure in the Holmes household, a fact about which I am
not always wholly honest. To paraphrase Kipling:

> For Belial Machiavelli kept
> The little fact a secret, and,
> Though o'er his minor sins she wept,
> Poor Lizie did not understand
> That Thatch — sixteen-three and grey –
> Absorbed one-third her husband's pay.

We have simply been together, in good times and in bad, on
baked limestone or sombre stables, too long for me to forsake him
now. Lloyd admired horses for their 'beauty of form, willingness
to exert themselves at our slightest bidding, helplessness, absolute
dependence on us for their every need. A good horse always gives
of his best without stint. He will suffer hunger, thirst, pain, and
still work on till he drops.' I do not much care if Thatch is no
Einstein, or if a bin-liner caught in a hedge occasionally persuades
him to decant me. On that dreadful Néry day he carried me through
the Forest of Compiègne, down the long, sinister shuttered high
street of Béthisy St Martin, past gardens garrisoned by a bestiary
full of dogs (I am fond of terriers, but soon took the view that
one persistent yapper would have looked well beginning his hoof-
powered orbit), across a level crossing and on up *le Haut de la Justice*
where the gibbet once stood, and still had to be asked not to trot
up the track out of the gully.

We are sometimes too anthropomorphic about horses, and strive
to bestow on them human attributes they can never possess. I admire
Thatch for what he is: big, strong, gentle and trusting, and the fact
that he would stretch out over his stable door to nuzzle any provider
of Polo mints worries me not at all. After that endless grooming,
feeding and tacking up I begin to understand how the cavalryman

felt about his steed. I now know why, amongst all the acts of petty governmental meanness at the war's end, the decision to sell Army horses locally — rather than to spend money shipping them home — caused such resentment. In Palestine, the Australian Light Horse, who always took an oblique view of discipline, simply refused to betray their trusted friends to be worked to death. They held a brigade race meeting, and every trooper shot his horse the next day. Some British cavalry did the same: George Barrow, who had protested at the order, turned a blind eye to it. One Australian waved two calloused fingers at the establishment in an unforgettable couplet:

> Maybe I'll be court-martialled,
> But I'm damned if I'm inclined
> To go back to Australia
> And leave my horse behind.

Good on you, mate. In 1930 Brigadier Geoffrey Brooke was appointed to command the cavalry brigade in Egypt, and his wife Dorothy, appalled at the plight of the ex-service horses she saw around the streets of Cairo, established the Old War Horse Memorial Hospital which, as the Brooke Hospital for Animals, still thrives today.

Strong bonds link the cavalryman to his horse. Tom Bridges, who got through a number of chargers in his time, affectionately remembered an old bay Waler, that he had bought when sold off by the RHA. He found him a quiet home in India, and was surprised to see him in the gunner lines at Ladysmith in 1900, but at once took him on again. 'His adventurous life ended at the Relief of Mafeking,' grieved Bridges, 'when he was shot dead with my groom on his back. I trust he roams the Fields of Asphodel and perchance rubs noses and exchanges reminiscences with other equine heroes, Bucephalus, Copenhagen, Marengo, Vonolel, Black Bess and their like. Though only a ranker he could tell them a few things for he was a tough customer.'

There was a particular poignancy when death plucked a rider from his horse's back. One amateur poet commemorated a Canadian field artillery driver, killed at Ypres, with the prayer:

> Grant that I die where bursting shrapnel sings
> My team upon a gallop toward the foe.

When Richard Chant of the 5th Dragoon Guards — who knew

more than a little about gallops towards the foe — reminisced on his time in the Army he paid special tribute to his comrades who had died as a trooper ought.

> So good luck to all the Pals I know
> That's had the life-long run
> Especially those who took the Jump
> On the back of his long-faced Chum.

Riding the Retreat did more than bring me very close to my own long-faced chum. It reminded me of Clausewitz's wise warning that: 'If no one had the right to give his views on military operations except when he is frozen, or faint from heat and thirst, or depressed from privation and fatigue, objective and accurate views would be even rarer than they are. But they would at least be subjectively valid, for the speaker's experience would precisely determine his judgement.' I have far more sympathy for the combatants of August 1914 — British, French and German — than I ever did before. I was fit and well-fed, and the fact that I was short of sleep was nobody's fault but my own. There were no uhlans snapping at my heels, no sergeant-major laying into me, no shells screaming overhead to hammer my comrades into meat and entrails and threaten my own all too fragile existence. My decisions cost nobody his life, and I had to endure neither the impotent anguish of watching a plan falter nor the secret misery of knowing that I could never fulfil the promise others saw in me.

I have lost count of the number of military cemeteries I have visited since I first became a military historian, and of the tens of thousands of men — most of whom enjoyed a much shorter life than mine — whose graves I have passed. Thatch carried me past dozens while I rode the Retreat. Their crisp greensward and uniform headstones can so easily blunt our sensibilities: every grave, every one of those nameless names on one of the Memorials to the Missing, represents a human life. Indeed, Sir Martin Lindsay, who fought from Normandy to Germany with the Gordon Highlanders in the Second World War, thought that soldiers should be buried by their comrades and not subsequently reinterred in a military cemetery 'where the grave-stones will remain for posterity and their bodies will be dressed by the right, regimented in death'.

What are we to make of these regiments of dead who mean little to the HGV driver grinding his gears up the hill towards Desolation Farm, or the farmer more concerned with the Common Agricultural

Policy than the chalky relics of humanity turned up by each spring ploughing? Should we bulldoze the lot, because they represent bad old days, and are constant reminders of a murderous past that might make European unity more difficult to attain? Far from it. Let us not spurn the sacrifice of those who died for issues that seem distant to us, but celebrate their courage and their fortitude, for surely by recognising our common past we may hope to achieve a common future.

I drove Thatch into the yard at Newton Valence at 4.30 that Sunday afternoon, to an enthusiastic welcome from a stable-yard full of small girls, my youngest daughter, Corinna, prominent amongst them. I divested the old rogue of his travelling kit, led him into his stall, and stood quietly with him for a moment, thinking of all those miles we had covered. He stared gravely into my eyes, blew branny breath into my face, gently placed a hoof on my foot, and stood on me.

Select Bibliography

Unpublished Sources

The Public Record Office
Unit War Diaries in WO 95

The Imperial War Museum
Papers of:
Brigadier E. W. S. Balfour, 5th Dragoon Guards
Major C. L. Brereton, Royal Field Artillery
Lieutenant-Colonel Tom Butt, King's Own Yorkshire Light Infantry
Lieutenant John Campbell, Royal Horse Artillery
Lieutenant-Colonel G. A. Carden, Royal Field Artillery
Private William Clarke, The Queen's Bays
Sergeant T. H. Cubbon, The King's Liverpool Regiment, attached 3rd Division Cyclist Company
Second-Lieutenant William Edgington, Royal Field Artillery
Brigadier-General G. T. C. Edwards, 20th Hussars
Field-Marshal The Earl of Ypres (Sir John French), General Headquarters
Private R. G. Garrod, 20th Hussars
Bombardier Thomas Langston, Royal Field Artillery
Major E. G. Lutyens, Royal Field Artillery
Major W. J. Nicholson, Royal Horse Artillery
Captain John Norwood VC, 5th Dragoon Guards
Captain H. B. Owens, Royal Army Medical Corps
Captain Percy Snelling, 12th Lancers
B. E. Todhunter, Remount Purchasing Officer
Private A. Wells, 9th Lancers
Lieutenant Neville Woodroffe, Irish Guards

The Liddle Collection, University of Leeds
Papers or recordings of:

Captain Sir Roger Chance, 4th Dragoon Guards

Private Richard Chant, 5th Dragoon Guards

Lieutenant Colonel T. H. Clayton-Nunn, The Royal West Kent Regiment

Corporal Harry Easton, 9th Lancers

Lieutenant-Colonel K. B. Godsell, Royal Engineers

Lieutenant T. L. Horn, 16th Lancers

Sergeant Frederick Luke VC, Royal Field Artillery

Company Quartermaster-Sergeant E. M. Lyons, Warwickshire Regiment and
Army Service Corps

Major-General R. C. Money, The Cameronians

Brigadier-General C. de Sausmarez, Royal Garrison Artillery

Second-Lieutenant Kenneth Tallerman, Royal Field Artillery

Lieutenant-Colonel North Whitehead, Army Service Corps

Privately owned papers of:

Brigadier E. H. W. Backhouse, The Suffolk Regiment

Major Wilfrid Dugmore, The Cheshire Regiment

Miss Edith F. Maudslay, Women's Remount Depot

Brigadier J. A. C. Pennycuick, Royal Engineers

Mr Keith Simpson allowed me to consult the questionnaires completed at his
request in 1977 by selected surviving First World War officers. I found
that of Lieutenant-Colonel Alan Hanbury-Sparrow, The Royal Berkshire
Regiment, especially useful.

Published Sources

Books

Andrew, A. W., *Cavalry Tactics of Today* (London 1903)

Anglesey, Marquess of, *A History of the British Cavalry 1816-1919* (4 vols, London
1973-82)

Arthur, Sir George, *Not Worth Reading* (London 1938)

Ascoli, David, *The Mons Star* (London 1981)

Ashurst, George *My Bit* (Ramsbury 1987)

Baker, P. S., *Animal War Heroes* (London 1933)

Barnett, Correlli, *The Swordbearers: Studies in Supreme Command in the First World
War* (London 1963)

Barrow, Sir George, *The Fire of Life* (London 1941)

Beaumont, Harry, *Old Contemptible* (London 1967)

Beckett, Ian F. W., and Simpson, Keith, (Eds) *A Nation in Arms* (London 1985)

Bernhardi, F. von, *Cavalry in Future Wars* (London 1906)

Bidwell, Shelford, and Graham, Dominick, *Fire-Power: British Army Weapons and
Theories of War 1904-1945* (London 1982)

Binding, Rudolf, *A Fatalist at War* (London 1929)

Birch, Noel, *Modern Riding* (London 1909)

Birdwood, Lord, *Khaki and Gown* (London 1941)

Blenkinsop, L. J., and Rainey, J. W., *History of the Great War . . . ,Veterinary Services* (London 1925)

Bloch, Marc, *Memoirs of War, 1914–15* (London 1980)

Bloem, Walter, *The Advance from Mons* (London 1938)

Bond, Brian, *The Victorian Army and the Staff College* (London 1971)

Brack, F. de, *Light Cavalry Out-Posts* (London 1876)

Brereton, J. M., *The Horse in War* (Newton Abbot 1976)

Bridges, Sir Tom, *Alarms and Excursions* (London 1938)

Chatwin, Bruce, *What am I doing here* (London 1989)

Coleman, Frederic, *From Mons to Ypres with French* (London 1916)

Congreve, Billy, *Armageddon Road: A VC's Diary 1914–1916* (Ed Terry Norman) (London 1982)

Craster, J. M., (Ed) *'Fifteen Rounds a Minute': The Grenadiers at War, August to December 1914* (London 1976)

Denison, G. T., *A History of Cavalry* (London 1877)

Edmonds, J. E., *History of the Great War . . . Military Operations, France and Belgium 1914*, Vol I (London 1922)

Edwards, F. M., *Notes on the Training, Equipment, and Organisation of Cavalry for War* (London 1910)

Farndale, Martin, *The History of the Royal Regiment of Artillery: The Western Front 1914–18* (Woolwich 1986)

Farrar-Hockley, Anthony, *Death of an Army* (London 1967)

Gibbs, Philip, *The Soul of the War* (London 1915)

Gleichen, Count E., *The Doings of The Fifteenth Infantry Brigade* (Edinburgh 1917)

Gough, Sir Hubert, *Soldiering On* (London 1954)

Haig, Douglas, *Cavalry Studies* (London 1907)

Hanbury-Sparrow, A. A., *The Land-Locked Lake* (London 1932)

Hatton, S. F., *Yarns of a Yeoman* (London ND)

Haythornthwaite, Philip J., *World War One: 1914* (London 1989)

Hohenlohe-Ingelfingen, Prince Kraft zu, *Conversations on Cavalry* (London ND) *Letters on Cavalry* (London 1893)

Holmes, Richard, *The Little Field-Marshal: Sir John French* (London 1981)

Home, Archibald, *The Diary of a World War I Cavalry Officer* (London 1985)

Horne, Pamela, *Rural Life in England in The First World War* (New York 1984)

Huguet, V., *Britain and the War* (London 1922)

Kluck, Alexander von, *The March on Paris* (London 1920)

Kournakoff, Sergei, *Savage Squadrons* (London 1936)

Litauer, Vladimir S., *Russian Hussar* (London 1965)

Lloyd, R. A., *A Trooper in the 'Tins'* (London 1938)

Lucy, John, *There's a Devil in the Drum* (London 1938)

Macdonald, Lyn, *1914* (London 1987)

Martin, A. A., *A Surgeon in Khaki* (London 1915)

Maude, F. N., *Cavalry: Its Past and Future* (London 1903)

Maze, Paul, *A Frenchman in Khaki* (London 1934)

Mons, Anzac and Kut, by an MP (A. N. H. Herbert) (London 1919)

Nagel, Fritz, *Fritz: The World War I Memoirs of a German Lieutenant* (Huntington, West Virginia 1980)

Osburn, Arthur, *Unwilling Passenger* (London 1932)

Porch, Douglas, *The March to the Marne* (Oxford 1981)

Poseck, M. von, *The German Cavalry in 1914 in Belgium and France* (Berlin 1932)

Putkowski, Julian, and Sykes, Julian, *Shot at Dawn* (London 1989)

Richards, Frank, *Old Soldiers Never Die* (London 1933)

Rifleman, A., (*pseud.* M. F. Crum) *The Question of Mounted Infantry* (London 1909)

Rimington, M. F., *Our Cavalry* (London 1912)

Ritter, Gerhard, *The Schlieffen Plan* (Munich 1956)

Robertson, Sir William, *From Private to Field-Marshal* (London 1921)

Russell, J. C., *Cavalry Service* (London ND)

Shephard, Ernest, *A Sergeant-Major's War* (Ed Bruce Rossor) (Ramsbury 1987)

Simpson, Keith, *The Old Contemptibles* (London 1981)

Smith-Dorrien, Sir Horace, *Memories of Forty-Eight Years' Service* (London 1925)

Smithers, A. J., *The Man Who Disobeyed: Sir Horace Smith-Dorrien and his Enemies* (London 1970)

Spears, E. L., *Liaison 1914* (London 1930)

Terraine, John, *Mons: The Retreat to Victory* (London 1960)

(Ed) *General Jack's Diary 1914–18* (London 1964)

Travers, Tim, *The Killing Ground* (London 1987)

Tuchman, Barbara W., *A Distant Mirror: The Calamitous Fourteenth Century* (London 1978)

Tylden, G., *Horses and Saddlery* (London 1965)

Watson, W. H. L., *Adventures of a Dispatch Rider* (London 1915)

Wedd, A. F., (Ed) *German Students' War Letters* (London 1929)

Wood, Sir Evelyn, *Achievements of Cavalry* (London 1900)

Pamphlets

Cavalry Training (1912)

Cavalry Combat (US Army Cavalry School, Harrisburg, Pennsylvania, 1937)

Field Artillery Training (1914)

Field Service Pocket Book (1913)

Field Service Regulations Part I Operations (1909)

Infantry Training (4-Company Organization) (1914)

Articles

Becke, A. F., 'Néry 1914' *Journal of the Royal Artillery* October 1928

Bethune, E. C., 'The Uses of Cavalry and Mounted Infantry in Modern Warfare' *Journal of the Royal United Services Institute* February 1906

Molyneaux, E. M. J., 'The British Cavalry: Some Suggestions' *Journal of the Royal United Services Institute* June 1904

'New Acquisitions' *Newsletter of the Friends of the National Army Museum* Spring 1993

Simpson, Keith, 'Capper and the Offensive Spirit' *Journal of the Royal United Services Institute* June 1973

Singleton, John, 'Britain's Military Use of Horses' *Past and Present* No 139 May 1993

Spiers, E. M., 'The British Cavalry 1902–14' *Journal of the Society for Army Historical Research* Summer 1979

INDEX